Abandoned and Forgotten

An Orphan Girl's Tale of Survival
During World War II

Evelyne Tannehill

Abandoned and Forgotten:
An Orphan Girl's Tale of Survival During World War II

Published by Wheatmark®
610 East Delano Street, Suite 104
Tucson, Arizona 85705 U.S.A.
www.wheatmark.com

Publisher's Cataloging-In-Publication Data
(Prepared by The Donohue Group, Inc.)

Tannehill, Evelyne.
  Abandoned and forgotten : an orphan girl's tale of survival during World War II / by Evelyne Tannehill.

  p. : ill., map ; cm.

  ISBN-13: 978-1-58736-693-2
  ISBN-10: 1-58736-693-2

1. Tannehill, Evelyne—Childhood and youth. 2. World War, 1939–1945—Children—Prussia (Germany)—Biography. 3. World War, 1939–1945—Personal narratives, Prussian. 4. World War, 1939–1945—Prussia (Germany)—Biography. 5. Girls—Prussia (Germany)—Biography. I. Title.

D810.C4 T36 2006
940.531/61/092 B   2006931480

In loving memory of my parents, Anna and Herbert, and the thousands of other innocent people who perished during World War II

Oct 15, 2009

To Gail,
With best wishes,

Evelyne Tannehill

GERMANY - 1940

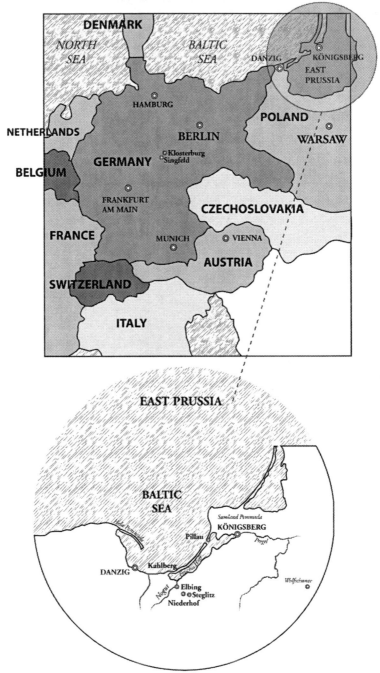

Where it all happened

CONTENTS

The New Germans

Epilogue

PROLOGUE

THE HUMAN COST OF WORLD War II reached into the millions.

Over forty million people lost their lives, and millions more were displaced and lost their homes. Hundreds of thousands were raped, beaten, mutilated, starved, and murdered for no other reason than being the wrong nationality or religion, having opposing political affiliations, or simply being in the way. The entire world was affected by this war, and nothing has been the same since.

In a sense, World War II was a continuation of World War I, or at least, the seeds for it had been planted then. After Germany's defeat in 1918, the Allies were determined that Germany should remain so weak it would never be a threat to any nation again. The victors imposed reparation penalties on Germany beyond the country's ability to pay, at the same time choking its economic comeback by levying heavy restrictions on its manufacturing capabilities. The result was high unemployment, unfathomable inflation, extreme poverty, and a serious breakdown of law and order.

It was easy for a man like Adolph Hitler to rise to power in that environment. He promised something to everyone and, in the end, delivered nothing. He betrayed all those who had put him into power.

He took over the German government by trickery, lies, and sheer force of his will. He promised the Western nations he would destroy communism and so, in the beginning, received financial support from them. He promised the German industrialists a powerful comeback and received their backing. He promised to restore the military to its former prestige. He promised to make the streets safe again by eradicating crime. Above all, he promised to restore Germany to its former glory, and for that he received the people's loyalty and respect. The one thing Hitler did not reveal was how he intended to fulfill these seductive promises.

He was the hero of the time, the savior. He put food on the table, created jobs, and gave the people hope. The populace drank it in and became intoxicated with visions of a glorious future. No one asked or anticipated the price or sacrifices that would be necessary to achieve this glorious future.

Hitler was committed to his aggressive expansionism that went far beyond getting back the territories Germany had been forced to cede after losing World War I. Men joined the military willingly and enthusiastically to free the *Vaterland* of its shackles and regain *Lebensraum*, living space. Germany embarked on a war on several fronts, a war it could not and did not win.

Many books have been written about World War II, especially about battles won or lost, where they were fought, the casualties, and the heroic feats by soldiers. It is not often, however, that we read about the immeasurable suffering and sacrifices of the innocent German civilian populace—in my case, what happened to a simple farming family.

This is my story of growing up in the German province of East Prussia by the Baltic Sea during those tumultuous times. It is also my story of coming of age in a troubled world that had been turned upside down, a world where nothing was normal. It is told through the eyes of the woman I have become. The story relates what happens when law and order break down, and killing is a virtue rather than a sin—when human decency is exposed to the test of conscience, when desperation deadens all feeling of pity, when good and evil fight it out behind the scenes on their own battlefield, when compassion loses to human greed, and self-preservation is the only thing that matters. It is not a pretty tale, but once I lived it.

THE GERMANS

CHAPTER ONE

IT IS MY NINTH BIRTHDAY. It is snowing and the temperature hovers near freezing. My mother and I struggle with a sled heaped with food supplies and warm bedding as we flee from the Russians, the enemy. We are in a procession with hundreds of women and children pulling sleds loaded with infants, young children, and sparse possessions. We make little progress. Our feet sink into the powdery snow. Suddenly, we hear a droning sound like a hundred angry bees. Airplanes appear from everywhere in the cloudless sky. They are Russian planes with large red hammer-and-sickle symbols under their shiny wings. The planes look like enormous silver birds as the sun reflects on the hard metal. I look up and see the laughing faces of young boy pilots in brown fur hats as they zoom in on us. Violent explosions shake the earth. People scream. I scream. I try to run but am stuck in a sea of white. I throw myself to the ground and bury my face in the icy snow. I cry out for my mother and look up, searching for her. Blood splatters all around me. Body parts fly through the air, some of them landing on my back like heavy fists. The ground is covered with severed arms, legs, and heads, while the snow melts under me and turns into a pool of blood. Its nauseating, sweet smell penetrates my nostrils. I am drowning in it and continue to call for Mother, but she is not there. I come up for one last breath of air and see her stretched out on a gurney under a white sheet. She is dead. I fight to stay afloat, but something heavy is pulling me down. I am drowning. Just before passing out, I awaken, gasping for air. My heart pounds wildly in my throat, and I am drenched in the sweat of fear, a fear so real that I am frightened even after I realize it was just a nightmare, the same nightmare that has haunted me for over sixty years.

MY FAMILY CALLED ME EVA. Not until much later did I learn my name was actually Evelyne, but then there was so much I did not know. The history of my family, and who I was, unfolded itself slowly in bits and pieces. I entered the world in 1936, the youngest of five children, on a small farm by the Baltic Sea in the province of East Prussia, Germany. I spent my childhood years in carefree oblivion in the outdoors, roaming through the countryside among the farm animals, unencumbered by boundaries and the limited freedom city children experience. By the time I reached the age of human aware-ness, Germany was already deeply embroiled in World War II.

In the beginning, we remained relatively untouched by the battles being fought in the East at the Russian front. But when the war finally did reach us, it came suddenly and with full force, sweeping over us like a giant tidal wave with ever-increasing momentum, pushing before it a panic-stricken mass of fleeing humanity. A massive exodus of people stampeded west for the frozen waters of the Baltic Sea, across which they hoped to reach safety. When the panic ended, a hush settled over the obliterated landscape. Death and devastation lay in its path, and an eerie stillness hung over the blood-soaked land. Only here and there a surviving crazed dog, cat, or farm animal remained, witness to these cataclysmic events, but hunger and starva-tion soon silenced them, too.

By January 1945, it was evident that Germany was losing the war. The Russian army had advanced into Germany. Battles now fought on German soil took on catastrophic dimensions. Yet the radio still blasted out encouraging news, telling the unsuspecting populace that the setbacks were only temporary, and that the German armed forces were doing a valiant job holding the enemy at bay. These newscasts were supposed to calm the population and avoid panic. However, the events surrounding us spoke more clearly of what was happening in those tragic final days. By the time my parents realized the end was closing in on us, civilians were no longer allowed to flee without written evacuation orders from their local party leaders. The penalty for disobedience was death.

In the meantime, our farm was overrun with refugees from the eastern part of East Prussia. In the summer and fall of 1944, the refugees had been people from the Baltic countries. Now they were Germans, and the stories they told contradicted every news broadcast we heard. This had a sobering effect on my parents, and we, too, prepared to flee to the West. What we did not know at the time was that the Red Army had already broken through the German lines and had surrounded our part of East Prussia in a pincer maneuver. They blocked all avenues to safety, thus condemning most of the East Prussian population to an unfathomably cruel fate. While waiting for the official evacuation orders that never were issued, thousands and thousands paid with their lives.

My mother, the youngest of seven children, had been born in 1898 in the village of Niederhof. She had three brothers and three sisters. Niederhof was mainly a railroad depot and never had more than two hundred inhabitants; most of them were employed by the railroad. We owned one of the only two farms in this village. Although small, Niederhof had a bakery, a butcher shop, a post office, and a grocery store, which also served as a tavern, or a *Gasthaus* as the locals called it. However, it did not have a school. My mother attended school in the one-room schoolhouse in the neighboring village of Steglitz, just as children from generations before her had done.

Rittmeyer, my mother's maiden name, was well represented in the area. Relatives and cousins surrounded us. Going back far enough, we were related to the entire village of Steglitz to one degree or another, but we had little interaction with any of these relatives. Family feuds, petty jealousies, and opposing political affiliations kept the Rittmeyer clan fractured. The rift between the siblings widened when Mother inherited the ancestral farm after she married my father, Herbert Rapp, a city boy and "foreigner" at that, which made him even less popular with our country relatives. She turned her back on most of them, or more likely, it was the other way around, and focused her attention and affection on her newly acquired family, who embraced and loved her.

My parents met by chance. Looking to buy a farm, Father heard that my grandparents' property was for sale. When he met Anna, their youngest daughter, my mother to be, he fell in love at first sight. So, instead of buying the farm, he married the farmer's daughter.

Father was born in 1894, one of five children. His oldest sister, Aunt Kaethe, married a man from the western part of Germany and settled near her husband's family. They owned a grocery store. Father came next and Aunt Elsbeth, Uncle Eduard, and Aunt Gertrude followed. They lived in Elbing, a commercial center of one hundred thousand inhabitants near the Baltic Sea. The last three siblings never married, and we, their brother's children, became their adopted family.

When Father turned sixteen, the age of emancipation at that time, he turned his lifelong dream of immigrating to America into reality. His family knew adventure was in his blood and gave him their blessings. He left home in 1910, when immigration to the United States was still easy, and did not return until some time in 1922. Up to that point, he had enjoyed all the benefits and comforts of home a middle-class family could provide. His family had owned a brewery that my grandmother had sold after my grandfather's early death. She had invested the proceeds in real estate, which she managed very wisely.

After he returned to Germany, Father took to country life naturally. He made many improvements and positive changes on the farm, and, over time, turned it into a showplace. His head was full of new creative ideas he had brought back from America, where he had been a land surveyor in the states of Alabama and Florida. He fell in love with America, a love that lasted until the end of his life.

When World War I broke out, Father decided not to return to Germany and became an American citizen. Only my grandmother's serious illness brought the prodigal son back to his dying mother's bedside. She survived. By this time, Father had met my mother, and our fates were sealed. We were to be born in Germany, by a German mother and a naturalized American citizen father, thus giving us dual citizenship. And so, we spent our childhood years in the province of East Prussia, that piece of Germany by the Baltic Sea, which lay north of Poland. The free city state of Danzig and the Polish Corridor separated East Prussia from the main part of Germany, referred to as the *Reich* at that time.

In order to retain his American citizenship, Father had to return to the United States every five years to report to the immigration authorities and prove he was in the country. These two or three months' absences were hard on Mother. The jet age had not yet arrived, and the long ocean voyage and land travel alone took several weeks. He made his last trip to the United States in 1938, the year Hitler started his campaign to conquer Europe. Father saw the gathering war clouds on the horizon, and he planned to bring the family to America and make it our permanent home.

While Father was making the necessary arrangements in America, Hitler declared war on Poland and closed Germany's borders, making emigrating difficult. At the same time, Hitler sent out a call into the world for all loyal Germans to return to the *Vaterland* and be part of rebuilding it to its former greatness. In exchange, "foreigners" such as my father would be allowed to leave Germany with their families. Five transport ships with German expatriates who answered Hitler's call were to come from the United States via Lisbon, Portugal. The same ships were to return with families who wanted to get out of Germany. We were slated to be on the last ship. Father leased the farm and land, and then he crated our belongings according to German customs regulations.

Our new home was to be Foley, Alabama, where Father had lived for some time. He had located a pecan farm owned by a widow anxious to lease or sell, and he had made arrangements to lease the property with an option to buy. Hitler's limitation on the amount of currency that could be taken out of the country complicated the transaction, but Father had managed to take enough cash with him to secure the deal. He had followed up with clandestine payments through his American Consul friend.

While Father made the necessary arrangements in the United States for the family's upcoming move, Mother was busy getting her paperwork processed, since she would be traveling with a German passport. We children, thanks to our father, were automatically recognized as American citizens and did not require special German travel permits. Mother's passport was issued March 18, 1938. On the first page was stamped, "Good for emigration to the United States of North America. Passport expires March 17, 1943."

Our family planned to make the big move within a few weeks. However, it did not come to pass. Only the first two transport ships left for the United States. When Hitler invaded Poland, all further transactions of exchange were canceled, and the German borders were closed.

I was only two years old when all this took place and have no memories of Father's return from his last trip to America, but his arrival at the Niederhof station in cowboy attire from head to toe, complete with ten-gallon hat, boots, and chaps became something of a legend. For years after, people talked about that crazy, tall cowboy farmer who seemed to have stepped straight out of an American western movie. Father's unorthodox behavior and eccentric appearance, mainly for the benefit of his children, did leave a comical and lasting impression on the inhabitants of Niederhof who had witnessed this strange family reunion. It set him and our family apart from the locals. In the early years of Hitler's rise to power, Father was merely an aberration among the German citizenry. However, as Hitler tightened his grip on the populace, Father's foreignness and his refusal to march with the masses turned into a detriment for the family. He became a man to be watched and to stay clear of, a sentiment that intensified as the war progressed.

CHAPTER TWO

COMPARED WITH OTHER FARMS, OUR property was of average size. It was located just two blocks from the railroad station, along the tree-lined highway paralleling the railroad tracks that formed the main artery to and from the *Reich*. At any given time, we had between twenty-five and thirty dairy cows, thirty to forty pigs, somewhere between three hundred to five hundred chickens, over a dozen horses, several calves and foals, and flocks of geese, ducks, and turkeys. Father improved the farm's productivity by concentrating on rotating crops, using better fertilizing procedures, and replacing old equipment with more modern implements, some of which he imported from America. Neighboring farmers often came to inspect the new machinery and foreign gadgets he acquired and to learn about the innovative ideas he used.

Ours was a mix of a dairy and grain farm. The one hundred and fifty acres consisted of grazing land, agricultural acreage, and some forestland. Father grew rye, oats, wheat, and feed corn, as well as potatoes, turnips, sugar beets, and produce. What we did not need for our own use, Father sold in Elbing. Our main income, however, came from dairy products.

Although we had live-in farmhands and outside help during harvest time, Mother and Father pitched in wherever and whenever needed. Spring, summer, and fall—the time for sowing, growing, and reaping—were months of frenzied activity, since so much depended on the weather. In winter, Father did the threshing, repaired equipment, mended harnesses, and fattened up the pigs. It was also a time for rest and partying.

The farm prospered and the family was productive. My parents and older siblings were well settled into their rhythmic routine by the time I was born. My brother Erwin, sister Vera, and brothers Douglas and Henry preceded me in birth. We arrived at rather close intervals, with only nine years age difference between Erwin and me. Tall for our ages, we also inherited both our parents' blue eyes and fine blond hair. I longed to have long, thick braids like my playmates, but my thin hair had the texture of fine silk. I envied my contemporaries' voluptuous crowns of elaborate tresses as I succumbed to regular haircuts "to make my hair grow in thick," Mother promised. But it never did.

As the youngest in the family, I was the most spoiled and the most neglected at the same time. While my parents focused their attention on the needs of my older siblings, and the war made life increasingly more difficult, the care of my youngest brother, Henry, and me fell to Lene and Soscha, our household help. They came from an area in Poland that had changed hands between Germany and Poland many times during the course of history. They spoke both languages and were considered *Volksdeutsch*, meaning they had some German blood running in their veins.

Lene, our *Kindermaedchen*, the children's nurse, also helped in the household. I adored her because she paid attention to me. On Sundays she wore pretty dresses with bright flowers and used lipstick. She let me try on her dangly earrings, which I usually screwed on so tightly that my earlobes turned numb. I delighted in the way they tickled my neck. Best of all, I liked her crank-up gramophone with a big funnel tube for a speaker.

When Lene's Polish boyfriend came to call on her, she laughed and flirted with him, and they kissed while dancing the tango, her passion. I enjoyed watching their rhythmic leg movements. When the music slowed, Lene called over her friend's shoulder, "Crank up the gramophone, Eva! Hurry! Don't let the music stop!" And they continued to twist and twirl their bodies in perfect unison. Sometimes Soscha joined in and danced with a broom for a partner. I giggled when she pretended the broom was a live partner, and hugged and kissed the handle.

On laundry days, Lene propped me up on the old mangle that stood in a corner of the laundry kitchen, probably to keep me out of the way. But I did not mind. From this vantage point, I watched the sheets, tablecloths, and towels boil in the big kettle and make their journey through the many tubs of water before ending up in the electric spinner, the only labor-saving device in the room. The mangle, an enormous wooden box filled with heavy rocks, resembled our flatbed milk wagon on stilts instead of wheels. Two smooth, fence-post size rollers, around which Lene and Soscha wrapped the wrinkled sheets and tablecloths, separated the top from the smooth bottom platform. Lene would lift me on top and say, "We need you up there for the extra weight." Then I would get a ride while she and Soscha pushed this rock monster back and forth, and I pressed down hard, thinking of the extra weight.

When I was five, Lene married her Polish friend, who had joined the German army. She went away with him and took the magic music box with her. I missed her and hoped she would visit us occasionally, but she never did.

Soscha remained with us until the end of the war. Her real name was Sofia, but we called her Soscha. She was a stocky young woman, somewhere in her early twenties, simple minded, and easily sweet-talked in and out of anything, which considerably reduced the discipline in Henry's and my life. We enjoyed our loosely watched-over childhood like two wild puppies. However, when our misdeeds required punishment, it came swiftly in the form of a severe spanking, a spanking that kept us out of trouble for a long time.

My happiest memories are closely connected with my father's siblings, Aunt Elsbeth, Aunt Gertrude, Uncle Eduard, and my grandmother, whom we called Oma. We rarely spent a weekend without them. They arrived from Elbing, about a half-hour train ride away, on time for our main midday meal, which on Sundays was always a culinary feast served on Mother's good china. In the afternoon, during the warm summer months, we drank coffee and ate pastries in a cozy, lilac-shaded corner of the garden, my favorite place. The day usually ended with a light, cold supper. All week, I looked forward to Sundays, because the aunts always brought little presents for Henry and me. This routine varied little from weekend to weekend. In the mornings, Henry and I ran to the station, dressed in our Sunday finery, to meet our grandmother, aunts, and uncle. My heart always beat faster when I heard the train whistle in the distance, announcing their arrival. The minute they saw us, Aunt Elsbeth would call out, "Have you cooked enough kisses to go around?"

"Yes, hundreds and hundreds," I usually said, eager to prove it. The exuberance with which they collected the kisses and doled out hugs often overwhelmed me. Aunt Elsbeth, especially, squeezed so hard that the air threatened to escape from my lungs. They loved us, their brother's children, and we loved them in return. Back at the farm, we would not give them any peace until they distributed the goodies, usually little bags of sweets. Sometimes other treasures appeared: a box of much-prized colored pencils, an occasional coloring book, chalk, or a ribbon for my doll.

We passed the day feasting on Mother's good cooking, followed by the traditional afternoon stroll to admire nature, breathe the fresh country air, and, as the aunts claimed, to help the digestion. In the evening, we escorted them back to the station and passed out more hugs and kisses. By then, Aunt Elsbeth's squeezes had lost much of their power. Once settled in their compartment, Aunt Elsbeth would lower the window and call out to Henry and me, "Don't forget to cook lots more kisses for us."

Often the aunts brought friends of the family with them. Mother knew how to set a festive table, and the city people enjoyed our wholesome country meals. A weekend without guests was rare. I usually went to the station anyway, hoping an unannounced visitor might surprise us. Sometimes my parents received reciprocal invitations from their city friends, which rarely included me. I had to stay home in Soscha's and Lene's care.

Our "company" weekends, with the many courses of good food and great variety of cakes and fancy pastries, offered a most welcome change from our much-hated, monotonous "one-pot" weekly fare. Weekday meals consisted of meat, potatoes, and dried or fresh vegetables all cooked together. On Sundays, we feasted on roasted goose, duck, chicken, pork, and sometimes turkey, and always dessert, which never appeared during the week. For Sunday supper, we had sandwiches with cheese and our own smoked sausage, with homemade apple or berry ciders to drink. During the week, we faced scrambled eggs and potatoes fried in bacon grease and milk soup with *Klunckern*, a small, sweet flour dumpling. This fare never varied: every evening it was the same, except on "company" Sundays.

We had little interaction with Mother's side of the family. All her siblings were married, owned farms, and had many children. They lived in the surrounding small villages, which quickly gave way to the fields and meadows around them. Unpaved, dusty roads led to the hamlet-like communities that had been in existence for several hundred years. Thickly thatched roofs covered their wooden farm buildings. I have only vague memories of visiting these aunts, uncles, and cousins. Their ancient, musty-smelling homes and buildings made a far greater impression on me than did the little-known relatives who occupied these houses of wood and straw. The stoic adults, mostly dressed in black, always seemed to be in mourning for some departed family member. Simple people, solidly anchored in village traditions, they often relegated what they did not understand to the realm of superstition.

With their low ceilings, lace-covered windows, dark rooms, worn wooden floors, and doorways through which my tall father had to duck, the buildings looked like they belonged in a fairy tale. I can still see those wonderful old farmhouses, but I cannot recall a single face of the relatives who lived in them.

On Mother's dresser stood a photograph of my maternal grandfather, an old man with a tousled, bushy white beard that reached down to his chest. I was not at all sure I would have liked to know him. He stared at me with strict, penetrating eyes that made me think he knew all my secrets.

As Germany became more and more embroiled in its European conquests and needed its able-bodied men for the war efforts, Polish nationals replaced our German help. Most of them had a rudimentary knowledge of the German language, and communication was not a problem. They did not necessarily come to us willingly. Under a form of forced labor, they received regular pay with free room and board. Although they were allowed to move about freely, they needed official permission to leave us. Hitler's war government mandated food production, and the farmers produced what the state dictated with the labor available. This marked the beginning of the government's takeover of our lives.

My parents never replaced Lene, and so I turned to Soscha for my needs. Mother was busy running our large household, and my older siblings took little notice of me. I was that "pain-in-the-neck little sister," useless as a playmate and mostly in everyone's way. But kind-hearted Soscha tolerated my incessant pestering and tyrannical demands good naturedly. I clung to her. She was barely literate, which I turned to my advantage. I could always commandeer her attention with the many stories and fairy tales with which Grandmother filled my head.

Yes, Oma, my sweet, little, moonfaced grandmother, could tell fantastic stories, and I was her most attentive listener. Immediately after her arrival on Sundays, I would greet her with, "Oma, do you have another story?" She would nod and say, "Later, Evchen, later." I had to wait for the adults to exchange news, endure the drawn-out meal, with its accompanying small talk and laughter, and maybe even a little nap for Oma. But ultimately, she settled in with me, and sometimes Henry as well, and then the stories spilled out of her. I would snuggle up against her small body or crawl into her lap and play with the little bun her gray hair formed at the nape of her neck, slowly pulling out all the hairpins that held it together. But she always caught on to me before it fell apart.

Oma's were not the timeless and familiar fairy tales of the Hans Christian Anderson or Brothers Grimm genre; hers were gory and spooky stories, not to be found in any children's books. She dug deep into her bottomless well of superstition, legends, and ghost stories that formed an integral part of East Prussian daily life. Her stories dealt with good and evil characters, and with the severe punishment of disobedient children. She told tales of ghosts slipping through keyholes at midnight, headless riders galloping across fields, and pretty nymphs sliding to earth on moonbeams during the night.

She always began with, "Now, Evchen, have you been a good girl since the last time I saw you?"

"Oh, *ja*, Oma. I didn't get spanked once," I would reassure her, careful not to tell her of any narrow escapes I may have had.

Then she would start, often retelling the same tales, enhancing the plot with new twists and surprise endings. My favorite story was about a girl without hands.

"You know, once upon a time there was this beautiful little girl, about your age," Oma would say, "who could not resist stealing apples from other people's trees. Then, one night, the fairy of virtue and honesty appeared at her bedside and hacked off both her hands." The goose bumps on my arms started to prickle in anticipation of the next gruesome details. "After that, the girl roamed the neighbor's garden during starlit nights and tried to pick more apples, which had turned to gold, but she couldn't do it without hands."

"Was blood dripping from them?" I would ask every time.

Oma took her cues from my many questions and spun tales of adventurous trials and tribulations the protagonist had to go through before she repented and became a shining model of goodness. In her fairy-tale world, animals talked, people lived in haunted houses, fire-spewing dragons guarded castles, and the spirits of the dead roamed the countryside. My vivid imagination embellished her stories with the necessary ingredients to make them more frightening than she intended. Her ghost stories held a special fascination.

"Is it really true? Can you really see ghosts?" I asked repeatedly.

"True just as I'm sitting in this chair. But they don't appear to just anyone. You have to be special to be able to see them," she would reply, with a twinkle in her eyes.

"Oh," I would say every time and hold on to her more tightly.

With her loving arms around me, I felt safe. Her stories took root in me. However, they did not mold me into a more obedient child; instead, they made me fear the dark when the characters of her tales became larger than life. During moonlit nights, the dancing shadows of the old, gnarled apple trees outside our bedroom windows turned into scary, ghost-like apparitions. By the time Oma died, my head teemed with horror tales and was peopled with enough evil characters to turn my dreams into endless, frightening nightmares.

My father was the more affectionate of my parents. For a hug, a kiss, and a few minutes in his lap, he risked Mother's wrath by raiding the pantry for sweets, cakes, or pastries. This was especially reward-ing on Saturday evenings, when the larder was full in anticipation of Sunday's guests. He would cut a slice out of the fanciest layer cakes, and then he would face Mother the next morning with a guilty grin on his face and say, "Annchen, wouldn't you rather the children eat your cakes than all those people who descend upon us all the time?"

My playground was the farm and the railroad station, with its comings and goings. My playmates were the children of the farm workers and the railroad employees. I cannot remember ever meeting any of their fathers, who were soldiers at the front. Fortunately, my American citizen father was exempt from conscription into the military and kept out of politics. He never abandoned his dream of eventually resettling his family in America. During many of our company Sundays, he brought out his picture postcard collection of the New World. He had piles of them, and many fascinating stories to go with them. For me, they represented a land of mystery, with buildings countless stories high. How did people get to the top floor of those buildings? My aunts lived on the third floor of their apartment building, and that was a climb.

"They have a lift, an elevator," Father explained.

I envisioned a couple of strong men in the basement of the building, pulling a thick rope to make this curious contraption with people trapped inside go up and down. Then, there were pictures of trees with orange tennis balls (oranges) and clusters of yellow sausages (bananas), and exotic birds of all sizes and vivid colors like those that existed only in my coloring books. The pictures hinted of a world very different from the one I knew.

CHAPTER THREE

WHEN IT BECAME APPARENT THAT neither Aunt Elsbeth nor Aunt Gertrude was interested in marriage, although they had many suitors, my grandfather had insisted they take up some type of profession. At a time when daughters either married or were doomed to spinsterhood in a relative's household, helping raise the children, my aunts quickly and gladly complied with their father's ultimatum. They became telegraph operators and worked for the German telegraph, a government-controlled department of the post office system. Almost all communication was done either by letter or, when urgent, by telegram. Few people owned a telephone, including us.

One thing was certain: the aunts were not going to subjugate their freedom to tyrannical husbands, as I overheard Aunt Gertrude say more than once. It turned out to be the best thing they could have done. Unknowingly, they set the course for their own survival. They did not become war widows as did so many of their contemporaries, and they had a skill for supporting themselves after the family lost everything at the end of the war.

Uncle Eduard remained a bachelor as well. Early diabetes and a chronic heart dysfunction exempted him from military service. He managed the family apartment buildings and became Oma's travel companion.

The aunts took full advantage of their financial independence. While Aunt Gertrude squandered her earnings on rare books, objects of art, and precious jewelry, the more practical Aunt Elsbeth had a vacation home built in Kahlberg, a resort by the Baltic Sea. It became our summer paradise. We spent most of our vacations there. Occasionally, my parents joined us on weekends.

The trip to Kahlberg was a special adventure in itself. First, there was the short train ride to Elbing. I felt the excitement mount in me as we headed straight for the busy pier at the Elbing River, where an excursion steamer awaited us. From there, we glided along the calm river for six or seven kilometers. Then, we crossed the ten-kilometer-wide *Frische Haff* and threw dry bread to the seagulls that greeted us. As we passed the lone lighthouse at the halfway point where the gulls lived, we listened to their pained cries in the wind. Oma, who had a tale to tell about everything, referred to them as the souls of the many sailors who had drowned in storms.

The *Frische Haff,* as it then was called, is a freshwater inland sea, which stretches for seventy kilometers along the East Prussian coast. An equally long, two- to three-kilometer-wide spit of land, heavily wooded with pine trees and covered with immense, shifting dunes, separates it from the vast Baltic Sea. Only a narrow opening to the north allows the fresh and salt waters to mix. Because of the low salinity of the water, its shallowness, and the harshness of the Nordic winters, the sea freezes during the cold months. The colder the winter, the more this thick ice sheet comes alive, breaks up in parts, and turns into a treacherous place.

Each winter, it became a challenging sport to traverse these frozen waters on foot and be the first person to cross from Elbing to Kahlberg without breaking through the ice. Enthusiasts looked forward to the race despite the hidden dangers. All winter long, there was ice sailing and skating on this wide expanse of solid ice. We did not participate in these popular diversions; we only heard the aunts talk about them. For us, only the warm summer months by the sea mattered. We swam in the cold Baltic water, combed the miles of beaches for golden amber that so readily washed ashore after a storm, built sand castles, and collected sea shells and pine cones. None of us knew then that these turbulent waters would become East Prussia's biggest graveyard.

By the time I started first grade in the one-room schoolhouse in Steglitz, my older siblings were already attending private schools in Elbing, where they were slated for higher education, which usually started after fourth grade. Only Henry still attended the country school, but he, too, soon transferred to one of the city schools.

Our maid, Soscha, not Mother, enrolled me on that first day of learning. Rain the night before had turned the two-kilometer-long dirt road to Steglitz into a quagmire of mud. Faithful Soscha propped me up on one of my brothers' bicycles and delivered me dry and clean. Henry brought me home, and from then on, I was on my own.

I quickly fell in with the Niederhof children and never had to make the long walk to school alone. We trudged along the well-worn path in hot, cold, rainy, snowy, and freezing weather. School was not to be missed, and the only way to get there was on foot. It was comforting and exciting to share the one-room school with all the other grades. I liked to listen to the older children's lessons, which were a lot more interesting than my tedious assignments.

Only the first four grades had a sizable number of students. The upper grades were smaller, because many students, like my older siblings, left for the various private schools of higher education in Elbing. Our teachers were masters at juggling their time and attention among the varied requirements characteristic of a one-room school, for these included not only lessons but also the enforcement of discipline. Sitting still over our assignments was torture for us free-spirited country children, who, until then, had roamed about freely.

School was a happy time for me. A diligent student, I was eager to learn how to read so that I could finally delve into all those mysterious books the aunts gave my brothers and sister. Only my left-handedness slowed me down. To be left-handed was still considered abnormal. Mother and my teachers tried hard to make a right-handed person out of me, but with minimal success.

I owned few toys. Shortages of all types began to appear even in the early stages of the war, with toys being the most expendable. A jump rope, a ball, colored pencils, coloring books, and my doll were my most prized possessions. Each spring, Father hitched a horse to the milk wagon and took us to the sandpit outside Steglitz to get a load of sand, which he dumped in our yard by the stable. We looked forward to this momentous occasion almost as much as Christmas. It marked the end of school and promised long, warm summer days filled with untroubled play and adventure in the wide-open outdoors.

We brought friends along, which turned it into an adventure. We liked to climb to the top and roll down the incline while the sand gave away under us until we landed at the bottom, a few pounds heavier with sand in our shoes and pockets. Once it was in our yard, the sand pile became the playground for the entire neighborhood. We

baked fancy cakes and decorated them with tiny pebbles. Occasionally, I snatched an egg from the hen house to make the sand more
binding. We built elaborate medieval castles and fairy-tale villages.
When Henry and his friends joined in, the sand pile became a battlefield with intricate fortifications and an extensive bunker system, a
sign of how the war had started to sneak into our games. By the end
of summer, there usually was barely a trace of sand left, which meant
school was about to start again.

When we tired of the sand pile, we played hopscotch, picked wild
flowers along the creek, or wove dandelion wreaths and decorated
our heads with them. We chased butterflies and collected bugs. On
rainy days, we gathered worms and fed them to the pigs. We played
ball and the universal game of statue, and we invented new twists
and angles to old games. We made up different words to the songs
we knew. We taxed our imaginations to the limit to keep ourselves
entertained.

Our farm was by far the most popular playground around. We
played hide-and-go-seek in the empty stables when the animals were
out to pasture, or jumped from the barn rafters into the soft piles of
straw below. We built a network of intricate passageways in the hayloft
and tunneled our way from one end to the other. When not by the
sea in Kahlberg, we went bathing in the nearby millstream, a shallow,
gurgling creek with hidden deep spots. Since none of us knew how to
swim, it was a miracle no one drowned. Most of the time, our parents
were unaware of where we were or what we were doing. As long as we
showed up at mealtimes, all was well, and hunger always brought us
to the dinner table on time.

Sometimes Henry and his friends included me in their boys'
games. We roasted potatoes over clandestinely built fires the boys had
started with a magnifying glass. We stuffed dry reeds with fresh hay
and smoked them like cigarettes. When I had no one to play with, I
lay on the garden lawn, watching the clouds sail across the sky as they
formed into characters out of Oma's stories.

During our long Baltic winters, the newly fallen snow replaced
the sand pile. We went sledding, built snowmen, and slid along the
slick ice on the frozen pond. The cold never stopped us from enjoying
the outdoors. Occasionally, Erwin tied our sleds together and hitched
Matzka, our black mare, to them. We made the rounds, picked up

neighboring kids, and raced happily through the wintry countryside. Or, we went to the railroad station and tied our sleds to the wagons or sleighs that came to pick up arriving passengers, hitching an exhilarating ride halfway to the next village. Sometimes the drivers gave us the whip and yelled, "Get away from there, you pesky little brats!" But more often they indulged us and pulled us along.

Our games were simple fun. The word boredom did not exist in our vocabulary.

The most memorable event each year was Christmas. When Mother brought out the Advent calendar and put up the traditional Advent wreath with its four red candles, we knew it would not be long before the *Weichnachtsmann*, Santa Claus, arrived. On St. Nicholas Day, the beginning of December, we put our shoes, the high-ankle ones that held more, by our beds for St. Nick to fill with candy. If we had been bad, we found a chunk of coal instead. There always was a little piece of coal mixed in with my candy. As the big event drew nearer, Mother baked cookies and sweet cakes that made the whole house smell of exotic spices.

A day or two before Christmas Eve, my brothers went into our forest to cut down a pine tree. When I was old enough, they pulled me along on a sled. The most exciting part was the search for the perfect tree, which always seemed to be in the next grove. On Christmas Eve, we decorated it with glittering tinsel, colorful ornaments, and real wax candles. Then, a bell rang outside, and the *Weichnachtsmann* appeared with his rod, a reminder to be good, and passed out presents. Mother lit the candles on the tree, and we opened our gifts. We each also received a plateful of Christmas cookies with a few pieces of the traditional homemade *Marzipan*, a type of almond-paste candy, mixed in.

For me, Christmas did not start until the aunts, uncle, and Oma arrived on Christmas Day, their suitcase filled with extra presents that had nothing to do with the *Weihnachtsmann*. Their well-chosen books for our individual ages were high on our wish list.

On New Year's Eve, or the day before, we took down the Christmas tree. It was bad luck to leave it up into the New Year.

We children shared one big room that served as playroom during the day and was turned into a dormitory at night, when it resembled the bedroom of the seven dwarves. Beds lined the walls, and an enormous, tall dresser standing between the two windows left space for little else. We played games and did our homework around a heavy oak table in the center of the room.

Although I did not exist for my older siblings during the day, they took great delight in mercilessly teasing and frightening me at night. They played on my fear of the dark and expanded on Oma's wild stories by adding their own scary details. On many a stormy night, I went to sleep with visions of a devil so grotesque that I came close to suffocating under my feather coverlet as I tried to hide from him.

My brothers' story was always the same. Erwin or Douglas would say, "You better watch out, Eva; if you're not good, the devil will come and get you. He's ugly and mean and limps because he has only one human foot. The other one is a split horse's hoof. His deformed body is all covered with coarse black hair. He has a hideous human face and the head of an animal with dangerous, pointed horns. And he has a long tail that he whips around on the floor."

"Can he really talk?" I asked every time, from under the covers.

"Oh, yes, he can talk and he can tell what you're thinking."

This freakish devil became so real, I could almost hear the swooshing sound of his tail.

Another favorite joke my brothers loved to play on me, a joke more frightening than funny, was the story of the man with the wooden leg. As we lay in the dark, Erwin or Douglas would start with, "There was this man who had a wooden leg. Every night he took it off and parked it by the side of his bed. One night, he awoke and found his leg missing. He called out, 'Who stole my wooooden leeeeg? Who stole my wooooden leeeeg?'" The storytelling brother would repeat this query several times in a low, drawn-out voice. My body would stiffen with fear in anticipation of what would come next. Then, suddenly, two firm hands would grab me in the dark and shake me, and my other brother would say, "You stole my wooden leg!" They pulled this trick on me time and again, and although I knew what was coming, it frightened me every time.

On Sunday mornings, we slept late. I loved those times when my brothers and sister talked about school and city life, of which I knew nothing. When we felt hungry, they sent me to check the old grandfather clock in the dining room for the time. I had not yet learned how to read the clock, but all I needed to tell them was on which number the big and little hand rested. From that, they figured out the correct time. Sometimes I had to go back more than once to get it right, and in the process I learned to tell time.

That was in the early years of my childhood. But, one by one, my siblings disappeared from that overpopulated bedroom. My sister, Vera, left first when she transferred to the girls' *Gymnasium*, the equivalent of middle and high school, in Elbing. As the war escalated and train service became unreliable, she no longer commuted and, instead, lived with family friends in the city.

I was very jealous of my sister. Father idolized her, and Mother was always making pretty things for her. Even the aunts parted with some treasures to help keep my sister in fine clothes. She had tennis and dance lessons, and when rationing cards appeared in the early 1940s, most of my coupons went to keep her beautifully dressed, while I got her hand-me-downs. They were well worth waiting for, but I had to wait ages before I grew into them. She and Mother went to the beauty parlor in the city for haircuts and permanents. I received my haircuts, and no perms, from the barber who came to the farm regularly to cut the boys' and Father's hair. I resented it and was very vocal with my tearful protests, but it did me no good. Mother always consoled me with, "You're not old enough. Your time will come."

Despite our seven-year age difference, I was competing with my sister for attention. I wanted the things she had. I wanted the pretty clothes and the colorfully embroidered sweaters Mother made for her. Most of all, I wanted my sister to notice me. I adored her like a princess one admires from afar, but she rarely took notice of me. The gap in our ages was too great. We lived in different worlds. She had become the sophisticated city girl, while I still was that ugly little country bumpkin. We lived in the same house with the same loving parents, but the war interfered, and we did not really grow up together. As a result, I have few memories of any intimate interaction with my siblings, except with my youngest brother, Henry.

Erwin and Douglas commuted to their schools in Elbing. They left home early in the morning and returned in the late afternoon. Evenings, they were busy with homework. I should have felt closest to Henry, who was barely eighteen months older than I, but we fought more than we played together. He did not like school and often neglected his homework. I became the carrier of distress notes between teacher and Mother on his account. Hoping to get Henry into a more learning-inducing environment, Mother finally pulled him out of our little country school and put him into a private elementary school in Elbing. He, too, boarded with family friends in the city. Erwin and Douglas eventually moved into one of the upstairs bedrooms, which left me alone in the children's room, among all the empty beds. But I am getting ahead of my story.

CHAPTER FOUR

THE RHYTHM OF OUR LIVES moved in tune with the farm, the cycles of planting and harvesting, the coming and going of the seasons, and the natural world around us. But dark war clouds were gathering and our idyllic life was about to change. By the beginning of 1940, Germany was irrevocably committed to the path Hitler had chosen. With each successful conquest, the need and greed for more *Lebensraum*, living space, increased. When the populace finally awoke from its trance, Hitler controlled the country with his *Gestapo*, or secret police, and his SS troops, the military elite. He spread a net so tightly over the nation that there was no escaping from its grip. You either fell into line or faced serious consequences.

The first changes were subtle. The male teachers in our little school were drafted into military service and were replaced with young, single females. Fuel shortages appeared, and we could no longer drive our Opel without a special permit. I loved our Sunday outings in the shiny black car. Sitting on Mother's lap in the back seat, I pushed my feet into the driver's backrest and shouted, "Faster, Papa, faster!" Father got so irritated, he threatened to stop and drop me along the road. Then I pouted and whispered into Mother's ear, "Make him go faster, Mutti!"

Sometimes, we drove to Elbing, the big city, to visit Oma and the aunts and, occasionally, called on friends. To own a car in the late 1930s and early 1940s was a rarity among the farmers, and, I suspect, Father enjoyed showing off his toy.

When we could no longer drive the car on the streets, Father drove it in the farmyard on Sundays. We went around and around in a circle and made the startled chickens scramble to safety. Afterwards, Father lovingly wiped the vehicle clean, parked it in the garage, and locked the door until the next weekend. Occasionally, Father bribed one of his city connections into slipping him a canister of *Benzin*. Eventually all fuel sources dried up, and the car remained in the garage even on Sundays, and we reverted to the horse-and-buggy age. Father dusted off the old upholstered carriage, and we made our social calls at a much slower and less exciting pace.

Father had big remodeling plans, which he could not complete because of the war. He intended to modernize the farm. When he married Mother, they had no running water in the house or stable. The animals were watered by hand, and the large, clay cistern in the kitchen had to be refilled daily. We had a drafty double outhouse, one for the family and one for the help. All this was about to change with indoor plumbing installed in one of the storage rooms. Mother talked about an enormous, four-legged bathtub, a toilet that flushed, and a porcelain sink with running hot water for washing our hands. There would be no more freezing sessions in the privy during long, cold winters, and we would all be able to take leisurely, hot baths without having to haul endless buckets of heated water to the tub.

Father started his ambitious project with the stable. Workmen dug up the entire yard into a network of deep trenches in which they laid iron water pipes to keep them from freezing. Then they installed a unique watering system inside the building. Each animal got its own water fountain. An animal just had to press its pointed snout into the round bowl in front of it, and a spring released water for as long as the animal held it down. Father was very proud of this new system. As soon as our Sunday visitors arrived, they had to submit to an inspection tour before they were allowed to sit down at the dinner table. Even neighboring farmers came to look at this unique system.

When it was time to start on the indoor plumbing, the war had already broken out, and with it went our dreams of long, lingering baths and responding to nature's calls in warm comfort. Ultimately, we did get cold running water to the kitchen, but the luxury bathroom remained a fantasy. The future looked uncertain, and many plans and dreams had to be put on hold.

Mother, however, did get a new kitchen stove. The old built-in tile stove was a large green monster that occupied an entire corner of the kitchen. It took a whole day to tear it out. She then had a cast-iron stove, still wood fired, with the usual cooking holes that could be enlarged or reduced with iron rings, but it was half the size of the old one and freed up valuable space.

The kitchen, the hub of the household, stayed busy from early morning until the late evening hours, with daily meal preparations for our large family and farmhands. In addition, summer brought the endless process of canning and preserving fruits, vegetables, and berries from Mother's garden.

In winter, we did the butchering. After the war started, Father had to obtain a government permit. The size of our family and how much live-in help we had determined how often we were allowed to kill a pig, and how many kilos it could weigh. The rest of the pigs went to a centralized slaughterhouse at government-established prices. Hitler needed to feed his growing army.

Butchering days were exciting; they occurred in November and again in March. Since we had no refrigeration, butchering had to be done in the colder months. I was not allowed to witness the killing, but I always managed to sneak a peek anyway. First, Father knocked the unsuspecting pig out with the blunt side of an axe. Then, the help tied its hind legs together with a thick rope and pulled the rope over a rafter in the shed, where Father stabbed the pig in the main artery in the neck and let the blood run into a large bucket. As the pig squealed for its life, I ran for mine while everyone wondered where I had come from in the first place.

After Mother and Soscha gutted and cleaned the animal, we waited for the meat inspector with his special microscope. He put thin slices of flesh under a fine lens and checked it for trichinosis. Then, the real job began. We sliced, diced, and ground the meat, stuffed sausage casings, and hung them in the attic smoke room. The rest was preserved in glass jars or salted away. We all pitched in. Even I got to crank the meat grinder, probably because it kept me occupied and prevented me from falling into tubs of boiling water or getting caught on one of the mean-looking meat hooks.

As the war intensified, we were issued ration cards for food, clothing, and many household items. But shortages made it difficult to redeem them. Meat, especially, was scarce in the cities. The East Prussian farmer, however, never experienced that type of deprivation. We had meat with every meal until the very end of the war. When we ran out of our quota of pork, the chickens and other fowl were on standby to keep us well supplied. Occasionally, Father quietly butchered a calf.

My brother Erwin raised rabbits. For a long time I did not know we ate them, thinking they were his pets. I loved to go to the rabbit shed, stick my hands into their wire cages, and stroke their soft, warm fur. I brought the animals juicy dandelion greens and fresh clover and talked to them. Then, one Sunday, I overheard a guest say to Mother, "Annchen, this rabbit is delicious. You must let me have the recipe."

I dropped my fork. "You mean Erwin's rabbit?" I looked at Mother accusingly. "You said it was chicken."

"Now, Evchen, it tastes just like chicken."

"Not any more," I protested and ran from the table. From then on, I counted the rabbits every Sunday morning, and if any were missing, I refused to eat the meat. No one could convince me any longer we were eating chicken, duck, or goose.

One by one, the men disappeared from among our Sunday guests. Only occasionally did a husband accompany his wife, and then in uniform. I admired their spiffy outfits and secretly hoped Father, too, would get a uniform, but he never did.

On each April 20, Hitler's birthday, and other holidays, swastika flags flew everywhere. Father, however, hung out the old black, white, and red-striped pre-Hitler flag. I loved the new red banner with the white circle and black swastika in the center, and I thought it was the most attractive of all flags as it gracefully fluttered in the breeze. I thought we were too poor to buy a new flag and felt ashamed. I did not know this was Father's silent way of protesting. One day, an official showed up and warned him. "Herr Rapp," he said to Father, "that old rag has to come down. You're headed for trouble if you keep this up."

Father obeyed, but he refused to fly Hitler's banner.

The next change was more drastic. It probably coincided with Hitler's invasion of Russia in April 1941. Our Polish farmhands were issued "Germanization" papers and drafted into the German military. At the same time, a German soldier appeared with a group of twenty English prisoners of war, captured during the battle of Dunkirk. They replaced the Poles. Father talked to these men who wore strange brown uniforms. I watched his lips move but did not understand the words. That was how I learned Father was fluent in English.

Father's animated conversation with the British captives lasted several minutes while the guard stood by, looking as puzzled as I was. Charlie, Jimmy, and Mack stayed with us; the others were distributed among the farmers in Steglitz. We paid a monthly fee to the German government for the prisoners. They, in turn, received *Lagergeld*, prison money, with which they bought personal items of clothing and toilet articles in a stalag prison camp store near Elbing.

We housed our men upstairs, where they shared one room. The guard also lived with us for a time. Every day, he went to Steglitz to check on his charges and made sure they were kept locked up during the night.

Father had chosen his men well. They accepted their imprisonment philosophically. Working on a farm far away from bomb-targeted cities, where food was still plentiful, where English was spoken, and the master was sympathetic to their plight, was better than facing death on the battlefield, they told Father. The men settled in with us and quickly became part of our family. They had a fair grasp of the German language. Before long, even we children could communicate with them. They were not required to wear a special type of prison garb but could keep their dapper khaki uniforms, which made them easily recognizable as British war prisoners.

Jimmy was a career soldier, had officer status, was married, but had no children. A mechanic by trade, he could fix anything, and he became Father's right hand. Mack shared Mother's love of gardening and spent many an evening helping her make a showplace of her flower garden. Charlie was the "chef." Many a Sunday he concocted special dishes for our ubiquitous guests.

Charlie was my favorite. He was affectionate, like Father, and loved children. I readily gave him a hug or two whenever he asked. In the evenings, we children moved freely in and out of their quarters. Jimmy helped Erwin, Douglas, and Vera with their English lessons. My parents, however, knew to be careful, because it was strictly forbidden to fraternize with the "enemy."

The first prisoner guard who roomed with us was not a member of the Nazi party, or a big Hitler fan. He befriended the English, as we referred to them, and kept a closed eye to their comings and goings in our household, which made life easier for everyone. He took his meals with our family, while Soscha and the prisoners and whatever other help we had ate in the kitchen, where a small children's table and bench were set up for Henry and me as well. We did not get to join my parents and older siblings at the dinner table until after we started school. The help ate the same food as we did, even on Sundays. After supper, Erwin and Douglas often played cards with the English, and sometimes Father and the guard joined them.

We lived in harmony with our involuntary help and their guard. And so we entered the war years with optimism. The German military was winning on every front, and we expected a short war.

Every three months, the English received enormous food packages through CARE (Cooperative for American Relief Everywhere) via the Swiss Red Cross. The distribution of the goods was strictly supervised by neutral foreign officials according to the Geneva Convention for the fair treatment of all war prisoners. The boxes arrived at the stalag camp near Elbing, where Father picked them up. The wooden crates were so large and heavy it took several men to haul them up the steep stairway to the attic, where the guard distributed the contents to our men, as well as to the other prisoners in Steglitz. Food items, the likes of which we rarely saw during the later war years, filled the crates—cocoa powder, powdered milk, tins of sardines, cans of corned beef, fancy crackers, special teas, real coffee, and most amazing of all, a variety of chocolate bars—along with big bars of soap, medical supplies such as bandages, ointments, and salves, and cigarettes. The CARE packages, along with gift packages from the prisoners' families, continued to arrive for as long as the English were with us.

Charlie, a nonsmoker, accumulated enough cigarettes to trade them with the guard for an accordion. From then on, in the evenings, we heard music upstairs. Mack played his harmonica, and Jimmy pretended to play the drums with spoons on the back of a chair, or he sang along in his low baritone voice. I loved to listen to the strange words he belted out. Even my parents lifted their heads and listened to the foreign melodies drifting down to us. Father sometimes hummed along, because he had learned some of the songs in America.

The English not only shared their music with us, but also those long-missed delicacies from their CARE packages. Foreign tins and boxes lined our pantry shelves. Charlie was especially generous with his chocolate bars. He often called out to me, "Little Eva, I've got something for you." I knew immediately what he meant and flew into his arms, doling out hugs with equal generosity.

Every Christmas Eve, all three men came down and joined us in the celebration. They appeared with their arms full of chocolate bars for us children and real coffee beans for Mother, which they had saved all year. Even Soscha was not forgotten.

Although Germany now fought on several fronts, we remained sheltered from the war. Living in the country was, in many respects, like living on an island, untouched by air raids, power outages, and other disruptions. My brothers were still too young to be drafted into the military, and the Party left Father, the foreigner, alone for the time being.

We did, however, suffer one early war casualty. In the summer of 1941, an army jeep drove into our yard, and two men in military uniform, with bright Nazi badges proudly pinned to their chests, jumped out. They wanted the tires from our car. Not bothering to take them off the rims, they removed the wheels, loaded them onto the army vehicle, and drove off, ignoring my baffled Father's protests. A month later, they returned with the wheels, remounted them, and drove off with our car.

I remember that day well. Father was not home, and Mother fought hard to stop them from taking his beloved Opel away. She refused to sign the papers the officers spread before her. One of the men read the document to her, an agreement of sorts, while Mother listened with tears in her eyes. I sat under the sewing table, playing dress up with the clothes in the mending basket and peeking out every time the men raised their voices. They were issuing warnings: "Think of the repercussions for the family if you don't sign! Think of your children! We will take the car anyway, whether you sign or not. It will be better for you to sign." One officer was waving a red flag in front of Mother, but she failed to notice it. When I stepped into the room to be admired in my new ensemble, the conversation stopped. There I stood in Mother's full length, pink corset, bra portion stuffed with rags as I had seen Lene do, and a multitude of garters dangling around my knees. To complete the effect, I had put on Father's gray felt hat with a black ribbon hanging over one ear. Mother blushed. I think the officers blushed as well. Then, they broke out in a roar of laughter. It relieved the tension. One of the men pulled an orange from his brief case, handed it to me, and said, chuckling, "You look very grown up." He looked at Mother and added, "Think of that little girl and sign!" She picked up the pen and signed the document. The officers drove off with our car, and we never saw it again. Still in my dress-up attire, I ran after them and watched them drive away, holding on to the orange, which looked curiously similar to those orange tennis balls on Father's picture postcards of America. That orange was the most delicious fruit I had ever tasted, even more delicious than Charlie's chocolate bars.

Shortly after that, the military confiscated our best horses. That was a far greater blow than losing the family car, since all the farm work was done manually. We owned no tractor or power-driven farm equipment. From then on, even our occasional Sunday outings by horse and carriage stopped.

In the meantime, the masses still showed up by the thousands to watch Hitler deliver his impassioned speeches during his many public appearances. There was fire in his inciting words, but few saw the ashes descending upon them like a smoke screen. Except for Father, that is, who seemed to sense hard times ahead. He often would shake his head and say to Mother, "Annchen, Annchen, this can't end well! What is going to become of us?"

CHAPTER FIVE

EAST PRUSSIA WAS STAUNCHLY PROTESTANT, and so were my parents. However, I have no memory of them attending religious services. And since religion was not part of our school curriculum, I had no exposure to any type of biblical learning. Until the age of twelve, I was never inside a church.

Just once Mother tried to show me the inside of the red brick church that stood in the center of the cemetery where my maternal grandparents lay buried, but the big wooden doors were locked.

Much later I learned that Father had had a falling out with the local pastor over the pastor's enthusiastic support for Hitler and vowed never to set foot in his church again.

Erwin and Vera, however, attended confirmation classes in a church in Elbing and were confirmed. We almost did not make my sister's confirmation because we had missed the train. Mother had gotten shoe polish all over her good dress when she helped me tie my shoelaces. By the time she changed clothes, we were late. My brothers and sister hurried ahead, perhaps in hopes of holding up the train, but German trains wait for no one. My parents and I ran after my siblings. We still had a long way to go when we heard the whistle announcing the train's arrival. We turned the last corner just in time to watch the train pull away in a cloud of steam. Mother gave me a stern look and an additional scolding. Father, always the calmer one, hitched the horses to the old carriage and we raced to the city in a steady gallop. The ceremony had already begun when we arrived, and Mother quietly slipped through the church door. Father refused to enter the building, and I had to stay with him as punishment. He turned to me and said, "Let's go find an ice cream man. It'll be our secret." He tied the horses to the hitching post, and we were off.

We returned just as the worshipers poured out of the church. Father winked at me and said, "Remember, not a word to anyone." Thrilled to be sharing a secret with Father, I no longer cared about being banished from the church. And so I missed my second chance to see the inside of a place of worship. It would be years before the opportunity presented itself again.

Most of the farmers, however, did attend the little country church where my maternal grandparents had been buried. The congregation consisted of people from several communities, and many of the members had a long commute by horse and buggy or on foot. The pastor, a German-speaking Lithuanian refugee, was an older man with a disability, which exempted him from being drafted into the military. He held religious services for his ever-diminishing congregation until the end of the war. He also gave Bible classes for the children in Steglitz, but we did not attend those voluntary lessons because they were held in the evening, and it was too far for us to go, especially in the winter.

To be a member of the Hitler Youth, on the other hand, was mandatory for every young child. It was the new cult that replaced religion. Teachers made school difficult for those who did not attend the group meetings. They harassed mothers if they kept their older children home to help on the farm during the absence of their fathers and accepted no excuse.

The program was divided into two groups. Ten- to fourteen-year-old boys belonged to the *Deutsches Jungvolk*, German Youth. At the age of fourteen, they transferred into the Hitler *Jugend*, Hitler Youth. My oldest brother Erwin finished the first four years and then belonged to the Hitler *Jugend*, along with his friends and contemporaries. A seventeen-year-old railroad official's son, who had earned several merit badges, was their leader. The group met every Wednesday afternoon in the school building in the winter, and on the sports ground in the summer. On meeting days, there usually was no homework.

The early phase of the Hitler Youth program was exciting and fun. The leaders put emphasis on sports and physical fitness, thus harnessing the energy of the young. After the war started, the boys trained for military service. The members had to listen to long lectures praising Hitler's great accomplishments and were thoroughly indoctrinated into his philosophy. To become members, they underwent a special ritual. Once a month, on Sunday mornings, all groups from the surrounding villages met on the grounds in front of the only church in the area and held a rally. They endured long propaganda speeches, marched to the beat of drums, learned to shoot, and played war games with great fanfare, while drowning out the pastor's sermon inside the church. The minister and parents were annoyed, but they remained powerless to put a stop to this calculated choice of time and place for the noisy group meetings. The boys, however, enjoyed the large get-togethers; they probably found them a lot more exciting than sitting on hard benches and listening to dull sermons. I admired my brother in his special uniform of short, black corduroy pants, light brown shirt, and black tie. He looked so grown up. Father, on the other hand, was upset about those brainwashing sessions, as he called them.

My sister belonged to the Hitler Youth as well, but the girls' group was called *Bund Deutscher Maedchen*, League of German Girls. Their sport activities resembled those of the boys', but instead of learning to shoot guns, they were initiated into the virtues of becoming good wives and mothers. Their leaders encouraged them to keep diaries of all the wonderful things Hitler was doing for the country. In the later war years, the focus shifted to knitting wool socks and mittens for the soldiers at the front and making bandages for the wounded. The girls also sewed rag dolls for war orphans, which my sister did on our old treadle sewing machine. Mother gave the doll natural black curls by covering her head with unraveled knitting yarn. I wanted that doll more than anything and thought my sister would surprise me with it. When that did not happen, I hoped it would appear under the Christmas tree. But it was not there either. Instead, it ended up under some war orphan's tree.

The enthusiasm with which my sister attended her group meetings and the camaraderie she shared with her peers left me envious. I looked forward to the time when I, too, would be part of all those exciting activities and have my very own brand new white blouse, navy blue pleated skirt, and black tie. Most of all, I wanted that black tie. But my role as the youngest sibling was to wait for my time to come, Mother's favorite final words.

I still had a lot of growing up to do. While my sister was already throwing amorous glances at my older brothers' friends, I still believed the stork delivered babies. Ours were the only storks in Niederhof. They built their enormous nest on the steep barn roof. All summer long, I kept a careful eye on the pair, hoping to catch them making that special delivery. Never once did I see them flying through the air with a diapered bundle in their long beaks. When I questioned Mother, she said, "They deliver the babies during the night." Once I watched a neighbor's calf being born, but I did not make the connection between the two.

The storks' arrival, sometime in April, was always an occasion for rejoicing. For me, it marked the beginning of summer. My year did not have four seasons; it only had summer and winter, and the arrival and departure of the storks marked the division between the two. All summer long, I watched them carry twigs and grasses to their nest, and when the babies, usually two, hatched, the parent storks brought gigantic frogs and other critters to them. Periodically, the babies broke the silence with the joyful clatter of their long pointed beaks. Once we found one of their unbroken eggs on the ground. We brought it into the house and asked Soscha to boil it.

She raised her eyebrows and said, "What if there already is a little stork inside?"

Erwin held the egg to his ear and shook his head. "I don't think so. I can't hear anything."

Then Douglas, Henry, and I, too, listened to the egg and decided there couldn't possibly be a little stork inside. But Soscha refused to boil it, so Erwin did.

"Do you think fifteen minutes is long enough?" he asked Soscha.

"I don't know, but I think it's long enough to kill the baby inside."

I held my breath when Erwin reached for a big ladle and fished the egg out of the kettle. Filled with suspense, I leaned closer as he cautiously removed the shell. The egg white was hard and shiny and revealed no sign of feathers. He cut it in half, exposing a yoke the size of a hen's egg. He pushed it into our faces and said, "Here, you taste it first!" But we could not force ourselves to eat even a tiny bite. Henry finally said, "Let's feed it to the pigs." They seemed to like it, as the nearest pigs fought over it and quickly devoured it.

I never got close enough to the storks to see just how big they really were, so they never bothered me. But our farm animals frightened me. The geese flapped their wings and chased after me, hissing and making a loud racket whenever I got too close to them. The gander was the worst. He probably singled me out because I was the smallest human who crossed his territory. After he nabbed me in the cheeks, the ones you sit on, I picked a more circuitous route to get past him. The tom turkey also made my life miserable. He got all puffed up whenever he saw me. One day, one of our roosters held me hostage on Father's hay rake. I sensed he was calculating the best angle for his assault. Just when I thought he had changed his mind, he jumped on my head from behind, buried his sharp claws in my scalp, and tore a piece of skin from my forehead. It took years for the ugly red scar to disappear. But I got even with him. Whenever he mounted one of the hens, I chased him off with a big stick to protect the poor helpless chicken. When Father caught me in the act, he scolded me and said, "Leave the rooster alone! He's only doing his job." But I still managed to occasionally interrupt his duty calls.

Danger lurked everywhere on the farm. One day when I took a shortcut across a neighbor's field, a raging bull charged after me. I ran, screaming, which only made him angrier. Luckily, a stranger stopped his car along the road, jumped out, and distracted the bull. From then on, I avoided anything with horns, not to speak of the horses, which towered over me like four-legged giants. I did not even reach their round underbellies, and their shod hoofs looked too much like the devil's feet from my brothers' scary stories. The entire farmyard seemed populated with potential enemies.

Charlie, who saw me flee from my torturers, finally came to my aid. He took me by the hand one evening, and together we called on the farm's denizens. He lifted me up and pushed me in front of our mare, Matzka, and said, "Touch her nose! She likes to have her nose stroked. You'll see."

I cautiously ran my hand over the velvety, black skin between her nostrils and was surprised how warm and soft it felt, softer even than Mother's silk Sunday dress. She held her head perfectly still, and Charlie repeated, "See, I told you. She likes it."

Then he took me to the cows. Their horns were pleasantly smooth. In the chicken coop, he guided my hand under the hens' feathery bodies and had me feel for eggs. And so I slowly lost my fear of the animals. But there was nothing we could do about the gander. He remained my enemy, and I gave him all the room he desired. With the pigs, I was on neutral ground, because they were always penned up. But then, one day, they cornered Schnurribart, my cat, in one of their pens. He hissed furiously at the puzzled pigs. Fearing for his life, I quickly opened the gate to help him escape. He leaped past me. Frightened, I ran after him, the squealing pigs at my heels. Thereafter, no one could ever convince me pigs were harmless, not even Charlie.

Schnurribart, my big, fat, gray and white tomcat, and I had a special relationship. When he was so inclined, he let me dress him in doll clothes, put a bonnet on his head, and take him for walks in my doll buggy. Sometimes, he even fell asleep. But other times, when he had enough of my mothering, he jumped out of the buggy and took off, clad in a dress and ribbons. He looked funny as he furiously tried to rip off the clothes. He ran and rolled on the ground, tearing away at the ribbons, leaving a trail of tattered shreds in his path. By the time I saw him again in the house, he had shed the entire outfit. The minute he spotted me, he made a beeline under the couch and stayed there. During the long winter evenings, he often curled up on my lap and purred, while I scratched his back and whispered tender endearments into his perked-up ears.

His favorite pastime, however, was sitting on the window sill, letting the gentle rays of the sun warm his soft fur, while eyeing the chickens scurrying around the yard. He was too lazy to chase after them, but he loved to chase after mice and rats. He usually returned looking battered, with a squirming mouse or rat clenched between his teeth, which he proudly deposited at the back door and played with until he had tortured it to death.

Mumchen, Henry's slender red calico cat, was Schnurribart's mate. She produced a litter of kittens once a year, sometimes twice. She picked the oddest places for delivering them. We never knew where she had rid herself of the heavy burden until she proudly deposited her new-born offspring at the back door. Once, after she had been missing for several days, we found her and her babies inside a drawer among the socks, a little wobbly from lack of food. Another time, she dropped her litter in one of the hen's nests in the chicken coop.

It was always a mystery to me how she had a bunch of kittens one day, and a few days later they were gone, until I overheard Mother tell Erwin it was time to drown the kittens. Upset and worried, I followed him and watched, horrified, as he dropped them one by one into a bucket of water. I cried and made Mother promise they would not do the same with Schnurribart and Mumchen if they did not stop having so many children.

"Don't worry," Mother reassured me. "They have a job to do. They have to catch mice."

We put both cats out before bedtime each evening so they could do their duty. In the morning, we usually found several dead mice neatly deposited by the back door, as though the two cats had tried to prove their usefulness. By far the better hunter, Schnurribart also went after our abundant birds. He sat for hours in the apple trees and pounced on the unsuspecting feathery fliers. But his favorite activity must have been keeping the neighborhood female cats pregnant. Every time one of my friend's cats had kittens, their mother accused Schnurribart of being the father. Not sure whether I should be proud of him, or if he needed a good scolding, I let him be.

During the winter, Fraulein Erna, a matronly professional seamstress, appeared on the farm. She usually stayed with us for an entire month and helped Mother sew clothes for us. They cut out patterns, sewed and ripped, and sewed from early morning until the late evening hours. Occasionally, even I got something new, and so did my doll. I collected fabric scraps from the floor, and Mother taught me to sew them together. I was a quick learner and enjoyed it tremendously. Mother often praised me and said, "Evchen, you are gifted. Some day you'll be able to take over the sewing for the entire family."

I learned how to knit at Mother's knee as well. Knitting was her true hobby, and we all had many beautiful sweaters. She also liked to read, and she somehow managed to combine the two. She usually sat at her mending table under an enormous asparagus fern that hung like a green halo above her bent head, a library book propped up before her and a knitting project in her hands. The needles danced wildly between her busy fingers, only breaking rhythm when she turned the pages of her book without missing a stitch. Each time she started a new knitting project, she made up pattern samples first, which she gave to me to practice on. I learned to knit before I learned to read and write. But to this day, I have not mastered the art of reading and knitting at the same time the way Mother did.

The harness mender turned up at the farm during the winter months as well. He stayed for as long as he was needed and spent his days in the stable, patching saddles and repairing harnesses with enormous needles. He smelled of leather and had a shiny bald head and big, bulging eyes, giving him a sinister expression that reminded me of the evil characters out of Oma's stories. Sitting at the dinner table next to him, I was afraid his eyes would pop out and drop into my soup plate. When I called him an ugly ogre, Mother yanked me out of my chair and gave me a severe spanking with the rug beater. She deposited me in the kitchen with Soscha and the English, and imposed house arrest on me for the remainder of the day.

That really was not as much of a punishment as Mother intended. The spanking smarted all right, but eating with Charlie in the kitchen was a lot more fun than sitting quietly at the family dinner table next to a man who frightened me and put all kinds of scary thoughts into my head.

Charlie had always been my champion, but that day he played a trick on me. For my sixth birthday, the aunts had given me a book called *Schlaraffenland*, a tale of a land where roasted pigs ran around with forks and knives stuck in their backs, rivers flowed with milk and honey, and mountains were made of solid chocolate. Smoked sausage fences surrounded cake houses. Instead of leaves, trees grew every kind of candy. The air swarmed with roasted fowl and birds, which flew directly into your open mouth. Clothes of every style and color grew on special trees. When you tugged at the hem of the one you wanted, it dropped right over your body without your having to raise an arm or a leg. To get to this wondrous land, you had to travel far, and in order to enter it, you had to eat your way through an enormous wall of rice pudding. Colorful illustrations made the tale appear even more exotic. It was a place I would have liked to visit.

I had shown Charlie the book about this land of abundance and asked him if he knew where it might be. I was sure he knew the answer because he came from a faraway land. But he always had to think about it. So, this time, as I sat there next to him, still smarting from the spanking and hinting at running away, he looked at me and said, "You know, Eva, I have figured out where this *Schlaraffenland* is. Go put on your coat and boots, and we'll go and find it!"

"Right now?" I asked, surprised.

"Yes, right now."

It did not take me long to get ready. When I returned to the kitchen, all four of them—Charlie, Jimmy, Mack, and Soscha—broke out with peals of laughter. I had not just **gotten** ready, but I had also packed a few extra things in a basket for the long journey. I was about to ask if we could bring Schnurribart along when Mother stuck her head through the door, wondering what was going on. She took one look at me and asked, "Where do you think you are going?"

"Charlie and I are going to find …" She did not let me finish but grabbed me by the neck, pushed me into the children's room, and said, "You're not going anywhere. You're spending the rest of the day in this room!"

Charlie did not come to my rescue. I was mad at him and did not speak to him for several days. But I weakened as the pieces of choco-late with which he tempted me grew larger. Soon I forgave him and doled out hugs again. Later, Charlie confessed that there really was no *Schlaraffenland*, and that it existed only in people's minds. He tried to explain to me that adults, too, needed to fantasize about things they did not have or could not have during those difficult war years. It was a bit over my head. The real war's full fury had not yet touched me.

That same year I also learned there was no *Weihnachtsmann*. When he stood before me, wearing Father's fur-lined coat, fur turned out, I scrutinized this yearly visitor more carefully and burst out, "How come you're wearing Father's coat? Is that you, Papa?" He cut his visit short, and Father reappeared shortly thereafter. But that was not such a traumatic revelation. I always had known that most of the presents, at least the ones that mattered, came out of my aunts' suitcase.

The chimney sweep, however, was real. He came yearly, blacker than the soot on the bottom of our pots and pans, his gear slung over his shoulder, working his way from rooftop to rooftop. We children teased him mercilessly because of his blackness, but he took it good-naturedly. When he became tired of us, he threatened, "I'm going to drop you down the chimney, and then you'll be even blacker than I, and your parents will think you're my children, and you'll have to come home with me." That usually stopped us.

Spring cleaning coincided with the arrival of the storks. Mother and Soscha rolled up the rugs, hung them over a line outside, and beat the dust out of them with the wicker rug beater. They moved and rearranged furniture, waxed the floors, washed windows inside and out, and replaced the heavy winter curtains with lacey summer ones to let in the sunshine. Then the plowing and planting began, and we commenced a new cycle. But the war was coming our way at an ever-increasing speed.

CHAPTER SIX

BY THE SUMMER OF 1941, Great Britain stood alone against Hitler's fury. Germany had taken over Austria, Czechoslovakia, Poland, Hungary, Romania, and Bulgaria. Greece and Yugoslavia followed soon after. In the West, Hitler's forces invaded Holland, Belgium, Norway, Denmark, and parts of France with little resistance. Mussolini entered a nonaggression pact with Hitler and joined the Germans in their conquests of the Balkans and North Africa.

In June of the same year, Hitler attacked Russia. This crucial act started a chain of events that eventually brought Germany to its knees, and the country's population learned the true meaning of sacrifices, loss of lives, and inconceivable suffering. The first year of the Russian campaign held easy victories until the German forces reached Stalingrad. It marked the turning point of the war, and became Hitler's undoing.

The first news reports of Germany's setbacks at Stalingrad reached us as sketchy, distorted, and gilded with half truths about the magnitude of military defeats and losses. Mail from the Russian front arrived censored and unstamped. People who had information about the true situation at the Russian front did not talk for fear of being turned in. Spreading demoralizing news was tantamount to treason and punishable with a prison sentence. While the official news media pounded out glowing reports of glorious victories, families silently mourned their dead and missing. Transports with severely wounded and disabled soldiers came through Niederhof carrying hundreds and then thousands, and these soldiers dared whisper the truth. Their tales alarmed the population and put them in an uneasy mood. The Hitler euphoria dampened and changed to silent hostility, as mothers and young wives lived in fear of that dreaded telegram from military headquarters. If they received letters from their loved ones, it was old news, and they still did not know if their sons and husbands lived or lay buried in some unmarked grave. Even Aunt Gertrude grew less vocal about her wonderful Hitler.

At home, there were not enough medical facilities to accommodate the wounded. The military converted my siblings' schools into makeshift hospitals. Erwin, Douglas, and Vera transferred to other schools, attending only half-day classes. They rode their bicycles to the city instead of using trains; locomotives now pulled hospital cars. Only commuter trains for the employed still ran regularly in the mornings and again in the evenings, but were not always reliable because of increased bombings. Although the war cut my siblings' school time in half, their actual days were considerably longer. They came home hungry and tired, and in the winter months, well after dark.

Troops appeared everywhere, and our little railroad station turned into a bustling hub of activity, with young soldiers in training at a nearby boot camp and the continuous loading of the thoroughbred horses for which our area was known. Disciplined columns of soldiers marched past our farm, singing patriotic songs. I ran alongside and watched them lift their shiny boots in perfect unison.

Our Sunday gatherings grew fewer and smaller, the atmosphere increasingly subdued. People talked in whispers. I lived in a world where secrets abounded. I became curious about what went on around me and listened to the adults' conversations with greater interest, although they talked in code.

We did not own a radio. True, undistorted news reached us slowly and often came filtered down through our visitors. When the Japanese attacked Pearl Harbor in December 1941, and Hitler declared war on the United States, Father was elated and said, "The war won't go on much longer, and Germany will lose."

Mother turned ashen. "Shut your mouth, Herbert! Someone might hear you."

Events proved Father only half right. The war raged on for another three-and-a-half years. Air attacks on major cities in the *Reich* escalated. But East Prussia, Germany's breadbasket, had little industry and stayed relatively unaffected by the devastating bombings. Our farm remained a safe place. We lived sheltered from the war. The only major inconveniences we faced were the disruption of train service and the many shortages.

We received blackout orders, and our world went dark at night. Cars and locomotives had to dim their headlights. Father covered the stable windows with empty potato sacks. During the summer months, the blackouts posed no problem for me, but as the days grew shorter, my fear of the dark became my nemesis. Many times, I received a thorough spanking for turning on the light in the children's room before closing the wooden shutters. But I continued to break the rule, until the night guard, who made sure the village blended into the night, caught me. He issued a severe warning to my parents and hit them with a steep fine. That evening, I received more than a spanking. Mother put me under house arrest for a whole week. But she lost track of time. The week lasted only a couple of days. From then on, I stayed out of dark rooms and waited for someone else to close the shutters.

Other disturbing stories trickled down to us. One Sunday, my aunts Elsbeth and Gertrude brought a widow friend with them. She had lost her husband before the war and had raised her two daughters alone. The distraught woman did not finish a single sentence without a spell of hysteria. The widow's story resembled Oma's many tales. Her younger daughter lived in a mental institution, victim of some type of hereditary genetic disorder. When the older daughter applied for a marriage license, she had to submit to sterilization. I did not know what sterilization meant, but sensed from the conversation it had something to do with having babies. Her fiancé broke the engagement because he wanted children. I wanted to cry out, "Our stork could have brought them a baby!" but remained quiet. I was beginning to have doubts about that stork business. The daughter grew despondent after her evil prince, as I thought of him, left her, and she turned on the gas stove and killed herself.

Father, outraged, exclaimed, "Hitler is a madman. The world has gone crazy! What will those fanatics think of next?" I never heard him vent his feelings so openly.

Aunt Elsbeth pressed her hand on Father's arm and said, "Now, Herbert, calm down! That's dangerous talk. There's nothing you can do."

Father became increasingly bold and once spoke out against Hitler while drinking a beer or two with the local men at the *Gasthaus*. When he repeated his prediction that the war could not last much longer and that Germany would lose, the two men warned him to keep his unsolicited, incendiary opinions to himself and accused him of being unpatriotic. Often, other people who started to grumble were put into their places with the reprimand, "Don't talk like Herr Rapp, that foreigner."

Hitler demanded conformity. Father, not a conformist, sensed hard times ahead and kept voicing his dark premonitions. However, the *Fuehrer* still had an enthusiastic following among those who had not yet felt the sting of the war, especially among the impressionable young, who were so easily led and misled. They felt a strong kinship with him.

My eighteen-year-old cousin, Kurt-Heinz, Aunt Kaethe's only living child, was drafted into military service when the Russian campaign began and was soon called to the Russian front. He visited us on the way to his unit. He was Oma's first-born grandchild and her favorite. The aunts, too, adored their *Bubchen*, a little lad, a pet name Aunt Gertrude had bestowed on him the first day she had laid eyes on him after he entered the world. The prospects of his coming back alive did not look promising, and the family already grieved for him. I had no memory of ever meeting him before this visit, but I was glad I was related to him. I wanted all my playmates to come and admire him in his handsome uniform, but they met my invitation with indifference. I did not fully realize they had their own valiant fathers, uncles, brothers, or cousins—all of whom also were fighting in foreign places—to boast about.

My friends Ursula and Gerda had already lost their father. He had been a soldier only a short time when a single bullet in his chest killed him. An old military uniform hung in the back of their mother's closet. We looked for the blood-encrusted bullet hole but found none. Ursula finally concluded that it must have been her grandfather's uniform, because she could not really remember her father.

We became more and more preoccupied with what it would be like to die for the *Vaterland*, words we heard over and over again. What would it be like to have bombs fall from the sky, and what would an explosion sound like? All the talk about blown-to-pieces bodies and humans charred beyond recognition frightened us, but it did not stop us from spying on the adults' hushed conversations, trying to make sense of it all.

In school, our teacher never talked about the war, but we felt the effects in the classroom. We practiced writing the alphabet and numbers on slate boards, because paper was in short supply. We memorized the words to patriotic songs, the same songs we would be forbidden to sing after the war ended. We girls received instructions in sewing and made samplers. In third grade, knitting and crocheting became part of our curriculum. Soon, we would be making things for the soldiers at the front, the teacher told us. Most of us had already learned the rudiments of those things from our mothers.

For my seventh birthday, Aunt Gertrude gave me the *Struwwelpeter*, a book meant to teach children the consequences of disobedience. Filled with meaningful rhymes and graphic pictures directed at naughty children, it told of the incurable thumb sucker who reverted to his bad habit every time his parents left him alone at home. One day, a tailor appeared with enormous scissors and cut off the boy's thumbs, leaving him standing with blood dripping from his hands and his thumbs bouncing on the floor. Then, there was the girl who liked to play with matches, until she caught on fire and burned to a heap of ashes; her two cats watched helplessly, shedding so many tears that they formed a puddle. Or, there were the boys who taunted a black Moor because of his blackness. Saint *Nikolaus* came along and dunked them into his giant inkwell until they came out blacker than the Moor. The *Struwwelpeter* himself was a disheveled-looking boy with an unwieldy mass of hair and claws for nails because he did not let anyone comb his hair or cut his nails. I believed all these stories and the many more that were just as explicit and frightening.

The book's message provided food for our mischievous thoughts and made us cautious during those abnormal times. It was, in a sense, a definitive children's self-guide to keep us out of trouble in an environment where discipline was weakened by the absence of fathers. We grew up in an atmosphere with emphasis on self-reliance, and the *Struwwelpeter* helped steer us through the troubled waters of our loosely supervised childhood.

After I started first grade, my circle of friends expanded. My new friend Katarina lived in a small villa. I was convinced her parents were very rich because they had indoor plumbing. Katarina and her older siblings had an entire toy-filled room dedicated as the children's play room. She owned many dolls, with an extensive wardrobe, doll furniture, and two sets of little dishes, one for every day and fine china for special occasions. We all competed for her friendship just to get our hands on all those wonderful toys. None of my other friends had so many things, and neither did I.

I saw Katarina's father, a high-ranking officer in the military, only once, when her family picked him up at the station. He had many shiny medals pinned to the jacket of his neat uniform, and he looked handsome and gentlemanly, unlike my father, who always walked around in wrinkled old corduroy pants and smelled of hay and the stable. I wished my father could have a uniform just like Katarina's father had.

I asked Mother one day, "Are we very poor?"

"What do you mean, very poor?"

"Katarina has so many toys. You should see them. They even have a movie screen, and sometimes her brother shows us pictures of black people in Africa. Is it true that there are real black people like the one in the *Struwwelpeter*?"

Mother thought for a minute and said, "Yes, there are black people in Africa. There are people of all colors all over the world."

"Are they in Africa too?" I wanted to know.

"Yes, in Africa too."

Mother went back to counting the stitches on her knitting and ignored my further probing. I did not know what to make of this newly revealed world of color. Yellow people, red people, green people, black people. What did they look like? Oma had never talked of such curiosities. I decided to ask her the next time she came to see us.

But Grandmother, her health failing, no longer joined the aunts on their visits. She was the only grandparent I knew, and I missed the time and attention she had always so patiently devoted to me. Occasionally, my parents took me along to Elbing to visit her. When I begged her for another story she brushed me off with, "Some other time, Evchen, I'm too tired right now."

The visits to Oma's house were special. I got to drink sweet tea out of a clear glass in an ornate golden holder, while I claimed her black cane rocking chair. When I became tired, I snuggled up with their white polar bear rug in front of the old grandfather clock, but not before Aunt Elsbeth rendered the bear rug harmless by tying a string around his gaping mouth. Then, I could stare into the open cavity, examine his sharp teeth, and poke my fingers into his glass eyes.

During these trips to Elbing, I slowly became accustomed to the strangeness of city life. But I never lost my fear of that overpopulated world, with the squeezed-together buildings, the din of traffic, and the clanging of the many streetcars going in all directions. As soon as we got off the train in the city, I felt disoriented and held on tightly to Mother's hand. Once in the safety of Grandmother's house, I often ventured downstairs, sat on the front steps, and watched the busy city life unfold in front of me. I did not dare walk to the nearest corner, since I was afraid of not finding my way back. If a friendly passerby talked to me, I ran into the building and hid. The city felt like a great big giant with gaseous breath, a breath so different from the pleasant aroma of dried grass and potato fields, the sweet smell of ripe apples, and the scents of the many flower blossoms in Mother's garden. I was apprehensive about the day when I, too, would be attending school in Elbing. How would I find my way in that web-like maze? How did my brothers and sister do it? They seemed so grown up and worldly, and I felt small, ignorant, and frightened. And if not so little any more, I was still quite ignorant and naïve, which did not help me when the war finally shattered our lives.

But at that time, I had no inkling of what the future held. I lived in the moment. Neither the war nor the *Struwwelpeter* squelched my curiosity or hunger for experimentation. On laundry days, Mother let me iron handkerchiefs. With the iron still warm, but unplugged, she thought I could do no harm. But she was mistaken. One time, while she sat by the sunny window, engrossed in her knitting, I did what I was told not to do. I plugged the iron in again and left it resting on the blanket that served as an ironing surface. Mother did not even look up. Then I went to look for my doll. As I reentered the room Mother raised her head, sniffed the air, and exclaimed, "Something is burning!"

I lunged for the iron, lifted it up, and watched the blanket go up in flames. Mother jumped up, got tangled in the ball of yarn that had tumbled to the floor, and caught herself at the edge of the table. She rolled up the blanket, pulled the electric plug from the socket, and yanked the iron out of my hand. Luckily for me, both her hands were full. I ran out of the room, flew past a puzzled Soscha in the kitchen, and shouted, "I didn't know it would catch fire. I only plugged it in for a little while!"

I made myself invisible for the rest of the day and came to the supper table prepared for punishment. But Mother showed no anger. Instead, she took both my hands, looked imploringly into my shifting eyes, and said, "Evchen, Evchen, you could have burned the house down. I hope you've learned a lesson."

I had not learned a lesson. Mother not only gave me another chance with the iron, but she also left me alone in the room. This time, I plugged the iron in just long enough to make that swishing sound when I tested it with the spit on my fingers the way Mother did. I was about to do an experiment. The aunts had given me a book called *Max und Moritz*, a story of two mischievous boys whose sole mission in life was to play tricks on unsuspecting adults. In one of their capers, they sawed the wooden bridge to the village tailor's house in half. Then, they taunted him until he came running with his long ruler in pursuit of the two culprits. The bridge collapsed, and the tailor fell into the creek. Two geese came along and pulled him out of the frigid water. Soaked through, he could not warm up until his sympathetic wife stretched him out on the ironing table and ran the hot iron up and down his shivering body. Intrigued by the story, I decided to iron my body, starting with my thigh. I let out a scream, fled to the shed, and hid in the old carriage, writhing in pain. Jimmy, our English prisoner, stuck his head through the door, and asked, "What's the matter, Eva? What did you do this time?"

"My leg—it hurts. I can't walk."

He looked at the red outline the iron had made on my thigh and asked, alarmed, "What happened? What did you do?"

"I wanted to iron myself like in *Max und Moritz*."

He scooped me up in his arms and carried me upstairs to his quarters, all the while telling me, "You silly girl. Don't you know anything, you silly girl?"

He sat me down at the edge of his bed, rummaged through his magic duffel bag, and brought out a jar of soothing ointment and a big roll of white bandages, which he applied to my thigh. In less than a minute, the pain was gone and a happy smile erased my tears. I put my arms around his neck, squeezed hard, and whispered into his ear, "Don't tell Mother, pleeeease!"

Mother did not need to be told with the all-too-visible evidence. To my surprise, I did not receive a spanking this time either, but it put a permanent stop to my ironing career.

CHAPTER SEVEN

AFTER HITLER DECLARED WAR ON the United States, diplomatic relations between the two countries ceased. This had serious consequences for our family. Suddenly, Father was not merely an eccentric foreigner—he became the enemy. The American consulate shut down, foreign officials left the country, and with them went Father's protective umbrella. Although he had planned to make another trip to the United States, he now could not follow through. He turned to the American consul in Switzerland and wrote many letters, with Jimmy's help, explaining his untenable situation. He fought to retain his American citizenship, which, after his family, was the thing most dear to him, as he often said.

He succeeded at least in going on record as having tried. The consul requested a family portrait for the records. We got to stay home from school on that special "photo" day. As usual, we rushed around getting ready in time to catch the train. For these family events, my sister always had to help Henry and me get dressed. She rebelled regularly. "Learn something from this," Mother told her. "Don't have so many children when you get married."

We did not miss the train that time, but we had to make the usual run for it. We never walked to the station on these family outings and quite often only managed to catch the train because it was late. We arrived at the photographers at the appointed hour. It turned out to be a lucky family portrait. Everyone had their eyes open and displayed just a trace of a smile. Only Father looked into the camera with a sad and solemn expression. Our recorded images made it into the "Rapp family" file at the American Embassy in Switzerland. The records lay there and collected dust until the end of the war. They disappeared for a time and later became the subject of a long search.

By then, Germany was at war against half the world. And so the German people allowed the country's history to be reshaped by the man they put into power, the man who promised to pull them out of that devastating depression of the 1920s. And he did. The price, however, for the new, short-lived prosperity was going up by the month, by the week, and in the end by the day!

Centralization and government control became the new catch-words. Farmers were urged to raise sheep for wool and grow flax for linen. Hitler needed these commodities to keep his soldiers clothed. Father was no longer free to make his own arrangements and do business with whomever he pleased, nor were we allowed to process our milk to make cream and butter. The local dairy shut down and became a butter and cheese storage facility for the military. A truck now picked up our milk and delivered it to a central dairy in Elbing. In return, the driver left us a canister or two of skimmed milk for our calves and family consumption.

The German defeat at Stalingrad roused the civilian popula-tion out of its blind euphoria. The turning tide divided the country between those who still believed in Hitler's magic powers and the disillusioned who, win or lose, wished for a quick end to the war. As the death toll and number of missing in battle rose, the population's morale sank and an oppressive mood hung over the country.

These upheavals went mostly unnoticed by us children. We only felt the excitement around us. The stench of death did not reach our nostrils. I was just young enough to absorb much of what I heard and saw without the trepidation and alarm the adults felt. My head was still full of fairy tales, and I saw much of what happened around me with that "and they lived happily ever after" expectation.

Niederhof was inundated with military, and the station waiting rooms overflowed with tired travelers, waiting for connecting trains that might or might not materialize. We children hung out at the station by the hour and watched the excitement that often overwhelmed us. Up to that time, we had lived an insular life in the deep-seated traditions of simple country people. Then, suddenly, everything was in a state of turmoil and agitation. Troop transports heading for the Russian front became a daily sight. We waved to the soldiers. They waved back through the lowered compartment windows, shouting victory slogans and singing happy songs as they slowly passed through Niederhof.

Trains coming from the Russian front brought back the wounded. They did not wave back at us, nor did they sing happy songs. We saw them lying between white sheets, with bandaged heads and limbs; they stared at us through closed windows, bewildered expressions on their gaunt faces. Sometimes these unscheduled trains sat for hours on sidetracks, waiting for a locomotive or clearance to continue the soldiers' painful journey. We rushed over and gawked at the men. I asked Mother about these transports, but she offered no explanation and told me to stay away from there, which had exactly the opposite effect. The station attracted us like a magnet. Often a string of flat cars loaded with war machines stood on a sidetrack for several days. We looked with awe at these firmly secured, towering monsters.

On our way home from school one day, the gatekeeper at the railroad crossing shouted from her tower, "Children, are you coming to watch Hitler's train? He's coming through Niederhof this afternoon."

I ran home, dropped my satchel, gulped down my meal, and headed for the station. To see the *Fuehrer* in person would give me something to brag about in school. I did not tell Mother about the momentous event. Hitler was not popular at our house. I had figured that out a long time ago. My parents did not realize how much I heard of things that were not meant for my ears. We received conflicting messages from the adults. In school the teacher praised Hitler, at home he was ridiculed and condemned, and with our innate children's sensibility, we knew not to question either.

A cloud of excitement hovered over the small group gathered for the event. Every time a piercing whistle announced the approach of a train, we craned our necks expectantly, only to discover it was just an ordinary transport or freight train. When Hitler's train finally did arrive, we did not immediately recognize it as "the train"; it looked that insignificant. First, a locomotive passed with two red swastika flags mounted at the front. From that we knew it was an official train, but there was no accompanying fanfare. Then came a flatcar with an anti-aircraft gun aimed at the sky. Two passenger cars, windows closed and heavily draped, followed. Another flatcar with an anti-aircraft gun brought up the rear. I expected the train to consist of an endless string of cars and many, many soldiers waving to us from their open windows, with the *Fuehrer* in their midst also waving at us. As it was, we saw no sign that Hitler might be sitting behind one of the draped windows. No hand appeared to push the curtains aside; no face showed itself.

People mumbled disappointment and felt just as cheated as I did. After the long boring wait, I had nothing to boast about in school. Just as we started to disperse, a second train pulled past us, identical to the first with an engine sporting two red flags, a flatcar with a gun, two passenger cars with heavily draped windows, and, at the end, another flatcar with a second gun. And again, nothing indicated that the passenger cars were occupied.

"I bet he wasn't in either one," I heard a man say. "What a clever trick."

"*Ja*, he's probably sitting in his bunker at the *Wolfsschanze,* Wolf's Lair," the reply came. "He doesn't want anyone to know where he is these sad days."

So I did not get to see Hitler after all.

By spring of 1943, it seemed as though every male was a soldier, except for my father and my friends' grandfathers. Twice as many army units now marched in goosestep past our farm, often stopping to rest along the tree-lined highway. We children brought them cool water from our well to refill their canteens, and we listened to their talk. Father asked them about their destination, but they did not answer him. They were marching into the unknown. When they wrote home, they could not mention where they were. All mail arrived unstamped and censored. Families only knew that their loved ones were fighting either at the western or eastern front. My cousin, Kurt-Heinz, was at the eastern front, where the fighting was the fiercest and the casualties were the highest. His chances for survival were slim. Oma worried, the aunts worried, and my parents worried about my teenage brothers. Father feared that if the war lasted much longer, they, too, would be drafted into the military despite their American citizenship.

Another summer arrived. The news from the Russian front turned more and more gloomy. The Russians were forcing the Germans into a slow but steady retreat. Our life, however, remained outwardly unchanged. The big family event that year was the acquisition of a console gramophone. My father bought it from a Jewish business friend in Elbing, who had managed to evade persecution so far because of his influential Christian wife. Worried, the friend was now secretly turning everything he owned into cash. "So they can get out of Germany," Father whispered to Mother, pointing his chin in an uncertain direction, adding, "Switzerland."

Other precious things appeared at the farm, including a large oil painting, valuable pieces of crystal, and china. Mother shook her head and said, "Herbert, you are going to get us into trouble. Remember what happened to those farmers in Steglitz! Where are we going to put all that stuff? The kids need shoes. Find us some sturdy shoes instead."

"Annchen, they're our friends. They need money. Their lives are in danger. It may already be too late for them. They're not safe in Germany any more."

"Well," Mother changed the subject, "it'll be nice to have music in the house."

Mother was right about the trouble part. Several years earlier, a couple of farmers from Steglitz had ignored the new ordinance forbidding all Germans to do business with Jews and had sold their produce to them. When they were found out, their names and pictures appeared in the local newspaper. The headlines read, "Insolent Steglitz farmers do business with Jews," as though they had committed the crime of the century. (I got this piece of information from one of the "guilty" farmers' sons some fifty years later, when I asked him what that had been all about. Fortunately, there were no serious repercussions for them other than being called Jew-friends for a time.)

Along with the gramophone came a large collection of records. Now we had music in the house, and my parents gave a big, rollicking party. No one could have guessed that it would be their last celebration, an anniversary perhaps, or Father's fiftieth birthday, or maybe Mother's forty-fifth. Cheerful people filled the house one more time, women with their soldier husbands on leave and some without partners. Even Aunt Gertrude brought her much-older male friend. Boisterous laughter rippled through the rooms as it had during happier times. Mother and English Charlie prepared a feast of meats and pastries. After dinner, the men rolled up the living room rug and pushed the furniture against the wall. Mother sprinkled talc on the parquet floor, and the broom dance began. The women without mates danced with brooms as partners. When the music stopped, they dropped their brooms and wildly scrambled for real partners.

Father thrilled me and pulled me onto the floor for the first dance, but the rest of the evening I got one of the brooms. The men were popular that night since there were so few of them. The party ended with a nostalgic sing-along session of old folk melodies and sentimental songs glorifying the beauty of East Prussia, our homeland. The magical fairy-tale evening provided a happy interlude in my parents' troubled life.

Father had one more gratifying moment before the Gestapo caught up with him. A few years earlier, he had planted a fruit orchard. That summer, one of the fledgling apple trees produced a single red apple. Every morning he visited the "fruit of his labor," and warned us that woe would be upon us if we dared so much as touch that apple. Then, the wind blew it off the tree one stormy night. Father brought the apple into the house, held it under Mother's nose, and said, "Drink in that aroma, Anna. Isn't it the best thing you've ever inhaled?" I got to smell it too, but would have much rather taken a big bite out of it. He asked Mother for a bit of string, returned to the orchard, and tied the apple to the tree high enough so at least I could not reach it. It hung there until it rotted and fell to the ground, where the geese fought over it.

"You should have let the kids each have a bite," Mother reproached him. Father looked at her with a sparkle in his eyes and said, "Next year, the trees will be laden with fruit. You just wait and see."

That summer of 1943, Henry and I got our first pair of *Klappersandalen*, literally translated as clattering sandals. The sandals consisted of three pieces of wood nailed together with strips of leather and enough straps and hardware to hold them on our feet. For the entire season, we ran around in this new wartime footwear. We held contests to see who could make the loudest clatter while running a race. It shortened the sandals' life considerably and kept Charlie, a clever shoe repairer, busy. From then on, we only received new school shoes, bought with ration coupons and not always readily available.

When school was out that summer, we headed for the sea. Aunt Elsbeth now worked for the post office in Kahlberg and lived there year around. Her doll house, as we children called it, became our home for another glorious, fun-filled summer. We spent our days on the beach. Lazy and spoiled, we only showed up for meal times, sat around a set table, and waited for the food to appear, food that Aunt

Elsbeth prepared single handedly. I still had not learned how to swim. The beach was miles long, and the water was shallow for many yards out, providing safe footing. Henry and I waded in the surf, built sand bunkers, and wrote our names on them with pinecones.

When Father was with us, he swam out for long distances and did not return for what seemed like hours. Mother worried and scolded him when he suddenly reappeared, not from the water where she scanned the horizon, but from behind her where she did not expect him. He threw his arms around her still slender waist and pulled her close to him, whispering something into her ear, evoking happy laughter from both of them. I liked to watch them. They never were that relaxed and happy at home on the farm.

The season in Kahlberg ended with a special concert at the pavilion. Mother came for the final festivity, as well as Aunt Gertrude, Erwin, Douglas, and Vera. Henry was already installed with family friends in Elbing for the upcoming school year. Children my age were not allowed to go to the concert, at least so they told me. The dilemma was what to do with me. They worked on me with the most attractive bribery ploys I had yet experienced. Erwin gave me his gold pocket watch to play with, which must have cost him a great deal of anxiety. Douglas promised to take me fishing the next time he went, although he did not specify when that would be. Aunt Gertrude let me have one of her treasured books, the coffee-table kind, with a lot of colorful pictures of flowers and birds. Aunt Elsbeth promised to buy me ice cream cones, lots of ice cream cones, if I would just be a good girl and go to bed early. Mother promised that someone would come and check on me, so I never would really be alone for long. Besides, the curfew did not allow young children on the streets after dark. They left out the word "unaccompanied," but I did not know the difference. It all sounded extremely attractive, especially the ice cream cones. I promised to be a good girl.

After they left, the house creaked and moaned. I crawled deeper under the covers, clenching Erwin's watch tightly between my sweaty fingers. The shadows in the corners took on eerie shapes. Pinecones dropped on the roof, which, in my mind, quickly turned into dancing ghosts. When the hoot of an owl cut through the night air, I panicked and jumped out of bed, threw my clothes back on, and rushed to the door. It was locked. I screamed for Mother, the aunts, and my brothers, but no one appeared. The walls threatened to cave in on me. I pried a window open, moved the geraniums in the flower box out of the way, jumped into the garden, and raced along the sandy path until I reached the busy pier. Cautious about the watchman, who, according to Mother, looked for stray children like me, I stayed at the pier until it started to turn really dark. Then, I sneaked over to the pavilion, climbed the many flights of stairs to the top of the hill, plopped myself on a freshly painted white bench near the entrance, and waited. I heard music inside and knew once it stopped they would all come out; instead, they applauded and the music started all over again. A lump crawled into my stomach. What would happen to me if I missed them, or worse, if they had left early?

The double doors finally swung open and a noisy crowd emerged. With so many people pouring out all at once, I panicked again. How would I find my way home through that ghost-infested forest if I missed them? Suddenly, there they were, talking, laughing, and having a good time. They did not even notice me. I thought about following them home and watching their surprise at my disappearance. That might lessen the punishment I was sure to receive. But rather than risking losing them in the darkness, I faced them. They froze and stared down at me as if I were one of those frightening ghosts that had pursued me all evening. Before Mother could say anything, I flew into her open arms and sobbed, "I was frightened. The room was so dark and full of ghosts that made all kinds of scary noises. They were coming to get me."

Mother stroked my head and said, "Now, now, Evchen. It's all right. You're safe now."

I did not receive the expected spanking, not even a reprimand, and Mother never left me home alone again.

The next time Aunt Elsbeth came to visit us on the farm, she remarked to Father about the incident and chastised him about the lack of discipline among us children.

"*Ach*, leave them be," Father said, with a hint of premonition in his voice. "Let them enjoy what's left of their lives. Who knows what the future holds for them."

CHAPTER EIGHT

THE STEGLITZ FARMERS STOOD AT the outer perimeter of politics. In Niederhof, with its petty bureaucrats, the opposite was true. The Nazis pressured the civilian population to join the Party, which most of them did, if not by conviction, at least for reasons of expedience and convenience. Career advancements were a near impossibility if civilians did not belong to the Party, and certain high positions were closed to them altogether.

Father did not join the pack and became more and more of an outsider. He no longer felt welcome at the *Gasthaus*, he told Mother.

"Herbert, you've got to learn to control your tongue. It's not safe to speak your mind. You don't know who you can trust any more. Someone is sure to make trouble for you."

Mother's prediction came true all too soon. One day, two men from the Gestapo drove up to the farm in a shiny black car. I thought they were returning our Opel. Instead, they took Father away with them to their headquarters in Elbing for questioning. He did not return that evening, or the following day, or the next week. Since I was too young to understand the seriousness of the situation, Mother told me that Father had gone on a long trip and would not come home for a while. Over time, however, I picked up enough bits and pieces to know something was amiss, but I did not know if it was good or bad. I overheard a conversation between Aunt Elsbeth and Mother during which they referred to Father being in the *Gefaengnis*, the German word for jail. I had no idea what a jail was, or where it was, but from all the secrecy and whispering, I gathered it was a place of great importance. News spread in Niederhof that they had finally caught up with that "foreign agitator," Herr Rapp.

"Eva, where is your father?" my playmates' mothers asked.

"He's in jail," I proudly told them, convinced jail was a very desirable place to be. They gave me that all knowing look and said, "Ah," or, "Oh," or, "Really," and added, "Why, what has he done?"

"I don't know, but Mother said he'll be gone a long time," I answered with an air of importance.

In the meantime, the Gestapo, Hitler's secret police, held Father and considered him a red tag prisoner, a political incarcerate, and an enemy of the state. It was a serious charge, and few such prisoners ever saw their families again. Father's false friends from the *Gasthaus* had betrayed him. Their accusations were many. Father had spoken out against Hitler in public, a charge serious enough to earn him a prison term. He had turned the knob on the radio at the *Gasthaus*, searching for a foreign station, an absolutely forbidden act. People overheard him speaking English with the prisoners in our home. That put him under suspicion of espionage against the country. He absolutely refused to renounce his American citizenship, which he repeatedly was asked to do. In the pettiest accusation of all, he was suspected of skimming the cream off the milk before sending it to the dairy. That represented a crime against the people. This serious situation placed our entire family in peril. The investigation dragged on for several months. The authorities never came up with anything concrete, nor did the records at the central dairy reveal any irregularities, which could easily be verified since the milk canisters were marked with identifying numbers and could be traced to their source.

No one explained Father's sudden absence to me. I probably would not have understood. Even when word got back to Mother that I was telling everyone in Niederhof that Father was in jail, she gave no explanation. Instead, she threatened to lock me in the windowless chimney room if I continued to tell so many tales. The chimney room was the punishment of last resort. My siblings were well acquainted with that pitch-dark, sooty room, but I had not yet experienced it. The threat alone silenced me.

I missed Father's affection, the tender nightly sessions in his lap, and our raids on the pantry. Mother was stingy with her hugs, and she rarely showed her feelings. But I forced myself on her, transferring the love and longing I held cooped up for Father to her. I needed that physical contact, and with Father gone she now became the focus of my existence, with English Charlie as the backup. I went upstairs to see him every evening before bedtime. He made the pain less painful with his endless supply of chocolates.

Things changed after they took Father away. Now only the aunts showed up on Sundays, but less often, because they had to work longer hours and weekends. Oma and Uncle Eduard did not come at all any more. Aunt Elsbeth, our anchor during Father's incarceration, was relentless in enlisting the family's influential connections in Elbing for help. Father was not allowed visitors. Gestapo people showed up repeatedly at the farm, always unannounced, and demanded to see the books and records, which they pored over a single page at a time. They searched our English prisoners' room, went through their possessions, questioned them individually about Father's activities, put Soscha under scrutiny, and interrogated the people in Niederhof.

Whenever the Gestapo searched the prisoners' room, my sister and Soscha hurriedly cleared all the British goods that were sitting on the pantry shelves, thanks to Charlie's, Jimmy's, and Mack's generosity. The authorities' accusation of Father's fraternizing with the enemy might have been given sufficient ground if they had discovered those supplies.

Mother held up and carried on during those months of uncertainty. For a long time, we did not know who Father's accusers were. Normal human relations were breaking down everywhere. No one trusted anyone. If in the past people spoke in whispers and behind closed doors, they now did not speak at all for fear of being reported. Neighbors betrayed neighbors, and friends were not safe from their friends. No one knew who their friends were, as Father's situation proved.

So the summer of 1943 ended, and we children faced a new school year, a year quite different from the others. Erwin, along with his entire class, spent his last year of school in the *Heimatflak*, the Home Defense Corps, a type of boot camp for sixteen- to seventeen-year-old boys. They were called upon to prove themselves to the *Vaterland* as future brave soldiers. Aunt Gertrude, now totally disillusioned with Hitler, had a different view and referred to the young boys as "Hitler's next generation of cannon fodder."

In the *Heimatflak*, Erwin learned to operate an anti-aircraft gun and identify enemy planes. His buddies and he were to protect the home front, while most of their fathers fought the enemy on more distant battlefields. At sixteen, the boys were old enough to shoot a gun but too young to smoke cigarettes. Put into uniforms, they lived in army barracks at the outskirts of Elbing. Teachers came to the compound for half-day class instruction and book learning. The balance of the time was devoted to soldiering.

I was proud of my brother. Finally, a member of our family wore a uniform. He transformed overnight from a gawky kid into a handsome boy soldier. I wanted to parade him around Niederhof so my friends could see my soldier brother.

Erwin came home whenever he had leave. Sometimes, he brought his best friend, Dieter. Dieter's widowed mother had moved away from Elbing, and our farm became his home away from home. He always brought a radio and an accordion with him. On Sunday afternoons, he often joined the English in the stable for their music sessions. They kept the windows and doors tightly shut for fear of being heard, because the prisoners were supposed to be locked up when not working, especially on Sundays.

These musical interludes created suspenseful moments with Father gone, but Mother never stopped them. Only once did they almost get caught by a surprise inspection. Henry, however, saw the soldiers coming and warned the English. The prisoners made the instruments disappear, grabbed shovels and pitchforks, and cleaned the stalls. We had the most immaculate stable for miles around.

Often, when the English's melancholy melodies reached Mother's ears, she stopped what she was doing and listened. Her face softened while she gazed wistfully into space and whispered, "How beautiful." It seemed as if the music reached her hardening heart and liberated her innermost feelings. Always more affectionate with me during those moments, she often beckoned to me, saying, "Come here, Evchen! Give me a hug!" She embraced and squeezed me almost as hard as Aunt Elsbeth had the habit of doing. I relished those times, and I pressed my head into her soft breast and listened to the rhythmic beat of her heart.

Sometimes, on Sunday mornings, I got to listen to the *Children's Hour* on Dieter's radio, my first acquaintance with this curious apparatus. I could not figure out how the people got into such a small box. Mother said, "The voices come through the air." I looked over my shoulders to check the room for ghosts.

Erwin and Jimmy rigged up a makeshift antenna, which they ran to the top of one of the old apple trees in the garden, and tried to get an English channel, much to Mother's chagrin. Occasionally, they picked up pieces of news contradicting Hitler's grossly exaggerated reports of advancements and victories in North Africa and at the Russian front.

At school we had a new teacher, Fraulein Eckers, a long-haired, blond beauty with sparkly blue eyes and a soft voice. She looked very young, not much older than my sister. I adored her. Contrary to the old male teacher, who always was quick to punish the slightest transgression, she was kind and indulging.

That year in third grade, we practiced more reading and writing, and school became a lot more fun. More aware of the world around me, I noticed, for the first time, the imposing Hitler portrait hanging on the wall behind Fraulein Eckers' desk. A big red swastika flag stood in the corner behind the blackboard. I touched it once and was surprised by its softness.

One day, Fraulein Eckers brought a gas mask to school and announced, "Today we're going to learn how to breathe with this mask."

"What's it for?" one of the younger children wanted to know. "Are we going to have to keep it on all the time?"

"No, no. We're only practicing so you'll know what to do if you ever need to use it."

"It's to keep you from getting gassed," the girl next to me whispered in my ear. "My grandmother in Berlin has one of those things hanging in her closet."

I tried it on and, afraid I might suffocate, inhaled deeply. It felt strange. We laughed at one another because we looked like pigs with big goggle eyes and rubber snouts. The teacher laughed with us and encouraged us to make a game out of it, since some of the younger children were afraid to put on the mask.

A few weeks later, Fraulein Eckers issued each of us a bankbook and said, "We're going to learn to save money. The first school day of each month will be 'saving day.' I want you to save your pocket money and bring it to school, and I will enter it in your bankbook. You will be saving money for the *Fuehrer*."

I did not receive such a curious thing called pocket money, but

Mother gave me a few coins whenever I remembered to ask. The teacher duly entered the amount in my little blue book. She praised us for our patriotism. I would have much rather exchanged those pennies for a licorice stick at the *Gasthaus* and sometimes did.

Aunt Elsbeth appeared on the farm more frequently. Each time, Mother killed and cleaned a few chickens, which disappeared in Aunt Elsbeth's bottomless bag, along with a dozen or two eggs and fresh produce from our garden. Mother was not as adept at killing chickens as Father was. Occasionally, one would slip out of her hands and run around with its head cut off, leaving a trail of blood until it fell over. Aunt Elsbeth would quickly cover her eyes and say, "Oh, how horrible. Those poor birds."

"It's only a reflex, Elschen. Don't worry, they can't feel a thing," Mother would console her.

I suspect most of those chickens ended up on the dinner table of the people who worked on Father's case, because so many landed in Aunt Elsbeth's big bag. Mother joked about it and said, "You know, Elschen, every time the chickens see you entering the yard, they run and hide."

No one discussed Father's incarceration in front of us children, and I no longer told people he was in that special place called jail. After a while, they stopped asking about him. They knew more about Father than I did.

Life went on and brought hardships, heartbreaks, and despair to everyone. Bombs now fell continuously on cities. Not only soldiers, but also civilians, perished by the hundreds and thousands. No family remained untouched by death. Children were separated from their mothers and sent to the country, where they would be safe from the threatening skies above. Younger ones stayed with relatives, and older ones went into group camps, where they attended school part-time, helped out on farms, made bandages, and contributed to the war effort. East Prussia, with its quiet bucolic life, became the air raid shelter for the rest of the country. No bombs had reached us yet, but their victims arrived by the thousands, all in need of food and shelter.

CHAPTER NINE

NEWS OF CONTINUED SETBACKS AT the Russian front reached us almost daily during the winter of 1943–1944. But, as yet, we had no inkling of the greater danger headed our way. Their homes leveled by bombs, the homeless arrived by the trainloads, not just children but entire families dependent on relatives or strangers. Everyone who had room to spare was forced to take in evacuees, as we referred to these newly dispossessed families. The rift between the "haves" and the innocent "have-nots" widened with each new arrival, and resentment grew between the two. With no extra room in our farmhouse, we did not have to accommodate any evacuees.

Grandparents took care of grandchildren, while mothers stayed behind in the cities to work as aides, nurses, clerks in the military, and factory workers, jobs the fighting men had vacated. Labor shortages were acute. At school, our classes grew larger and became more interesting. The city children brought the outside world to our tranquil, little island of peace. They were well acquainted with the war's terrors, something we had yet to experience.

Erwin, Vera, and Henry now lived in Elbing, and Father was behind bars. Douglas commuted to school, and I made my daily journey to Steglitz with my schoolmates. The house felt empty. Still very much afraid of the dark, I did not like sleeping alone in the big children's room and would have liked very much to have a refugee family with many children move in with us.

After Father's incarceration, Mother no longer bought our staples at the local *Gasthaus*. Instead, she shopped in another village some five kilometers away, often taking me along. A once-simple errand became a major undertaking and took up a good part of the day. I loved to lie in the back of the milk wagon and watch the tangled branches move past as the little patches of blue sky peeked through; it was like looking through a gigantic kaleidoscope. The merchant woman never let us leave without handing me a licorice stick, for the long journey home she would say.

On laundry day, I had the job of keeping the ducks, geese, and chickens off the bed sheets and tablecloths Mother would spread out to bleach on the grass. One day, I took the rug beater and finally got even with the gander. He now gave me a wide berth.

During Father's incarceration, the mothers of my little friends kept me at bay. They often met me at the door with, "Christa," or "Waltraut," or whoever else, "is not home right now," when I very well knew they were. Katarina's mother did not even open the door, but Katarina watched from behind the lace curtains. The sudden standoff hurt and left me confused.

One day, some boys threw rocks at Henry and me and called us "damned foreigners." Douglas chased after them.

"Did you beat them up?" I asked, anxious for revenge.

"No, but I think they won't bother you any more." It felt good to have a big, protective brother.

That fall and winter was the unhappiest time of my young childhood. The doors to my friends' homes remained shut. We still walked to school together and, occasionally, gathered at the railroad station to watch the ever-increasing activities. But I spent many lonely hours looking out the window, getting lost in a fairy-tale world with Schnurribart at my side.

I played house with him under the big dining table in the family room and became well acquainted with the underside of our furniture. When he tried to escape my tyrannical household, I tied him to the table leg and kept him prisoner. But, smart and cunning, he always managed to wrestle free.

One cold day when the wind howled outside, I decided to trim his whiskers. He got suspicious when he heard that beguiling quality in my voice and made himself scarce. Instead, I practiced on Mother's hand-embroidered tablecloth in the parlor and cut off the fringe. When Mother saw what I had done, she turned pale and shouted, "Oh, no, Eva! Oh, no!"

I dropped the scissors and started to bawl as if I had already received the spanking that awaited me. Mother, however, sat down on the nearest chair rested her elbows on the newly trimmed table-cloth, covered her face with both hands, and wept. It was the first time I saw her cry. It frightened me. I threw my arms around her neck and whimpered, "I'm sorry, Mutti, but no one will play with me."

"What am I going to do with you? Don't you have any sense at all?"

"The fringe was all messed up. Maybe I should have just combed it."

"You should have kept your hands off the scissors. That's what you should have done."

It took a long time before I got back into her good graces. But as time passed, the de-fringed tablecloth received a new hem and became the subject of many a family joke.

One day, a picture postcard of a little girl sitting under an umbrella arrived addressed to Evchen Rapp, in Niederhof. It was from Aunt Elsbeth. The message consisted of a single line: "If you write to me regularly, I will send you a pretty postcard in return." I accepted the challenge enthusiastically and wrote to her about Schnurribart's exploits like, "Today Schnurribart fell out of the old apple tree, trying to catch a bird. I thought he had killed himself, but he walked away with only a limp." He did so many funny things that I always had something to tell. Aunt Elsbeth kept her word, and soon I had a colorful postcard collection of animals and fairy-tale characters.

By October 1943, the first bombers reached East Prussia. Even in Elbing, occasional air-raid warnings now cut through the night. Jarred out of their sleep, Erwin and his comrades ran to the anti-aircraft guns. The young *Heimatflak* recruits aimed their guns upward and shot a round of ammunition into the sky, but by that time, the hostile planes were long gone. They were headed for bigger, more-important targets with vital war-manufacturing facilities. The brave, young boy soldiers, however, could boast about how they finally got to shoot at the enemy.

The government stopped publishing casualty reports. The dead were buried where they fell, and on the vast Russian plains, they were often left for the enemy to dispose of. Never had the country's future looked darker. Soldiers came back from the battlefield dragging their mutilated, disfigured bodies. The one-armed and one-legged veterans were pressed back into service on the home front as prisoner guards or drill sergeants for the young boys in the *Heimatflak*. As long as there was life left in these half men, they remained on active duty.

No more able-bodied males between the ages of seventeen and fifty remained at home. They all fought for the *Fuehrer* and *Vaterland*, and more likely for their lives. At home on the farms and in the factories, the women took over the men's jobs and kept the country going, along with thousands and thousands of prisoners of war providing the labor. On our farm Jimmy, Charlie, and Mack not only ran the farm while Father was held in jail, but they ran it efficiently. They had been with us two and one-half years and knew what needed to be done. Mother relied heavily on them, and they did all they could to help make her life easier.

Fall came and went. The storks fled south, and I continued my lonely search for new friends among the evacuee children, whose doors were not slammed in my face. I befriended Irmgard, who lived with her grandparents in an attic room in Katarina's villa. A back stairway led to their crowded quarters, so I could visit without having to bother Katarina's mother. Irmgard's grandfather, who looked ancient with his long, white beard, taught us the art of paper folding. We made hats, boats, airplanes, butterflies, and all sorts of neat things out of old newspapers. I worried that Katarina, with her vast accumulation of toys, would lure my new friend away from me. But Irmgard, a city child, preferred our farm to Katarina's toy-filled paradise.

Our Sundays remained quiet. Occasionally, Vera brought school friends home. My brother Erwin and his friend, Dieter, joined them when on leave. They filled the house with mirth and laughter, playing board and card games. Sometimes they let me join in. When aunts Elsbeth and Gertrude showed up, they complained about being tired from working long night shifts and taking care of Oma, whose health was rapidly failing.

Another winter arrived. The days turned shorter and grayer, and the skies stayed overcast for weeks. Then, it started to snow. At first, you could count the large crystalline flakes, but they quickly gathered momentum and soon obliterated everything from view. I stood by the window and watched the outside world turn white. When my cat rubbed against my ankles, I held him to the windowpane and said, "Look, Schnurribart, the snow fairy is shaking out her beds. Soon it will be Christmas!" But he wiggled free and hid behind the big tile stove, probably afraid I might put him out for the night.

Winter tried hard to conquer the land. Snow fell for several days, making the countryside glisten and sparkle in the sunlight. After that, the weather warmed, the mantle of snow melted, and the earth turned into mush. Days of torrential rains followed and flooded the low-lying fields and meadows. A heavy frost turned everything into a sleek, frozen lake as far as the eye could see. This vast expanse of ice looked eerie, broken up only by half-exposed fence posts and a single row of barbed wire, over which we could easily step. We brought out our sleds and captured the moment. Opening our coats wide, we caught the wind in our improvised sails and glided across the mirror-slick ice. Only hunger and cold brought us home before dark.

The thermometer stayed below freezing for days, and our children's room felt as frigid as the outside. We warmed bricks on top of the stove, wrapped them in newspaper, and took them to bed. Only the kitchen and living room were heated for lack of fuel.

Mother told me Father would not be home for Christmas, nor would Erwin. My brother had to defend the home front. We often saw enemy planes fly over and listened for explosions in the direction of Elbing. When the earth did not tremble and the sky remained silent, we knew Father, Erwin, and the aunts were safe.

My brother Douglas faced problems in school. The principal, a staunch Nazi, declared he would not tolerate a "foreigner" in his school and pressured Douglas to renounce his American citizenship. The students picked up on it and called my brother an American asshole. It was extremely disconcerting for him, because he loved school and was a good student with an excellent record.

Father's investigation came to a stalemate. The local investigating official continued to appear at the farm and relentlessly harassed Mother. He went over the books time and again, and he questioned the English and Soscha over and over, looking for inconsistencies. Mother became so distraught that she refused to see him.

"Tell him I'm not home," she said to Soscha when he entered the yard again. "Tell him I've gone to Elbing!"

She gave me a warning look and said, "Don't you breathe a word!"

She turned to escape to the attic, hesitated, and grabbed my arm. "You'd better come with me!" she said.

Shivering from the cold, we sat on the old cedar chest and waited. Mother reached for a coarse woolen throw hanging behind the door and threw it over our shoulders. She put her arm around me and sighed. "That man will be the death of me yet."

"What does he want? Why are you afraid of him, Mutti?" I asked.

"He's an evil man." She quickly corrected herself and added, "He just doesn't like us."

"It's okay," Soscha called from downstairs. "You can come down now."

Mother did not always manage to avoid her pursuer. At those times, she bit her lip and calmly produced the documents he asked to see. She was always in a bad mood after he left.

I missed Father. However, the ostracism by my friends held a far greater sting. Most of their fathers were gone also, but I did not know the difference between their honorable absence and my father's dishonorable situation in the greater scheme of the times.

Then one Sunday, Mother brought out the Advent wreath and handed me the Advent calendar from the previous year. Days later, the kitchen was once again filled with the various good smells of holiday baking. When the much-awaited day arrived, it was not the same happy Christmas I remembered. Even the tree looked smaller and less brilliant. We received our traditional plate of cookies and candy, and the English came down, their arms heaped with bags of real coffee, cocoa, tins of sardines, and other rarities for Mother—and chocolate bars for us children.

The aunts surprised us the day after Christmas. When I saw them enter the yard, I flew out of the house, shouting, "They're here! Aunt Elsbeth and Aunt Gertrude are here!"

I threw myself into Aunt Elsbeth's arms, all the while eyeing that big suitcase they had brought with them. The aunts were such a large part of our lives that Christmas was not complete without them. I received a book called *Tales of 1001 Nights* and a box of decals that came with it. I could not decide which I liked best, the stories or the decals. They both revealed a world so exotic it defied imagination— wish-granting genies in lamps, flying carpets, men in dresses, and women wrapped in gossamer scarves. Did such a world really exist? Aunt Gertrude said, "Maybe."

Aunt Elsbeth also brought good news about Father. "Be patient, Annchen," she said. "Herbert will be home soon. But you've got to tell him to keep his mouth shut." A hopeful smile replaced the bitter lines on Mother's face.

On New Year's Eve, we visited my brother Erwin and his friend, Dieter, at their army barracks in Elbing. Mother made deep-fried *Bismarks*, jelly doughnuts, the traditional New Year's Eve treat in our family. She put a penny inside one of them. It would bring a whole year of good luck to the one who got it. She filled a few others with pepper, salt, and mustard as a joke.

Young boys in uniform packed the dining hall. Mother turned to Dieter's mother, who had come from Danzig for the occasion, and said, "Look at our boys. They're mere children, and already they are sitting behind guns." To me they looked like grown men in their matching uniforms.

The singing and merrymaking lasted into the night. I had never seen so many people gathered in one place, all of them having such a noisy good time. I sat next to Mother in a corner booth, fighting to stay awake, trying not to miss anything. But the sandman won. I awoke the next morning at home in my bed.

"Who got the *Bismark* with the penny?" I asked Mother.

She pressed a *Bismark* into my hand and said, "I saved the lucky one for you. Be careful not to swallow the penny."

CHAPTER TEN

After Christmas, we learned our vacation had been extended by a week to conserve fuel. When we returned to school in the middle of January 1944, the cast-iron stove in the middle of the room remained cold. We kept our coats and hats on, and we could see the steam of our breath in the frigid air. When the temperature sank to below freezing, and we still had no fuel, Fraulein Eckers took us to her cozy little upstairs quarters, built a roaring fire in her stove, and read to us while we warmed ourselves by the crackling fire.

Nothing could be done about the fuel shortage, but we still ate well. I traded my sandwiches of freshly baked rye bread and homemade sausage with my new friend, Irmgard, for dry hard rolls with jam, and we both thought we got the better end of the exchange.

Oversized placards with war slogans aimed at boosting the nation's plunging morale appeared everywhere. Above the station entrance hung a banner reading, *Raeder muessen rollen fuer den Sieg*, wheels must roll towards victory. On the platform side, a banner read, *Fuehrer befiel, wir folgen*, leader, give us orders, we'll obey. We shouted these slogans at the tired travelers passing through. Most of them ignored us, some called us ignorant brats, and others sent damning curses our way.

When I came home from school one day, I found Father sitting with Mother at the dinner table. He had been released that morning. "Papa," I shouted, "You're home!" and flew into his open arms.

He stroked my head and repeated, "Oh, how you've grown. Oh my, how you've grown."

"*Ja*, but she isn't getting any smarter," Mother said. "She has no sense at all."

"How was jail, Papa?" I asked. "Was it nice?"

Father shot Mother a questioning glance. She shook her head and said, "That child's ears and eyes are too big for her own good." She turned to me with a raised finger and added, "And you talk too much. From now on you don't repeat a thing of what goes on in this house. You understand?"

Mother's angry outburst surprised me. I knew I had tested her patience repeatedly, but this was such a happy moment, and I had not done anything lately to upset her.

Father came to my defense and said, "Annchen, leave her be. She's only a little girl. She doesn't understand. How can you expect her to understand the things we don't even fully understand?" He pushed me off his knee, pointed to my dinner plate, and added, "I've brought you something."

Next to my plate lay a brown, cone-shaped paper bag filled with black licorice candy, my favorite.

Father told Mother his acquittal had largely been the result of the family's connections in high places. When the judge finally released him, he took Father aside and warned, "You've made many enemies who would like to see your undoing. Be careful what you say in front of your neighbors."

A changed man, Father would have nothing more to do with anyone in Niederhof or in Steglitz, not even Mother's many relatives. The war had reached us in the form of betrayal and persecution.

Although free again, Father now had to report to the *Ortsgruppenleiter*, the Nazi group leader with several villages under his jurisdiction, and sign an affidavit stating he had not engaged in any act of espionage or sabotage against Germany that week.

Hitler's tight grip on the population left no place to hide. Nothing went unnoticed or unreported. There was the *Blockleiter*, block leader, with three to four farmers under him. Then came the *Zellenleiter*, cell leader, who presided over half a village. Above him stood the *Ortsgruppenleiter*, the man before whom Father made his weekly appearances. Next came the *Kreisleiter*, county leader, and above him, the most powerful man, the *Gauleiter*, who oversaw the whole province of East Prussia. This hierarchy, enacted everywhere, enabled Hitler to control the nation.

My eighth birthday came and went. I received another bag of licorice candy from my parents. The aunts and Oma sent a book about fire-spewing mountains, quakes in the earth that opened up chasms as wide as rivers, and ocean waves higher than the skyscrapers on Father's picture post cards of America. When I told my friends of these amazing wonders, they accused me of making up stories. I needed my wise grandmother to explain it all. However, by the time I saw her again, she had died. It seemed to me she had died quite suddenly, but in truth, she had had a long bout with breast cancer.

I got to stay home from school on the day of her funeral, my first exposure to death. I was anxious to see what Oma looked like dead. The weather hinted of spring. Mother, Douglas, and I managed to get to the station on time to catch the train. Erwin got leave for the day, Vera and Henry were already in Elbing, and Father had gone the day before.

The apartment was quiet, and the drapes were drawn when we entered. The aunts welcomed us in whispers as though afraid to awaken Oma. Aunt Elsbeth showed us into the living room, where Oma lay stretched out in a silver coffin. Father sat by her side, head bowed and tears in his eyes. Seeing him cry for the first time startled me. Aunt Elsbeth led me to the coffin. Oma lay under a shiny cover, her lifeless face as white as the hair on her head, her bony, frail hands folded on her chest. I stared at her mask-like expression and waited for her eyes to open. I expected her to smile when she saw me, but she did not stir. Aunt Elsbeth took my reluctant hand, laid it on Oma's folded hands, and said, "Say goodbye to Oma. She'll be gone for a long, long time."

I shuddered. Her hands were stiff and cold, very cold. Suddenly, I was afraid of her. She had entered the world of ghosts and demons, the same world she introduced me to while she was still alive.

After we left for the cemetery, a hearse picked up Oma's coffin. When we arrived at the little funeral chapel, she was already there, as if by magic. The chapel was filled with people I did not recognize, mostly women dressed in black.

After what seemed like an endless sermon, we left the chapel and followed the men who carried the coffin to the burial site. A deep hole awaited Oma. The carriers lowered her into the ground and everyone, including me, threw a handful of dirt into the dark abyss. It made an eerie, hollow sound, as though Oma no longer lay in the coffin.

Aunt Gertrude, the once-ardent Hitler supporter, came full

circle. She became more vocal with her anti-Hitler talk than Father. Father's unjust persecution and incarceration had killed the last seeds of her enthusiasm for the *Fuehrer*. After that, she referred to Hitler as a power-hungry, bloodthirsty, murdering maniac, and called him such every time Hitler's name was mentioned. Father squelched her angry outbursts the same way he had previously tried to silence her prior blind passion for Hitler. "Trudchen, don't talk like that in my house," he said. "I don't want that man's name mentioned under my roof. I've had enough trouble."

Aunt Gertrude stroked Father's arm and said, "I know, I know, Herbert. It's just so hard to watch. To see our land destroyed and not be able to do anything about it. I'm so tired of those endless telegrams coming through the telegraph about another lost son, father, or uncle. And all those bombing victims. Where is it going to end?"

"I don't care how you feel. Just keep it to yourself. One session in jail is enough for me."

But Father had not totally learned his lesson. He often sat by Dieter's radio with one ear glued to the speaker, fiddling with the dials, listening intently. The volume was always turned so low that the drop of a pin might have been more audible than what came out of that talking box. "Herbert, be sensible. You're going to get into trouble again," Mother warned him repeatedly. "What good is it to listen to the outside world? You can't change anything."

"I just want this war to end. How much longer is this murdering of children going to last? Think of the boys, Annchen. Erwin will be next to go to the front. He's not even seventeen and is already sitting in a bunker behind a gun."

The aunts visited more often now. Father said they were afraid of air raids. Mother disagreed, saying, "They are coming to fill their stomachs with a good meal."

"They do like your cooking, Annchen," Father teased.

Aunt Gertrude, not very domestic, liked to lift the lids from the pots and inhale the delicious aromas. The stable, however, was her favorite place. She loved the smell of warm milk, straw, hay, and dung. I thought the odor was downright unpleasant and wondered how my richly bejeweled, perfumed, and immaculately groomed aunt could mistake the acrid stable air for something pleasant. I liked to trail behind her, though, because she made everything smell better, especially the stable. She would inhale the pungent air and exclaim, "Ah, that aroma—it's heaven." Then, she would turn to Father and say something like, "As long as you have this, Herbert, your family will never go hungry."

Father did not agree. "If it weren't for this," he'd say, "we'd be in America now. We should have run when we had the chance. I don't like what is happening in this country."

"At least you're eating, Herbert," Aunt Gertrude said, "Germany is starving and bleeding from a multitude of wounds. There is a lot of tragedy out there. You'd be surprised what comes over the telegraph. I can't talk about it. But believe me, it's bad. At least you're safe here in the country. Be glad of it."

My parents and the aunts speculated a lot about when the dreadful war would end. The widows were getting younger, and so were the military casualties. Often, during the night, the droning sound of enemy planes on another bombing mission roused us out of our deep slumber. The planes always came at night.

With Father home again, Mother seemed happier and more relaxed. Then, one day when I came home from school, our English prisoners were gone. I thought they had run away and was mad at Charlie for not saying good-bye to me. Mother handed me a little package, awkwardly wrapped in newspaper, and said, "Charlie left this for you."

It was a small red ball and a chocolate bar.

"Why did they run away?" I asked, tears in my eyes.

"They didn't run away, Evchen. A man came and took them to a big prison camp."

"Why? Didn't they like it here any more?"

"No, no, no," Mother said, a bit irritated. "They'll be with other English prisoners. They will be happy there."

Two days later, a German soldier delivered three French prisoners to replace the English. None of the other farmers lost their English men; we were the only ones singled out.

We did not have the same close relationship with the French. Although they spoke some German, they were uncommunicative and kept to themselves. I no longer made nightly trips upstairs as I had done to see Charlie, and I pestered Father instead. In the evenings, while he read the newspaper, I climbed behind him on his desk chair and played hairdresser. I combed his thinning gray hair up and down and sideways, set it in rollers, and twisted it around a little comb to make him look like one of our roosters. At times, I got his hair so tangled up that Mother had to come to our rescue and pick the hairs one by one from the little comb. Occasionally, this task required the aid of scissors. Father patiently submitted to both of us without complaint. Mother finally said, "Herbert, if you let that child continue to play with your hair, you're not going to have any left on your head."

"We have bigger worries," Father said.

Douglas's school principal would not ease off my brother; he kept up his threats to kick Douglas out of school if he did not renounce his American citizenship. Fortunately, the school year ended early, and Douglas came home for the summer. Father arranged for him to live with Frau Teichert, a widow friend in Koenigsberg in the eastern-most corner of East Prussia, near the Lithuanian border, where he would be unknown.

Frau Teichert's husband had died before the war, and her soldier son had drowned at sea the year before, when enemy torpedoes hit his tanker. She wrote that she would be more than happy to take in my brother. Relieved, Father said to Mother, "Koenigsberg is far enough away. No one will know Douglas there."

"I just hope it's far enough so the bombers can't reach there," Mother said, with a worried frown.

"It is. It is," replied Father, reassuring her.

By late spring, endless caravans of Lithuanian refugees, all people of strong German origins, pushed passed our farm, each strange-looking wagon piled high with belongings and a cow or two tied to the back. They were fleeing from the advancing Red Army. Groups of twos, threes, or more, sometimes entire villages, moved past us, often stopping to rest along the road in front of our property. They unhitched their horses and let them graze along the road. Father gave them food and animal feed. They often stayed overnight in our barn. All summer long, they came in an endless exodus. They told unsettling tales of brutal rape and random murder by the Red Army. People refused to believe their stories and thought them to be gross exaggerations told in the hopes of encouraging the Germans to be more charitable. Many refugees were headed west to the farthest reaches of Germany, the farthest away from the Russians, as one frightened

Lithuanian told Father. Then, the gypsies came and things started to disappear from the farm during the night.

We acquired Senta, a German shepherd, to guard our property. We kept her chained during the day, but at night she had free reign. She had a mean bark, and the thefts stopped. I loved her from the day she arrived, and brought her food and crawled into the doghouse with her. I rested my head on her belly and talked to her, and she always perked up her ears as though she understood every loving word. But Schnurribart was absolutely petrified of her.

One day, I unchained Senta and brought her into the house to show her where I lived. Schnurribart was sitting on the windowsill, soaking up the warm sun, when Senta spotted him and made a giant leap after him. Schnurribart tried to jump through the window glass and almost broke his neck. He raced around the room and, in desperation, clawed up Mother's lace curtains, tearing them to shreds. He ended up on top of the drapery rod, hissing like a snake, while Senta leapt into the air, trying to get at him. She knocked over several chairs and Mother's mahogany flower stand. I screamed, "Senta, no! Schnurribart, no!" But the chase made them deaf to my pleas. Mother came running, and instead of going after Senta and the cat, she came after me, grabbed me by the neck, and deposited me in the black chimney room. It was my first experience in that dreaded room. The chimney room was a sooty, pitch-dark chamber, allowing access to the main chimney. I spent the most terrifying half-hour of my life in there. I went in screaming, with dug-in heels, and came out docile and cured, vowing I would never do anything that would have me repeat the experience. Mother gave me a stern look and said, "I've had it with you. The next time you'll spend the whole day in there. Don't you ever unchain that dog again!"

CHAPTER ELEVEN

"*HEIL* HITLER!" THOSE WERE MY proud words.

The young girl who delivered our newspapers taught me to ride a bicycle. Eager to show the world how accomplished I was, I rode with one hand on the handlebars and the other raised toward the sky and shouted, "*Heil* Hitler!" I became the friendliest child in the village. Whenever I could lay claim to my sister's bicycle, I pedaled through Niederhof, saluting locals and strangers alike with this newly discovered national greeting.

Heil Hitler, the official form of salutation between adults since the *Fuehrer* came into power in the 1930s, was not used by young children, except by me, the new show-off and the family's vocal Hitler fan.

When I demonstrated my dexterity on the bicycle to my parents, Father looked pained, shook his head, and grumbled. Mother said, "*Ach*, let her be. She doesn't know what it means. Besides, it's good for our public image."

Hitler's birthday in April 1944 was a subdued affair compared to those of the previous years. Once-ardent Hitler supporters who were parents or relatives of fallen soldiers now refused to fly the flag, just like Father. An official showed up at our farm and issued the usual warning about the missing flag, but his threat had lost its bite. Doubts about Hitler's sanity surfaced even among Party members. Rumors circulated that Hitler suffered from megalomania.

Then the most alarming rumors of all reached us—rumors about the gassing of Jews. The media squelched these stories as enemy propaganda. Aunt Gertrude refused to believe them and accused Hitler's adversaries of spreading vicious lies. But Father said, "That man will kill his mother to serve his purpose."

"No, Herbert, I don't believe that. The man is mad, but not that mad."

"*Ja*, just keep burying your head in the sand and maybe it will all go away," Father said.

Rumors or fact, our life in Niederhof and Steglitz remained relatively untouched by the violent, disruptive upheavals the war created all around us. For us, the war was mainly an inconvenience. Bombing victims continued to arrive in droves and were distributed among the villagers. These city people were totally surprised by how at peace our area appeared, while the cities in the *Reich* were going up in flames. When they saw the abundance of food on the farms, they thought they had arrived in *Schlaraffenland*, the land of plenty.

My parents invited Helmut and Dora, distant cousins Henry's and my age, to spend the summer with us. Their mother stayed behind in the city somewhere in the *Reich*. Henry, too, came home for the summer, and I no longer slept alone in the children's room.

Erwin also came home, his tour of duty in the *Heimatflak* over. Father quietly obtained an American passport for him through the American consul in Switzerland. As a documented U.S. citizen, he could not be drafted into the military. His friend, Dieter, on the other hand, graduated directly into soldierhood and immediately left for the eastern front. Barely seventeen, he now held a rifle in his hands and was ordered to fight for the *Vaterland*; if necessary, he was expected to "die on the field of honor," as Hitler called it. To die for a "greater Germany" was all a soldier's life was worth anymore. While Dieter, the child soldier, dodged bullets on the battle field, Erwin now had to accompany Father on his weekly appearances before the *Gauleiter*.

Erwin also had to serve the country by doing guard duty at home. He and his guard buddy, a German Pole, patrolled the area from nine in the evening until midnight. They looked in on the English prisoners in Steglitz, to make sure they were locked up, and joked with them through the open windows. They checked the railroad tracks for sabotage, watched for surreptitiously started fires, and kept an eye out for suspicious-looking characters roaming the countryside.

The country teemed with Russian, French, and English prisoners of war, and the civilian population grew uneasy with so many foreigners in their midst while their own men fought at the front. These aliens ran the farms and factories, and they also did all the manual labor. Germany was crowded with stalag camps, as the war prisons were called. Even in Niederhof, one of these labor camps sprang up overnight. One day, there was an empty meadow, and a few days later there were a hundred Russian prisoners locked up in crudely erected barracks. Every day, these men repaired railroad tracks between Niederhof and Elbing. On weekends, the farmers enlisted them to help with the harvesting.

We children had strict orders to stay away from the prison camp, which had exactly the opposite effect. Fascinated by these Mongolian faces in tattered rags, we stood glued to the chain link fence and stared at them, openmouthed.

One day, when Henry and I were standing outside the fence, a dark-skinned prisoner slipped a coarsely whittled stick doll through the fence, holding it concealed in the palm of his hand. I backed away, frightened. His face broke into a thousand wrinkles as he smiled, pointing his bearded chin toward the neighbor's apple trees across the street. Henry got the message and said, "He wants us to bring him apples."

A high fence surrounded the apple orchard, but with enough coaxing from a long stick, a few green apples dropped on our side of the barrier. We secretly brought the coveted fruit to our new "enemy" friend, looking out for the guards, who were quick to chase us away. The prisoner grabbed the apples and hid them under the rags on his body. His happy face gave us an unexpected surge of pleasure. We continued to deliver the forbidden fruit until the branches on the neighbor's apple tree were bare on our side of the fence. We would have gladly raided our own fledgling fruit orchard, but Father's prediction did not come true. Only one of the apple trees bore fruit, and Father had counted every one of them.

Some time at the beginning of that summer, my cousin Kurt-Heinz was released from the military. He still had all his body parts, but his lungs were badly damaged. He stayed with Aunt Elsbeth in Kahlberg to recuperate before continuing his arduous journey home. Incessant bombings knocked out major transportation routes faster than they could be repaired. A trip normally covered in eight hours now took two days on overcrowded trains. Also, travel of any length now required travel permits, and often there were no officials around to issue them.

Kurt-Heinz had suffered through a long Russian winter at below freezing temperatures. Night after night, he had slept under his jeep, inhaling exhaust fumes, poisoning his lungs while trying to keep from freezing to death. He had contracted double pneumonia and came back exhausted, emaciated, and traumatized.

"Our army at the Russian front is bleeding to death, Uncle Herbert," I overheard him confide to Father. "Our losses are great, greater than anyone can imagine."

My cousin took most of the summer to regain strength to continue his journey home. The doctors diagnosed him with the onset of tuberculosis, a double-edged blessing. It kept him out of the trenches, but now he was fighting a more insidious enemy.

My cousin's stay in Kahlberg inspired Aunt Elsbeth to open up her little summer haven to other recuperating soldiers. That meant we would not spend the usual month by the sea. Instead, we went swimming in the mill creek with our evacuee cousins. Helmut and Dora were city children who had lived all their lives fenced in by cement walls. We taught them to climb trees, jump across extra-wide creeks without falling in, and chase butterflies. They had never heard a rooster crow so early in the morning. I showed Dora how to befriend the farm animals, just as Charlie had done with me. She learned to handle the gander, who thought he had found a new victim to terrorize. We adopted Mother's newly hatched ducklings, took them to the meadow, and fed them fresh clover. They became so used to our coddling, they cackled and ran after us whenever they spotted us. We often had to sneak out of the house so they would not see us.

We caught dragonflies and grasshoppers, and fed them to the ducklings. Dora liked to chase our storks as they picked worms behind the plow in the field. When it rained, we changed the children's room into a playhouse and turned the chairs on their sides to form a train, which unlike Hitler's trains, always ran and never was late. The boys played with my older brothers' train and Erector Set. The children's room always resembled a miniature world of something else. On sunny warm days, Dora and I played with our dolls in the igloo-like haystacks in the fields and pretended our imaginary husbands, my brother Henry and my cousin, Helmut, were off to war.

When Mother killed a goose and chopped off its head, Dora ran into the house, crying and wanting to go home. However, when the goose appeared on the dinner table, she ate with relish. Mother chuckled and teased her about it.

When thunderstorms sent their distant rumblings our way, we were terrified and did not move from Mother's side. Even the farmers respected and feared these violent storms in the lowlands.

We introduced our city cousins to a multitude of new experiences, not all positive in their mother's view. She came to refer to Henry and me as the "wild ones" in Niederhof. However, Dora and Helmut remembered that summer of 1944 as the most exciting, fun-filled time in their young lives.

One Sunday, Aunt Elsbeth and Aunt Gertrude showed up on the farm, agitated and excited. They had heard of an unsuccessful assassination attempt on Hitler's life. Aunt Gertrude said, "It's a miracle he survived. That man has made a pact with the devil."

"Innocent boys are dying by the thousands, and he has to live," Father said. "Only a miracle can save us now."

From that day on, a vinegar bottle sat next to Father's plate with each meal. He generously sprinkled that sour liquid on all his food. When Mother tried to get him to stop spoiling his meals, he explained, "I need it to settle my stomach."

The slightest things upset him. He missed our English prisoners. I often heard him say, "Charlie would not have done that," or "Jimmy would have known what to do."

It riled Father when the guard came around more often to check on the French prisoners. But there was no danger of our being caught on too intimate terms with those prisoners. They remained aloof.

The guard brought a black armband with a big *P* in a yellow circle for Soscha. The *P* stood for "Polish origin" to help the officials distinguish between pure Germans and Poles. Soscha was now required to wear this band over her sleeve every time she left the farm. When some minor officials showed up to count our cattle and chickens to ensure we were delivering the proper amount of milk and eggs, Father would have sent Senta after them if Mother had not interfered. "Calm down, Herbert," she said. "That won't help Soscha. They're only doing their job."

At the end of summer, our cousins rejoined their mother in the city, and Douglas, Henry, and I got to spend the last week of our vacation in Kahlberg. Wispy white clouds sailed across the sky, the sun beamed its warmth-emanating smile, and the wind seemed to be merely practicing for the approaching colder months.

Aunt Elsbeth took me to work with her and let me talk on the telephone to Aunt Gertrude in Elbing; it was my first telephone conversation. I kept looking over my shoulder, certain that Aunt Gertrude was hiding somewhere in the room.

We spent the entire week by the sea. At age eight, I got my first swimsuit and was proud to finally be grown up enough to warrant such a garment. Until then, I had run naked in the breeze and the surf like all the other children my age. However, I quickly reverted to being a little nudist again. One day, while I was rinsing the sand out of the suit, the surf pulled it from my grip and carried it away. Screaming for help, I watched it float out to sea. Douglas, thinking I was drowning, came running, but it was too late to save the garment. I was devastated, because I knew I would not get another one that summer. However, nude children on the beach were a common sight. Nobody stopped and gawked at me the way I stared at the many men with mutilated bodies and grotesquely scarred faces. I saw a man with not just one arm, but no arms. Others hobbled awkwardly on their crutches in the sand, their short stumps flip-flopping back and forth. One man left his crutches behind and scooted into the water on his buttocks. I worried he might drown and ran after Douglas for help. But my brother said, "Don't worry; he can float."

I started to have nightmares about armless, legless, one-eyed ghosts.

Our week in Kahlberg ended all too soon. We came home windblown and tanned. I was surprised to see Frau Teichert had moved in with us. A terrifying bombing raid on Koenigsberg had leveled her house to the ground one night while she was in an air-raid shelter. When the raid ended, the entire city was in flames. She arrived on our farm with just one small suitcase.

With Koenigsberg bombed, my brother Douglas no longer had an alternative for the upcoming school year. When he returned to his school in Elbing, the principal refused to accept him. "If you want to continue your schooling here," he said, "you'll have to renounce your American citizenship."

The American consul in Switzerland advised my distraught father to cooperate with the principal. His letter read, "Don't worry; your son is still a minor. They can't make it stick. Sign the document and let the boy get on with his education. The war can't last too much longer."

My brother, the minor, not Father, signed the troublesome piece of paper and the school principal's harassment stopped.

In my school, we had a new teacher, even younger than Fraulein Eckers, and many more evacuee children. These big-city newcomers intimidated us, especially those from Berlin. Backward and shy, we country children perceived them as mouthy and brazen. We did not have enough textbooks to go around and had to share books with them.

When a barn in the neighboring village burned down, word quickly spread that children from Berlin had deliberately set the fire. Douglas and I ran across the fields to get a better look at the enormous blaze. People rushed around wildly, frantically trying to save what they could from the farmhouse before it, too, went up in flames. With no firemen or fire trucks, the fire devoured the barn filled with the summer's harvest in just minutes. I looked on, bewildered, and could not believe a fire could grow to such enormous size.

"Those damned Berliners with their bratty children!" an angry woman shouted. "I wish they would go back to where they came from."

An old man tried to calm her, but out of her mind with rage, she continued to curse the brazen Berliners. Douglas talked to the people near us and learned the irate woman owned the burning property, and that, indeed, the careless Berlin evacuee children assigned to her farm had been playing with matches in the barn when the fire got away from them. Word among the villagers now was, "If you have to house evacuees, make sure they're not loudmouthed, arrogant Berliners. They're the worst."

But they kept arriving because Berlin was now the main bombing target. Tensions mounted as grievances between locals and newcomers grew. Overcrowding and a general feeling of helplessness caused tempers to flare, with people on each side resenting the situation in which they involuntarily found themselves.

With Frau Teichert now living with us, we did not have to take in any strangers. But Father did put up a bombing victim, a woman with her three-year-old son, in our farm workers' building. The very pregnant woman had an enormous belly. Irmgard and I befriended her while she took her child for afternoon walks in a stroller. She talked a lot about her unborn child, how she hoped it would be a girl, what she would name her, and, above all, the wish that the baby would still have a father when it was born. We, however, were not interested in the woman's hope-filled dreams; we were dying to find out how that huge thing got in her stomach and, more frightening, how it would get out. We hinted at our ignorance about childbirth and our eagerness to learn more, but the woman cleverly circumvented the subject by alluding to the stork, miracles that happened during the night, and finding the baby on one's doorsteps when least expected.

Irmgard and I knew there was a lot more to this baby business. Since the adults would not clear up the mystery, we embarked on our own search for information. English Charlie might have been a good source, but he was gone. Soscha told me to ask Mother, but Mother stuck by her stork, and Irmgard's grandmother said we were too young for such questions. We asked the more sophisticated evacuee children and, with much conjecturing and guessing, we came up with our own answer. Babies came from kissing boys on the mouth. At least that was how they got in the stomach. Then, after a certain length of time, a month or two at most, the doctor cut the stomach open and took the baby out. We vowed none of us would ever have babies. And so our quest for carnal knowledge dead-ended in a heap of erroneous assumptions and misinformation.

Fall 1944 arrived early. The storks departed and the leaves on the trees changed color. The influx of refugees from the Baltic countries slowed to a trickle. However, many Russians from the Ukraine followed and threw in their lot with the Germans. At the same time, transports with thousands of captured Russian soldiers passed through Niederhof. It was unsettling, this "friend or foe" situation. The horror stories from the eastern front mounted, and fear of the Red Army grew. The draft age was lowered at one end and raised at the other. All able-bodied men between the ages of sixteen and sixty were now in uniform.

North Africa, Paris, and Rome were lost, and the Russians drew ever closer to the East Prussian border. Defeat stared Germany in the face, and yet, somehow, life went on.

After a second, more devastating bombing attack on Koenigsberg, only three days after the first, Frau Teichert went back to check on her demolished property, hoping to find a few surviving mementos. She returned, holding on to one useless saucer from her good china.

"There's nothing but rubble," she told Mother. "And my things? Disintegrated! Gone! Nothing left but broken bricks and melted glass. It's all gone!" Mother handed her a handkerchief. Wiping her tears, Frau Teichert continued, "How am I going to go on? I've nothing. It's all destroyed."

Frau Teichert talked often about her shattered life and dreams, tears always close to the surface. Mother, with her mending spread out in her lap, listened in silence, unable to provide comfort to her new companion. Perhaps she struggled with her own concerns and life's terrible realities. The war had become the killer of dreams. Our time of grace was rapidly running out, but we still had no inkling of the full fury the war would unleash on us.

Aunt Elsbeth stopped sending postcards. Instead, she sent a set of tickets to the children's theater in Elbing for Henry and me. It was a memorable day. We took the train, which miraculously not only ran as scheduled but pulled into the station on time. The theater, an ornate old building, was outfitted with rows and rows of red velvet seats with cushioned armrests. Smiling angels' heads protruded from the ceiling, golden moldings lined the walls, and an array of crystal chandeliers sparkled above us. I felt as if I had entered the realm of princes and princesses. An old woman ushered us to our seats, just a few rows from center stage. I sank into the soft upholstery, certain I was dreaming. Then, the lights went out, the heavy curtains swished open, and the room fell silent. A lone actor stepped into the spotlight, faced us, and started to speak. As the story unfolded, it drew me in, and the world around me disappeared. Never before had I experienced anything so captivating, and I wished for nothing more than that Aunt Elsbeth would keep sending us theater tickets.

I started to like Elbing, with its unexpected hidden treasures, and begged Mother to take me along on her periodic shopping trips. She referred to these excursions as chasing after the pot of gold at the end of the rainbow. Anything made of metal, like razor blades, sewing and knitting needles, safety pins, and kitchen utensils, was next to impossible to obtain, even with ration coupons. That day, Mother chased after light bulbs. We combed the city from one end to the other and found only one store with the coveted item in stock. But they sold only one bulb per person, although Mother had coupons for four. At the end of our futile pursuit, we returned to that store. Mother stopped at the door, handed me a coupon, and said, "You go in there and ask for another light bulb! They won't remember you."

Petrified, I felt certain the saleswomen would recognize me and punish Mother for cheating. My knees wobbled as Mother pushed me through the door. I laid the coupon and money on the counter, cleared my throat, and said with downcast eyes, "I want one light bulb, please."

The saleswoman studied me and asked, "Haven't you been in here with your mother?"

"No, that wasn't me," I lied, avoiding her eyes.

"Oh, yes it was. I think you've been here before."

I started to whimper and was about to turn and run, when the other saleslady said, "Ah, give her a light bulb. What difference does it make? When they're gone, they're gone."

I grabbed the bulb and hurried for the door.

"Wait! Here is your change," the woman called after me. She put the money into my hand and said, "It's okay. Don't be afraid."

Feeling victorious and grown-up, I handed my prize to Mother. But she merely bit her lips and said nothing. It was an empty triumph.

At school, our teacher told us to bring in old clothes and reusable materials, like pots and pans, harness pieces, or anything else made of iron and other metals, to be exchanged for points. There were no points by my name.

"We have nothing to spare," Mother said. "How can we let go of things when we can't get anything to replace them?"

That certainly was the case with our clothes. When a garment no longer fit or had served its purpose, Mother ripped it apart and remade it into something new. Our seamstress, Fraulein Erna, now worked in a factory and no longer came to sew for us. Mother enlisted Soscha to help her. They took things apart, pressed the wrinkles out of the salvageable pieces of fabric, and sewed them back together. I started to look more and more like a patchwork quilt. But I loved my colorful clothes. They were new to me and looked interesting.

By October 1944, the trees stood naked once again. The days turned chilly, and all signs pointed to a colder than normal winter. We no longer lingered on our way home from school, and at night, we took heated bricks to bed as we had done the previous winter.

CHAPTER TWELVE

IT HAPPENED!

The Red Army broke through the lines and set foot on German soil. The army unleashed its full fury on its first victims in the villages along the East Prussian border. The day of retaliation had arrived, and no German could expect mercy. The Russians occupied and held a strip of land a hundred and fifty kilometers long and forty kilometers deep. Drunk with victory and a desire for revenge, they committed the most unimaginable atrocities. Stalin himself had ordered the Russian soldiers to kill every German they encountered. He told his army they would not be held accountable for any crime against the German people. "Do to them as they did to us," he commanded.

Russia did not sign the Fair Treatment of Prisoners' Act, and they did not differentiate between soldiers and civilians. To them, every German was the enemy, including the unborn. They mass raped the women, dismembered many of them, and mutilated their bodies. Even girls as young as eight years old did not escape defilement. They destroyed everything in their path. All of East Prussia was in a state of shock and panic. For days, terror reigned, and the raping and killing continued until the German military succeeded in pushing the Red Army back.

Calm returned, and an uneasy mood settled over East Prussia. Hitler no longer appeared in public, but his propaganda minister, Goebbels, made impassioned speeches to reassure the population. He told them that the military situation had been stabilized, and that they had nothing to worry about. No Russian would ever set foot on German soil again. Hitler vowed not to give up one meter of German land without defending it to the death. Goebbels spoke of powerful new secret weapons. His speeches were loaded with great promises. The population believed him. They needed to believe.

The farsighted, however, packed their possessions and fled to the *Reich* to live with relatives. They disappeared quietly. But the farmers could not up and leave. They were bound to their land and animals.

Every able-bodied male, no matter what age, was now drafted into the *Volksturm*, the People's Army, a new branch of the military. Old men, together with fifteen- and sixteen-year-old boys from the *Heimatflak*, were to defend the home front. Irmgard's grandfather was called to report for military service in Elbing. He received a shovel and had to dig trenches. Each farmer had to provide a vehicle with a driver to assist in the hasty effort. It appeared that the beginning of the end of the war would take place in East Prussia, the province closest to the Russian border. The populace held its breath and hoped for a miracle.

Irmgard's teary-eyed grandmother talked of committing suicide if anything happened to her beloved life's companion, as she referred to her husband. I never saw her without a wet handkerchief twisted between her nervous fingers.

Father spent more and more time playing with the dials on Dieter's radio. When he found something forbidden, he sent me out of the room and told me to close the door. Mother and he talked a lot, their voices lowered to mere whispers. When I entered the room, they stopped abruptly. I could feel the tension building up all around me. Mother no longer read books, and Father no longer allowed me to play hairdresser with his hair. He got irritated and told me to go play with my doll.

"But she doesn't have any hair," I protested.

"I won't have any either if this continues," he shot back.

Senta barked so much during the nights that, at times, she even awakened me. I often overheard Father and Erwin talk about being out with her during the night, checking on strange noises and chasing after suspicious shadows. Sometimes we found empty nests in the chicken house, a cow or two that gave no milk, and briquettes missing from the woodshed.

Father secured the doors to the stable and barn as best he could, with no locks available. Mother, concerned about the thefts, asked, "Will the authorities believe us that we are being stolen blind by the riffraff running around during the night? Will they still expect us to deliver the required quota to them when half of it has been stolen from us? How can we stop this?"

"Thank heaven we have Senta," Father said.

Pictures of atrocities committed by the Red Army during its short stay on German soil appeared in newspapers and were flashed across newsreels in movie houses. They were meant to instill fear of the Russians and steel the Germans' resolve not to give up, but to clench their fists and fight to save the *Vaterland*. Hitler hoped the Red Army would exhaust itself. But a colossus was building up along the East Prussian border. The Russian divisions outnumbered the Germans three to one. The German army could not hold them back for long. Our reprieve was temporary. Veiled and distorted news reached us from the eastern front. The radio only reported military successes and never mentioned defeats. Hospitals overflowed with wounded. Soldiers died by the thousands each day, while our daily life continued. We neither knew nor suspected how little time we had left before everything would cave in on us.

Events that once might have made headline news now were everyday occurrences. Deaths, continuous defeats, nightly bombings, and shortages of every kind became integral parts of everyday life. We grew inured to hardships. Everyone thought only about how to escape the approaching Russians and not fall into the hands of the Red Army. But the Nazi Party forbade any talk about flight and threatened jail sentences for those who tried to flee or prepare for it without official orders. The Party officials held us hostage.

Premonitions of disaster plagued Father. Bad dreams kept him awake nights. He worried about my sister. At almost sixteen, she would be a prime target for the raping Russians. It was a time of agonizing worry for my parents, while I was just starting to experience life with a greater awareness and few concerns.

By December, we knew that the winter of 1944–1945 would be one of the coldest in years. The thermometer stayed below freezing for weeks. School let out a whole week earlier for Christmas vacation, and we did not have to return until the middle of January. The teacher handed us our savings books. She looked at each one and praised the individual owners for having been so diligent. When she looked at mine, she shook her head and asked with a hint of suspicion in her voice, "And what have you been doing with your money? There is hardly anything in here."

I blushed with discomfort and searched for a believable excuse. I could not make myself tell her I had converted some of Hitler's pennies into licorice sticks and thought of a hundred excuses, all equally weak. However, she did not seem to expect an answer. She said, "I put a note in here to remind your mother that it is your duty to save money for the *Fuehrer*."

I did not give my savings book to Mother; I hid it among my toys and hoped she had forgotten about it. I would have liked to forget about it also. Those licorice sticks weighed heavily on my mind. While that troublesome savings book remained in the teacher's hands, I felt safe from being discovered. Now, my conscience nagged at me. I had a brilliant idea. I burned the book in the cooking stove and watched, relieved, as it turned into ashes. Christmas was just around the corner, and I stopped listening to that small voice in my head. But I learned the painful lesson that every act has a consequence, and that there was such a thing as a conscience.

The lowland did not flood the way it had the year before. There was no ice sailing or sledding this winter. My evacuee friend, Irmgard, left for the city to spend Christmas with her mother. Katarina's villa, where I had slowly regained entry after Father's release from prison, was boarded up with shutters. It looked as if Katarina and her family would be gone for a long time. Irmgard's grandmother told me their father had sent them the necessary travel papers, and they had left for the *Reich* to be with relatives for Christmas. When I told Mother about it, she just said, "*Ja*, the Nazis have access to everything." She gave Father a meaningful look that only he could interpret and added, "You can bet they won't be back soon. They're going to wait it out in the *Reich*."

Mother brought out the old Christmas calendar and put up the Advent wreath with its four candles. The kitchen was filled with the many smells of Christmas baking once again. One day, I caught my brother Erwin making tiny furniture with his jigsaw. I was sure I would finally get the much-wished-for dollhouse for Christmas, and I waited for the big day to arrive with more than the usual impatience.

My sister, Vera, and my brother Henry also got out of school early. The family was united again. We did not go into the forest to cut the usual tree, and as we had the year before, we celebrated Christmas Eve without the aunts and uncle. But I was happy, because next to my plate of cookies and sweets sat a dollhouse, complete with Erwin's handmade furniture. I wanted to stay up all night and play with my new miniature house. Mother propped it up on a chair by my bed so I would stop fussing and go to bed willingly.

Several days after Christmas, the aunts and uncle arrived with their magic suitcase filled with books and gifts. At the very bottom was a tiny doll in a cradle to go with my dollhouse. Clever Soscha supplied me with dried peas and lentils for food and eggshells for dishes. She carpeted all the rooms with scraps of fabric and said, "Now you have a real villa." My dollhouse absorbed all my attention. For once, I stayed out of everyone's way, and Mother praised me for being unusually good.

On New Year's Day, the aunts came back to pick up the valuables and important documents they had given Father for safekeeping in case of a bombing attack on Elbing. They were agitated and looked as though they had not slept in a long time. They spent the afternoon engrossed in lengthy conversations with my parents. Even though no military information passed through the lines of their telegraph office, they picked up much vital information from private communications. They learned the Russians were advancing again at alarming speed, and not enough military strength remained on the German side to hold them off much longer.

"As soon as you get your official evacuation papers, you get out of here!" Aunt Elsbeth urged Father. "Pack now! Be ready! It could happen any day."

"I can't just up and leave. What about the animals? Who'll take care of them?" Father shook his head. "It's easy enough for you. You don't even have a dog or a cat. I've got a stable full of cows, calves, and horses. Who's going to feed them and milk the cows? They'll perish. It's all I have. I can't just up and leave."

"Hitler will make peace," Mother interjected. "When they realize all is lost, they'll surrender. Then we won't have to flee."

"Besides, Elschen," Father said, "I've talked with the English prisoner who works at the *Gasthaus*. He's advised me that no matter what happens, to stay put. He thinks that with my American citizenship papers, we'll be better off with the Russians rather than fleeing with the Germans. I've given it a lot of thought. I think he's right."

"Have you forgotten what the Russians did when they set foot on German soil last October?" Aunt Elsbeth persisted. "Do you think they'll stop and ask who or what you are, Herbert? Whether you're a Nazi or American? They're hungry for revenge. They'll shoot you first or rape your wife and daughter while they make you watch. They won't bother with questions."

"Well, we don't have to make any decisions this very moment. We can't do anything until we get orders to evacuate. The only thing that's official right now is that we'll be shot on the spot if we try to flee without a permit," Father concluded.

The aunts' visit did settle one important issue. In the event we were forced to flee, we would all meet at their sister's, Aunt Kaethe's, in the *Reich*.

"We're lucky to have relatives far away from here where it's safer," Aunt Elsbeth said. I had never met this Aunt Kaethe and only knew she was my cousin Kurt-Heinz's mother.

And so the year ended without the usual fanfare to usher in 1945. We walked the aunts to the station, only to find their train had been taken off the schedule, but that another train would make an unscheduled stop in Niederhof an hour later. We repeated this ritual twice more before a train finally pulled into the station, so overcrowded that the aunts feared they might have to spend the night with us. Only when Father shouted to the passengers that the aunts would be getting off at the next stop did people make room for them.

We said a teary goodbye. Aunt Elsbeth squeezed me harder and held me longer than usual. We stayed and watched the train pull out and disappear in the darkness of the frosty night. We walked home in silence, I preoccupied with my dollhouse and my parents steeped in more disturbing thoughts.

I returned to school with an uneasy conscience about my savings book, which no longer existed. Our teacher was not there, and many students were missing. Katarina and my new friend, Irmgard, had not returned either. The mayor of Steglitz came to tell us to go home. "Your teacher is stranded in the *Reich*," he said. "There has been a bombing attack where she lives, and the trains aren't running." He paused, searching for words, then added, "Just go home! There will be no school for a while."

This had never happened before: another vacation, and an indefinite one at that. I rushed home to tell my parents the exciting news, certain they would not believe me without a written note from the mayor. But Mother was not at all surprised to see me. She looked at Father and asked, "Does this mean we'll be notified to evacuate?"

"We're not going anywhere. We can't leave this place," Father said and stomped out of the room. Mother looked lost. She sat down and sighed. Her eyes remained dry, but her lips quivered. I felt heaviness in my chest. Things were not right. I bundled up and went out to look for Schnurribart.

The next day, a biting wind brought flurries of snow. I stood by the window and watched the flakes perform their whimsical dance before they reached the ground. Snow fell all day and night. The next day, although sunny and bright, stayed cold, and the windows frosted over. I made peepholes by blowing my warm breath on the icy glass. Paths, which the French prisoners had shoveled in the deep snow, crisscrossed the yard. Cozy and warm in my room, I was glad I had my dollhouse and Schnurribart.

One by one, my siblings appeared; their schools, too, had been closed until further notice. Tension continued to build in our household. My parents argued a lot, and I could feel their wavering indecision. Father paced the room like a pent-up animal. He would throw up his arms and say, "I don't know, Anna. I just don't know what to expect next. We can't believe what we hear on the radio. All signs point to approaching disaster."

It continued to snow off and on for several days. Icicles formed on the eaves during the freezing nights. The countryside looked white and pristine. We built snowmen in Mother's flower garden and lined them up in a row, like soldiers standing at attention. Even Erwin and Vera joined in the fun.

Then, one morning, I looked out the windows and saw a line of German refugees stretched out for as far as I could see. I watched the overloaded wagons move past our farm and felt like something inexplicable was about to happen. The entire world appeared to be on the move. Old men and both French and English prisoners drove the vehicles. Women and their children sat on top of their belongings. An icy wind blew over them and pushed them on. Some people walked, perhaps to lighten their loads or to keep from freezing. By the end of the day, wagons that had stopped for the night filled our yard. One man told Father they had slipped through cross fire between the Red Army and the Germans. He said, "I tell you, the Russians will be here any day. There is no holding them back."

Over two million people lived in East Prussia in January 1945, and they all seemed to have taken to the road overnight. They headed west for the *Reich* or north to the Baltic seaports in hopes of finding a ship that would take them to safety. The easternmost population of East Prussia had received evacuation orders, which were to be issued town by town and village by village. But the war reached us with such speed we had no time for anything. Nothing had been prepared for or organized. The Russians broke through the lines and were advancing fast.

We, too, were caught by surprise. Father had managed to sidestep the many traps in Hitler's Germany, but he was about to embark on a far more dangerous journey.

Within a few days, the highway was clogged and traffic crawled. A road that could barely handle two passing vehicles now extended to four narrow lanes. Retreating German tanks, military cars, and moveable equipment took up the center lanes. The refugees, forced onto the shoulders and often entirely off the road, traveled by all means of transportation. The fortunate ones had horse-drawn wagons or sleds. Several families often shared one vehicle. Others made do with whatever they could round up or quickly put together. They used anything into which a few belongings could be loaded: baby buggies, handcarts, bicycles, even wheelbarrows. Many simply plowed through the snow on foot, with rucksacks of provisions on their backs and extra layers of clothing. Broken-down and overturned vehicles brought everything to a near standstill. Panic broke out, and mass hysteria ruled. A frenzied effort to keep moving was the norm of the day. An iron determination to escape the advancing Russians pushed the people ahead.

Our farm was soon overrun with strangers. The refugees made rest stops on our property, often begging for food and feed and water for their horses. My parents did what they could. The able moved on;

the sick and exhausted stayed behind. New arrivals appeared by the hour. They descended upon us like locusts and acted as if they owned our place. Soon every room, every corner of the house, the stable, and the barn, crawled with people. Our family retreated to the children's room, along with whatever provisions Mother was able to stow away before these hungry, uninvited guests got to them. Strangers took over the kitchen. Aliens slept in our beds. They helped themselves freely to our food and to whatever else they could use. Crammed together, we fell over each other in our little room. Mother spread bedding on the floor for us to sleep on. She stopped trying to get into the kitchen to cook our meals. Instead, she had a little electric burner set up in the room, on which she warmed up some food and milk for us. The government dairy truck had stopped making pickups, so we had plenty of milk.

To watch our property being taken over by strangers and commandeered by soldiers devastated my parents. All niceties and social graces were quickly forgotten. Everyone was out for himself. There had been so little time to prepare for this shocking turn of events. Just two weeks earlier, the official radio had blasted out news of great German victories at the eastern front to create a false sense of security. Less than a month ago, we had celebrated a happy Christmas, with good food and little gifts. The aunts had talked about an eventual evacuation, but they also had talked about the latest movies they had seen and about getting children's theater tickets for Henry and me. Then, suddenly, everything collapsed.

On January 21, 1945, my ninth birthday, my uncle appeared on his bicycle. Commuter trains had stopped running altogether. The railroad, now totally under the control of the military, was used for transporting soldiers and supplies to and from the front. If an engine could be spared, it was made available to help evacuate the civilian population. My uncle brought news that a refugee train was being put together for our area. He urged my parents to get on it. But Father's excuse remained the same. "We have no evacuation orders. We can't leave."

"Forget the orders. It's too late for that. You've got to get out. At least get Vera and the little ones out of harm's way. The Russians are at our doorsteps. They're raping the women and looting, killing, and destroying everything in their path. Look at these masses of humanity. Aren't you listening to their stories? Can't you see the fear in their faces? The Russians have broken through the lines. It's not a matter of weeks or days. It could be only hours before they're here. Save your family! Get out, Herbert! Pull your head out of the sand! Face reality!"

Father shook his head. "I can't leave!"

"Can't you hear the distant rumblings? That's not thunder. That's the enemy. They're here. It's over for Germany. We're finished."

Uncle Eduard cut his visit short. Before he left, he gave me the most beautiful doll I had ever seen for my birthday. It was a present from my aunts. She had real hair, her eyes opened and shut, her eyelashes were genuine, and her celluloid arms and legs moved. She was clad in the softest red velvet dress. How had they come by such a treasure when you could not even get a light bulb or a bar of soap? She looked like a princess next to the rag dolls Mother had sewn together for me. I named her Elsbeth, after my aunt, and I loved her.

My uncle's visit did bring results. With forceful insistence by Father and great reluctance on Mother's part, they decided to put my sister and Frau Teichert on that train, but not Henry and me. No one could have known how devastating a decision that was to be for the two of us.

The next day, the train pulled into the Niederhof station in the late afternoon. Since it was packed full, there seemed no way of getting Vera and Frau Teichert on. But Father pushed them by sheer force into the crowded compartment, ignoring the loud protests from the squeezed-together passengers. We stayed until, after a long delay, the train finally pulled away. Father sighed as it slowly disappeared in the distance. It was the last transport to leave our area before the Russians cut off the lines to the *Reich*. My parents would never know whether it reached safety.

Shocked into a decision, Father said to Mother, "Eduard is right. It's over for us. We've got to get away from here. The German military is retreating. There are tanks everywhere. The road is so plugged, they're crossing the fields. They're headed for Elbing. I think they're getting ready to defend the city."

"Elbing? We've got to go through Elbing to get out," Mother said. "We'll get caught right in the middle of a battle. We'll all be killed!"

"We'll take the back roads and get there faster. We'll have to go by sled. The snow is too deep for the wagon. Besides, traffic is crawling on the highway and the military is pushing the refugees off the road. People have dumped stuff right and left. You should see the things. Furniture! China! Food and clothing! I even saw a sewing machine in the ditch."

Father sat down, ran his hands through his thin gray hair, and stared past all of us. Mother sat down next to him, wrung her hands, and cried.

We packed the next day. Mother sent me to empty out drawers and gather up her sewing supplies, knitting needles, safety pins, and a much-prized crystal vase from the parlor, while she and Soscha concentrated on food supplies, warm clothing, and bedding. I had to elbow my way through the strange new occupants of our house. A woman stopped me, scolded me, and relieved me of the items I had gathered up in my apron.

"I live here. These things belong to my mother," I told her.

"We all live here now," she replied and slapped my face. I ran to Mother, crying.

Mother was outraged. "Show me the brazen woman. This is still our house!"

She took me by the hand and dragged me through the rooms, but I could not point out the woman among the strangers. They all looked alike, with their dark clothes and grief-stricken faces.

Despite all the confusion, we managed to get our most important belongings packed. Our pantry was full of metal storage containers, barrels, and earthenware of various shapes and sizes, which eased the process. Father brought down the old cedar chest, and Mother filled it with clothes and valuables. Things were ready to be loaded on the sled the next morning.

That was our last night on our farm. I listened to my parents' whispered conversation, and heard Mother weeping quietly. Our whole life was suddenly turned upside down. Yet, I felt a secret excitement and was full of anticipation. We were about to embark on a great adventure. New experiences awaited us. I cuddled my precious new doll and dreamt of becoming a refugee.

We awoke to a clear but frosty morning. The temperature stayed below freezing all day. However, the sun shone brightly and put a friendly face on everything. Mother took it as a good omen. We had a busy morning. Father shuffled things around, unloading and reloading the articles several times. Mother, irritated, shouted, "For God's sake, Herbert, if you continue like this we'll never get out of here."

The French prisoners mucked the stable and fed the animals one last time, and Mother prepared a quick meal for us. We ate while one of my brothers stood guard over our loaded sled, because the refugees had taken to stealing.

"We can't even lock up the house," Mother said. "Every room is full of strangers. As soon as we pull out of here, the place will be ransacked."

"It already has been," Father said.

Father gave our French prisoners the choice to come with us or stay behind and take their chances with the Russians. They seemed as afraid of the Red Army as everyone else, and they opted to flee with us.

While Father and the French hitched the horses to the sled, Henry and I frantically looked for Schnurribart and Mumchen. They had become skittish with so many strangers in the house and had hidden in the stable most of the time. They did not come running when we called them.

"Don't worry," Mother said. "They're hiding. They don't want to come along. They'll be all right. There're plenty of mice around. They won't starve."

I panicked. It never occurred to me that we would leave without them. I kept calling Schnurribart, but he did not show up. I overcame my shyness and asked the strangers in the house. No one had seen the cats. I cried, pouted, and refused to leave without Schnurribart. Mother remained unmoved. "Even if you find him," she said. "he stays here with Mumchen!"

"Do you think they're hiding together?"

"I'm sure they are." Mother stroked my head and added, "We won't be gone long." Her words calmed me, but it did not make that uneasy feeling in my stomach go away.

The last thing Father did was untie the cows and open all the doors to the stable, barn, pig sty, and chicken coop, so the animals might be able to fend for themselves and, hopefully, find food and water on their own. It was his final farewell to a way of life.

The horrors that followed were to be indelibly inscribed in my memory. We did not know then that we would be uprooted for good, and that it meant a parting forever.

THE RUSSIANS

CHAPTER ONE

THE SUN HAD ALREADY STARTED to descend when we finally departed. Perched on top of our belongings, dressed like mummies in triple layers of clothing, we pulled out of the yard and left our home in the hands of strangers. We could only hope it would still all be there when we returned. The sled groaned under its weight. My brothers and the French prisoners followed on foot.

I kept calling for Schnurribart, hoping he would show up at the last minute. Then I noticed Senta was not with us either. "What about Senta? Isn't she coming?" I asked. "Who's going to take care of her? She doesn't eat mice."

"Senta has to stay and guard the farm," Father said. "The people will take care of her."

By the sternness in his voice I knew it was useless to pursue it any further, and I clung to my doll.

We immediately met our first major obstacle: crossing the clogged highway to get to the other side and pick up the less-traveled country road, our planned escape route. I watched the slow flow of vehicles, bumper to bumper, as if they were tied together. We had gone only thirty meters and were stuck already.

"Look at them," Father said, more to himself than to any of us. "They're running from the Russians, afraid of their revenge. There'll be hell to pay. Last October was only a taste of what we can expect."

Father gave the horses the whip and charged into the maelstrom. Caught up in the flood of traffic, a soldier in a moving jeep pointed his gun in Father's direction, shouting, "I'll shoot you if you don't get out of the way immediately!" He stood up and continued, "You cowardly deserter. Get off the sled and fight for the *Vaterland* instead of running like a scared woman! I ought to come and yank you down and make you fight."

Mother cried out. She knew the soldier had the authority to shoot anyone who refused to obey. He was merely following Hitler's orders. However, before the soldier could make his threat a reality, we were on the other side of the road and well out of the way.

As Father hurried the horses along the side road we saw German soldiers all around us, their guns pointed in the direction of the approaching enemy, ready to defend the railroad station.

"*Ach*," Father said. "The Russians must be very close."

When we came to the railroad crossing, the gates were down. A hospital transport packed with wounded soldiers and refugees slowly crawled past us. A freight train followed, loaded with army equipment and more soldiers, who were actually firing in the direction of the advancing Red Army.

"The Russians are right behind us. You better hurry!" a soldier shouted. "You'll get caught in the crossfire if you don't get out of the way fast!"

A biting wind whipped the snow across the tracks while we stood and waited for the transports to pass. Suddenly, we heard heavy artillery fire in the distance just as the last car cleared the tracks. Father gave a loud sigh and said, "Finally! I was afraid they would block the crossing forever." When the gates did not go up, Father screamed at the gatekeeper in the tower, "For God's sake, woman, raise the gates!" But nothing happened. Father ordered the French and my brothers to hold up the gates manually while we pulled across.

"Those gates have been down all day," Mother said. "There never was a keeper in the tower. Everyone is running. I just hope it's not too late for us."

As we moved along, we spotted German tanks racing across the fields, which put us in an even greater hurry. Father spurred the horses on. Steam escaped their nostrils as they strained under their heavy burden. When the sun disappeared below the horizon, the icy wind died down. We had barely covered the two kilometers to Steglitz. The village looked peaceful and quiet compared to the frenzied chaos in Niederhof. All we could think of was to keep moving.

When dusk faded into night, we could barely distinguish the road from the snow-covered fields. Father slowed the pace and proceeded more carefully. Explosions rocked the earth behind us, turning the sky into a kaleidoscope of reds and yellows from the many fires in the distance. A ghostly silence followed each muffled detonation. All of Niederhof seemed ablaze. "Oh, my God. They've blown up the whole village," Father said. "The soldier did not exaggerate. The Russians are at our heels."

Shivering from cold and fear as the demons of the night emerged, I realized being a refugee would not be the exciting adventure I had envisioned.

When the church steeple of the next village greeted us at the horizon, our spirits lifted. The frosty night air had penetrated my many layers of clothing, and my hands and feet had turned numb. Streaks of light flashed across the sky and lit up the entire village, stretched before us under a heavy blanket of snow.

Suddenly, two soldiers jumped out of a trench alongside the road and pointed their guns at us, shouting, "*Halt*, stop!" We panicked. We could not tell if they were Germans or Russians until one of them said, "You can't go beyond this point. The Red Army has broken through. We're surrounded. They're entrenched just outside Elbing. There is no escaping. Find shelter as fast as you can!"

We knew the Russians were close behind us, but in front of us, too? We were so near Elbing, but where else could we go? We had headed right into a noose, and now the loop had closed. Trapped and cut off from all alternative routes into the *Reich*, we could not move in any direction. To go back home seemed an even more perilous trap, judging from the glow of fires spread across the sky. The soldiers did not allow us to pass.

"A unit of German troops is entrenched behind us," they said. "We're going to make our stand here."

Father decided to turn in at a farmer friend's near where we were. Finding our way to the isolated property was difficult in the feature-less landscape, with all road markers deeply buried in snow. We crept along by the light of an almost-full moon. Suddenly, the sled jerked hard, and we all flew through the air, landing in a soft snowbank. The horses had strayed into a ditch, pulling the sled down with them. I heard the clatter of breaking china. Miraculously, no one had been hurt. Even the horses had escaped injury. The sled held together, but our belongings lay scattered in the deep snow. The men quickly righted and reloaded the vehicle. The skittish horses struggled to their feet on their own. I was heartbroken because my new doll was missing. She lay somewhere, deeply buried in the shadowy snow.

"Don't worry," Mother consoled me. "We'll come back and look for her after the snow melts."

I felt like a mother who had just lost her first child.

We received a less than enthusiastic welcome at the Hagen farm. Other refugees had arrived earlier in the day. They, too, had been turned back by the German military, and instead of returning home, had headed for the nearest cover. The group consisted of Herr and Frau Weber and their soldier son Kurt, who had lost his right leg above the knee a month earlier and was on crutches. The others included Herr Weber's portly sister, Frau Leitzel, and her daughter, Fraulein Gretchen, a nurse, who took care of her cousin Kurt's wound. The widow, Frau Kehr, her nine-year-old daughter, Helga, three young sisters from Elbing, and Franz Ehrlich, a distant relative of the Hagens, completed the group. The small Hagen farm already overflowed with people when all eleven of us arrived, thus more than doubling its refuge-seeking occupants. The elderly Herr and Frau Hagen were shrouded in black. They had lost their only son at the Russian front the year before.

With the quiet rhythm of our daily lives blown apart, we settled in as best we could. Fate had thrown us together, and together we waited for what was to come. We spread straw on the floor for sleeping. Exhausted and shaken to the core, we spent our first night as refugees only five kilometers from home.

The Hagen farm was so isolated it did not even have electricity. However, it did have plenty of kerosene lamps. "It's a good thing we have them," Father said. "There probably is no electricity any more. I'm sure all public utilities in the area have been abandoned."

We had brought a fair amount of provisions with us. The women took turns in the kitchen, taking care of their own. Our French prisoners shared the Hagens' Polish boy's quarters, and Soscha shared a bed with their Polish maid.

Three uneventful days passed. We claimed our space and established a loose order. The weather remained clear and bitterly cold, with the thermometer hovering around minus ten degrees Celsius. We did not know what to expect. We heard salvos of cannons in the direction of Elbing. Every night, we stepped out and watched fireballs, flares, and signal rockets go off, lighting up the sky like silent fireworks. Mother shivered and wondered out loud about the tragic dramas unfolding all around us. Occasionally, explosions ripped through the stillness. A cold, round moon stood high above us. I trembled with fear and clung to Mother.

No more refugees arrived at the Hagen farm who might have brought news with them. Fear kept the men from venturing out to the nearest village to gather information. We stayed put and waited.

The third morning, we heard a dog whining outside. Father opened the back door and found Senta pacing back and forth. She leaped all over us, thrilled to see us. I secretly hoped my cat, Schnurribart, would show up next.

"How touching," Frau Weber said. "That animal followed you and found you all the way out here. That's amazing! It'll be good to have a dog around. She'll warn us of any surprise visitors."

We kept her locked up in the stable day and night for fear the Russians or Germans would shoot her if she chased after them, as she was bound to do. But Senta had turned into a timid animal and stayed crouched in a corner.

On the fourth day, we faced the first Russians. They bolted through the door and stood before us with aimed guns. "*Germansky Soldat* here, German soldiers here?" they asked.

We sat tense with fear while they searched the rooms. To our surprise, they were polite and almost friendly. The officer in charge spoke some German, and we relaxed a little. Father told him we were American citizens and showed him our papers. The officer patted him on the back, called him comrade, and said, "You put *Americanski* flag on door. Make you safe."

They stayed no more than ten minutes and left as suddenly as they appeared. We breathed more easily.

We did have an American flag, which my parents had carefully packed and brought with them, but now we could not find it. However, with or without the flag, things looked hopeful, and Father speculated that the horror newsreels about Russian atrocities a few months earlier had been propaganda after all.

The young Ehrlich, however, saw the real danger. He was well known in the area as a bully and a gun-wielding Nazi Party boy. Like so many SS Party members, he often put himself above the law and took advantage of his position. He knew the Hagens' Polish boy would soon turn him in to the Russians. He stole one of the Hagens' horses and fled during one night.

My father, on the other hand, remained optimistic and relied on our American citizenship papers for immunity, certain those precious documents would be our passports to safety. How naive he was! He wanted us to return to our farm, but Mother would not hear of it. "Where would we stay?" she asked. "By now all those refugees will have taken over the entire house. We'll be guests in our own home."

Father would not be dissuaded and said, "Annchen, I've got to go and see for myself, to check on the animals and find out what's happened. Besides, for all we know the Russians have burned down all of Niederhof. We may no longer have a home to return to."

With his valuable American papers in his pocket, he set out on foot the next morning. He did not return all day. Mother was beside herself with worry as we watched day turn into night, and still no Father. Another hour passed. Mother sat by the window and stared into the darkness outside. We all did. Then, suddenly, Father walked in through the back door while we were watching from the front windows. It was a moment of indescribable joy. Mother vowed we would never be separated again.

Father sat down, shook his head, and groped for words. "The place has been vandalized. Our animals are gone, and the farm is crawling with strangers. They told me the Russians slaughtered most of our cows to feed their troops and took the rest with them. The German military blew up the post office, the dairy, and the *Gasthaus* to deprive the Red Army of the food stored there. Those were the fires we saw. They said the dairy burned for days because of all the butter stored in the cellar. I tell you the countryside is littered with the dead. It must have been terrible. The Russians just ran over everything in their bloodthirsty fury—people, animals, wagons, and whatever else was in their way. They caught up with one of those trains we had met at the crossing. It's still sitting on the tracks, shot to pieces. I stumbled over snow-covered corpses in the field. I can't put into words what I saw. It's a nightmare out there."

"What are we going to do? We can't stay here. We'll run out of food." Mother said.

"We can't go back. There're Russians everywhere. I had to hide from them. Elbing is still under siege, and there are ongoing skirmishes all around us. We're lucky to be alive, to have escaped all that. We're safer here!"

I listened, horrified, trying to make sense of Father's words. He stopped and, with trembling hands, wiped the moisture from his eyes. "And those soldiers we saw entrenched by the railroad crossing," he continued, "dead! Not shot, beaten to death. They probably ran out of ammunition. Beaten to a pulp. Clothes and boots ripped off. Their intestines hanging out and ..."

"Herbert, enough, enough! The children!" Mother stopped him.

Father did not stop, but he did change the subject. "The refugees on our farm told me one of our Poles came looking for us. He wanted to help us with the Russians, to vouch for us."

"It probably was our old Stefan," Mother guessed. "Bless that loyal soul."

Father handed Mother our family photo album and said, "Here! I found it trampled on the floor. It may be all we'll have left to remind us of our home." He also produced an enormous chunk of frozen butter wrapped in a flour sack.

"I dug it out of the dairy ruins," he said. "There's a whole basement full of this stuff. It's frozen solid; it'll keep. We're lucky it didn't all burn. As soon as it is safe, we'll go back and get more."

CHAPTER TWO

IT STARTED TO SNOW AGAIN, and the outside world looked deceivingly peaceful. The adults speculated on the outcome of the war; they never totally gave up hope that the Germans might yet push the Red Army back, and that we would be able to continue our flight. However, our second encounter with the Russians a few days later quickly shattered that hope. The Russians appeared, like the first, from out of nowhere, kicked the door open with brute force, and charged into the room. Their eyes flashed with hatred, murder, and lust. Their fingers were poised on the triggers of their weapons, ready to shoot. We were paralyzed with fear. There were nine or ten of them, itching for action. "*Frauen, Frauen*, women, women," they shouted and grabbed Fraulein Gretchen, the three sisters, and Frau Kehr and dragged them to the back of the house. The women screamed and fought, but were powerless against the men's savage force.

"They're going to kill us," the youngest sister kept repeating as she tried to wrestle free. "They're going to kill us." One of the soldiers pushed the rest of us into a corner and held us at gunpoint, while the others ransacked the house, looking for valuables. They turned the furniture over, picked the upholstery apart, kicked in the cabinets, yanked open drawers, and dumped our measly bundles from home on top of it all, shouting, "Give me watch! Give me gold! Give me silver! Give me *papyrossa*, cigarettes." They were especially crazy for cigarettes.

All the while, the women's screams from the back room echoed through the house. Kurt swore under his breath and raised one of his crutches, trying to hit a soldier, but his mother caught his arm, leaned to his ear, and whispered, "Stop! You're going to get us all killed."

Not understanding rape, I thought the Russians were torturing the women before killing them, like Schnurribart often did with the mice he brought home. Not until much later did I figure out why the women always ran into hiding when Russian soldiers appeared. I was glad Mother was safely at my side. What would Father have done if the soldiers had taken her, too, and what would the Russians have done to him if he had tried to protect her?

This nightmare seemed to last forever. The crazed soldiers alternated between pillaging and continuous raping; everyone got his turn at everything. They brutally kicked Kurt around and showered him with angry Russian curses, the meaning of which we could only guess. One man found an old World War I saber at the bottom of a drawer. With his young face beet red, he pulled the gleaming blade out of its scabbard and lunged forward, shouting, "You hide weapon to kill Russians," and brought it down on my brother's shoulder. Douglas winced with pain. I screamed, thinking he had split my brother in half, but the blade had landed on the flat side. I dug my fingernails deep into Mother's arm. She cringed and pried them loose one by one, only for me to dig in deeper.

Then, the soldiers slapped our French prisoners around. They searched their belongings and shouted, "You traitor! Why you not fight? You work for Hitler! You help kill Russians!"

Full of hatred for all that was German, these Russians came as avengers. They were on German soil; the time for retribution had arrived. Hungry for revenge, they unleashed their pent-up anger and hatred, leaving all of us, including the French, shaken and much sobered.

The women rejoined us, their clothes ripped, their hair in disarray, and their eyes red from crying. They had been gagged, held down, beaten, forced into submission, and raped over and over again. Father turned to Mother and said, "That would have been our Vera's fate. Wherever she may be at this moment, dead or alive, it's got to be better than this."

"Are we going to be killed?" I asked, the violence still ringing in my ears.

Father stooped down, put his arms around me, and said, "Not as long as I'm alive."

This traumatic experience jarred us into action. The next day, we gathered up the valuables the adults had wisely hidden before the Russian arrived, along with containers of smoked sausages, salted meats, and other nonperishable staples, and hid them in the hayloft. The looters had missed Herr Hagen's hunting rifle, which he had wrapped in a waterproof tarp and hidden in the rain gutter of the farmhouse. They also had missed Frau Kehr's wedding ring. She had never removed it from her finger during her marriage or widowhood. Now, nothing would budge it from her hand, not grease, soap, or ice. Nothing. "It's got to come off," she said. "The Russians will cut off my finger to get it."

Herr Weber found a crude rasp in the tool shed and filed the ring in two. She sighed when it finally fell from her bleeding finger and quickly sewed it into the hem of her dress.

From then on, Russian soldiers appeared almost daily at the Hagen farm, looking for loot, raping the women, and terrorizing us. One group rounded up our French prisoners, beat them with the butts of their guns, and lined them up against the barn, ready to shoot them. Soscha and the Hagens' maid ran out and pleaded for their lives. Instead, they marched the French off at gunpoint. Dumbfounded, Father said, "The French were their allies. They were taken prisoner while fighting against the common enemy. What's the meaning of this?"

Soscha later told us the Russians intended to punish the French for hiding out with us instead of surrendering to them. Father, too, had expected the French to take off at their first opportunity, but he guessed they were reluctant to make use of their freedom after witnessing the Russians' brutalities. Now that they were gone, Father was glad to no longer be responsible for them. However, we often wondered if they ever got home to their families, or if the Russians shot them after all and blamed it on the Germans.

That same week, the Russians carried off all our horses, and just as they were leaving, they took Senta as well. I was devastated. She went growling, with her paws dug in, but they beat her into submission. They told the stable boy, Soscha, and the Hagens' Polish maid to go back to their homes in Poland. The two women opted to stay with us, while the boy took off immediately, but not before threatening the Hagens, saying, "I'll be back with the Russians and have you shot for what you've done!"

The Hagens looked at him with perplexed apathy and said nothing.

They had been despondent ever since we had arrived. Apparently, the boy had made earlier threats, but we never learned the details of his grievances. Father suspected the Hagens' son, a staunch Nazi, had manhandled the boy in the past, and he now promised to take revenge on the parents.

The next morning, Herr and Frau Hagen were missing. We searched the property and saw no sign of them. Douglas found foot-prints in the new snow that had accumulated during the night. They led to the nearby forest, but soon the prints dwindled from two pair to one. Father and Erwin joined him, and together they followed the tracks into the woods.

They returned half an hour later, stunned by their discovery. The couple had committed murder/suicide. They found them inside a shelter, where they had carried out their final act in privacy. Herr Hagen had shot his wife through the forehead and then had shot himself in the mouth. His stiff body lay slumped over hers, with the rifle still in his hands. A half-empty bottle of brandy lay next to them. "He must have carried her most of the way," Father concluded. The men buried the couple together, along with the gun, at the spot where they had found them. There were no coffins, no ceremony, and no marker. The Hagens had departed from us without a note, not even a hint of their intent. Mother said, "They're at peace now. They had nothing left to live for. I'm sure they're spared a great deal more suffering."

Shortly after that, early one evening, two German soldiers knocked at our back door. They were a pitiful sight, these once-proud marchers in their crisp uniforms. They trembled from cold, and fear spilled out of their every pore. Unshaven, gaunt from hunger, uniforms dirty and torn, they were nervous and edgy, and so were we. They were hungry and lost. We gave them food and some of Herr Hagen's clothes, and then we begged them to be off quickly.

"Don't try to hide out in one of the farm buildings during the night; we will turn you in to the Russians if you do," Herr Weber threatened. If Russian soldiers had shown up at that moment, they would have killed all of us. We were relieved to watch them hurry off.

To this day, I can still see the fearful expression on their childlike faces. They were so young, boys rather than men. "Will they make it to safety? Will their lives be spared, or are they already measured in only hours or days?" Mother mused.

Death stood at everyone's door, made its relentless demands, and claimed its due. In this war, death was the overwhelming victor, and we were its silent witnesses.

The two young boy soldiers, however, had brought news. They confirmed that East Prussia was totally cut off from the *Reich*, with the Red Army entrenched in the abandoned German fortifications and strongholds. Elbing had not yet fallen, but artillery bombarded the city relentlessly from the heights above and reduced it into a blazing inferno. Now we knew that the explosions we had heard and the nightly red skies we had seen were from Elbing, only ten kilometers away. The soldiers also told us Russian bombers were reducing the *Haff* ice to floating islands to prevent the German military from escaping across those frozen waters. The Germans, on the other hand, tried to keep this escape route open by creating passageways from several strategic cities along the coast. They marked safe routes across the treacherous expanse by boring holes into the ice and sticking stakes into them, so that the fleeing populace could reach the waiting rescue ships on the other side of the peninsula. Many refugees had made it across, but many more had perished; they had either been caught in the Russians' bombardment, or had simply lost their way in the dense fog and had frozen to death. These freezing waters might have been our icy grave as well. Instead, we sat on an isolated farm, alive but uncertain about our future.

CHAPTER THREE

AFTER DAYS OF SEARCHING, PART of our precious American flag showed up as a decorative ornament in the blouse pocket of the Hagens' Polish maid. She had ruined it by cutting it into handkerchief-size pieces. Although he was extremely upset, Father did not dare confront her. We had learned from the Hagen incident not to antagonize the Poles. It now was commonplace for the Poles to denounce any Germans against whom they had a grievance. The Poles knew everything about the local civilians: who belonged to the SS or the Gestapo, what they did, and above all, how they treated their prisoner labor.

The Russians took full advantage of this information. The witch-hunt was on, with no one exempt from interrogation, arrest, imprisonment, or if the soldiers felt like it, from being shot. While the first Russians were fighting soldiers, those who followed were the clean-up force. We called them the "sweepers." They looked for German soldiers in hiding, Nazi Party and SS members, or anyone who might be considered an enemy of the new Russian order.

A week after his sly disappearance, a much-subdued Ehrlich returned without his horse, naked terror reflected in his face. He had gotten caught in the middle of a battle between the two opposing armies. His horse had been shot from under him, and he had barely escaped with his life. He was tired, hungry, cold, and very frightened. He stayed two days and then fled again during the night, this time without a horse. We never saw him again.

"*Frauen, Frauen*! Women, women! *Uhren, Uhren*! Watches, watches!" became the Russians' new war cry. They held us at gunpoint, rummaged through our possessions, took whatever appealed to them, and repeatedly raped the young women. They committed the most odious acts without inhibition or restraint, while Mother pushed my head into her lap to keep me from seeing.

"I'm going to kill myself if one of those dirty animals tries to touch me again," Fraulein Gretchen said after another brutal rape session. "They stink of sweat and urine." Grimacing with disgust, she added, "Those beasts haven't washed in months."

Defenseless and helpless, the women desperately tried to alter their appearance by dusting their hair with flour and pulling it back into severe buns. They pillaged through Frau Hagen's wardrobe for long black skirts and dresses, anything to help transform themselves into "old women." Only Frau Weber's, Frau Leitzel's and Mother's efforts produced visible results, but they had age on their side. As long as the younger women were around, the older ones were spared. I lived in terror that they would hurt Mother, too.

Shortly after the Hagens' murder/suicide, their Polish stable boy reappeared with two Russians to make good his threat. He had convinced the soldiers that Herr Hagen and his son, although dead, had been Nazis. When Father told them the Hagens had committed suicide, they turned violent.

"You damn Germans! You're lying! You're protecting them! Where are they hiding? We'll shoot all of you if you don't show us where they are!"

"We buried them in the forest where we found them. We'll show you their grave." Father offered.

Not satisfied, the Russians searched the house and the farm buildings. The Pole knew the property well and left no corner unchecked. Fortunately, they never discovered our hiding place in the hayloft. In the end, they demanded to be taken to the burial site.

"We're going to dig them up! There better be bodies there or else it will be your grave!" the Pole threatened, red with rage.

Father and Erwin led them into the woods. Mother, edgy and nervous, said, "I hope they won't shoot them anyway."

We listened for gunshots and were relieved when all five of them emerged from the looming forest. Once the Russians saw the gravesite, they departed, satisfied. They never asked how the Hagens had committed suicide, so the issue of the gun did not come up.

In early February, the Russians took Father and my brother Erwin away to report to headquarters in the next village for official registration and documentation, the new requirement for all German males over the age of fifteen, or so they said. The Russians conducted themselves in such a business-like way that we believed them. Father and Erwin were to be back the same day. We stood by the window and watched them trudge through the deep snow, Erwin in the new shiny boots he had received for Christmas and Father in his warm fur hat.

A low, leaden sky promised more snow. Mother put her hand on my shoulder and squeezed it continuously. Her face convulsed with emotion, but she did not cry. We waited all day for Father's and Erwin's return, but night descended over the frozen earth without a sign of them. We continued our watch late into the moonless night. When I awoke the next morning, they still had not returned. We watched for them throughout that day, and the next, and the next. Mother became more and more distraught. After a week, we stopped looking for them, but Mother never gave up hope. I was obsessed with fear that the Russians would take Mother next.

The official call for registration and documentation had been a ruse. "That American citizenship document isn't worth the paper it's written on," Mother said. "They took them anyway. It's been our undoing. First the Germans, and now the Russians."

A few days later, the Russians came for the three sisters. They did not return either. Since they had no kin waiting for them at the Hagen farm, they might have returned to Elbing, their hometown, at least so Mother reasoned. Herr Weber was spared because he was paralyzed on one side from a stroke and walked with a cane. He carried his arm in a sling to appear more disabled and started to grow a beard. The Russians paid little attention to him.

Kurt, on the other hand, was often physically manhandled. They cursed him and beat him with the stocks of their rifles. Sometimes they took away his crutches and pushed him to the floor. Other times they spat in his face, kicked him in the groin, and screamed, "You goddamned German swine!" I buried my head in Mother's side and flinched every time they hit him. Kurt bore the abuse in silence, while helpless Herr and Frau Weber watched.

Barely three weeks had passed and so much had happened. The Hagens were dead; Father, Erwin, the three sisters, and Ehrlich had not come back; the French prisoners had been led away at gunpoint; and the Hagens' stable boy now worked for the Russians.

Soscha and the Hagens' Polish girl disappeared one night as well. They left without saying good-bye. The adults reasoned they were afraid that the Russians' treatment of the French might also become their lot if they did not disassociate themselves from us. Our group had shrunk by half, and by doubling up, we all now had a bed to sleep in.

Mother coped. Every now and then, she voiced her anguish to no one in particular. "Will they ever return? Will we ever see them again?"

Our food supply was shrinking, and we started rationing. The Russians had not only relieved us of our valuables, but they also had emptied the Hagens' larder. No soup kitchens traveled with the Red Army. They lived off the land and helped themselves to whatever they found on the farms. When soldiers came to get a load of hay for their horses, we decided to change our hiding place and buried everything under the big woodpile in the shed.

We worked fast. We children were the lookouts and had to give warnings of suspicious movements from any direction, while the adults carried the trunks and containers to the new hiding place. This time, we included important documents in the cache. Luckily, no visitors surprised us. We replaced the wood at random so that the pile looked undisturbed. For the time being, we still had the Hagens' cows and a few chickens. But we feared that soon they, too, would be taken away from us, just as had happened with the horses.

We continued to live in perpetual suspense. After the soldiers abducted the three sisters, Fraulein Gretchen and Frau Kehr became the targets of the Russians' continuous raping. Pretty Fraulein Gretchen, in her early twenties, especially caught their eyes. Even in her disguise, she looked desirable. Frau Kehr, on the other hand, although still young, had a child, and the soldiers sometimes left her alone. Both were lucky that the Russians had not abducted them with the other women.

Kurt's stump became infected. Whenever soldiers appeared, Fraulein Gretchen quickly undid the outer bandages to expose the pus and blood-stained layers, hoping to evoke compassion. He contorted his face in pain, but it rarely deterred the Russians from torturing him, physically and emotionally. Once, one soldier hit his raw stump with the butt of his gun. It was the only time I heard Kurt scream.

My brother, Douglas, did not escape their clutches either. On a day like all others, five or six soldiers appeared out of nowhere. We were getting better at detecting their approach, but still they surprised us. They were searching for German soldiers. Douglas, tall for his age, apparently looked like a deserter to them. They grabbed him and started to walk off with him.

Mother ran after them and pleaded, "Oh, please don't take him. He's just a boy! He's not even fourteen." But their hearts were encased in steel. They took him anyway.

Mother cried as she watched them disappear. I think part of her died that day. Now she wept often, silently. She would stare into space and clutch me in her arms as though afraid of losing me, too. My brother was so young.

Many a night I heard Mother sob, her body jerking against mine, arms locked around me. I felt her hot tears on my back. Grief overshadowed her existence. Half of our family had been yanked away from her, and she did not know their fate.

"Will we ever see them again? Are they still alive, or have they been killed?" These unanswered questions gnawed at Mother's soul, and she voiced them often to no one in particular.

The Russians did not promise Douglas's release after the "official registration," but we watched for him anyway.

"Why would they take such a young child? Surely they will send him home when they find out his age," Mother hoped, her gaze lost in another place and time. She was certain Erwin had not kept his shiny black boots. "Did they at least give him a pair of shoes to replace them? Are they getting enough to eat?" she often worried.

We could do nothing but wait. Always on the lookout for approaching soldiers, we never let down our guard. If a visit was imminent, we braced ourselves for whatever might happen. We children, Helga, Henry, and I, had to stay at our mothers' sides, preferably in their laps. If time allowed, Frau Kehr hid in the attic or cellar and Fraulein Gretchen stretched out on the couch, which had been carefully prepared to look like a sickbed, always ready for its "patient."

If the soldiers intended rape, Fraulein Gretchen went through her sick act. Her nurse's training helped her make it look very convincing. She bent over, pressed her hands into her stomach, gasped for air, and rolled her eyes as if about to faint. Agonized moans and groans, or a few screams, accompanied her performance. The more aggressive the soldiers' behavior, the more animated Fraulein Gretchen's act became. One time, they yanked her off the couch and forced her to her feet. She cried out in pain. Frau Leitzel rushed to her side and caught her as she fainted in her mother's arms. I was convinced this time it was not an act; her performance appeared that real. The soldiers turned away, cursing, and joined their comrades. They rarely touched her any more. Sickness of any kind was a deterrent. But when drunk, they forgot all caution.

From the Russians' frequent visits, we guessed fighting still raged around us. The occasional distant rumblings and red flare-ups in the night sky confirmed our surmise. Much later, we learned that German forces had fought hard to hold the key cities along the Baltic Sea to keep open the escape routes for the civilians. They could do no more. According to later statistics, their action allowed several hundred thousand German citizens to escape to the West between the end of January and the middle of March 1945. Ships from the coastal cities picked up these refugees. However, many of the rescue vessels ran into mines or were torpedoed, and then sunk with their doomed cargo.

CHAPTER FOUR

BARELY A MONTH HAD PASSED—A terrifying month—since we had fled from home. We knew only one thing for certain: we could expect no mercy from the Russians, who considered us their prey and fair game for any savage act. If they killed us, there would be no witnesses, no one to report our fate, and no one to bury our bodies. Our kin, if they survived, would never know what had happened to us. Law and order no longer existed.

After the Russians took Douglas away, the job of feeding and watering the cows fell to Henry. One afternoon, he came running back to the house, trembling. "I heard noises up in the hay loft. Somebody is hiding up there!"

"You are imagining things," Herr Weber chided. "Are you trying to get out of your chores?"

"Something is going on up there!" Henry persisted and refused to go back. Herr Weber was forced to go and check for himself. He grumbled. He did not know how he would make it up the ladder with his disability. But the adults agreed that if German soldiers were hiding in the hayloft, it would take an adult to ferret them out.

"Let's hope it's a false alarm," Herr Weber said. He grabbed Henry by the arm and headed for the barn.

We waited uneasily. If the stowaways had guns, they might shoot if caught by surprise. When the two returned, we surmised from the expression on Herr Weber's face that Henry had been right.

"Tell us! Tell us!" Frau Weber probed. "Did you see anyone? Did you talk to them?"

"No! But hay has been built up against the back wall. Somebody has been, or still is, up there," Herr Weber said. "Whoever they are, they're clever. During the night, they milk the cows and steal our eggs from the chicken house, and during the day, they hide. We'll have to pry them out. The Russians will kill us all if they discover them. They won't ask questions; they'll just shoot."

Herr Weber came up with a simple but effective solution. He had Henry set food on the ledge of the loft. Then Herr Weber called out, "We know you're hiding up there. We've put out food for you. There are women and children on this farm. You're putting all of us in grave danger. If you're not gone by morning, we'll turn you in to the first Russians who show up on these premises!"

The next morning, we were edgy and nervous. Had the defectors left? Had somebody really been up there? Herr Weber and Henry went to check. The food was gone, and the wall of hay was down. We never knew who they were, or how many.

By now, the Russians had taken most of our chickens as well. We tried to hide the remainder, but chickens are difficult to control. In the end, they all fell prey to the marauding Red Army. We were running out of flour and other staples. The women became innovative. They soaked feed grain overnight and added it to the bread dough, with tasty and crunchy results. Nervous tension always filled the air on bread-baking day, but baking days were our lucky days. Soldiers appeared only once and took all our freshly baked loaves. Frau Leitzel had just enough time to hide a loaf in the chimney. We retrieved it, covered with soot, but it filled our stomachs that evening.

Articles of clothing disappeared along with all the other things the Russians took. The women cut up drapes and sheets, and sewed them together to replace the stolen garments. Mother unraveled a knitted tablecloth that had graced our dining room table at home. I had always admired its intricate design from my under-the-table vantage point, and I had been tempted to cut off the black beads at the end of the fringe to make a necklace for my doll. I had thought if I cut off every other one, no one would notice. Now, Mother unraveled it to knit a sweater for me, and I no longer cared about the beads. My doll was gone.

A week later, two Russians appeared and rounded up the Hagens' cattle. The adults had talked about butchering a cow; now that opportunity vanished and so did our precious milk. The soldiers went straight to the stable, untied the animals, and drove them into the yard; then the soldiers entered the house. Frau Weber and Mother begged them to leave at least one animal for us. Their pleas fell on hardened hearts. Instead, one of them pointed at Frau Kehr, Helga, Henry, and me and said, "You go with us. You help drive cows to next village. Cows go to Russia. You hurry!"

We barely had time to put on warm clothes. Mother held on to one of the soldier's arms and pleaded, "Please don't take my children! Please!" But he shouted at us, "*Dawai, dawai*, hurry, hurry," and pushed us out of the house. Mother stood in the doorway, with tears in her eyes, and called after Frau Kehr, "Be sure you bring them back to me." Frightened and upset, I held on to Frau Kehr's coat. I did not understand why Mother did not come with us. Today, I know she had never given up hope that Father, Erwin, and Douglas would return, and so she needed to be there. She provided the center to which we all would return. If she were gone, how would we find each other? How would we ever be reunited? It was a heartbreaking predicament for Mother.

We took off in the direction of Steglitz and assumed it to be our destination. Our path led us by the edge of the forest where the Hagens lay buried. Can they see us drive their cows away, I wondered uncomfortably? Will their ghosts rise from their cold grave and haunt the empty stables? I shuddered as my childhood phantoms resurfaced. When I saw Steglitz appear at the horizon, I knew we would get home well before dark.

Most of the snow had thawed. The puddles that had formed in the road reflected the sky with its ragged clouds. My feet had become wet minutes after we had left. The Russians remained silent, only occasionally exchanging a few words. As we got closer to Steglitz, the path split. They stopped and debated between them. When they steered us away from Steglitz, my heart sank. Frau Kehr, unfamiliar with the area, asked Henry, "Where are we going? How far is it to the next village?"

Henry had only a vague idea, and I, who had never been beyond Steglitz, had no idea at all. We trudged along, driving the cows before us. By afternoon, we were hungry and tired. The temperature dropped, and cold penetrated my body. We knew we would not get back the same day and merely hoped to arrive at the village soon, whatever its name, and get food and warm shelter.

We arrived at dusk in a village, much larger than Steglitz. Mass confusion reigned, with cattle and soldiers everywhere. Animals rounded up from surrounding areas were separated into two groups. The good, sturdy stock would go to Russia, and the weak animals would be slaughtered to supply the fighting forces. Entrails and waste were heaped high in several piles. The stench from the mix of blood, urine, dung, and rotting flesh took my breath away. Frau Kehr assessed the situation and said, "We've got to find a way to get out of here fast—if we don't die from the stench first."

Women and children milled around aimlessly. They, too, had been forced into service as cattle drivers. People spread contradictory rumors, ranging from having to take the cattle to the nearest railroad station for loading to having to drive them on foot all the way to Russia.

We left our charges at one of the farms and found shelter in the overcrowded house. The Russians did not give us anything to eat, but when a soldier ordered Frau Kehr to help with the milking, she returned with a bowl of milk.

She pulled us aside and said in a low voice, "Stay out of the Russians' way and keep out of sight. We're going to get away from here before dawn, but first we need to get some rest."

We found a small storage room with a twin bed in the back of the house that at one time might have been a servant's quarters. We three females crawled into bed, while Henry settled for the cold, hard floor. Sleep came quickly, and we remained undisturbed all night. Frau Kehr awakened us before dawn. She put her finger to her lips and whispered, "Now! Be very, very quiet and follow me!"

Having slept in our clothes, we were ready in seconds. Stepping over sleeping bodies, we made our way through the house in the semidarkness. Someone was snoring in the corner of the room. When we reached the hallway, we heard footsteps coming from the living room. A stream of light from a slightly ajar door guided us along. A few Russians stood around the yard, but they paid no attention to us. Our getaway was unexpectedly easy. We headed in the direction from which we had come the previous day and did not slow our pace until the village was well behind us. As dawn approached and shafts of sunlight turned the sky red, we watched for patrolling soldiers.

We left the road, crossed a field, and headed for cover in the forest. We hoped to avoid Steglitz by taking a shortcut through the woods. Among the dense trees, we were less sure of our direction. The rustling of dry leaves under our feet put us on guard. We tried to walk lightly, all four of us walking in step, but the silence around us magnified every sound. The cover we had hoped for vanished with each noisy step.

Two shots rang out in quick succession and threw us into panic. A third whistled right past us and ricocheted against a rock. We leaped for cover behind a rocky outcrop. Frau Kehr held Helga close to her.

"Oh, my God! Oh, my God! They're going to hunt us down like wild animals," she cried out.

I thought my heart would jump out of my chest from fear. Would it hurt to have a bullet pierce my body? I longed for Mother, and at the same time I was angry with her for not coming with us. We cowered behind the rocks, frozen into position, not daring to move, and listened. We heard faint voices, but they were moving away from us and soon faded altogether.

We stayed in our hiding place for minutes, hours, I could not tell. Nothing seemed real, not the trees or the silence—only my fear was real. My hands stiffened from cold, and pain clenched my stomach. I was hungry. We waited and listened. When Frau Kehr decided to risk coming out of hiding, we were driven by fear. All we could think about was to keep moving in that endless forest. Finally, we came to a clearing and a field. They looked familiar. We recognized landmarks and discovered we had returned to the same spot where we had entered an hour or two earlier. We had lost our sense of direction after taking cover behind the protective boulders and had come full circle. I cried when we started over again, but I fell into step.

I was possessed by fear—fear of being shot at again, fear of never seeing Mother again, and fear of never finding our way out of that labyrinth-like forest, with its ghosts that would surely assail us during the night. We alternated between walking and running, and we no longer paid attention to the loud rustling under our feet. Eventually, we came to another clearing and field. We ran across and picked up a narrow path. Things looked familiar again. We were on the road from the day before, and home lay just beyond the next hill. When the Hagen farm came into view, we ran the last few meters and burst into the kitchen. A sorry, downcast group sat around the table and stared at us in disbelief. I flew into Mother's trembling arms. She pressed me to her breast.

"Evchen, my child, my child," she repeated between sobs, her eyes red from crying. "Evchen, my child."

It felt so good to be safely locked in Mother's embrace.

CHAPTER FIVE

SNOW CONTINUED TO FALL INTERMITTENTLY. We children stood by the window and watched the landscape turn white. We longed to go sledding, build snowmen, and make angels in the fresh snow, all the things we used to do during happier times. Fear kept us from venturing out. Danger lurked around every corner, behind every tree and building. We were as jittery as hunted deer. We did not dare cross the yard to the little outhouse next to the stable without an adult. We organized "outhouse" trips. There was safety in numbers, and we lived by that principle.

Cabin fever set in with all of us. We children had a particularly difficult time. Always on edge and tense, we fought at the slightest provocation. I missed my doll, the only toy I had been allowed to bring along. Helga still had her doll, but she was not eager to share. When she felt generous, we played house together, the doll being our baby. But we never strayed far from the adults, not even to go into an unoccupied adjoining room. An eerie atmosphere of doom hung over us day and night. Any sudden, unfamiliar noise threw us into panic.

We spent hours sorting the cattle feed, a mixture of oats, wheat, rye, lentils, peas, and chaff, we had found in the Hagens' storehouse. We separated the grains and cooked them for food. Luckily, the Russians had not taken the feed for their horses. Herr Weber insisted we save the cache under the woodpile for a last resort.

Russian soldiers now appeared less frequently, and we relaxed our guard. Friction developed between the women as old grievances surfaced. My parents had not been on speaking terms with the Webers for years, although we had been neighbors, and the two sisters-in-law had their own private quarrel going. In addition, Mother grew resentful that the Weber-Leitzel clan was still very much intact, whereas she had lost half her family. However, the underlying struggle for survival was the glue that held the group together.

By the middle of March, we still had no word from Father or my brothers, nor did we have information about the progress of the war. We no longer heard distant artillery rumbles. But on our nightly trips to the outhouse, we occasionally saw white phosphorous shells exploding in the distance. It was an eerie sight, like watching silent fireworks. From that, we guessed there were still some isolated skirmishes not far away. We lived in a state of limbo. Since the end of January, all commerce had stopped. Stores no longer existed. We were cut off from the central government, if it still functioned somewhere in the *Reich*. The enemy and thugs now held the law in their hands. Things we once took for granted, like electricity, sanitation, radio, and mail delivery, hospitals as well as any type of medical services, and schools, were all luxuries of the past. All elements that kept society functioning in a civilized and orderly way had vanished overnight.

The March weather alternated between snowing, thawing, and freezing. Some days were gloomy, gray, and depressing, and others were sunny, clear, and almost uplifting. On one such cloudless day, a lone Russian soldier appeared at our door. That was unusual since they had always come in numbers. An older man with a friendly demeanor, he had a fair command of the German language. He showed no interest in looting and ignored the women. He was more like a visitor who happened to be in the neighborhood and had decided to drop in. Within minutes, he and Herr Weber were engaged in a friendly conversation.

His name was Ivan. He was of German origin from a region in central Russia along the Volga River. His ancestors had settled there when Katherine the Great had opened up that territory to German immigrants.

Anxious for news about the war, Herr Weber assaulted him with questions. "Tell us what's happening at the front. Will the fighting be over soon? Will we be able to return to our farms?"

"*Weuna bald kaputt*, the war will be finished soon. *Hitler auch bald kaputt*, Hitler, too, will be finished soon." He shook his head and added, "War is bad thing. Too many people die. My people die. Your people die and everything *kaputt*, destroyed. What for? I want go home to my people. I no want be here. War over soon. I go home."

With much gesturing and filling in the missing words, we learned that Danzig, one of the last escape ports for East Prussian refugees, was about to fall, and with that victory, all East Prussia would be in Soviet hands. If we were to believe Ivan, we now were totally cut off from the *Reich*. We also learned that, while some Russian units were besieging Danzig, the main body of the Red Army was already halfway to Berlin, and the Germans were in full retreat. He guessed the war would be over in weeks. We had mixed feelings. That East Prussia was now Russian territory was disheartening, but that the fighting might be over soon, no matter the victor, encouraged us. We expected the end of the war to bring back order and a measure of safety into our precarious existence.

Ivan assured Mother that all German men who had been taken prisoner would be sent home as soon as the dismantling of East Prussia was completed. Not until much later did we learn the true meaning of the word "dismantlement." The Russians shipped every-thing movable and useable to their own country. Whole factories, equipment, large and small, and all livestock found a new home that way. Even railroad tracks were removed and transported east.

Renewed hope that Father and my brothers might be alive and might return brought Mother back to life. More cheerful now, many of her musings started with, "When we're all together again ..."

Ivan rose to leave, pointed into the distance, and said, "Other farms there. No people. Maybe you find food." He shook Herr Weber's hand and promised to return with bread for us.

We had made our first friend among the Russians. Ivan was our ray of hope. He had brought us more than just news of the outside world; he called our attention to other farms in the area. The adults decided to venture out and forage for food. The best and safest time was always the day immediately after a looting spree by the Russians.

We did not have to wait long. Soldiers appeared and unleashed their usual fury on us. For once, they left Fraulein Gretchen and Frau Kehr alone. Instead they demanded cigarettes and *Schnaps*, whiskey. They browbeat us until they became convinced we had neither, and they finally departed, grumbling.

The next day would be the day of our great adventure. Filled with anticipation, we children looked forward to the foray as if we had never seen the outside world. Since our arrival at the Hagen farm only six weeks ago, we had not ventured out, with the exception of our harrowing cattle drive. We were like caged animals about to be freed. The promise of great rewards gave us the courage to risk the hazards we might encounter. Herr Weber and Kurt stayed behind because of their disabilities. Unhappy, Kurt said, "I feel so useless. I ought to be out there fighting with my fellow soldiers. Instead I'm forced to sit here." He pounded the stump of his missing leg with his fist and continued, "I can't even fight back when these animals molest the women."

Frau Weber put her hand on his shoulders, "Look," she said, "losing your leg may well have saved your life. You could be dead by now or sitting in some prison in Siberia. One more fighting soldier would have made no difference in the outcome of the war. Our plight would still be the same."

Frau Leitzel remained with the men as a precautionary measure, just in case Russian soldiers showed up. If they found the two men alone, they might take them in for questioning, or worse, shoot them.

The weather cooperated. The sun seemed brighter that morning and the sky bluer. Water dripped from icicles at the eaves, and the new snow sparkled like a million stars. Henry found an old sled in the woodshed and called out, "Quick, let's ride down the hill before the others catch up with us!"

Helga and I jumped on, Henry pushed from behind, and together the three of us raced to the bottom, an exhilarating ride down the hill that had beckoned us all winter. We quickly pulled the sled back up and raced down a second time. For one brief moment, we were kids again, and it felt good. We made angels in the wet snow, took turns pulling each other along on the sled, and enjoyed our brief, newfound freedom.

Before we knew it, a farm appeared in view as we came over a hill. It sat like a lonely sentry, unprotected by trees and visible from all directions. We approached with caution and saw no signs of life. An eerie stillness hung over the grounds. As we entered the inner yard, we came upon the carcass of a horse, its rib cage picked clean by wild animals, and the innards gone. Only the head and hoofs were still covered with hide. As we approached the animal, a swarm of flies escaped from the rib cage and took flight.

"It's too early for flies. It's still winter. Where did they come from?" Frau Weber asked.

The flies marked the beginning of a new nemesis. The summer of 1945 turned out to be the year of the fly—horrible, monstrous flies. They inundated us. Dead bodies, animal carcasses, and rotting food littered the countryside. Burial had not yet begun, with soldiers on both sides still engaged in battle.

As we walked toward the farmhouse, we peeked through the open stable doors. A lone cow was calving in one of the stalls. We rushed in to assist her.

"Milk! We'll have milk again," Frau Weber called out. "And a newborn calf means meat!"

But the cow looked suspiciously motionless and quiet. She had died in the process of giving birth, and the calf had died with her. It had come out half way, head and front feet clearly visible. We could not tell how long ago this had occurred. Their eyes were glazed over, and their bodies cold and stiff, but the usual sweet odor of decay and decomposition was not yet present. The adults speculated whether the meat might still be safe to eat.

We had been there only a few minutes, and twice death had greeted us.

We cautiously entered the farmhouse through the back door by the kitchen and found it empty, but everything looked as though the people had just left. Pots stood on the stove, and kindling filled the woodbin. A dishcloth lay neatly draped over the dishpan, and a lone coffee cup sat on the dust-covered table. A chair was pulled back as though someone had just gotten up.

"Hello! Is anybody here?" Frau Kehr called out. "Hello?" No one replied.

We continued through a narrow hallway into the next room. A man's coat hung on the wall. The living room, like the kitchen, had the feel of a human presence about it. Frau Kehr called out once more, "Hello! Hello! Anyone here?" Again, silence.

The eerie stillness made me shiver. We had invaded someone else's domain, where we did not belong. I felt as though the owner might appear at any moment to challenge us. Only the undisturbed layer of dust on everything belied recent human habitation. We puzzled over the absence of signs of looting and the usual disarray. No furniture was turned upside down, no upholstery ripped or slashed, and even the beds remained neatly made. Had the Russians missed this farm altogether?

"Come see this!" Henry shouted from the storeroom off the kitchen. "Look at all this food."

We rushed to his side and could not believe what we saw. A sack of rye flour, a bin of sugar, salt, a few glass jars filled with fruits and vegetables, even a couple of dried up loaves of bread. We quickly loaded our sled.

Behind the kitchen, Mother discovered a stairway leading to the attic and said, "Maybe there is a smoke chamber up there like we have at home. We might find sausages, bacon, and other meats."

Frau Kehr and I followed her upstairs. Mother jerked to a sudden stop. "Oh, my God," she cried out. "Oh, my God!"

Then I saw it, too. A man dangled from a frayed rope slung over a rafter. Mother threw her hands over my eyes, but it was too late. I saw it all. I stood openmouthed and wide-eyed. Mother grabbed me and pushed me down the stairs, while my goose bumps developed goose bumps. I could not get down fast enough.

"Now, it all makes sense. Perhaps that's why the Russians have avoided this place," Fraulein Gretchen whispered. "Who knows what crimes have been committed here."

We rushed away from that house of death, pulling the loaded sled behind us. I kept looking over my shoulder, expecting the man's ghost to grab me and hold me back. I could not erase from my mind the bulging eyes and grotesque expression on his waxen face, his bare feet and arms dangling limp from his shoulders.

Much shaken, we concentrated on getting home quickly with our contraband. Even the bright sun and clear sky felt threatening. Reminded once more of our vulnerability and of how little our lives were worth, we took little joy in the success of our mission.

"There was something very strange about that place from the start," Frau Kehr said. "Very, very strange! I wonder how long he'll dangle there before someone buries him."

The adults speculated as to who he was—perhaps the owner of the farm, a passing stranger, or a worker—and what had driven him to that desperate act.

We were a short distance from the Hagen farm when two Russian twin-engine planes roared above our heads. The suddenness of their appearance startled us. We had not heard them coming. They dove down so low we could see the pilots' young, laughing faces. We looked up and watched as they circled and came back towards us. We heard the ratatatat of guns and realized the guns were aimed at us. Mother threw herself on the ground, pulling me with her. Exposed on top of the hill in the bright snow, we made easy targets. The exploding shells created a continuous racket. I screamed. Mother threw herself over me and tried to muffle my cries, as though we would be safer if we could not be heard. The incident lasted less than a minute, and the planes were gone. No one was harmed.

We rushed down the last hill. Before we reached the bottom, the planes returned. This time we did not stop and stare at the sky. We kept running. We made straight for the brush at the bottom of the ravine. Again, the guns went ratatatat above us. Now even the women screamed. The farm seemed miles away. The planes vanished as quickly as they had reappeared. We stayed under the brush and waited, but they did not return. Frau Weber, ashen from fright, shook her head and exclaimed, "Those brutes tried to kill us!"

We pulled ourselves up and darted up the last hill. When we realized we had abandoned the sled with its precious cargo on the other side of the ravine, Frau Kehr and Fraulein Gretchen rushed back and retrieved it while we waited, nervously watching the sky. We sprinted up the final stretch of the incline and did not stop until the sheltering farmhouse enveloped us. Mother fell into the nearest chair and let out a deep sigh, "What a day. We could all be dead. Were they just playing with us? Or were we plain lucky that their aim was so bad?"

"You saw their young faces. They were kids having fun with a new toy," Frau Weber said. "Just think if one of us had been seriously wounded. What would we have done without a doctor, a hospital, or medical supplies? We were more than lucky."

CHAPTER SIX

A SINGLE YELLOW CROCUS APPEARED in the Hagens' garden, and we rejoiced at this first sign of spring. We had been thrown together on the Hagens' isolated farm only two months ago, two months that seemed like an eternity. Ivan did not come back. Had Berlin fallen? Was the war over? Food remained our greatest concern. We found packets of seeds among the Hagens' supplies. Should we plant them, or should we leave the farm and return to our own farms? These were questions that could not be easily answered. We no longer heard or saw signs of war, but that did not mean it was over. We were sure of only one thing: East Prussia was now fully under Russian occupation. We opted to stay together and wait it out.

The conversation often returned to the ill-fated food foraging expedition of the week before. Frau Kehr, especially, was still greatly disturbed by our shocking discovery and ultimately hit upon what had been wrong in that attic. "You know," she said, "I don't think that man committed suicide. There was nothing under his dangling body. No tipped-over chair, no object of any kind that he might have kicked from under him. I think he was murdered. Somebody hung him from those rafters."

"If anyone wanted to kill him, why didn't they just shoot him as they threatened to do with the Hagens? It would have been faster and easier," Herr Weber argued.

"It could have been an act of revenge like the Hagens' boy intended for them. To watch the man struggle would have made the act more gratifying for the avenger," Frau Kehr reasoned.

The conversation was taking an uncomfortable turn. I pressed my fingers to my throat and envisioned being choked to death with a rope around my neck. I was learning about the many painful ways of dying. They all frightened me.

Then, one day, a small miracle happened. Our Senta limped into the yard. She plopped down by the back door and let out agonized yelps. She had been shot in the hip.

"I can't believe it," Mother said, shaking her head.

"What an amazing animal," Frau Weber marveled.

"Let's hide her so the Russians won't take her away again," I pleaded.

"Come here, Senta!" I called and held out my hand to her. But she eyed us carefully and growled, allowing no one to touch her. We coaxed her into the barn with food and made a bed of straw for her in a sheltered corner. She gulped down the food and collapsed. We wondered how far this brave, loyal animal had traveled to find her way back to us.

I covered Senta's quivering body with a warm blanket and decided to nurse her to help her get well. She would replace my lost doll. She would be mine. All mine. I made all kinds of promises to her, if she would only get well. I lay down at her side and stayed with her until Mother came looking for me.

My happiness was short. When Russian soldiers showed up the next day, Herr Weber told Henry to ask them to shoot Senta because we did not have enough food for her. I was devastated.

Shortly thereafter, a single drunken Russian soldier staggered into the yard. He took a few steps, stopped, swayed, and looked around as though searching for something. We watched him uneasily through the living-room windows and expected others to materialize, but none did. A lone soldier was rarely a bold one. This much we had learned from past experience, but a drunken soldier could be unpredictable and quick to wave a loaded gun at us. An unsteady hand made that gun more dangerous, even if the soldier only meant to frighten us.

"What do you think this one is up to?" Herr Weber wondered. "It's strange that he won't come into the house."

When he spotted the woodshed, his stride steadied as he headed for it. He disappeared inside, leaving the door wide open. We could not see him, but we saw pieces of wood fly past the open door. He was uncovering our cache.

"How does he know where to look, where to search for loot?" Frau Leitzel asked, alarmed.

"They know where to look by now. They've figured out all the hiding places." Frau Weber said. "They've had enough experience poking in all the corners, ripping up floors and whatever else, obviously with success."

She was right. One group of soldiers had even knocked a hole in the wall of one of the Hagens' attic storage rooms, looking for crawl spaces, false walls, or any other possible place of concealment. In any event, our hiding place was about to be uncovered.

"Our last possessions are under that pile. Our money. Our documents. My jewelry. It's all we have left," Frau Leitzel whispered, as though she was afraid she might give away the secret by speaking out loud. "We've got to distract him or lure him away from there somehow."

"Let's kill the bastard," Herr Weber said. "He's alone and drunk. It'll be easy to overcome him."

Kurt jumped up and waved one of his crutches in the air. "Are you out of your mind? What will we do with the body? They'll surely come looking for him."

Herr Weber turned away from the window and gave Kurt a determined look. "We'll knock him out with an axe and then strangle him. That'll leave no tell-tale signs of blood."

"And then what? We still have to get rid of the body!"

"We'll bury him in the ground in the barn under the straw," Herr Weber suggested.

I listened, horrified, and held on to Mother as the dangerous plan evolved. For the first time, the adults thought of taking positive offensive action. But the women were not so easily persuaded to abet this act of murder. They voiced a lot of what-ifs, while the wood continued to fly past the open door. Suddenly, we heard the roar of an approaching engine, and a jeep filled with soldiers came into view. They called out to our man. He stuck his head through the shed door and waved to them. They exchanged words, which turned into a shouting match. He gave in, hurried toward the jeep, and jumped in, and they drove off.

Kurt wiped his forehead and said, "That was a close one. Can you imagine what they would have done to us if they had caught us in the act of killing him?"

"They would have torn us apart limb by limb. Shooting would have been too merciful for us," Frau Kehr replied.

I shuddered.

This incident made it clear that the woodpile was no longer a safe place for our valuables. We had to find a new hiding place and find it quickly.

The next day brought another lone Russian visitor. With a rucksack carelessly slung over one shoulder and a rifle over the other, he walked into the house with just a hint of caution. He leaned his rifle against the table and emptied his rucksack on the table. Potatoes, onions, and an enormous slab of bacon came into view. My eyes feasted on the bacon, and I began to salivate. Is this for us, I wondered? With sign language he gave Mother and Frau Weber to understand he wanted these things prepared into a meal. They quickly built a crackling fire in the kitchen stove. Mother and Frau Weber cooked up everything he had brought: the entire slab of bacon, the onions, and all the potatoes, enough food for a dozen hungry men. A most intoxicating aroma permeated the air.

The soldier attacked the meal with relish, ignoring us. I watched with hungry eyes, longing for just a little taste of those wonderful greasy potatoes. He ate and ate. I feared there would be nothing left for us, while he replenished his plate repeatedly. Finally, he dropped his fork, looked up, and pushed the remainder of the food toward us. He did not speak. He just nodded and gestured for us to eat. We hesitated. We had been toyed with too often and distrusted any considerate act. He rose, slung the rifle over his shoulder, picked up the empty rucksack, and departed with a content smile on his unshaven face. The instant the door closed behind him, we pounced on the food and devoured it like hungry animals, a feast reminiscent of happier times.

"Let us pray for this man's return," Herr Weber said.

A few days later, Ivan reappeared. Delighted to see him, we greeted him like an old friend. He did not bring bread as he had promised, but he brought something much more precious. He carried his rifle over his shoulder in the usual soldierly fashion; from the top of it dangled my doll, her red dress faded to a deep pink and her hair matted. I ran toward him and reached for my doll. Startled, he took a quick step back. Mother pointed to the doll and said, "Ivan, that's my daughter's doll. Where did you find her?"

Ivan smiled and said, "I find in ditch over there." He pointed his chin away from the farm and added, "I think she belong here."

He slipped the rifle from his shoulder and pushed the dangling doll in front of me. Petrified of the pointed gun, I froze. Ivan recognized my fear, lifted the doll from the rifle, and laid her in my open arms. He stroked my head and said, "*Keine Angst, Maedchen*, don't be afraid, little girl." Happiness reentered my world. The spring melt had at long last released my doll from her frozen resting place, just as Mother had promised.

Ivan brought us less optimistic news than the bits of information he had given us earlier. The Russians were still fighting for Berlin. However, Elbing had been blown to pieces by artillery fire and rockets.

"Oh, dear," Mother said, "I hope Elsbeth, Gertrude, and Edward got out of there in time."

Danzig had fallen, as had all the other coastal cities. Both sides were still fighting hard on land and sea. The Russians constantly bombarded the ships and retreating army on the Baltic Sea. Most of the Soviet fighting forces were concentrating on the final assault on Berlin. Ivan ended his report with these words: "It not long, and you be free of Hitler. Him dirty swine."

For once, we agreed with the Russians.

Ivan and Herr Weber talked a long time about the unfairness of war. His family, too, had suffered a great deal at the hands of the Germans, but he made the distinction of referring to the "bad Germans" as Nazis. He left without promising to return.

The Hagen farm remained our prison. A constant, gnawing fear of the unknown and what lay ahead was our prison guard. We felt powerless in the face of the cataclysmic storm that had lit upon us with such fury. Our lives had deteriorated to the basic instincts of survival—eating, sleeping, and keeping warm. Only a quick end to the war would bring new meaning into our hopeless existence.

The key to our staying alive was food in our stomachs. That fact drove all our activities. We went on another search for food. We did not return to the place of death, as Frau Kehr called the site of our first effort. We had seen other farms that day and picked the nearest one. We did not take the sled for lack of snow but brought empty potato sacks instead. Watching the heavens, we hurried across the fields. Danger lurked everywhere. However, this excursion proved uneventful as well as less gainful. We found the farm deserted and ransacked, furniture toppled over, upholstery slashed to shreds, and broken glass ground into the wooden floor under our feet. Even the bedding had been slit open. A layer of white goose down rested on everything like a light dusting of snow.

We encountered no surprises, but the destruction unsettled us. Although I was only nine years old, I began to perceive the drama of this war in a broader spectrum. People had lived in this house. Tragedy had touched them, also.

"I wonder what happened here," Mother said. "Did the people get away?"

"They're probably waiting out the war in some strangers' house just as we are. Or maybe they've been dragged off to Siberia," Frau Weber speculated.

"Let's just hope we find food. That's all that matters anymore. If only we could find some meat. That's what I miss most," Frau Kehr said.

With memories of our previous excursion still fresh in our minds, we carefully searched the house with uneasy feelings. An eerie mystery hovered over everything. Even in their silence, the rooms screamed of violence; it greeted us everywhere as we rummaged through the debris. Family heirlooms lay trampled and defaced under our feet. Mother picked up a framed photo, perhaps of an ancestor. The face of an old man with that stoic, turn-of-the century look so common for that time showed through the broken glass. He had a long, white beard, like my grandfather had had, and his eyes looked kindly at us as though he forgave us for intruding.

Henry came running with a large bucket of honey, still unopened, and shouted, "Look what I found!"

We were ecstatic.

"Where did you find it?" Frau Weber asked and added, "Let's open it and make sure it's really honey. I can't believe the Russians overlooked it. Where was it?"

"I found it in the stable. It sat on a shelf all by itself. Maybe the Russians thought it was empty."

"Miracles still happen. Good boy, Henry," Mother said.

We found more feed, similar to what we had located in the

Hagens' storehouse. Mother searched the smoke chamber in the attic and spotted a large tin of salt. We filled our sacks and containers with grain and headed back, happy with our meager spoils. On the long walk home, Helga said to Henry, "You're the hero of the day." She turned to her mother and added, "We better eat the honey right away before the Russians take it away from us."

All the way home we talked about honey sandwiches and fantasized how wonderful they would taste.

The weather warmed up, and a full week passed with high blue skies and glorious sunshine. Although the nights remained frosty, the days hinted of the approaching spring. We continued our search for food. There were more isolated farms near us than we had realized. We planned to visit them all.

A strong, biting wind had come up and rattled the windowpanes on the day of our third expedition. The sky looked threatening, but that did not deter us. This farm was tucked away in a hidden glen, surrounded by old oak trees. Their naked limbs afforded us a partially unobstructed view of the buildings and the grounds. The only perceivable movements were from the branches, dancing in the gusts of wind.

"I think there is smoke coming out of that chimney," Frau Weber said.

We focused on the roof, but it appeared to be an illusion created by moving clouds and swaying limbs. With sharpened senses, we pushed ahead, ever mindful of any sudden surprises. The yard was deserted. A loose shutter flapped in an uneven rhythm against a wall somewhere, and a broken-down milk wagon stood next to the wooden barn. Leaning against one of the back wheels sat a dead German soldier, slumped over as though in deep thought. Caked blood clung to his pants and bare feet. Someone had stripped off his boots. Blood clotted around a hole in his stomach. The sight sent cold shivers up my spine. Mother steered me away and said, "Death, nothing but death everywhere. Who will notify his family? He's only a youngster!"

"Let's check his identity. Maybe some day, when this is all over, we can notify his family," Frau Weber suggested.

But we got no further. Henry let out a loud scream and came running towards us, shouting, "There are Russian soldiers inside the house! They're going to shoot us!"

He sped past us, his face contorted with fear. Then we heard a shot. Terrified, we bolted after Henry. I expected a bullet to pierce through me any second. We struggled up the hill, never looking back once and never slowing down until the farm was long out of sight and all was quiet.

"I thought for sure our time had arrived," Fraulein Gretchen said.

"I told you I saw smoke coming from the chimney. I was right!" Frau Weber said.

Later, Henry told us that while we were deciding on what to do about the dead soldier's identity, he had walked up to the house and peeked through a window. As his gaze adjusted to the darkness inside, he found himself staring straight into the barrel of a rifle with two Russian soldiers positioned behind the weapon, ready to pull the trigger.

"They probably saw us coming and were waiting for us," Mother said. "Maybe our quick getaway caught them with equal surprise."

"Do you think they meant to shoot us?" Henry asked. "Or were they just warning us not to come near them?"

"Who knows. We're lucky they didn't come after us. They could have easily caught us if they had really wanted to."

We returned home unharmed but, once again, badly shaken.

We started to tap into our cache under the woodpile, grateful that the drunken soldier had not uncovered it. But the incident at the farm had left us with a sense of urgency.

"We've at least got to find a better hiding place for our valuables," Herr Weber said.

The adults debated what to do. The lack of watertight containers limited our options. They finally decided to dig a shallow hole in the Hagens' garden, make the site look like a newly dug grave, and mark it with a wooden cross to make it appear more authentic.

"They'll spot it immediately and will never believe it is a grave. You might as well write on the cross, 'Here lies what is left of our valuables,'" Fraulein Gretchen said.

"Why don't we bury the stuff in the barn under the straw, where we were going to dig a real grave only days ago?" Kurt suggested. "They'd have to do a lot of searching before they'd find anything."

"That's it. It'll not only be well hidden, but it'll stay dry," Frau Kehr said.

The plan of action was the same as before. We children watched out for unwelcome intruders; the women moved the straw and dug a hole in the dirt foundation, then recovered it with straw. The following day we would transfer the containers to their new hiding place. We spent an anxious night. The next day, we waited until late afternoon before we continued. Experience had taught us that the Russian soldiers usually came earlier in the day. The day started out raw and gray, and the weather felt like it could not decide whether to rain or snow. At noon, it started to drizzle.

Henry, Helga, and I worked at reducing the woodpile by aligning the pieces of splintered wood neatly against the wall just enough to make the final transfer of the containers a quick one. If Russians appeared, our activity would look innocent enough; we were straightening up the shed. We had fun doing it. We knew the adults were keeping careful watch over us. I even ventured to the outhouse alone.

When I came out, two young, sullen-faced soldiers jumped in front of me. I wanted to run, but my feet froze to the ground and a powerful bolt of fear left me paralyzed. One of the men pointed a long rifle at me, with a shiny bayonet attached to its muzzle. He pressed it against my trembling chest and twisted it back and forth. I felt the hardness of the steel blade getting ever closer to my skin as it bored a hole through my woolen dress. I backed against the brick wall, expecting him to thrust the sharp blade straight through my almost-stopped heart. I tried to scream, but the sound got stuck in my throat. Nothing came out. My world started to turn black while I desperately tried to call for Mother in a silent plea. The words would not form.

"Germansky soldat hier, German soldiers here?*"* one of them asked me.

Speech had left me. I shook my head in denial as my legs gave out from under me and I slid to the muddy ground. They gave me a contemptuous glance and walked toward the house.

Henry and Helga had heard the soldiers and emerged from the shed, their arms loaded with firewood, just as we had been instructed to do in case something like this happened. I picked myself up from the ground and, with wobbling legs, followed them to the house. Inside, I clung to Mother, never taking my eyes off the flashing bayonets. I could almost feel the pain of the sharp blades cutting me wide open. Not until the soldiers departed did I recover my voice. I pointed to the hole in my dress and said, "They tried to kill me with those long knives."

Mother pressed me against her breast, rocked me back and forth, and said, "Now, now, Evchen. It's okay. They're gone." She looked at the others and added, "They'll not leave us in peace until they've done away with us all. Where is it going to end? We're toys in their hands."

I realized that for one eternity-long minute I had faced death, and now I feared it more than ever.

We did not finish the transfer of our valuables that day. The adults completed the task the next morning at dawn, while we children dreamt our children's dreams, which were rapidly turning into nightmares.

CHAPTER SEVEN

HYACINTHS POPPED UP IN THE Hagens' little flower garden. Chirping birds announced the arrival of spring. With the promise of a kinder season, we hoped our lot might improve as well. The adults decided to take more drastic measures, or at least go to the nearest village and find out what was happening. We faced the quandary of how to go about it, and who would venture beyond our self-imposed confinement. Herr Weber's and Kurt's disabilities prevented them from taking charge. Even if they could have done so, as German males, they were liable to be picked up by Russian soldiers and hauled off. Frau Weber reminded them repeatedly of their good fortune at being alive and still with us.

"I'm going home to check on our farm," she said. "Maybe I can pick up news along the way. I'll skirt around the villages. The farm is close enough; I can make it back in the same day."

"Are you out of your mind?" Herr Weber asked, waving his good arm in the air. "There's no way I'll let you go. It's not just men. Any German wandering around is vulnerable to being picked up. Look what happened to the others. Have they returned? Not even a word from them."

"I'll take one of the children with me. They'll leave a mother with a child alone. We can't continue to just sit here. We'll starve to death if they don't kill us first. We'll never make it through another winter."

Frau Kehr volunteered to accompany Frau Weber. By morning, however, she backed out of her commitment. "I really don't care anymore what happens to us. Why should we expect to find a better situation anywhere else?"

Not discouraged, Frau Weber said, "We can't remain here forever. We've got to do something."

She picked Henry to be her child for the trip. Although reluctant to let him go, Mother agreed it was time to act.

"Our lives are in danger no matter where we are or what we're doing. Death will find us if it's meant to be," she said.

Mother packed a few provisions for their risky journey. Dark, threatening clouds raced across the sky and the wind howled. "Perfect weather for our undertaking," Frau Weber said, looking out of the kitchen window. "It'll keep the Russians from roaming the country-side."

Agitated and tense, we sat by the window all day, watching for their return. To everyone's surprise, they were back by midafternoon. We ran out to meet them, anxious for their report. They had not encountered a single human being, German or Russian, and so had brought back no news. But Frau Weber gave an upsetting report on what they had found on their farm.

"The place is torn apart. Ransacked. Broken-down wagons, sleds, and every type of conveyance are scattered all over the place. The debris are knee deep." She sat down, shaking, and continued, "You can't imagine the sight. The yard is covered with spoiled food, clothing, dishes, tools, and whatnot. It looks like a violent storm had swept over the area, lifted everything up, and deposited it all on our property. Everything is just lying there, rotting. We even saw a couple of dead dogs, half-eaten by rats or mice or who knows what. You can't imagine the stench."

"What about the buildings? Are they still standing?" Herr Weber asked, impatient for details.

Frau Weber put her hand on his lifeless arm and replied, "Oh, *ja*. There are a few holes in the walls and most of the windows are blown out, but they're standing. We even have a couple of shot-to-pieces German tanks in the field behind the stable. The place looks like a combat zone. It must have been terrible what transpired there."

"Thank God we got away," Herr Weber said.

The Weber property stood only a few kilometers from our farm, along the same main highway. Frau Weber confirmed what Father had told us when he had gone back to check on our farm in January. The Russians had pushed through along the highway, forcing the Germans into retreat from city to village to city, leaving nothing but destruction in their path.

"We could all be dead," Mother said.

Still unable to make a decision, we did nothing. We allowed the events to spill over us, like trees in an ever-increasing storm, each gust weakening our ability to withstand its force. We knew eventually it would uproot and destroy us. But we were about to be jolted out of our stupor the very next week.

Mother had picked a small bouquet of newly opened daffodils and arranged them in a glass jar. They cheered the room like a ray of sunlight and stood like brave little soldiers in the face of our doom, a small thing, yet so uplifting. Perhaps it was the magic of spring, earth's renewal and rebirth. We greeted the change of seasons like a long-awaited, most-welcome guest, a guest named hope. Nature exploded all around us. Trees began to bud, and plants started to sprout in the garden. Each day, the sun inched higher in the sky, with its comforting warmth, and erased the last remnants of snow.

The adults reminisced about the good life we once had enjoyed. They always seemed happier when they talked about better times. Even we children felt lighter as they recalled the past and shared their dreams and hopes. Those days seemed so long ago, yet only three months had passed since we all came together on the Hagen farm. Frau Kehr spoke of how her husband had fallen at the Russian front early in the war, and what good had it served. Nothing had been gained and so much had been lost. She looked up from her work and gazed out the window.

"Oh, my God! Here they come again!" she cried out.

We looked up, alarmed, and watched the yard fill with Russian soldiers. Their numbers seemed endless.

"It's a whole damn unit," Kurt said, with dread. "This group looks ugly. I think we're in for it this time."

The soldiers stormed into the house before Fraulein Gretchen reached her "sickbed" couch. The room shrank as they piled in, and the walls closed in on us. We knew immediately Kurt's prediction was about to come true, and we huddled closer together. These men looked like new, untamed recruits. They charged into the room, wild eyed and primed for action.

Some of them disappeared into the stable, the barn, and the shed, and then they searched the buildings. Those in the house poked their guns into the bedding and upholstery. One soldier herded us into a corner of the room and held us at gunpoint. Others eyed Fraulein Gretchen. They forced her to stand, caressed her breasts, and pinched her buttocks and thighs. They laughed and bantered among themselves while watching her terror-stricken face. One man ripped her eyeglasses from her face and slipped them into his pocket.

"Please, please don't take my glasses. I can't see without them," she begged, but he ignored her.

Another soldier joined our guard and reached for his pistol, which was carelessly tucked in his leather belt. He placed himself directly in front of Mother, pointed the weapon within inches of her head, and shouted, "Give me watch! You find watch or I shoot!"

I pressed myself against her tense body and stayed glued to her. I stared at the weapon and saw nothing but one great big round hole, ever expanding. As it grew, I shrank until I thought it would swallow me. My heart threatened to explode in my chest. Trembling, I dug deeper into Mother's side and whimpered, "Will it hurt when he shoots us? I don't want him to kill us."

Then, something totally out of character happened. The soldier winked at me. Feeling the tension drain from Mother's body, I relaxed. But the soldier did not lower his weapon. Instead, he repeated over and over, "Give me watch. I want clock, or I kill you!"

While these words still hung in the air, an officer stepped into the room. We recognized him as such by his authoritative demeanor and how he handled the men. He directed some stern words in Russian at our antagonist, who immediately lowered his gun, turned his back on us, and stomped out of the room. Kurt took heart, hobbled up to the officer, and begged for the return of Fraulein Gretchen's glasses. A loud exchange of words exploded between the officer and the guilty party. This soldier was not so easily persuaded. The officer pushed him into the kitchen, and more shouting ensued. He reappeared with Fraulein Gretchen's glasses and handed them to her, smiling.

Then, a truck backed into the yard, and the soldiers loaded it with hay. They took our bread, the legumes we had so patiently sorted, and Henry's bucket of honey and heaved them on top. The officer rounded up his men and gave orders to depart. Henry ran after the officer and pleaded, "Please, don't take our honey." I feared the man might get angry and beat my brother. To everyone's surprise, Henry returned with the honey container in hand and a victorious grin on his face.

"When is this going to end?" Mother asked. "How in God's name are we supposed to produce a clock, a watch, or whatever else they want? Don't they know by now there have been so many others before them looking for the same things?"

Luckily, the soldiers had overlooked the bag of unsorted feed. The next morning, we started over and hoped for a quiet day. By midday, however, we heard the sound of an approaching engine. A military truck pulled into the yard and came to a jerky halt; a gang of soldiers spilled out from the back. We immediately recognized them as the men from the day before, not as many, with the officer conspicuously absent. The men had obviously been drinking. Their gleeful banter and gales of laughter reached us before they staggered into the house. Again, Kurt sized up the situations correctly when he said, "Brace yourselves! These guys are trouble."

They burst into the room. Fraulein Gretchen had barely reached her couch and pulled the covers over herself. Two soldiers grabbed her by the arm, yanked her up, and dragged her to her feet, while another group singled out Frau Kehr and pushed both women into one of the bedrooms. Kurt clenched his fists in helpless anger, as he always did when the soldiers molested Fraulein Gretchen. Frau Weber controlled him in her usual calm way by quickly putting a firm hand on his shoulder and pressing hard to keep him down. "You make one move," she said, "and it will be the end of all of us. Control yourself!"

Then things happened fast. Another soldier waved his pistol at the remaining women and us children. He forced us up a steep ladder leading to the attic off the kitchen hallway. We pulled ourselves up, one by one. Terrified, I kept missing the rungs. Mother guided my feet and pushed me up from behind. The soldier pulled the trap door down and locked it from the other side. I watched the trap door, expecting him to return with a rope to hang us from the rafters, like the man on that ill-fated farm. As long as it stayed shut, I felt safe.

We remained quiet and listened for clues to tell us what was happening downstairs. Helga started to cry, repeating over and over, "They're going to hurt my mother again! They're going to hurt my mother again!"

Mother tried to console her, but she would not let anyone touch her. Frau Leitzel whimpered and tried to pry the trap door open, but it would not budge. Frau Weber propped herself up on a box under the little round attic window. Since it faced away from the yard, she could see nothing. Agitated, she paced back and forth, and said, "I don't think this is going to end well. I have this terrible feeling in my gut." Only Mother stayed calm.

We heard a great coming and going downstairs. Doors slammed, and the Russians' voices thundered through the rooms. Frau Kehr's and Fraulein Gretchen's intermittent screams reached us like sharp daggers. By now I had some idea of what was happening to them, and I gathered from the raging tempest that the whole house was being turned upside down.

"Your leg is rotting in Russia, you Nazi swine," a soldier shouted at Kurt. "How many Russians have you killed? How many Russian women have you raped?"

"You took my food! You burned down my house. You beat my father. You killed my brother. You even killed my dog," somebody else screamed.

They accused Kurt of all the wrongs any German had ever done to their country and their families. It seemed as if they were making him pay for all the suffering their nation had endured at the hands of the Nazis. They beat him. We heard Herr Weber's pained plea to spare his son. A loud exchange of words between the Russians followed. A door slammed, and the voices faded towards the stable. Filled with anxiety, we listened. We were afraid the truck engine would start, and they would take Herr Weber and Kurt with them. Instead, a single shot rang out. I clung to Mother, shaking, Frau Leitzel gasped for air, and the blood drained from Frau Weber's face. "Oh, my God, what have they done?" she wailed.

A second shot followed. My heart skipped several beats. Helga panicked and screamed, "They've shot my mother," and repeatedly knocked her head against the roof. We listened. Would there be another shot and another? The gun remained silent. Soldiers' voices, no longer so merry and gay, reached us from the yard. The engine coughed several times, and the truck drove off. A feeling of foreboding settled over us as we heard the roar of the engine fade. What awaited us downstairs?

We sat there, afraid to move. Then the latch on the trap door rattled, the door swung open, and Fraulein Gretchen's disheveled head appeared.

"Oh, Gretchen, you're alive. I've died a thousand deaths up here. I was so worried," Frau Leitzel whimpered.

One by one, we made our way down. Frau Kehr sat by the kitchen table, her face frozen into a mask of stone as she stared wide-eyed and stupefied at the wall.

"I'm going to dig up the Hagens' gun and shoot the next bastard who comes near me. I need a gun. I've got to get a gun," she kept repeating. Helga ran to her, threw her arms around her, and sobbed, "Mama! Mama!"

Kurt and Herr Weber were not in the house. We rushed to the stable. The door hung open. Frau Weber called out for the men. There was no answer. Then we saw Kurt in one of the empty stalls sprawled out on his back in a pool of blood, shot through the heart. The blood formed a little rivulet from the stall into the drain. It was so red and looked so thick. Kurt's glassy stare was fixed at the ceiling, and his arms were spread out at his sides, as if he wanted to make an angel, as we children used to do in the snow. His leg was bent awkwardly under him; his crutches were missing. Frau Weber fell to her knees and placed her gray head on his still warm body, but her eyes remained dry.

"Oh, no, not both of them!" Frau Leitzel cried out.

Herr Weber lay stretched out in the doorway to the hayloft, also on his back, shot between the eyes. We conjectured later he must have followed the Russians when they took Kurt at gunpoint to the stable. When he pleaded for his son's life, they simply shot him, too. Mercifully, the shots had been perfectly aimed and found their targets. Both men had died instantly.

Mother, Frau Kehr, and we children quickly returned to the house. Frau Weber, Frau Leitzel, and Fraulein Gretchen stayed with the bodies to be alone with their loved ones, to mourn the husband, the son, the brother, and the cousin.

Back at the house, we now saw the chaos we had not immediately noticed when we had come down from the attic. Not one piece of furniture stood in its original place. Even the beds had been broken down, the mattresses slashed, and the bedding ripped apart. Floorboards had been pried loose in some places and the curtains had been yanked down. Our clothing was scattered throughout, and the so tediously sorted lentils, peas, and barley rolled under our feet, all mixed up again, with the unsorted sack of feed dumped on top of everything. In the middle of it all lay my doll, my little Elsbeth. She, too, like those men in the stable, had met a tragic end. Her head had been smashed, crushed under a soldier's boot. Her glass eyes lay among the mixed grains and stared at me accusingly, as if to say, "You shouldn't have left me behind."

Death had passed by our door many times, but this time it had entered and had made its claim. Its suddenness and violence left us dazed. Frau Weber bore her grief with saintly stoicism. But Fraulein Gretchen and Frau Kehr were on the brink of falling apart. They had been raped again and again by the smelly, sweaty men, their clothes torn from their bodies. They looked like two shrunken wallflowers with no more fight left in them. Frau Kehr's obsession with the Hagens' gun took on new life. "Why don't we get that gun and put an end to all of us?" she asked. "I just can't face another day like this."

The need to bury the bodies brought us back to reality. The next morning, we dug a grave in the flower garden, large enough to accommodate both father and son. A dark sky loomed above us. The ground was soft and wet from the spring thaw. It started to drizzle. The women wrapped the bodies in bed sheets and brought them to the gravesite in a wheelbarrow. I watched with an uneasy feeling as they wrestled with the mummy-like bundles and dropped them into the shallow hole.

"Rest in peace, my loved ones," Frau Weber said, wiping moisture from her eyes.

We pushed the earth over the bodies and made the gravesite look like a newly planted flowerbed by scattering the contents of seed packets we found in the storeroom. We speared the empty envelopes with sticks and stuck them on the little mound. Frau Weber studied one of them and said, "Forget-me-nots—how fitting."

After the burial, we cleaned up the chaos the soldiers had created and took inventory of our remaining possessions. We did not think we had had anything left the Russians could possibly want, but we were mistaken. The kitchen silverware was gone. They took some of the smaller pieces of furniture and our oil lamps, a loss of some consequence. Now we faced dark evenings. "Thank heaven the days are getting longer," Frau Leitzel said.

We carefully swept the grain, lentils, and peas together and collected them in containers. At least we still had that, but we needed to act, to do something. We had held out on the Hagen farm and teetered between panic and submission far too long. It was time to leave this unlucky place.

Ivan gave us the final nudge. He turned up a few days after the shooting, quietly and alone, as he had the two times before. He sensed immediately something was amiss. Looking around, he asked, "Where is old man?"

Frau Weber broke down crying, her first good cry.

"He lies dead and buried in the garden," Frau Leitzel said. "His son is there with him. Your soldiers killed them."

Ivan shook his head. "War a terrible thing. Too many people die. Take me to old man grave!"

We led him into the garden and showed him the "flower bed" gravesite. He removed his fur cap and folded his dark hands as if in silent prayer.

Back in the house, he sat down with us and gave us advice. "You leave this place. Go to village. You safe there. Village has commandant. Food in village. Many cows. You get milk and meat. Go away from here!"

He worked himself into a veritable tirade, and we understood the sense of urgency he tried to instill in us. He had an aura of reassuring kindness about him. We trusted him. He left quickly, and we never saw him again. But we decided to follow his advice and leave the Hagen farm.

CHAPTER EIGHT

IVAN HAD POINTED TOWARDS STEGLITZ when he had urged us to leave the Hagen farm. Situated away from the main highway between the Webers', the Leitzels', and our property, it seemed the safest choice. From there, we would explore the possibility of returning to our own homes.

Getting ready did not take long. Our belongings had shrunk to the clothes on our backs and what lay buried in the barn. We took what we could carry and hoped to return with help to retrieve the containers from their hiding place.

The morning of our departure was unseasonably warm, and a heavy fog blanketed the fields. We stopped at the lone grave in the Hagens' budding garden one last time. Tears quivered on Frau Weber's cheeks as she picked two red tulips and gently laid them on the earthen mound. She raised her head and said, "Maybe they're the lucky ones. What's left to live for? Our lives don't count for anything. One bullet and a life is snuffed out, like blowing out a candle. That quick! That easy!"

We, too, bade farewell to Kurt, Herr Weber, and the Hagens. Then, we grabbed the heavy bundles and set out on our journey into uncertainty, leaving behind that unhappy place, with all its tragic memories. For three months, we had lived in ignorance, cut off from the world. With the exception of Ivan, our only outside contact had been the vindictive Russians.

Stalin himself had given the order: "Kill, kill, kill! The only good German is a dead German. Rape their women! Take their things! Demolish everything in your path! Do to them as they did to us! Show no mercy!" Ivan told us so. "My comrade enjoy kill," he said. "I no like."

We were the first Germans the Russians had encountered, and so we became their first victims. We experienced the true meaning of revenge, hunger, and fear, and what life without law and order meant in an environment where no evil act was punished. Would we find deliverance? Were we escaping from the claws of hell or were we about to plunge more deeply into its bowels?

A dense fog veiled Steglitz in mystery. We stopped at the black-smith's deserted dwelling by the millstream. The windows were broken; the walls were covered with mold. Depositing our things inside, we set out in search of more comfortable shelter. Steglitz had been Mother's place of birth, and she hoped one of her many rela-tives would extend a helping hand. We did not know who had stayed behind, who had fled, or who was still alive. As we headed for Aunt Liesel's farm, we glimpsed a group of idle Russians in the fog, like ghosts floating in a cloud. Jittery and afraid, we stopped and watched them. To our surprise, they paid no attention to us.

"Didn't they see us, or don't they care?" Mother wondered. "Maybe things really will be better here!"

"God, let's hope so!" Frau Weber said. "Have you noticed those women and children by the well? They're not from here. It looks like this place is full of strangers."

By their furtive walk and downcast glances, we surmised not all had gone well in Steglitz either, although on the surface everything looked reassuringly normal. Plump chickens scratched in the dirt, and we heard horses neighing in a nearby stable.

"I hope we'll see a familiar face," Mother said, as she knocked on Aunt Liesel's door.

The door flew open and there stood Aunt Liesel. "Annchen! Oh, my God! Where did you come from? We thought you people got away. What happened? Where's the rest of the family?"

Mother embraced her and held her to her breast. "Oh, Liesel. It's all so sad. They're gone. The Russians took them away." Mother's eyes filled with tears as she continued, "Who knows where they are. I worry about them every minute of the day."

"Did they take Vera too"? Aunt Liesel asked.

"Herbert put her and Frau Teichert on a train at the very last minute. I don't know if they made it out." Mother shook her head. "We waited too long. Had we only known what awaited us!"

Aunt Liesel held Mother by the arms and said, "It's been crazy here. We were overrun by the Russians. They stormed in and lined up all the German soldiers from that ill-fated train and shot them. Then, they rounded up the village men and took them away. It all happened so fast. One day, a whole group of women, children, and wounded soldiers came running into the village, screaming, 'The Russians are coming! They're shooting at us!' I've never seen a more panicked group of people. I'll never forget the terror reflected in their faces." She pulled us into the kitchen and continued. "It was terrible. We were terrified. We did not know what to do, run, hide, or what. It was total chaos. There was no time for anything. We heard shooting, and there they were. They stampeded in here like wild animals, and all hell broke loose. Their rage was unbelievable. They tore everything apart, anxious for loot. 'You give me gold, silver, watches. Give me cigarettes, give me, give me,' they shouted. You should have seen them. Their pockets were bulging with loot. They could not get enough. And then they went after the women, screaming, '*Frauen! Frauen! Wo sind Frauen?* Women, women! Where are the women?' The women hid in a different place each night, but the soldiers found them and dragged them out of their hiding places. I thought I had died and entered purgatory. I can't put into words what we went through. You're lucky, Annchen, that you weren't here. Where have you been all this time, anyway?" she asked like an afterthought.

Then Mother opened up and told Aunt Liesel about our ordeal on the Hagen farm. "So here we are," she finished. "We need a place to stay. We left our things at the blacksmith's cottage. As you can see, there are many of us. Where can we go?"

Aunt Liesel's house was full of refugees. She had taken in as many survivors as she could from that unlucky train, while she had retreated to one room with her young son. She had lost an older son at Stalingrad, and her husband had been reported missing somewhere in Russia. Aunt Liesel fed us and put us up for the night. We would search for housing in the morning. It was another night like our first night at the Hagen farm. We spread straw on the floor under the table, and that was where Henry, Helga, and I slept. It was comforting to be surrounded by so many people.

That evening, the adults sat up in the kitchen by candlelight. The door had been left ajar, so we children picked up pieces of their conversation. A thin, flickering stream of light fell onto our crammed accommodations, while Aunt Liesel's words floated into our ears. And so the fate of Steglitz unfolded.

"We had no inkling of how close the Russians really were. Hitler's henchman, Goering, kept feeding us nothing but lies over the radio: stay put, stay calm, do not worry."

"*Ja*, we heard the same outrageous lies," Mother interjected.

"The very morning of the day the Russians broke into the village, the *Buergermeister*, the mayor, told us he had been at a meeting," Aunt Liesel continued. "Higher authorities informed him that the Germans had pushed the Red Army back. Then, that afternoon, all hell broke loose. The Russians came charging in right behind those frantic fleeing people from the train. The Red Army had caught up with it in Niederhof, shot the engine to pieces, killed the engineer, and cut down the people as they tried to flee. The wounded froze to death where they fell. Later, some people from the village ventured out to assess the extent of the massacre. They said the embankment and the field were covered with corpses and torn-off body parts. Shooting the victims was not enough."

"*Ach*, how terrible," Frau Weber said. "I can't listen to this without thinking of my poor Kurt and his father. The Russians tortured them with diabolical pleasure. We could hear the Russians beating and manhandling them before they shot them. Kurt would have been better off if a bullet had found him while fighting the beasts."

"I tell you those first Russians were mad with rage," Aunt Liesel said. "They couldn't spill enough blood, as long as it was German blood. You can go and see for yourself. The bodies are still lying there." She paused and added, "You know the Germans blew up the post office and the dairy in Niederhof before they retreated. Tons and tons of butter were stored there."

"We saw the fires on the day of our flight," Mother said. "I still can't believe we were just minutes ahead of the Russians. Tell me what happened to the Niederhof people?"

"Most of them got out on time. The railroad people had more information than we did. Our mayor knew a lot more, too, but he was warned not to divulge how things really stood. He sneaked his whole family out before Christmas. That should have been a warning to the rest of us. The refugees along the highway fled in all directions when the Russians swept through. An old man showed up here a month ago and told us there was a whole column of burned-out wagons lying in the middle of the highway. Russian tanks crushed everything in their path, people, animals, and vehicles. There are dead bodies everywhere, including Russian soldiers. Who is going to bury them all?" Aunt Liesel asked.

Aunt Liesel painted a most gruesome picture of those first days in Steglitz with the Russians. The Lithuanian pastor had shot himself before the Red Army ever got there. Then the Russians rounded up all remaining males and took them away for that "official registration." But first they went after the mayor and tortured him to death. Whole families committed suicide rather than submit to the revenge-seeking brutes. The blacksmith gassed his wife and their two little girls and then killed himself. The meat inspector drowned his three small children in the village pond, then shot his wife and himself. Their oldest son ran away.

"That poor boy was totally out of his mind," Aunt Liesel said. "He no longer knew what happened, or who he was. Maybe he was better off not remembering anything. That first week, we all reached the edge of insanity."

I absorbed enough nightmare material to keep me awake a long time, but eventually I fell into a fitful sleep.

The next morning Aunt Liesel continued over breakfast, "Had we only known what awaited us here, we would have abandoned everything and run for our lives. Instead, we sat here blind and deaf."

"*Ja*, it was unconscionable of Hitler and his gang to feed us all that propaganda," Mother said.

"It's unforgivable. We waited for those evacuation permits, not knowing how close the Russians really were," Aunt Liesel said. "But the mayor knew. He got his family out in time. We were sacrificed. All those dead people scattered in the field gave their lives for what? We were the first Germans these Russians had gotten hold of, and we took the full brunt of their fury. Oh, how they hated us."

"When they tortured the mayor to death," one of the refugees interrupted, "a soldier kept screaming in German each time he kicked him with his boot, 'this one is for my sister and mother you swine raped. This one is for the brother you shot. This one is for my uncle. This one is for all my friends you Nazis killed.' It was terrible."

"All that for a war that was forced on us," Aunt Liesel said. "Did anyone ask us if we wanted this war? My boy, Willie, and his father died at the front. They paid with their lives. Wasn't that enough? Now, the Russians are taking over our properties. We've nothing left."

The conversation turned to the present situation in the village and the Russian occupation. By the end of March, things had quieted down, Aunt Liesel explained. A Russian commandant had taken charge of the area. Headquartered on a neighboring farm, he was to keep order in Steglitz and the surrounding villages. Cows and other livestock the invading Russians had not slaughtered were rounded up and brought to Steglitz to be transported to Russia. The village women fed and milked the animals, and mucked the stables. They were rewarded with precious milk for their families and an occasional piece of meat. "All this is good," Aunt Liesel finished. "The Russians need us to do the work. I think after they got over their initial killing frenzy, they realized they better keep some of us alive to do the cleaning up and bury the dead. There is talk of a mass grave for the victims from that doomed train. That's one thing I don't want to be part of. Just the thought of it makes me shudder."

The search for housing proved difficult. Refugees filled the village. The Russians had confiscated the more desirable properties for their housing, forcing the owners out, who, in turn, had moved in with relatives or friends.

We ended up in the teacher's living quarters at the schoolhouse, where people had moved out and returned to Elbing. A Frau Schulze and her two young sons occupied one of the two rooms. We moved into the other and shared the kitchen. Our quarters were tighter than on the Hagen farm, but we felt safer.

We had a roof over our heads, but not much else. We needed bedding, mattresses, a table, chairs, pots and pans, and other household items. It all sat at the Hagen farm. If we did not go back for it right away, someone else surely would. Everyone needed something, if only to replace the things they had lost. To approach the Russians for help was unthinkable, but we did get help in a most unexpected way. While we belabored our predicament, a loud knock sounded at the door. We were startled. Accustomed to the Russians just charging in, we wondered if life was becoming civilized again. Mother opened the door and exclaimed, "Janek, what are you doing here?" She hugged him. "I thought you had returned to Poland."

"Well, I'm back. I heard about your arrival last night. I came to see if I can help you in any way," he said, grinning sheepishly.

Janek had worked on a farm in Steglitz during the early war years when we still had assigned Polish help. A friend of our Poles, he had spent much of his free time playing cards with them. Erwin and Douglas had often joined in. Father, too, had had a good relationship with all of them. Janek had not forgotten this. So, there he stood at the door, ready to help with his horse and wagon. He heard that East Prussia was to become part of Poland and had returned to the area to stake out his claim. In the meantime, he was glad to be able to help us.

We went back to the Hagen farm that same day and loaded Janek's wagon to capacity. On top of everything, we placed the Hagens' kitchen table upside down, tied a chair to each leg, and filled the center with bedding. We hand carried extra pots and household items. We knew there would be no returning for more. Janek made this one trip for us. "I'm going back to get the rest for myself," he said.

The wagon creaked under its heavy load, and the horse strained along the rutted dirt road as we made our way back to Steglitz. Despite Aunt Liesel's horror stories, we were optimistic that life was going to be better. Mother even saw the comical side of our situation and said, "We look like a bunch of gypsies, traveling from village to village."

Everyone laughed, and our spirits lifted.

CHAPTER NINE

WE SETTLED INTO THE SCHOOLHOUSE as best we could. Frau Kehr and her daughter moved in with Frau Schulze. The women worked for the Russians and brought home milk, cottage cheese, and occasionally, a piece of meat. I looked forward to meal times, when the seductive aromas emanating from the kitchen kept me at Frau Leitzel's side. She had taken over the cooking for all of us, including Frau Schulze and her little sons.

Slowly, our derailed lives got halfway back on track. Rumors circulated that the Russians had reached Berlin and were taking the city building by building. This meant the war would be over very soon.

The Russians brought in seed and potatoes to be planted. It was to be business as usual; the only difference was that we were now the enslaved. Aunt Liesel, especially, was very vocal about it. "We've been turned into laborers on our own farms," she lamented. "I never thought it would end this way. I'm a guest in my own house that's filled with strangers. I work on my own land for the enemy and have to beg for milk from my own cows. Imagine! My own cows! It breaks my heart. I wish we had burned the place down rather than letting it come to this."

After the spring thaw, the Russians commandeered a group of women to dig a mass grave near the site of the massacre and bury the dead. Thankfully, Mother was not among them, but Frau Kehr and Frau Schulze were. They returned to us, shocked by what they had seen. The bodies had lain there all winter, freezing, thawing, and freezing again, and now with the final thaw and exposure to the sun, they had started to decompose. The flesh separated from the bones when they tried to pull the corpses to the gravesite with dung picks. In some cases, only the skeletons remained, the flesh eaten away by wild animals.

"If I live to be a hundred, I'll never get the stench of those rotting bodies out of my nostrils. This war has made death ugly!" Frau Kehr said. "The worst were all the scattered limbs and severed heads. We gathered them up in a wheelbarrow and dumped them in the pit. I had to close my eyes to be able to do it."

"It was gruesome," Frau Schulze added. "Some of the bodies had been stripped naked and hacked to pieces. If those fields could speak, they would tell a terrifying tale. There was no way of identifying the bodies. How will their families ever know what happened to their loved ones?"

"They're better off not knowing," Mother said.

After the women finished clearing the fields, they moved to the highway, where they pulled the dead into the ditch and covered them with gravel.

Frau Schulze was talkative that evening. She told us her husband had died from a bullet wound at the Russian front. She had received the sad news the day before Christmas. "That was my Christmas present," she said. "Out of six years of marriage, I can count on one hand the months we had together. The boys never really knew their father. He was more like an uncle, someone who buzzed in and out of their lives. He fought on every front until the Russians got him. Every day, I lived in fear of receiving that dreaded telegram. When it finally arrived, it was almost a relief. I knew from the very beginning it would end this way."

She told us her husband had been an only child, and that his parents had committed suicide by taking rat poison shortly before the Russian invasion. Her own mother had died young, and her only brother had fallen in the Balkans early in the war. Her father had died of a broken heart; that was how she put it. "Now, here I am, all alone in the world. The boys keep me from giving up. I don't know what I would do if I didn't have them."

Frau Kehr and Frau Schulze became good friends in the following months. The common thread of their suffering from the loss of their mates so early in their marriages bound them together like sisters. But the relationship between Mother, Frau Weber, and Frau Leitzel started to deteriorate. They barely talked to each other anymore.

Every day, from early morning until late evening, Mother tended the cows or worked in the field. She only came home for the midday meal. I often followed her to make sure she had not disappeared. My greatest fear was that the Russians would take her away as well one day, leaving Henry and me behind. But life arranged itself into a predictable routine. I always knew where to find her and started to relax.

Despite the commandant's presence, the Russians continued to be a threat, especially when drunk. They had converted a large potato steamer into a primitive alcohol still and put one of the older village boys in charge of it. My brother, Henry, often kept him company. They made the first batches of alcohol from dried sugar-beet chips. When those were used up, they switched to grain and potatoes. In the evenings, soldiers from all around assembled by the still and let the much-sought-after liquid drip directly into their tin cups. Night after night, we heard their boisterous singing and call for *Frauen*, while the women trembled in their hiding places. During the day, the soldiers slept off their hangovers, only to start over again the next evening.

However, the alcohol also provided a blessing. When the Russians were not around, the boys siphoned off the first, purest batch and smuggled it to the village nurse, who used it as a disinfectant. This precious liquid was particularly effective in curing scabies, now rampant among the children. One boy had already died, and the nurse was able to save his brother's life by washing his sore-covered body with the pure alcohol.

After Frau Schulze drafted Helga into babysitting her sons, I befriended Inge and Traute, two refugee girls from Elbing, and spent my days with them, while Henry went off on his own adventures with the village boys. One day, two young Russians took them along in their jeep to Niederhof. My brother returned with a first-hand report about our farm. Niederhof, deserted and ransacked, looked like a ghost town. Our farm was still standing, with seven Russian graves in Mother's flower garden. The telegraph building, the dairy, and the *Gasthaus* lay in heaps of rubble, the wind howling through their windowless facades. The stationmaster had been shot; his rigid body still lay stretched out on the platform, face down, clutching the hand-signal in his fist. The highway had been cleared, but the ditches on both sides were piled high with broken-down wagons and their contents.

A week passed before Mother summoned up the courage to go

to our farm and see for herself. She took me along. An eerie still-ness hung over the empty village, but I felt like a hundred eyes were watching us. A frayed Hitler banner, reading *Volk ans Gewehr*, people get to your gun, flapped in the wind as it hung from the eaves of the gatehouse. Ankle-deep debris covered our yard. I held on to Mother, afraid of getting stuck in them.

The Russian graves were lined up in a straight row in the garden where I once had played house with my little friends. A slender, red wooden pyramid-shaped cone, some three feet tall with a metal star nailed to the top, marked each dirt mound. Mother studied the scene and said, "Seven graves in my flower garden. One for each of us. How I wish it were so!"

I shuddered. I had heard much talk of parents killing their children, but I never considered Mother might foster such a thought. I nudged away from her side. She pulled me back, put her arm around me, and gently stroked my shoulder. Then, she noticed something and exclaimed, "My God, look at that! They've cut up my dining room set to make those markers! My beautiful dining room set!"

We entered the empty house with caution. Unfamiliar belong-ings of the long-vanished refugees littered the rooms. Food-encrusted plates sat on the kitchen table as though people had left in a hurry. Most of our furniture was still there, but the dining room was bare, with the exception of the grandfather clock. It stood in its rightful place between the two windows facing the Russian graves. I stared at the clock. Every numeral had a bullet hole in it; the hands had been shot off. In the children's bedroom, only the metal frames and bare bedsprings remained. I searched for my doll buggy, but it was gone. Walking through the ransacked rooms gave me an eerie feeling. The house no longer felt like home. Mother must have sensed it, too. Her eyes glistened with moisture. She sat down on a kitchen chair and surveyed the room. This had been her ancestral home, where she had been born. I was too young to guess what thoughts were going through her troubled mind. Perhaps she saw her whole life pass before her. How short her happiness had been, and how fragile and inconstant everything must have seemed.

Someone had started a fire in one of the upstairs rooms, but it must have died before incinerating the whole building. We checked the stable, the pigsty, and the chicken house, now hollow shells without the animals. Remnants of Mother's dining room set lay scattered on the tool-shed floor. She picked up a scrap of wood, massaged it between her fingers, and put it in her pocket.

I called for Schnurribart, my cat, but he did not appear.

"They probably caught him and ate him," Mother said, absentmindedly.

"Who ate him?" I shot back, alarmed.

She looked at me, startled, and groping for words, said, "The … the … wild animals."

But I knew what she had meant and cried over my poor cat. More than once, I had overheard people talking about butchering dogs and cats and eating them.

We rummaged through the debris in the yard and found an endless variety of things: a rusty electric iron, a water-soaked coffee mill, a meat grinder, a baby rattle, a snuff box, pieces of fine china, rotted feather beds, and many, many articles of clothing. Mother pulled up an oil painting of a young boy with curly blond hair, clear blue eyes, and an impish smile. "Such an innocent face," she murmured while resting the picture against the stable wall.

I lifted a girl's dress with white ruffles and red flowers all over from the debris. It looked my size. Mother said I could have it, its rightful owner being long gone. I did not know if she meant gone, like in gone away, or gone, like in dead, and was no longer sure I wanted the dress. But it was so pretty that I decided to keep it.

Mother found the cut-lace curtains she had made as a bride trampled into the floor in one of the rooms. They had graced our parlor windows during the summer months for as long as I could remember. Many times, I had tried to enlarge the holes by poking my fingers through the lace, and equally as many times I had received a thorough spanking for it. Now they hung over Mother's arm, soiled and wrinkled, and she did not seem to know what to do with them. "Will they ever adorn a room for us again?" she wondered out loud.

Just as we were leaving, Mumchen, Henry's cat, dashed across the yard. We called her. She stopped and looked at us. When we tried to catch her, she hissed and ran away. She recognized us, but she had turned wild.

Mother did not talk all the way home.

MY FEARLESS NEW FRIENDS, INGE and Traute, had a great sense of adventure. I could not believe my eyes when I saw the accumulation of treasures they had collected in a neighboring village only a kilometer away. Most of the thatch-roofed village had burned to the ground during the crossfire between the two fighting factions. My friends had found enough charred housewares, utensils, and pots and pans in the now-deserted houses to set up housekeeping in their backyard. They even rigged up a tent with blankets and played house the grown-up way, using real articles. I eagerly joined them on their raids. We were turning into little looters, just like the Russians. Discipline had fallen by the wayside. I always knew where Mother was, but she could only guess where I was or what I was doing. Under normal circumstances, we would have been in school, but schools did not exist any more. Only our fears of the Russians, of losing our mothers, and of being attacked by imaginary ghosts kept us from turning completely wild.

Henry and his friends were becoming little hooligans as well. They roamed the countryside, unrestrained in their own mischievous ways. War artifacts littered the ground, and the boys, braver than the girls, combed the fields for broken-down war equipment, artillery shells, and shrapnel. The hastily nailed-together barracks on the steep embankments above Steglitz were their favorite hangout. Live ammunition covered the area. The boys gathered the cartridges, stood them up, and detonated them with a hammer, shrapnel flying in all directions.

One day, Henry came running home, holding onto his chin, blood streaming down his neck and dripping from his elbow. A piece of shrapnel was lodged in his jaw. Mother jumped up from our midday meal, grabbed a dishcloth, and wiped his arm. "What have they done to you? Now they are even shooting little kids! Is there no mercy in this world?" she asked, trembling.

I ran for the village nurse, who removed the metal, cleansed the wound with the Russians' alcohol, and dressed and bound the wound as best she could. Fortunately, it was a clean puncture. The shrapnel had only scraped the jawbone, and the cut healed quickly. However, our supervision tightened from that day on.

I liked living in the schoolhouse, not having to attend classes, and although I did not miss school then, I would later on. Our quarters were tight, and conditions were crowded. Mother, Frau Weber, and

Frau Leitzel each had a bed. The rest of us slept on the floor. Woe was to the person who had to get up during the night and navigate past the stretched-out sleepers.

That summer, huge monster flies descended upon us. They appeared overnight, thousands of them, not a good omen. Fraulein Gretchen predicted disease was sure to follow. The unburied, rotting animal carcasses, human corpses, and spoiled food littering the landscape provided the perfect breeding ground. Within a few days, the built-in white tile kitchen stove turned black from the flies' droppings. We children held fly-catching contests by swatting them with rags and counting who had the most casualties.

Frau Leitzel declared her own war on the pests in an innovative way. She filled a glass jar three-quarters full with water. Then, she covered the opening with a slice of old bread, wrapped some paper over it with a piece of string, and poked a hole in the center, just big enough for a fly to crawl through and get to the bread. The pests discovered the bread in minutes. They slipped through the opening and attacked it from underneath. I watched them, fascinated by their unique ability to walk upside down. When the bread turned black with feasting flies, Frau Leitzel shook the jar, and the flies dropped into the water and drowned. She paraded the jar filled with casualties around and exclaimed triumphantly, "There must be at least a hundred flies in here!"

"*Ja*, and two hundred more will come to their funeral," Frau Weber countered.

One morning, I awoke with a whole flock of flies in my open mouth. Not realizing it, I bit down and felt them crunch between my teeth. When I rinsed my mouth, little black spots speckled my spit. When I told Mother she said, "I hope you won't get sick. Keep your mouth shut from now on." Apparently, she thought I had control over what I did in my sleep.

CHAPTER TEN

"*WEUNA KAPUTT*, THE WAR IS finished," a group of drunken, rabble-rousing soldiers shouted from their jeep as they drove into the village. They came to celebrate by the commandant's vodka still, while the women raced to their usual hiding places. But the men hunted them down and took them where they found them.

The Russians were on one last rampage, and their cry for *Frauen, Frauen*, women, women, could be heard from far away. No female was safe. The war may have ended for them, but not for us. The Russians wallowed in their victory, with the commandant heading these debaucheries. He cared only about getting the work done, not about our protection. We referred to him as the *Schnapskomandant*, the whiskey commandant. During the day, the Russians guarded the women while they worked, but during the night, they molested them.

When an officer shot and killed one of his own men in a drunken rage, he accused the villagers of the murder. The commandant rounded up the few remaining old, disabled men and had them taken away. They never came back. With that, the culprit went free, and justice was done.

Some of the women opted to become willing mistresses, under the protection of one soldier, rather than submit to a whole legion, but others preferred death to the endless raping.

The story of a particularly tragic incident in a neighboring village reached Steglitz. A young woman finally had had enough. When a group of soldiers tried to rape her again, she grabbed her baby, ran screaming through the village, and jumped into the well, clutching the infant in her arms. When the people fished them out, both mother and child were dead.

Our commandant was the first to acquire a "steady woman." A survivor of the train massacre with no family, she lived with him and thus escaped the continuous raping. We nicknamed her *Russenbraut*, Russian bride. When she walked past the schoolhouse one evening, I recognized Mother's dress on her. "Mutti, come look, the *Russenbraut* is wearing your good Sunday dress!" I called out.

"Now I've seen everything," Mother exclaimed, as we watched her stride by. "How did that dress ever find its way into her possession?"

"That's no mystery," Frau Weber said. "The Russians steal from one and give to another. She may not be the last one to wear your dress. When he's tired of her, he'll kick her out and keep the dress for the next one."

Yet another woman, the mother of eight young children, became a Russian soldier's live-in bedmate. He was kind to her and brought food for her hungry children. "It's the only way I can keep my children from starving," the woman told Mother. Her husband had been reported missing in action in December 1944, and she did what was expedient to guarantee the survival of her family. She eventually bore a *Russenkind*, a Russian child. However, by the time the child was born, the father had long vanished.

We, too, acquired a "protector" when Fraulein Gretchen took up with a Russian officer. Frau Schulze's quarters often served as the "entertainment" room, and what went on in there was only whispered about. The word soon spread that Fraulein Gretchen was off limits to any other soldiers. The protecting officer was an educated man, who spoke German fluently and had an elegant air about him. He often brought sweets for us children, and we looked forward to his visits. We were so bribable. The fact that it was German candy probably stolen from our own kind did not bother us. Fraulein Gretchen's mother, while not pleased with her daughter's activities, shrugged the whole affair off with the philosophical words, "One has to adjust to the times."

With the warmer weather, the women drove the cattle into the fields and stayed with them. Mother often took me along. Sometimes Lotte, Mother's distant cousin, accompanied us. While listening to them talk, I learned Mother was related by degrees to half the village, and that I, too, had many cousins I had not known existed. I even went to school with some of them without knowing I was related to them. The rift in Mother's family had widened to such an extent during the final war years that I did not know who my country relatives were.

Full of information, Lotte often asked Mother, "Did you hear what happened to so and so?" It did not matter whether Mother said yes or no; she would tell it anyway. When she mentioned Jozef, a sixteen-year-old Polish orphan boy who had worked for a farmer in Steglitz, my ears popped up, because I knew him. Illiterate and not very bright, he had been the object of many jokes in the village. Mother had not heard this story.

"Well, let me tell you. The day the first Russians appeared, he jumped on their bandwagon. He had a score to settle with everyone in the village and was well on his way to doing so, if the Russians had not killed him first."

"My God, what happened to him? What did he do?" Mother asked.

"He threatened everyone he would get even with them. He started with the last people he worked for by stealing his master's new leather boots. He paraded around in them like a peacock. When a Russian came across him in the street and saw the boots, he demanded that Jozef hand them over to him. Jozef refused. The soldier pulled out his gun and shot him on the spot." Lotte snapped her fingers and added, "Just like that."

"Just like that!" Mother repeated. "He was a Pole. The Poles are supposed to be their allies. Have they gone completely mad? Why didn't he just pull the boots off his feet?"

"He did, after he shot him," Lotte said with contempt in her voice. "Half the village witnessed it. I think the Russian was so surprised when Jozef refused to hand over the coveted boots that he shot him as a reflex. I tell you one thing, no one mourned over him. We were relieved to see him dead before he got to us. He was bad news. All that happened in February when the ground was still frozen. We had to bury him in the dung heap."

"Which one?" I gasped, wide-eyed.

From then on, I suspected every dung heap in the village of harboring a corpse. I envisioned a head, a foot, or a hand protruding from the mounds, and suddenly, all the old ghosts from Grandmother's fairy tales returned. When I told Inge and Traute what I had overheard, they wanted to check out the pile of manure behind each stable. I, on the other hand, gave the smelly mounds a wide berth.

Summer unfolded, and one sunny warm day followed another. We children reveled in the unlimited freedom and the endless vacation, with school attendance nowhere in sight. We made numerous trips to the burned-down village in search of more loot. Charred chimneys towered eerily into the sky, marking the sites where farmhouses once had stood.

Our collection of household items grew into an astounding accumulation that would have made a young bride green with envy. We played house in grand style, cutting up potatoes, gathering weeds and grass, and cooking all of it into a slimy green paste. I don't know how we got our hands on matches, but we did. We gave imaginary dinner parties using charred china and chipped glasses. The only pretend elements in our games were the guests.

The days ran together, with little distinction between weekdays and Sundays. Periodically, I would ask Mother, "Is today Sunday?" and if it was, I put on the ruffled dress I had found in our farmyard. Mother had washed and ironed it, and she had made it look like a Sunday dress. One day, I glimpsed my distorted reflection in the large window of the schoolroom. I saw a ghost-like apparition in the old wavy glass. The stiff ruffles over my shoulders looked like wings, and suddenly, my mirror image appeared to be floating toward heaven. It startled me. I saw the ghost of a dead girl, the rightful owner of the dress. Frightened, I ran into the house, tore off the garment, and never wore it again. The spirits of the dead hovered so close to the surface in my imagination that even a strange, distorted shadow could bring them to life.

One morning, a lone woman staggered into the village, pressing blood-soaked rags to her cheeks and crying out for help. We ran for the village nurse. The woman had been shot in the face. A bullet of unknown origin had entered one cheek and had come out the other. "I was walking along the highway," she labored with the words, "when I heard a gun go off. I felt nothing, until suddenly I noticed blood dripping from my face. I realized the bullet had found me. I ran across the field and hid in a ditch. Another shot zoomed over my head. I was sure it was the end of me!"

"What were you doing walking along the highway? You know it's dangerous with Russians everywhere. They could have killed you," the nurse chastised.

"I really don't care any longer what happens to me. They can't hurt me any more than they already have. I just want to go home to Elbing. I've been walking for days," the woman said, slurring the words. The bullet had taken out some of her teeth.

Later, when she could talk without effort, she told us her story, a familiar tale, yet it seemed more tragic, more touching. She told of a last-minute flight from Elbing when news had reached her that the Russians were about to take the city. She had hastily dressed her two babies in several layers of warm clothing, wrapped them in heavy bedding, loaded them on a sled, and joined the long lines of fleeing people. She had headed in the direction of Danzig, some fifty kilometers away, where she hoped to catch a transport ship and reach the *Reich* by sea. A retreating German unit had given her and her children a ride part of the way, but the soldiers were forced to drop them off near a village when they met up with Russian forces. She found shelter in the nearest barn and spent the night there. In the morning, while it was still dark and the children slept, she had ventured out into the village to beg for food. Suddenly, Russian tanks burst forth. They stopped, scooped her up, and dragged her with them into the village. When the soldiers encountered no more German resistance, they rounded up all the women and mass raped them. She hesitated at the word rape, but continued, "The Russians kept us locked up for two days. I pleaded with them to let me get my babies. Crazy with worry, I tried to run away, but they had posted a guard at the door. I went through a thousand hells. Then, they pulled out just as suddenly as they had appeared. I ran to the barn and called for the children, but there was no answer. I rushed to the spot where I had left them. Only the infant was there, frozen to death. The other child was gone. I found him behind the barn in the snow, frozen stiff. At that moment, my world went dark. The people in the village helped me bury their little bodies. I sleepwalked through the next weeks, and when the fog finally lifted, I started my long walk home. And now this," the woman concluded, stroking her bandaged face.

She stayed in one of the little cottages. The nurse came to see her daily and dressed her wounds with the Russian's alcohol. The village women provided meals for her, which we children faithfully delivered. When she developed a fever, and her mind clouded over, she talked to us, thinking we were her children. Other times she asked, "Who are you? Where am I? What am I doing here?"

With time, she did heal both in body and mind. My two friends, Irma and Traute, and I liked to visit her during her convalescence. She always seemed glad to see us. We brought her a cup, a plate, and utensils from our "household" collection. She may have told us her name, but we called her "the Patient." She never talked about her dead children again. But she liked to tell stories about the funny little Dachshund she had been forced to leave behind. One time, when she expounded on her dog's lovable traits, she added, "I can't believe that a dog would actually eat a human, but I saw it with my own eyes."

We thought she was hallucinating again.

"I stopped at this deserted farm one evening to spend the night," she said. "In the yard, I saw a big dog tearing at something. As I got closer, he looked up and growled. I stopped in horror. He was gnawing on a human corpse."

Goosebumps popped up on my arms as I thought of the crazed German shepherd that had strayed into Steglitz only a month earlier. No one could approach him without being met with a vicious growl. He chased after us kids whenever we got near him. He yelped and whined throughout the day and howled all night. We threw him scraps of food and hoped he would warm up to us, but he turned meaner each day. Then, he bit one of the boys in the leg. After that, we armed ourselves with sizeable sticks to ward him off.

The boys finally banded together and set upon ridding the village of the vicious animal. They lured it with food into a small stall in the schoolhouse barn. The dog, engrossed in gulping down his vittles, barely noticed the noose the boys slung around his neck. They dragged the helpless animal into an open area with exposed roof rafters, threw the rope over the lowest beam, and pulled him up. We girls were invited to witness the execution, and we did so out of curiosity and not without some feeling of vindictiveness. We did not believe the boys would actually carry out their sinister plan. So there we were, standing in the wings, silent participants in a most cruel act. I put my hands over my ears to drown out the animal's frantic wailing, watching his legs thrash the empty air and his writhing body twist and jerk at the end of the rope. The incident revealed how desensitized even we children had become.

None of the adults responded to the racket coming from the barn. Once the animal was silenced, they trickled to the scene of the crime. I expected the boys to be severely punished; instead, the adults just shook their heads. The mother of the bitten boy looked at the shepherd's motionless body and said, "Good riddance." The boys buried the animal behind the outhouse with much childish ceremony. When they wanted to add a cross to mark the site, the adults stopped them.

A few days later, a man who had been taken prisoner by the Russians during the first roundup in Steglitz drifted into the village. He had escaped from a prison camp in Poland and brought news of Father. He had seen Father in camp, but because of the guards and the thousands of men kept there, he never had made contact with him. He told Mother the prisoners were slated for transport to Siberia.

"Siberia? Who can survive Siberia?" Mother cried out. "If they took him there, we'll never see him again! Ivan lied to us. He knew all the time what was in store for our men."

CHAPTER ELEVEN

BY JUNE 1945, SIGNS POINTED to an exceptionally warm summer. The pungent aroma of each newly opened flower blossom lay heavy in the air, as though to atone for the bitter winter. But Mother seemed in a state of depression. Nothing cheered her.

She decided to make another visit to our farm. I followed her in a happy mood, hoping to find a doll hidden among all that litter, just waiting to be adopted.

When we reached Niederhof, we saw a few Poles milling around the station, but they took no notice of us. Our farm looked unchanged, deserted as before, and undisturbed in its silence. We walked through the rooms once more and ended up in Mother's flower garden. The lilac bushes, now in full bloom, yielded a rich, sweet scent. Weeds flourished on the Russian graves. A few flowers had fought their way through the rubbish. Mother seemed surprised at how quickly things had gone to seed without her nurturing touch. I spotted a small electric burner among the debris, perhaps the very same one Mother had used to heat our last meals before we fled. A week earlier, I would have eagerly added it to my household collection, but Mother's depressed mood dampened my enthusiasm.

She was not herself that day. Pensive and unnaturally quiet all morning, she now appeared listless and lethargic as well. She sat down on a tree stump, surveyed the desolation around us, and broke out sobbing. Her crying unnerved me. I had never seen her like that, and I sensed she had arrived at that fine line between sanity and insanity, between fighting and giving up. I knew by instinct this was a critical moment, and I let her be.

I lay down in the grass next to her and looked at the deep blue sky. A few scattered clouds floated across the translucent expanse like gossamer cloth. A gentle breeze brought a wave of heavy lilac scent with it. I inhaled the sweet air and retreated into my own world, waiting for Mother to find her way back. I watched her and noticed, for the first time, that her hair had turned as white as Oma's had been when she died. Renewed panic struck me. I was afraid Mother might also die. I tried to get her attention by saying, "I'm hungry. I'm tired. When are we going back?" She reacted to none of my proddings and continued staring despondently into space. I nudged her. She gave me a blank look, as though coming out of a dream, and said, "Oh, Evchen." She rose and reached for my hand. We walked back to Steglitz in silence, Mother never letting go of my hand, massaging it lovingly to the point of hurting.

The next day, Inge and Traute came looking for me. They planned another treasure hunt. No longer so skittish and afraid, I felt an exhilarating lightness during those glorious early summer days. I think the excitement of collecting our prizes far exceeded the satisfaction of possessing them. We were reclaiming our childhood, and exploration was such a great part of it.

Our expedition turned out to be fruitless. Poles had moved into one of the few surviving houses. Two boys stood solidly entrenched in the middle of the road, watching our approach. We aborted our planned raid. I consoled my friends with the promise of richer finds on our farm in Niederhof, where loot covered the ground just waiting to be collected.

On the way home, we took a shortcut across a field. My friends knew of a great swimming hole. The pond, merely a watering hole for cattle, held murky water. But water, any kind of water, proved temptation enough for a dip on this perfect day. We stripped down to our underwear and charged in. Barely wet, I stepped on a piece of glass and headed for dry land, bleeding from the deep gash. Inge, two years older and much smarter than Traute and I, took my underpants and wrapped them around my foot. I limped all the way home. The bleeding stopped, but the pain continued. Mother gave me a violent scolding, trying to impress upon me that even a harmless cut could have serious consequences during these perilous times without medical resources. My foot throbbed all night, but by morning, the pain had subsided considerably.

News of a case of typhoid fever spread through the village and left everyone terrified. Within a week, the patient died and many others had come down with this highly contagious disease. We found ourselves defenseless against the worst enemy of all, with no place to turn for help. The lack of sanitation and any type of medication, not even so much as an aspirin, left us wide-open to become its next victims. Houses remained locked, and people shunned each other, hoping to escape infection. Only the dedicated village nurse made her faithful rounds. However, she could only give basic sanitation instructions to prevent the disease from becoming an epidemic. The believers prayed, and others just waited, while the fever ravaged the village.

We heard free typhoid shots were being dispensed by the new Polish administration in a nearby town and decided to participate in the mass inoculation effort. We set out immediately, eager to be among the first before they ran out of the precious serum. The promise of immunity to the life-threatening illness enticed us along the ten kilometers on an unusually hot day. My foot started to hurt again, and I complained a lot. We arrived at the hospital by midday and were surprised to encounter no line in the newly opened facility. A white-uniformed Polish nurse ushered us into an examination room. Frau Leitzel looked around and said, "This looks just like the old days. It's a real hospital. I can't believe they're actually going to take care of us here. I expected things to be more primitive."

Frau Weber, more cynical, said, "Don't kid yourself. They don't care about us. They're afraid of catching typhoid. It's the great equalizer here. Otherwise, they would just as soon see us dead."

A doctor stepped into the room and addressed us in fluent German. Although he was a Pole, his command of our language must have built up Mother's confidence. She said, "Please look at my daughter's foot. She has a deep cut."

I had not expected this and prepared to run. I stared at the doctor, my new enemy, and feared him more than the Russians. However, he looked at me kindly and lifted me onto the examination table. Mother stepped closer and pushed me down. Before I could wrestle free, the doctor had a firm grip on my throbbing foot. I had never been in a hospital or seen an examination room; the ghostly white atmosphere terrified me. Two enormous light fixtures hung suspended from the ceiling, looking like giant, man-eating mushrooms out of Oma's fairy tales. The nurse removed a little brown bottle from a shelf and handed it to the doctor. I felt a piercing sting, ten times worse than the cut itself; before I knew it, a white bandage covered my foot, and I actually felt better.

"Now, was that so bad?" the doctor asked.

I remained quiet and kept my eyes on the nurse. She turned around and stood before me, holding a monster needle. I jumped from the table and flew out of the hospital into the street. Nothing and no one could stop me. No way would I submit to that giant needle. Hiding behind a tree, I kept a keen watch on the entrance, every nerve in my body on alert, but no one came looking for me.

At last, Mother and the others appeared in the doorway, but they did not call my name or make any attempt to find me. They did not linger either and headed straight for home. When it looked like they would leave me behind, I panicked and ran after them. Mother would have nothing to do with me. I walked beside her in silence, giving her pleading glances, but she stayed angry with me because I did not get the "life-saving" typhoid shot.

The next morning, Mother did not feel well and did not go to work. By afternoon, she was in bed. The other women, too, felt queasy and achy, but not sick enough to lie down. By the evening, Henry ached all over and retired early. The following day, both Mother and Henry did not get up, feeling no better. On the third day, Henry recovered, but Mother ran a fever. The dreaded typhoid had caught up with her.

Frau Leitzel monitored Mother's temperature, watching it rise until she was burning up with fever. While Mother fought for her life, she hallucinated about our missing family members. It was my first exposure to serious illness, and it frightened me. For days, Mother drifted in and out of delirium. My torture level rose and fell with her condition. When her mind was lucid, she was sweet and loving with me. However, when it clouded over, she escaped into another world. She tried to connect with her missing loved ones and made me search for letters from them. Sure that mail had arrived, she made me look under the bed, in drawers, and behind the furniture. When I came up with nothing, her wrath had no limit. "You're a bad girl! You're a disobedient brat! I'm going to have your father spank you!" she threatened. However, the most stinging threat of all was, "If you don't bring me those letters, I won't love you anymore."

Every day, her delusion differed. One day, she looked for Father's letter, the next Vera's, Erwin's, or Douglas's. But mostly it was Vera who occupied her tortured mind. Mother's anger was always greatest when I came up with nothing from my sister. I did not know what to do. I hated my sister for having gotten away, and I resented Mother for being so unfair. At times, she had unusual cravings. She sent me into the field to pick sorrel, a sour-tasting, long-leafed weed, which Frau Leitzel cooked into spinach-like soup. Always precise about where I could find these things, she sent me to a specific meadow for the sorrel, to Aunt Liesel's for a letter from Vera, or to wherever her delirious mind saw things.

She even wanted me to go to the Niederhof post office and confront the postmaster, who supposedly had kept the letters from her. In the beginning, I obeyed and went on these futile errands, but as her demands became more and more unreasonable, I gave up. Her fever lingered at a dangerously high level, and her lucid moments, those precious intervals, dwindled. Terrified Mother would die, I stayed at her side and lapped up every loving word she had for me. We were both fighting, she for her life and I for her love.

Mother held on tenaciously and fought with all her strength, but by the end of the second week she was losing her battle. Many people in the village had already succumbed to the disease. The consensus was that if the fever went beyond a certain degree and did not break in so many days, death was inevitable.

Always close to tears, I stayed near Mother. Whenever anyone inquired about her, I replied with a flood of tears.

Before death claimed Mother, she had to submit to one more beastly act of cruelty. East Prussia was being turned over to the Poles, and the Russians were pulling out for good. A wild, drunken troupe descended upon Steglitz to celebrate their departure. They tore the village apart. No woman was safe that day. Fraulein Gretchen's officer was among them, but he had stayed clear of our quarters since he had learned of Mother's illness. Instead, Fraulein Gretchen disappeared with him somewhere in the countryside.

One intoxicated soldier was not frightened away from Mother's sickbed. He staggered into the room and saw his opportunity. He lifted the bed covers and climbed into her bed, boots and all. Horrified, I ran into the kitchen and then into Frau Schulze's room, but everyone had mysteriously vanished. I went back and stayed alone with Mother and the molesting animal; I did not know what to do and looked on in disbelief. The soldier embraced Mother. She had a mysterious glow on her face as she looked at him. She smiled and said, "Herbert, you've come back!" Then, she looked my way and asked me to leave the room.

I ran out and called for help, but everyone had disappeared. Only the celebrating Russians milled about in the street. I headed for the nearest meadow, threw myself on the ground, and cried. When I returned, things had quieted down, and most of the soldiers were gone. Frau Weber and Frau Leitzel were back and acted like nothing had happened. I rushed to Mother's bedside. Her eyes were closed and her serene face had an aura of peace about it. I became hopeful of her recovery. As I sat at the edge of her bed, her feverish hand reached for mine. Her eyes opened, and she said, "Evchen, there you are. I've been looking for you. Listen to me carefully. Be a good girl, always. Do what Frau Weber and Frau Leitzel tell you. Be obedient. I don't want to, but I am leaving you. And always remember that I love you. Now, go find your brother and send him to me!" I knew she was saying good-bye and wanted so much to say something loving to her, but fear choked my words, and stinging tears flowed down my cheeks.

I dashed out. Where was Henry? I did not know where to look for him, but I let it be known that Mother wanted him. I did not return to Mother's side but went to my meadow instead. I lay down in the grass and watched the billowing clouds race across the sky, searching for friendly images. Only ogres and ghostly shapes appeared. Mother had held on longer than most of the other victims, but the seed of death was firmly planted in her, and I knew it would be only a matter of time, perhaps only hours, before she closed her eyes forever.

That evening, I had another uncontrollable crying spell. Fraulein Gretchen took me into her arms, rocked me back and forth, and said, "Don't worry, Eva. I'll take care of you. You'll be my little girl if your Mother doesn't pull through." Those comforting words calmed and reassured me.

Frau Leitzel awakened me in the morning with, "Wake up, Eva. Your mother is gone. She died during the night."

Although I knew this would happen, I lay stunned as the words slowly penetrated my consciousness. I looked at Mother's bed; it was empty. They had removed her body and laid it out in the school-room.

"Do you want to see her?" Frau Leitzel asked.

I shook my head, dressed hurriedly, ran back to my meadow, threw myself on the wet grass, and cried. What would happen to Henry and me now? Did Fraulein Gretchen really mean it? Would she adopt us? Would they take care of us? While Mother had been alive, I had never thought much beyond today, tomorrow, or next week. Now, with the passage of one night, everything had changed. I looked up at the sky, wishing I could float away on one of those puffy white clouds and join Mother.

I returned to the house and looked through the window of the schoolroom. Mother lay stretched across several pushed together desks, encased in the white sheets from her deathbed. She looked untouchable and unreachable. At that moment, I knew life would never be the same. My childhood ended with her death.

Mother was interred the following day. A few people joined the sad procession behind Janek's creaking cart. A shallow hole awaited her in the mayor's vegetable garden, which had been converted into a cemetery since Steglitz had none. She was buried alongside all the other typhoid victims.

THE POLES

CHAPTER ONE

I MISSED MOTHER. WHILE SHE was alive, I had felt guarded and protected. Now, I felt exposed and vulnerable. Fraulein Gretchen tried to console me, but only Mother would do. A deep pain crept into my heart whenever I looked at her empty bed. Then, one night, I saw her sitting at the edge of her bed, holding out her loving arms, inviting me to cuddle up with her—Mother was alive! I picked up my blanket, crawled in with her, and continued to dream. In the morning, I knew it had only been a dream, but I felt better. From then on I slept in her bed.

That day, I made my first visit to the mayor's vegetable garden. Mother's was the only unmarked grave. Crude wooden crosses with names burned into the raw wood identified the others. I tried to decipher the makeshift epitaphs, but did not recognize any names.

In time, I turned to Fraulein Gretchen to help me adjust to Mother's absence. But the heaviness in my stomach refused to go away. Mother's death had taught me the true value of her sacrificial love. I realized how much she had shielded Henry and me from the rawness of life.

I had not seen Inge and Traute during Mother's illness, nor had they come looking for me. Now, I missed them and rushed down to our hangout. Nothing was left of our play household. I called out for them. A dog started to bark in the house. The door opened, and a young woman with two small children appeared. She shouted something in Polish and sent the hound after me. I fled. Just as I felt the snarling beast nip at my heels, she called the vicious animal off. I did not stop running until I reached the safety of the schoolhouse. No one was there. I threw myself on Mother's bed and released a new reserve of tears.

"What happened to Inge and Traute?" I asked Frau Leitzel when she appeared in the kitchen with an armload of firewood.

"The Poles confiscated their house. They went back to Elbing."

I looked at her puzzled. "What does it mean, confiscated their house?"

"The Poles wanted their place, so they kicked them out. They are gone, child. They left several days ago. They were refugees from Elbing. They went home."

I thought of the Patient, whom I had not seen either during Mother's illness. I needed someone other than the people around me to share my grief. I knocked at her door. No one answered. I wanted to call out to her, but did not know her real name. I peeked through the foggy window glass. An empty room stared back at me. The Patient was gone. Even her bed was gone.

I asked Frau Leitzel if the Patient had returned to Elbing with Inge's and Traute's family. "No, no, child. She died. She lies buried next to your mother."

I did not recognize the Patient's name on the grave marker. I knew her only as the Patient. A special friend to Inge, Traute, and me, she had tried to enlighten us about sexual matters, things our mothers would not talk about. Now she, too, was gone.

Henry and I never talked about Mother. Perhaps by not acknowledging her death, it made her demise less finite. We coped in our own ways, Henry by prowling the countryside, looking for adventure, and I by constantly seeking acknowledgement and approval from Frau Weber, Frau Leitzel, and Fraulein Gretchen. We let events carry us along. Frau Leitzel stopped calling us by name and referred to us as "child," and in the general conversation we became the "Rapp children." It sounded cold, and it hurt.

Typhoid fever continued to run rampant, sparing only the hardiest. The mayor's vegetable garden quickly filled. Burials now took place in a new cemetery at the outskirts of the village. Thirty-six people died during that summer.

One day, the Russians shot off their guns and shouted, "Hitler *kaputt*! Hitler is finished!" That same day, an army truck drove up and delivered a black grand piano to the commandant's quarters. All night, we heard the soldiers' loud singing and boisterous merrymaking, all to the accompaniment of this new acquisition.

We knew nothing about the Yalta meeting and the Allies' agreement about Germany's new borders. Rumors circulated that East Prussia was to be part of Poland, and that all Germans would have to leave the area. Transports would be put together, and we would be shipped into what remained of the German *Reich*. But these statements remained only rumors.

The Russians had their personal agenda during those last weeks of the summer of 1945. Stalin had given them permission to send home packages with contraband as a reward for winning the war. They now searched for loot with renewed persistence. They descended upon us daily again, but instead of going after the women, they dug up the entire village, looking for buried treasure. They were amply rewarded with many lucky finds.

During this time, the Russians brought in German prisoners to drive the remaining cattle to Russia so that the livestock could be distributed among their own farmers. They loaded all the farm machinery on army trucks, along with people's furniture, and hauled everything away. They stripped East Prussia of everything of value before turning it over to the Poles.

The Poles appeared right behind them, walking around the village and taking inventory of what the Russians had left behind. First, they claimed the more desirable properties the Russians had vacated. We realized they would eventually take our schoolhouse, but we hoped for some form of resettlement procedure before we lost our home. We hoped in vain. One evening, a Polish family, husband, wife, and their little daughter, interrupted our supper. The man placed himself in front of us, crossed his arms over his chest, and said, "You have one hour to clear out of here! From now on this house belongs to us. The furniture stays. Take your clothes and food and get out!"

We sat dumbfounded, not knowing what to do or where to go. Helga pressed her doll to her chest when she saw the little Polish girl pointing to it. The girl's mother walked over to Helga, yanked the desired object out of her clutching arms, and handed it to her grinning daughter. Helga stomped her feet and screamed, "I want my doll back. I want my doll back." Frau Kehr reached for the coveted toy and pulled it away from its new owner. Helga took the doll and tried to escape into the other room. The father stepped in front of her, pulled a pistol from his pocket, pointed it at her, and said, "Give me that doll!"

Helga dropped it to the floor and ran out of the room, screaming. I watched with malicious glee. That doll had caused many hurt feelings between us. Now it belonged to someone else.

The Pole's gun convinced us he meant business. We had one hour. Where to go? We moved into the farmhouse across the street. Elbing refugees had moved out during the typhoid epidemic, and Poles had not yet claimed it. We frantically hand carried our most essential possessions across the road, while the clock ticked and the new proprietors watched. Before our time of grace expired, they placed themselves in the doorway and barred any further entry to the schoolhouse.

We quickly settled into our new accommodations. Frau Schulze did not come with us. She moved in with a Pole with whom she had started a relationship of convenience, as she put it. Our new quarters consisted of a large, sunny room and a spacious, windowless storeroom that was large enough to hold the two beds the Elbing refugees had left behind. At first, we shared the kitchen with two other families, who left for Elbing shortly thereafter. For the moment, we had a place to stay, but we knew it would only be a matter of time before another Polish family showed up and kicked us out.

Then the commandant disappeared with his German woman. The next day, a truck arrived and took the piano away. From that, we gathered he would not be back. Fraulein Gretchen's officer did not return either.

In the meantime, the winter wheat the Germans had planted the fall before turned a deep gold and needed to be harvested. With the machinery and horses gone, the women cut the wheat with scythes. The slow and tedious process left most of the precious grain to spoil.

During August 1945, the month of transition, more Poles arrived in droves and took over the entire village. However, the Russians remained in charge.

Helga and I were sitting on the kitchen windowsill one day when we overheard her mother and Frau Leitzel talking.

"*Ja*, that's our dilemma. The Poles are taking over and pushing us out. Where are we to go?" Frau Leitzel asked. "We'll end up in the street. Our money has no value here, and we have no Polish money. We don't even know if the trains into the *Reich* are running again."

Frau Kehr leaned closer to Frau Leitzel and lowered her voice, "I heard that those who have the means are getting out, but it's risky. Some people from Elbing tried to get away. They sold their remaining valuables to the Poles in exchange for train tickets for as close to the German border as they could get. The Germans boarded the train during the night. The same Poles who bought them the tickets lay in wait for them, kicked them off the train, and relieved them of the rest of their possessions. Then, they had the nerve to tell the Germans they were not allowed to leave without official permits from the new Polish government."

"Nothing makes sense anymore. First Hitler wouldn't let us flee without permits, and now the Poles won't let us go. Just when are we to receive those precious pieces of paper?" Frau Leitzel asked. "Where are we to live in the meantime? What are we supposed to eat until they are ready to let us go? Tell me that!"

The Russians no longer forced the women to work, and the Poles left us alone for the time being. We went into the fields and dug for potatoes missed during the initial harvest. Some days, we collected wheat and laid it out in the sun to dry.

After Fraulein Gretchen's officer vanished, two young Poles from Niederhof appeared on the scene. They spoke German and started to court Fraulein Gretchen and Frau Kehr. Occasionally, they brought us salt, sugar, or cooking oil. They also confirmed the earlier rumors: all Germans would eventually be expelled from the area, but they did not know when or how.

CHAPTER TWO

HENRY AND I REMAINED IN the Weber-Leitzel fold. We had a place to live, but Fraulein Gretchen was no replacement for Mother. There were no more gentle embraces, no more cuddling up with Mother, no more crawling into her lap at night. I needed to be hugged and kissed to make my world whole again. Instead, my universe was slowly freezing over. We remained the "Rapp children," the undesired burden. As the Russians pulled out and the threat of rape eased, there no longer was a need to borrow children for protection.

"I'm going to visit my sister tomorrow," Fraulein Gretchen announced one evening, "and I'm taking you with me, Eva."

To hear myself called by name was like a soft caress.

I was surprised to learn that Fraulein Gretchen had a sister, and that she knew where to find her during this time of displacement and upheaval.

We started early the next morning and headed out of Steglitz in a direction I had never been before. My familiar world ended after we passed the sandpit. Heavy dew coated the grass in the meadows, shade trees lined our sandy path, and birds cheered us on with their happy twitter. Puffy white clouds lingered in the blue sky and played hide and seek with the sun. It promised to be a singularly glorious day, one of those days when everything seemed perfect. Fraulein Gretchen was talkative. She had called me Eva, that sweet sound of one's name. She told me she would persuade her sister to come to Steglitz, and we would all try to flee to the *Reich*. I caught the "we" and felt reassured, but then she added, "You know I have two nieces around your age. My sister has two little daughters."

Already jealous of those nieces, I remained quiet.

The day turned hot after we left the shaded road to follow the railroad tracks. The parched ties burned my bare feet, and I kept stubbing my toes on the stones until they bled. Thirsty, I eyed Fraulein Gretchen's lean rucksack, hoping it contained something to drink and eat, but nothing materialized.

"It won't be long now," Fraulein Gretchen finally announced as a large stand of trees appeared into view. We quickened our steps and soon saw a little white gatehouse hidden among a cluster of old oaks. The gates and mechanism were ripped out. They had been another victim of the Russian dismantlement program, Fraulein Gretchen's sister later told us. The two sisters flew into each other's arms; the nieces clung to their aunt while she showered them with hugs and kisses.

"Oh, it's so good to see you. Mother and I have been so worried about you," Fraulein Gretchen said.

They ignored me as I stood and watched the happy reunion. Their pleasure was my agony. Their loving words for each other stung like nettles, and my heart sank as I felt Fraulein Gretchen slipping away from me.

Fraulein Gretchen called her sister Elfie; she finally nodded toward me and asked, "And who have you brought with you?"

"That's one of the Rapp children. Her mother died of typhoid fever. Her brother is with us, too," Fraulein Gretchen explained. She never mentioned my name, and I got the drift of their thoughts as they exchanged meaningful glances. Later, a curious niece asked my name. Tempted to say "child," I divulged it grudgingly. A stubborn defiance began to foment in my heart. I wanted to lash out and hurt back.

An older, kindly looking woman, whom the nieces called Oma, lived there as well. She was the mother of the missing father. After serving us a thin potato soup, the young family retreated into the other room and left me in the kitchen with the grandmother. When they emerged from their inner sanctum, it was suppertime. Fraulein Gretchen and Frau Elfie seemed edgy; the happy glow on their faces was gone. Our meal passed in uncomfortable silence. Only the girls displayed their pleasure at their aunt's presence with an occasional, "We are so glad you came," or, "We've missed you so much!"

As the sun slipped from the sky and the light began to fade, I realized we would stay the night. Sleeping arrangements were juggled around. The daughters slept in Oma's bed in the storeroom. The three women disappeared into the double-duty living and bedroom, and I slept on a bed of straw by the kitchen stove. I wanted so much to belong and would have given anything to share the girls' tight quarters. But I was tired and soon escaped into my child's land of dreams.

I awoke to a piercing scream. I had dreamt of the Russian soldier climbing into Mother's bed. I held my breath and listened. A single candle sat on the kitchen table and threw a dim, flickering light across the room. A fire crackled in the iron stove, and a giant kettle of water sent wafts of steam toward the low ceiling. Anxious voices and occasional moans came from the adjoining room. The door opened, and Oma appeared. I closed my eyes, pretending to be in a deep sleep. She emptied the dishpan into a bucket, replenished it with hot water from the kettle, and hurried back. The door clicked, and the voices became muffled again. I strained to pick up a clue as to what was going on in the next room, but the weight of sleep soon overcame me.

Oma was rekindling the fire in the stove when I awoke in the morning. I wondered if I had dreamt what I heard and saw during the night. About to question Oma, I saw bloody rags in the dishpan and thought something terrible must have happened to Frau Elfie. Not until much later, during hushed conversations between the adults, did I learn that Fraulein Gretchen had helped her sister abort an unwanted pregnancy. The village nurse had come to see Fraulein Gretchen before we left and talked to her with great urgency in her voice.

Frau Elfie did not come to the breakfast table. The girls told me their mother had become ill during the night. I grew edgy and anxious as morning slid into afternoon, and no one mentioned our departure. Fraulein Gretchen finally said, "We'll be staying here another day or two."

Fraulein Gretchen and the daughters spent the day at Frau Elfie's side. I asked Oma if the girls could come out and play. "You go play by yourself, child," she said. "Their mother needs them."

I meandered along a dirt road for a short distance and contemplated running away, but sensed the timing was not in my favor. They might not even notice I had gone. I lay down on the narrow strip of grass along the path and searched the clear sky for friendly cloud formations, but the wind had blown them all away. I fell asleep and awoke shivering from cold. The sun hung low in the sky when I returned to the guardhouse, feeling downhearted and rejected.

We stayed with Frau Elfie two more days. As we were leaving, Fraulein Gretchen promised to return in two days. Without me, I thought defiantly.

We arrived in Steglitz at dusk. Fraulein Gretchen was happy but anxious about her sister's well being, and I was unhappy and concerned about Henry's and my future. That evening, the women held a long discussion behind closed doors.

The next day, one of the village barns burned to the ground. Drunken soldiers had had a shooting contest, using the barn as their target. Filled with straw and hay, the building took only minutes to burst into flames. People raced into the house and carried their belongings to safety, for fear the whole farm would burn down, while the soldiers kept careful watch on their spirit factory in the adjoining stable.

We children watched this major event, awed by the speed of the destruction occurring before our eyes. I felt the heat of the dancing flames from a block away as they devoured the building.

"We'd all better bring our things to safety before the whole village burns down," somebody shouted, and we raced around frantically, gathering up our belongings. We had no fire equipment and no electricity to run the well pumps. Fortunately, the wind rested that day, sparing the village from total destruction.

Two days later, Fraulein Gretchen revisited her sister without me. I had quietly slipped out of the house after breakfast and had gone to Mother's grave. The little cemetery was full. All sites were identified with wooden crosses that one of the local women and her son had lovingly made. Mother's simple marker read "Anna Rapp, July 7, 1945." There was not enough room for her date of birth. At age forty-seven, death overtook her in her prime. She died without knowing whether her missing family members were dead or alive. Added to that, she had to leave Henry and me to fend for ourselves in a world turned hostile. But as I stood by her grave, I did not think of her final agony and moments of torture. I felt forsaken. A wave of resentment welled up in my breast. I could not forgive her for abandoning us.

When I returned to the schoolhouse, Frau Leitzel and Frau Weber were sitting and talking by the open window, doing mending. Their conversation stopped abruptly when I entered the room. Frau Leitzel glared at me and said, "Where have you been? You were supposed to go with Gretchen this morning. You are a useless child."

How could I tell them about the hurt in my heart, about the jealousy I felt of those two precious nieces? How could I explain to them that each gesture or word took on a new meaning, each slight was like a slap in my face? They did not notice how fragile my soul had become. The protective shield a parent provides had been ripped away from me, leaving me wide open to emotional torment. Even their abruptly halted conversation was a personal affront to me. There was no one to help me deal with Mother's sudden death, no one to help me put it into proper perspective. I missed the Patient. She would have known how to help me.

I did not answer Frau Leitzel and asked instead, "Where is Helga?"

"She and her mother went with Gretchen this morning. You weren't around," she said accusingly.

I said nothing but turned, ran into the field, and cried.

Two days later, Fraulein Gretchen, Frau Kehr, and Helga returned in a happy mood. I guessed that Frau Elfie had recovered.

CHAPTER THREE

At the end of summer, the Russians made their final pullout. They celebrated nonstop and were careless with their weapons. While we were eating breakfast in the kitchen one morning, a gun went off, and glass splintered in the adjoining room. We ducked and listened. A trembling Frau Kehr came rushing in and cried out, "They shot right through my bed. Come and look. They could have killed me if I had stayed in bed one minute longer."

The bullet had gone straight through Frau Kehr's bed pillow and had lodged in the opposite wall.

The Russians were on a rampage again. During the night, the Russians had assaulted the neighboring farm and pulled the inhabitants out of their beds. While holding a gun to their heads, they dismantled the furniture and loaded it on a truck, along with everything else the family owned.

"The gun clicked twice, but it didn't go off," one woman said. "They roared with laughter while we trembled."

"Maybe we're lucky to have so little," Frau Weber said. "I don't think they'll bother us any more."

We continued to gather wheat. The women plucked the grain from the stems, dried it in the sun, and ground the kernels in a coffee mill, turning out a coarse semblance of flour. They made vinegar from rhubarb and retrieved the cattle-salt they had kept hidden from the Russians. We dug up wild roots and collected dandelion greens. Helga and I gathered wild herbs, as well as linden blossoms and chamomile for tea. Thus, the clever, resourceful women kept all of us alive.

The Russians had shared some of their food with us, but the Poles were not as generous. When Helga and I collected green apples along the road, Polish children chased after us and relieved us of our bounty.

Our stay in the new quarters lasted less than three weeks before aggressive Poles stood before us and ordered us out. They allowed us to move into the attic, but they insisted we leave most of the furniture. Two old German sisters were already comfortably established in one of the upstairs rooms. Frau Kehr and Helga moved in with Frau Schulze and her Polish friend. We now had more space, but less furniture, and slept on mattresses on the floor.

At first, I was happy to see Frau Kehr and Helga gone. Helga and I had fought a lot, mostly initiated by me. Witnessing the loving relationship between mother and daughter, and their cuddling and hugging before bedtime, made my heart ache for Mother. After a while, however, I missed Helga. I wasn't sure if it was her companionship I missed, or that I no longer had anyone to torment and take my anger out on. I was crying out for attention and caring reassurances.

I stayed in bed one morning and faked sickness, hoping for sympathy. When I was unable to conjure up a fever, not even a little one, Frau Leitzel caught on to me. She pulled back my covers and commanded, "Get out of bed and get dressed! Go to your mother's grave and tell her you're sorry for your deceitful behavior! How long has it been since you visited your mother?"

Her well-aimed words hurt and made me resentful. The feeling spilled over to how I felt about Mother. Standing by her grave changed nothing. I always felt worse rather than better. I could not tame the deep anger festering in my soul. Why had she left us when we needed her most?

When I returned to the house, I saw a Russian soldier standing by the back door, vomiting all over the stairs. He steadied himself with one hand on the iron railing while wildly waving the other, tightly fisted, through the air, shouting curses in German aimed at the Russians. I did not dare walk around him for fear he might mistake me for one of those "damn Russians" he was swearing at. He focused his searching eyes on me and continued his tirade. "You goddamned Bolshevik. You lazy, good-for-nothing Rusky. You shit-eating communist *Schweinehund*." It was all in perfect German, but his words made little sense until I realized he must have learned those self-degrading expletives from the Germans, who at one time had cursed him that way. In his drunken stupor, he thought he was retaliating. I watched him, not sure what to do. When he ran out of his memorized repertoire, he stuck his head up the stairway and shouted, "Woman! You come down! I want woman!"

Finally, he passed out.

Two Poles came out of the stable, grabbed him by the shoulders, dragged him out of the yard, pulled him across the road, and dumped him in the ditch.

When I came upstairs, Frau Leitzel was surprised to see me and asked, "How did you get past that drunken animal?"

"Two men came from the stable and carried him off," I explained.

"The Poles are getting braver. They no longer fear the Russians," she said, shaking her head and adding, "How things have changed."

I befriended the two grandmotherly women who shared the attic with us. We called them the "spinners" because they each had a spinning wheel that they kept going day after day, making yarn out of Hitler's leftover sheep's wool. It was the one thing the Russians had no use for and the Poles had not yet discovered. When I told the women I knew how to knit, they gave me a pair of needles and yarn, and they started me on a scarf. I loved these two caring sisters; they reminded me of my Oma.

Our residence in the attic lasted barely two weeks. The downstairs Poles appeared before us one evening, embarrassed and fidgety, but with a definite and firm request. "Our parents are arriving in a few days, and we need this room." They let that sink in, and then the husband added, "I'll help you move with my horse and wagon."

Fraulein Gretchen's Polish friend urged us to come to Niederhof, where most of the railroad workers' housing was still unoccupied. "The Poles want the farms and the land," he said. "They're not interested in the little apartments at the station."

The Poles kept arriving in droves. First, the men appeared. Once they had zeroed in on the real estate they wanted, wives, children, in-laws, aunts, and uncles followed. They came from the eastern part of Poland along the Russian border, the part that now belonged to Russia. The Polish borders had been shifted to the west, into what used to be Germany. Russia ended up with a big slice of Poland on its western border, and Poland was compensated with a chunk of the eastern part of Germany. The Soviet Union gained territory, Poland shifted its borders, and Germany became a great deal smaller. Those were the rules of war: win the war, gain territory; lose the war, cede territory. It seemed fair enough on paper, but what was to happen to the German people trapped in the ceded territory? The world did not seem to know we existed. We were like loosely moored ships that got blown back out to sea with each new breeze.

To my delight, we did not wait for the parents' pending arrival but moved right away. Niederhof meant home to me, and surely once Father was released from prison, he would come looking for us in Niederhof.

At the railroad crossing, we passed a pile of weathered pianos sitting along the tracks. "My God, look at that," Frau Weber said. "Look at those beautiful pianos. Ruined! The Russians must have just abandoned them. What a pity." She almost cried. I, on the other hand, saw a potential playground and thought of how much fun it would be to run my fingers across those magic black-and-white keys.

We moved into the Hesse house, an idyllic little cottage that looked much like Aunt Elsbeth's summer home by the Baltic Sea. Separated from the main road by only a meadow, our new home afforded me a clear view of the highway from where I could watch for Father. I fantasized a lot about Father's homecoming and visualized the most tender, loving scenes—how he would take me into his arms and never let go. He became the knight in shining armor on that white horse out of Grandmother's fairy tales, the knight who would appear one day, sweep me up, and kiss all my fear and hurt away.

Niederhof was a lot more populated than we expected. We were surprised to see an occasional train pass through. The Poles were picking up the pieces and getting their newly acquired territory running. We learned from Fraulein Gretchen's friend that an ad-hoc Polish administration had been set up in Elbing as early as the beginning of April 1945. The Poles were now our new, unsympathetic masters. They had suffered a great deal under both the Germans and the Russians when those two nations had divided their country between them in 1939. The Poles were now free again, with many a score to settle. We quickly learned we could expect no mercy. Having lost their homes and properties at their eastern border to the Russians, these Poles now claimed what was promised to them as compensation in East Prussia.

They were told our farms were just sitting there, complete with furniture and equipment, waiting to be occupied. They arrived hungry for land, eager for a new life, and greedy for our things. They did not know the Russians had taken everything moveable with them.

The Hesse house consisted of two spacious rooms and a kitchen we did not have to share with anyone. It even contained a few forgotten pieces of furniture, including beds complete with mattresses.

"Let's hope they'll let us stay until we're ready to get out of here," Frau Leitzel exclaimed.

Frau Weber glanced around the blooming garden surrounding our new home and shook her head. "I don't think we'll be here very long. This is too ideal a place. Look at this beautiful garden and those asters. I'm surprised no one has picked them. It won't be long before there'll be that dreadful knock at the door, and we'll be sitting in the street again."

"Well, let's hope it won't happen too soon. Not until we're ready." Frau Leitzel said. Her words hinted of a planned getaway. "The Poles don't really want us around. We're just an unpleasant reminder that all this once belonged to us. But I tell you we won't make it through another winter. Not under the Poles."

"*Ja*, that's for sure," Frau Weber said. "The Russians at least gave us food. I don't think the Poles will. They don't seem to have much. If we could only lay our hands on those official documents they're always talking about. I don't understand why we can't just leave. Why are they holding us back?"

"Has it occurred to you that the Germans may not want us either?" Fraulein Gretchen asked.

We later learned Fraulein Gretchen was right. Germany was in ruins and unable to absorb mass migration from its lost territories.

Worried about what Frau Weber and Frau Leitzel intended to do with Henry and me, I spied on them. I hid under open windows and around corners. I pretended to fall asleep quickly at night and employed every ruse I could think of, but I learned nothing. Occasionally, Frau Elfie and the two nieces came up. Names of distant, unfamiliar cities such as Hamburg, Bremen, and Hanover were mentioned. I ardently hoped the plans being made behind those closed doors included Henry and me.

One day, while sitting on the front steps of the Hesse house watching our farm across the meadow, I made the disturbing discovery that it was inhabited. People were milling around the property, including children, and once a horse and wagon turned into our yard.

Fraulein Gretchen's male friend obtained a job for her at the railroad station. She would bring home a handful of potatoes, barely enough for a meal, or a half a loaf of bread, and occasionally, a small piece of meat. As the weather turned cooler and the trees started to lose their leaves, we worried about the approaching winter.

Henry located a whole subbasement full of briquettes in one of the station's storehouses. For an entire day, he and I hand carried this precious fuel from the far end of Niederhof to the Hesse house. When the Polish children noticed our activity, they stepped in front of us, waving heavy sticks, and forced us to drop the briquettes. When we attempted to sneak around our antagonists, they hurled stones at us.

A constant search for food defined our lives. Early each morning, Frau Weber and I combed the barren fields for potatoes. But other starving Germans had picked them clean. We ran into a group of women from as far away as Elbing. Hunger drove them farther and farther out.

"We think we'll be able to get out of here before winter sets in," one of the Elbing women told us.

"How?" Frau Weber asked, surprised.

"The trains are running again. You have to persuade a Pole to purchase your tickets for you."

"*Ja*, but people have tried it before. The same Poles who got them the tickets chased them off the train and robbed them in the bargain."

"The secret is to get on the train at a point where no one knows you," the woman confided. "For a watch, a ring, or some other valuable heirloom, you can bribe yourself out of here without those official papers."

That evening, the women talked into the night. Laboring to stay awake, I heard them mention Mother's trunk, which I had not seen since our last move. I had no idea what it contained. But, tired as always, I fell asleep within minutes.

CHAPTER FOUR

We were in the Hesse house only a few days before Fraulein Gretchen revisited her sister. She left early in the morning with her Polish friend. They did not return that evening, but Frau Leitzel did not appear worried.

The next morning, while I waited for Frau Weber to go with me into the fields, Henry came running across the meadow with a victorious smile on his face and a full canister of milk in hand. Jubilant, Frau Leitzel asked, "How did you come by this wonderful milk?"

"I went to see the people on our farm. They were very friendly. They gave me some bread and butter to eat, and they sent this milk for my sister."

"We'll have milk soup for supper tonight," Frau Leitzel said. "It'll be a feast. Maybe we can deal with those people, and they'll let us have some eggs, too."

Frau Weber and I headed out to forage for food late that day. Our pickings became slimmer with each trip. All day, I fantasized about that wonderful milk soup with flour dumplings awaiting us. On our return, an unexpected sight greeted me when we entered the house. Fraulein Gretchen, Frau Elfie, the grandmother, and the nieces sat around the kitchen table, eating my milk soup. I wanted to scream, but Frau Weber grabbed my arm and said, "Let's wash our hands, child, and join them."

When Frau Leitzel placed a bowl of soup in front of me, I could barely swallow. I kept my eyes fixed on my plate, refusing to acknowledge the nieces, who happily chatted away.

Frau Leitzel, the typical doting grandmother, could not do enough for her little angels, and the indulgent Auntie Gretchen completed this picture of family bliss. I watched with a sinking heart. Henry and

I had been replaced. If Fraulein Gretchen ever needed to borrow a child for protection, she now had her nieces.

The next morning, on our way into the field, I asked Frau Weber, "What's in Mother's trunk?"

"We don't know; the key is lost." she replied, eyeing me from the side.

"Why don't we pry it open and see?" Perhaps the trunk held enough treasure to buy freedom for all of us, I secretly hoped, and repeated, "Why don't we?"

"Why don't we what?"

"Pry the trunk open."

"We'll see. The key will turn up," she said evasively.

And so the elusive trunk remained a mystery, and I stayed watchful of every move the women made. Obsessed with fear of abandonment, I subjected each word they spoke to scrutiny and suspicion. The second night after Frau Elfie and her girls had joined us, I wet my bed. Unable to hide it, I feverishly hoped it would not happen again. I was sure a critical time had arrived for Henry and me, and that our fate would be decided soon.

Niederhof came alive with Poles. Trains arrived daily, and people spilled out of the compartments with entourages of family and relations; furniture and animals followed in freight cars days later. The new arrivals did not stay in Niederhof but headed for the villages where their advance scouts had staked out their new homesteads. Frau Leitzel shuffled around the house, wrung her nervous hands, and whimpered, "What are we going to do when they show up at our door again? This time we'll end up in someone's stable for sure, or worse, in a pigsty. That'll be the only place left for us."

"You might be right about that. They aren't bringing much live-stock with them. There'll be plenty of room in the stables for us," Frau Weber joked. Henry confirmed that assumption. The Poles on our farm owned only two cows, a calf, two horses, a colt, a pig, and a few chickens.

Our period of grace in the Hesse house lasted until the end of September. One evening, I was roused out of my sleep by loud, excited voices. Fraulein Gretchen's friend had come to warn us that we were about to lose our home again. The conversation took a disturbing turn. What was to be done about the Rapp children? My heart beat faster. I did not want to hear the answer and whimpered. The conversation halted, and the verdict on our future was left hanging in the air.

In the morning, we packed in a hurry. Fraulein Gretchen and her friend had zeroed in on our farm workers' housing, but all the windows had been blown out. Fraulein Gretchen's friend contacted the Poles on our farm for help. They agreed to fix the windows, but first they would have to find glass. Frau Weber gave them a dress of Mother's for their trouble. In the meantime, the Poles offered us one of the upstairs rooms on our farm.

All afternoon, we carried our possessions across the field and, to save time, deposited them in the laundry kitchen in the back of the house instead of lugging them up the steep stairway. We made many trips until late into the night. We moved everything: chairs, table, beds, and mattresses. We even took the briquettes Henry and I had so diligently hauled to the Hesse house. The room was piled high with our things. The Poles suggested that we leave it all right there until the windows were fixed in our new quarters. And since we would be very crowded upstairs, the farm's children, meaning Henry and me, could sleep with their children downstairs. I felt privileged to temporarily stay with the new occupants of our farm. However, we soon realized the door had been tightly shut behind us. We had no way back. Our exclusion happened so naturally, as if by mutual agreement. One day, we belonged to the Weber-Leitzel household; the next day, we were part of the Polish ménage. In the morning, I went upstairs to join the Germans for breakfast. Frau Leitzel dismissed me at the door with, "The girls are still sleeping. They'll come and get you if they want to play with you."

I waited all day for a signal, but none came. That evening, I tried again. Frau Leitzel let me in but said the girls had to go to bed, so my visit was brief and strained. I made one more attempt the following day and received the same standoffish response. The message was clear: I was no longer welcome. Then the feared moment arrived: the Weber-Leitzel household moved into our farm workers' housing and left Henry and me with the Poles. They had delivered us to our farm, and perhaps they thought their commitment to Mother, if they had made one, was now fulfilled.

The Ilowskis were a large family, consisting of Pan and Pani (Mr.

and Mrs.) Ilowski, somewhere in their middle thirties, their four children, and an aunt, whom they called Schotka. Schotka, in her early twenties, was Pan Ilowski's youngest sister. The oldest Ilowski child was fourteen-year-old Dorota. Walek, Henry's age, Kashia, my age, and three-year-old Stashek followed. They had arrived in Niederhof shortly after we had and were still in the process of settling in. Surprisingly, much of our furniture, farm equipment, and other items had survived and were now part of their household.

In the beginning, things went well enough. Henry and I ate with the family and slept with the children, Henry sharing a bed with Walek and I with Kashia. The parents spoke some German, which helped us adapt into this new and foreign environment. But the transition proved difficult and painful. Living on our farm among these alien people, I felt the loss of my parents and everything connected with the past more deeply. The hurt in my breast would not go away. I missed Frau Weber, Frau Leitzel, and Fraulein Gretchen.

Strife and discord ruled the Ilowski family. The father, a stern, short-tempered man, held everyone in check when he was around. He mysteriously disappeared for several days at a time. The mother was a small, gaunt woman, with mood swings vacillating between kindness and abuse. Then there was ill-tempered Dorota. Her unrestrained cruelty knew no limits. Schotka was a good person. Behind her kind eyes lived a gentle soul, and her every act hinted of a generous heart. Walek, a lazy, morose boy, tried hard to win his father's affection. He did not get along with Henry. Perhaps he saw a rival in my brother. Kashia and I slowly became friends.

After the Leitzel-Weber clan moved out, Pani Ilowski appeared in one of my sister's sweaters, and, over time, Mother's, Frau Weber's, and Frau Leitzel's dresses showed up on Dorota as well. It was torture to see our clothes on them. They had rummaged through our belongings during that first night and had taken what they wanted while we slept. I remembered Mother's trunk and asked Pani, "Did they leave my mother's trunk with you as well?"

Taken aback, she said. "No, there was no trunk. We never saw a trunk." She paused a minute and added, "You go and demand they hand it over to you."

From that short conversation, I gathered Mother's trunk was still in the Germans' possession. Pani insisted I go and claim it, and she sent Kashia and Walek along to help carry it. Frau Leitzel, outraged, shouted, "The nerve of them. They stole us blind and now they want more. You want your trunk? Go ask them for it! We don't have it."

Pani was irritated when I told her there was no trunk. The coveted trunk had disappeared, never to be seen again. Who had it was no longer important. It would have been of no benefit to Henry and me. Even if the Germans had turned it over to us, the Ilowskis would have quickly relieved us of anything valuable. The Poles now owned everything: our farm, our furniture, and our clothes. We stood before them, naked and afraid, and our welfare lay in their hands.

The farm grounds still looked very much like they had when Mother and I first had seen them. The Ilowskis had cleared the entrance to the yard and had made a path to the house and stable. Beyond that, the abandoned wreckage was still ankle deep. A sweet smell of decay, especially nauseating after a rain, hung over everything. Pan ordered us children to sift through the scattered litter and collect anything useable. Clothes, bedding, mattresses, linens, and draperies disintegrated in our hands. Most metal objects were rusted beyond saving. We salvaged only an occasional piece of china or glass. Pan collected all tools, no matter their condition. We loaded the rest of the debris on a wagon and hauled it to a newly created dump some distance away. When we finished the yard and its surrounding area, we moved to the ditch along the highway. The nauseating stench did not go away. We finally discovered that it emanated from the Russian graves. Pan and Henry doused them with kerosene and pushed extra dirt over the mounds.

"I bet those lazy, good-for-nothing Ruskies didn't bother to dig a hole," Pan said to Henry. "They probably just covered the bodies with dirt and were done with it."

When I heard Pan's words, my vivid imagination took over. In the evenings, when night swallowed day, the dead came alive. I saw the corpses push back the thin layer of earth like a blanket and slowly rise from their eerie place of rest. They turned into rattling skeletons with cocked machine guns and floated above the house and trees to the hoot of the owls looking for prey. I was afraid of the dark more than ever. And the nights were getting longer.

Living in our house without the familiar loved faces of my

missing family was bewildering and painful. The Ilowskis sent mixed messages. Sometimes, they treated us as part of the family, and other times they turned hostile and abusive. With time, we slipped into the role of indentured laborers. We were not free to walk away, as we were to find out.

Pan, illiterate as were the children, became mayor of Niederhof and the surrounding villages. Pani, the exception with an education, handled all Pan's paperwork. Government began to function, and life took on a semblance of normalcy for the Poles, while the fate of the dispossessed and forgotten Germans remained undecided.

Henry helped take care of the animals and became Pan's errand boy. He made many trips between villages. When Pan had to make a personal appearance somewhere, he often took Henry along.

I, on the other hand, became Dorota's whipping girl. She heaped chore after chore on me. Her commands echoed through the house: "Eva, go fetch a basket of potatoes! Eva, bring in firewood. Eva, we're out of water!"

Hauling the water was the worst. It had to be carried by the buck- etful to the house. I could only lift half a pail at a time, and so I made many trips to fill the clay cistern in the kitchen. If I brought too few potatoes, or too little firewood, or let the cistern go empty, Dorota would hit me across the back and push me out the door for more. While Kashia and Walek played, Henry and I were quickly initiated into the world of child labor.

A few weeks later, Schotka's handsome fiancé and his younger sister came to live with us. Gentle-mannered and soft-spoken, he had the warmest dark brown eyes. I liked him instantly. His sister, a cur- vaceous young woman, was a professional seamstress. She brought her sewing machine with her and immediately started to sew for the entire village. These three people became the bright rays of sun among the venomous Ilowskis. Schotka often shielded me from Dorota's fury. Unfortunately, their stay with us was short. Although the house was large enough for the two families, it could not accommodate the volatile temperaments and emotional explosions between the women. I did not yet know enough Polish to understand what their fighting was about, but I saw that Dorota more than liked Schotka's fiancé and tried to come between them.

Before the two families' final falling out, they united one last time in an ardent plea to the heavens to be spared from nature's destruction.

Fall had arrived in its full glory when a violent thunderstorm surprised us. Dark clouds gathered late that sultry afternoon and blocked the light from the sky. Jagged flashes of lightning streaked across the horizon, and faint rumbles of thunder reverberated in the distance. Soon, bolts of lightning and deafening thunderclaps exploded directly above us in quick succession, making the earth shake. With each flash, I feared the barn, the stable, or the house itself would go up in flames. The Poles hovered together in the darkness, and I crouched in a corner of the room, trembling, eyes tightly shut. I pressed my hands over my lids to make the dark even darker. I heard Pani beseeching the Father, the Son, and the Holy Ghost to protect the family. Dorota, Schotka, and the sister soon joined in. I forced my eyes open and saw them kneeling in a circle, holding hands with bowed heads in ardent prayer, while, between sentences, Pani kissed a silver Jesus on a wooden cross.

Then, the heavens opened and released a deluge, turning the yard into a giant puddle within minutes. In less than an hour, the storm's fury abated, and the thunder claps turned into distant rumbles again. Light returned to the sky, and the downpour stopped as suddenly as it had started. The women were visibly shaken by the intensity of the storm, and I was half out of my mind with fear. When they relaxed, so did I. It was still drizzling, but the worst was over. I hoped the Russians in the garden remained safely tucked away under their mounds. When I checked the next morning, the extra layer of dirt had been washed away, but the bodies seemed undisturbed. However, as I turned away, out of the corner of my eye—or was it my vivid imagination—I caught sight of a barely discernable shoe. From then on, my ghostly night visitors turned into shoe-clad skeletons that rattled me out of my sleep. The following morning, Pan and Henry doused the graves with more kerosene and pushed the extra dirt back.

With that danger over, the women started to fight again. When Schotka's fiancé found a job at the railway station, the two went to Elbing and returned as a married couple. The next day, they and the sister packed up their belongings and proceeded to move out. Pani locked all the doors to the house, trying to prevent them from taking their possessions with them. Schotka and her new husband were forced to move their things out through a window. That day, I saw Pani and Dorota at their worst, and I intuitively knew that Henry's and my journey through hell was just beginning.

CHAPTER FIVE

A BIT OF A CHILD still lived in Dorota. During Pan and Pani's absence one afternoon, she took me upstairs to Soscha's old room. She unlocked the door and there, in a cabinet, sat Mother's good china, her tea set, crystal, and many other beautiful things I did not recognize as ours. What the cabinet could not hold lay piled on a table. Behind the door, against the wall, leaned the oil painting of the little curly-haired boy that Mother had lifted from the debris. All that afternoon, Dorota and I played with these prized, delicate objects, and for a short moment, I saw a gentler side to her. Caught up in the spell, I told her, with great embellishment, of the wonderful dinner parties Mother had given in our house and of all the important people who had eaten from the precious china we were playing with. Captivated, she listened to my exaggerated stories, and I thought I had won her over. But the spell did not last. When I broke the cup to her favorite tea set, her face twisted in sudden rage. "God damn you, Eva," she screamed and punched me hard between the shoulder blades. I fled down the stairs. From then on, the treasure room remained locked, and I never entered it again—but Dorota often did.

As the autumn days turned chilly, I started to doubt Father's return. If he did not appear before the first snow, he surely would freeze to death in Siberia. Yet, I never stopped watching for him from my position on the milestone marker along the highway. Instead of Father, starving people from Elbing drifted into the village. News of the burned-down dairy in Niederhof had reached them. They heard that the cellar below the rubble was afloat with butter. However, nobody had told them the butter was long gone, and only a lingering foul stench remained.

Occasionally, Russian soldiers passed through Niederhof, pulling a canon or two behind their jeeps and heading for the newly formed East Germany. A group stayed overnight on our farm. When they learned Henry and I were German orphans, they wanted to take us along, but we feared them. When they pulled out the next day, we hid in the barn, and they departed without us. Had we known what awaited us, we would have taken our chances and gone with them.

Days turned into weeks, weeks lapsed into months, and Henry and I quickly learned Polish. We only saw Frau Weber and Frau Leitzel when Pani enlisted their help on laundry day, every four or five weeks. They barely acknowledged me. I still shared a bed with Kashia, which comforted me. I liked Kashia, and as I became more proficient in Polish, I introduced her to Grandmother's world of fairy tales. She was not familiar with any of them, not even "Hansel and Gretel" or "Little Red Riding Hood." In bed at night, I charmed her with my stories and lured her into a world of witchcraft and magic, princes and princesses, ogres and demons. Kashia had attended even less school than I, and she held me in awe because I could read and write and knew so many stories. When I ran out of tales to tell, I created new plots and changed the characters around. Little Red Riding Hood ended up living with the friendly wolf, while they did away with the grandmother, who really was a wicked witch in disguise. I did not win Kashia over completely, but I neutralized her away from the rest of the family's behavior. Sometimes, she even helped me with my chores.

Food, not as plentiful in the Ilowski house as it appeared at first, now became scarce. The family had not arrived in time for the spring planting and now had nothing to harvest. We lived off our farm's supplies from the winter before. Since the Russians never had settled in Niederhof, our hayloft was full of feed, and our potatoes had escaped the Russians' alcohol still. These two items became our mainstay until the next year's harvest. Occasionally, a chicken made it to our dinner table. When one of the horses died, Pani and Dorota hacked it to pieces, placed it into a large barrel, and left it outside to freeze.

When the first snow fell, I longed to join Kashia and Walek at play, to build snowmen and go sledding, but those carefree, childish activities were over for Henry and me. Our chores increased by the week. I scrubbed the kitchen floor, helped Dorota peel potatoes, and scoured pots and pans, which were always burned; Pani frequently rested and left Dorota in charge of the household and of me.

When Christmas arrived, we spent the day without gifts, guests, or a tree. Schotka, her husband, and his sister, who lived only two blocks away, were not invited. At dinnertime, Pani brought out the silver Jesus on the wooden cross and passed it around the table to be kissed. Afraid to let my lips touch it, I passed it on. Then Pani doled out the horsemeat. I attacked it as though afraid someone would steal it from me. The first chunk of meat lodged in my throat. It would not go down or come back up, blocking the air from my lungs. My knees wobbled and everything around me turned dark. I rose from the table and reached for Pani. She backed away, staring at me. They all did. My legs gave out, my head hit the wall, a lump of gristle flew out of my mouth, and I could breathe again. That day, I learned to chew my food well.

None of the special magic I remembered brightened this sad Christmas. After the meal, the family retreated into the living room, leaving Henry to tend to the animals and me to keep the fire going in the heating stove, that hungry monster. Built into the wall, it reached all the way to the ceiling on the other side and, when well fed, retained the heat until the next morning.

Henry joined me when he had finished with his chores and said, "Some Christmas, eh? You think we'll ever get away from here?"

I just shrugged my shoulders, fighting hard to hold back the tears.

So much had happened in just one year. We did not fully understand how it had happened, or why. Everyone we loved, or who loved us, was gone from our lives. But I once had known love and clung to the memory of it. If it had not been for the Poles' little religious ceremony, the Christmas of 1945 would have passed unnoticed by Henry and me.

Winter arrived with a vengeance. An icy wind howled outside and rattled the windows. Frost imprisoned the earth, and the cold took possession of me as well. I dreaded going out into that polar world without a warm coat or jacket, not to mention a hat or gloves. When Dorota sent me to fetch firewood, water, or potatoes, I returned shivering and eager to tend to the heating stove, just to be near its comforting warmth. At night, I dreamt of giant bonfires and a sun so brilliant that it penetrated walls and heated up every room in the house.

Two days after Christmas, Pani fell ill. She was resting on the sofa, while I was showing Kashia how to darn socks, when suddenly Pani pressed her hands into her stomach and let out an agonizing scream. Dorota rushed to her side and yelled, "Go boil some water! Hurry! I'll need a lot of hot water."

I moved fast and listened by the stove, puzzled. Dorota stuck her head through the door and shouted, "Get me some clean rags!"

I did not know where to look, but Kashia had already grabbed some towels. She knew what was happening and said, "The same thing happened last Christmas. You better not go in there. They'll get mad!"

We stood by the door, waiting for Dorota to come for the towels.

"Mother is having another dead baby," Kashia whispered in my ear.

"How do you know she's having a baby?" I asked, incredulous. "How do you know it's going to be dead?"

"Because she's had a lot of them. I mean a lot of dead ones." She moved closer to me and added, "The last one was a boy."

Pan vanished for several days. He reappeared drunk, wishing Pani and all her kind to hell. I thought he was going to hit her and could not tell if he was angry because the baby was dead, or because she was having so many of them.

Within a week, Pani's condition worsened. Her illness reminded me of when Mother had died: high fever, delirium, and irrational requests for strange foods. When the situation turned critical, Pan got on his horse and disappeared again, leaving Dorota to cope. She tirelessly tended to her mother and stayed by her bedside day and night. Kashia and I fetched ice from the creek, which Dorota wrapped in a towel and held to her mother's head. But Pani's fever would not break. I secretly wished that Dorota lay there, battling with death.

New Year's Day passed, and Pani's condition did not improve. Dorota brought out the family's silver Jesus and knelt at the sickbed, beseeching God and all the holy saints to spare her mother as she pressed the crucifix to Pani's lifeless lips. A drunken Pan resurfaced, checked on his animals, and vanished again, leaving Henry in charge of them. He never even looked in on Pani.

I did not want Pani to die and leave me at the mercy of Dorota. Anxious to help, I told Dorota that the Germans had a thermometer and volunteered to get it. I thought that taking Pani's temperature, as we had done with Mother, would help her.

Frau Weber flatly refused to hand over the thermometer. "Tell them to look for it among the things they stole from us! We don't have it anymore," she said and slammed the door in my face.

I did not dare relay Frau Weber's message; instead, I told Dorota the thermometer had been lost.

Pani did get well, eventually. The fever broke, her delirium passed, and the silver Jesus found a permanent place on the wall over Pani's bed. However, her recovery was slow. When Pan showed up again, there was none of the usual screaming and shouting. Even Dorota had mellowed somewhat.

During this period of calm, my tenth birthday came around. It passed unnoticed, unacknowledged, and uncelebrated. But I knew it was my birthday. I was now ten years old, Henry was eleven and a half, and we had not attended school for one whole year.

CHAPTER SIX

AFTER ONE OF HIS DISAPPEARANCES, Pan returned with several sacks of innocent-looking raw sheep's wool. These sacks ushered another dramatic episode into my traumatic life. Pani asked me if any of the German women knew how to spin yarn. I immediately thought of the two old sisters in Steglitz. Pan went to the village with his horse and wagon and returned with one of them. Beside myself with joy, I flew into the woman's arms. She did not recognize me and was taken aback by my unrestrained, emotional greeting. Tears of happiness ran down my cheeks. She looked at me, puzzled, and finally said, "Is that you, little Eva? How did you end up here? Where are the others?"

"They live over there," I said, pointing to the farm workers' housing complex. "They left Henry and me with the Ilowskis. You know, this is our farm," I added proudly.

She nodded and corrected me. "Hmm. So it was. So it was."

I floated through the days that followed in a state of bliss and stuck close to my new friend. Cantankerous Dorota never once touched me. I appealed to all the friendly fairies that this kind woman would not run out of wool to spin for a long, long time.

My guardian angel, as I thought of her, was a skillful spinner and a prolific storyteller. She was well acquainted with the secrets of folk medicine and old-wives'-tale cures for all types of afflictions. She knew of many wild plants and their healing powers, which caught Pani's attention, who often asked her advice on female problems. I helped translate, and since I did not know many of the Polish words or understand Pani's veiled questions, I made up some of the answers. Then Pani would say, "Ask her again. I don't think she understood right!" And so our spinner spun her tales, along with her yarn, and put us all under her spell. I called her Oma, because she reminded me of my beloved grandmother.

One evening, Pani and Dorota baked bread from a mixture of flour and soaked whole grain. Pani was generous that night. She cut into one of the warm loaves and gave each of us a tasty slice. We went to bed with happy stomachs.

During the night, I awoke to Oma's pained moans. I thought the coarse-grained bread might have given her a stomach-ache. She did not get out of bed in the morning. "Oh, my stomach," she cried out. "It's on fire!"

All day, she tossed and turned in agony. Pan brought out our old medicine chest and asked me to read the labels. Father's and Mother's and my siblings' names were written on the bottles. It was confounding how our things continued to turn up at the Ilowskis'.

"See if there's anything that says it's good for a stomach ache!" Pan ordered.

I carefully studied the writing, but I could not decipher anything beyond the names. I handed him a little brown bottle that read "Anna Rapp" and said, "This one!"

"Give her a spoonful of that two or three times a day," he instructed and left me with Oma.

Oma quieted down and greedily reached for my hand, guiding the bitter potion to her parched lips. She focused her gaze on me and said, "You're a good girl, Eva."

Her pain did not go away. Kashia and Walek refused to spend another night with the "raving" woman, and they left Henry and me alone in the room with her. Oma continued to rant like a mad woman and frightened me out of my mind. Before the night was over, the ghosts from the Russian graves rose and joined in the dance of the evil demons with which she was wrestling. Only the rising sun dispelled the madness that had entered my dreams. That morning, my bed was wet again. I strained my ears. Oma was quiet. I shuddered, thinking she had died during the night, but she waved a limp arm in the air.

I crawled out of bed, shivering. The room was freezing. Ice flowers covered the windowpanes and blocked out the weak winter sun. Oma's ashen face contorted with pain. She tried to speak but only mastered a moan or two. I gave her more of Mother's medicine and doubled the dose, hoping for better results. I checked the other bottles. The cough medicine looked familiar. I took a swig. It tasted like licorice and tickled my throat. I tasted away half the bottle and hid the rest for later consumption. While at it, I sampled some of the other potions, but they were bitter and hard to swallow.

Oma lived through another day, her tortured screams periodically echoing through the house. After a long silence, Pani sent me to check on her. She lay on the floor beside her bed, hands and feet pummeling the air. A foul odor reached me. She had defecated all over the floor and herself. I rushed away, terrified, and did not return to the room that night. I don't remember where I slept, but I did drink the rest of the cough syrup and probably rested peacefully in some dark corner of the house.

Oma died during that night. Pan opened all the windows to allow her soul to escape and let her body freeze to keep it from decomposing. The next day, he and Henry moved the frozen corpse into the storage room by the kitchen and laid it out on an old cot. They nailed together a crude box and buried her near the farm workers' housing, under a compost pile where the ground was soft. She had come to us alone, had died alone, and now left the world alone. My guardian angel was gone. Only the image of a grotesque old woman, lying on the floor and wrestling with death, remained imprinted in my mind. It followed me everywhere. I kept looking over my shoulder, afraid I might see her ghost. I thought I had killed her by pumping too much of Mother's medicine into her, but Pani said the fresh bread had caused her death. Today, I am sure she died of appendicitis.

Our relationship with the Ilowski family worsened after Oma's death. Kashia and Walek no longer slept with us. Henry and I now had to face that icy, cold "death room" alone. The days kept the demons at bay, but the nights whispered something else. Oma's death released the phantoms of my imagination once again, taking full possession of my mind.

Henry and I took solace in each other's presence and slept in the same bed. I held on tightly to him before falling asleep. As long as I had that human touch, ghosts stayed at bay. I had seen so much death and the many forms it took, and all had been grotesquely ugly.

In the middle of one stormy night, Henry and I awoke to a loud explosion in the attic. An excited Pan rushed into our room, pulled

Henry out of bed, handed him a kerosene lamp, and ordered him to go upstairs and check on what had happened. Another, much stronger explosion shook the building and rattled the windows. Deeply buried under the covers, I heard Pan shouting at Henry, who came rushing into the room, jumped into bed, and hid under the covers alongside me. He had seen nothing in the attic, but the second explosion had terrified him. We heard Pan and Pani shouting at one another. Pan came after Henry again, wanting him to go outside and check the farm buildings, but Henry clung to the bed. Pan left cursing. Petrified, I thought Oma was trying to come back to get me.

The next day, Henry told me the remaining post office facade had collapsed during the night, setting off explosives that had lain buried in the ruins. But I had Oma on my mind and refused to sleep in her death room one more night. I pleaded with Pani to let us sleep somewhere else. She banished us to our English prisoners' room upstairs, exchanging one frightening situation for an even more frightening one. The attic, with its many dark, mysterious corners and creaky beams, kept me awake most nights.

Shortly after Oma's death, Pan decided to ride to Steglitz to notify the other spinner of her sister's death.

"Do you want to come along and visit your mother's grave?" he asked, on a frosty winter day.

The opportunity to look up Frau Kehr and Frau Schulze and some of the other Germans thrilled us. An icy wind blew. Henry and I followed Pan through ankle-deep snow, while his horse kicked white powder into our faces. We reached Steglitz numb from cold and with freezing, wet feet.

Pan dropped us off at the deserted little cemetery and rode away. No recent footprints tracked the fresh blanket of snow. The individual mounds looked like freshly made white feather beds, while the crude crosses stood guard over the eternal sleepers. The cemetery presented a picture of peace and tranquility, an enclave away from the hard, cruel world that had come to meet us head on. As I stood shivering, I longed to be lying there with Mother, held in her protective embrace. I felt that even under the hard, frozen earth, nestled in her loving arms, I would be warm again. I brushed the clinging snow from the cross and was heartened to see her still-legible name. It would help her find her earthen bed when her spirit returned from its nightly searching journeys. I was convinced the dead only rested in their graves during the day, and that the nights belonged to them.

Cold and anxious to find Frau Kehr and Schulze, we did not linger long at Mother's grave. A Polish woman came to the door of Frau Schulze's cottage and said, "The Germans are gone. They left a long time ago."

"All of them?" Henry gasped.

"Yes, all of them. They disappeared one night."

"Where did they go?" I asked.

"Who knows. Maybe they went to Germany."

We stood there, not totally comprehending. How did the Germans manage to get away? How did they get the proper documents that allowed them to leave? Had Frau Weber and the others gone with them? We had not seen them in a long time.

I cried in helpless resignation. Even Henry, who never cried, shed some tears. Our visit to Mother's grave merely served to remind us that we had no emergency exit, and as cruel as the Ilowskis were, we had to be thankful to them for tolerating us on our farm, which now was theirs. And so our life among the Ilowskis continued to run its course.

That winter, Pan converted our old mush cooker into an alcohol still. Henry had learned a great deal about alcohol production from the Russians, and with his help, Pan connected a pipe to one end of the unit, ran it through a tub of cold water, and attached a bottle to the other end to collect the pure alcohol.

One day, when she was in a particularly good mood, Dorota took me with her to check on the fire under the still. An acrid, sour odor hung in the air. I watched the clear liquid go drip, drip into the attached bottle and asked her, "How long does it take for the bottle to get full?"

"All day," she said. "You want to taste it?"

She collected some in a metal cup, handed it to me, and said, "Here, Eva, try it! It's good. It'll make you feel warm all over."

To feel warm once again—those were magic words. I smelled the liquid; it was not unpleasant, but I could barely swallow it. My stomach convulsed, and for an instant I thought it would come back up. Instead, something wonderful happened. I felt a sense of well-being and took another sip. Warmth reached my toes. I wanted more.

Dorota laughed and gave it to me. The room began to rotate, and my legs grew unsteady. Dorota had to guide me down the stairs. Everything began to float, and I floated with it. I heard a voice say, "Eva, go feed the pigs!" I obeyed and promptly fell into the trough. I might have drowned in the few inches of slop if Henry had not been there to pull me out. I felt free and weightless. Comforting warmth took the place of the ever-present hunger pains. I lost all fear, soon wished the Poles to hell, and called on the demons and the devil himself to come and destroy the whole Ilowski family—with a few special requests for Dorota. Then, things turned ugly. Heavy fists hailed down on me, and my world turned black.

In the morning, I felt the ground under my feet again, but every part of my body hurt. My arms and legs were black-and-blue, and I shivered from cold. As my foggy mind cleared, I found myself hovering in a corner of the laundry kitchen. Someone had thrown a blanket over me. I vaguely remembered the profanities I had unleashed upon the Ilowskis, and how I had repeated some of Pan's swearing verbatim. I feared my punishment was not over with the blows I had already received.

But nothing happened. Dorota handed me an empty bucket and said, "We're out of water!" The others ignored me. Only Walek glanced my way and snickered. If not for the black-and-blue marks on my arms and legs and the awful pain, I might have thought I had had a nightmare.

Kashia later asked, "What made you drink father's alcohol? He was really angry." From that, I gathered he might have been responsible for at least some of my bruises.

Although Pan now had his own source of alcohol, he still disappeared periodically. When he was home, the slightest annoyance set him off. Sometimes, he turned violent and hit Pani, but she stood her ground, screamed, and fought back like a wildcat. Their fights usually ended behind the closed door of their bedroom.

As the days grew longer, winter loosened its grip on the frozen landscape. The snow melted, and water dripped from icicles hanging from the eaves and created puddles below. The air smelled sweet and hinted of spring. The sun heated the brick walls, and I often leaned against the stable and absorbed the comforting warmth, letting the gentle rays caress my face.

Then, one morning, I awoke with an excruciating toothache in one of my molars. For an entire week, I lived in agony. None of Dorota's threats, pushes, or shoves could budge me into doing my chores. I welcomed her abuse—it eased the pain. Pan finally took me aside and said, "Let me look at that tooth, Eva! Open your mouth! Which one is it?"

I pointed out first one tooth than another and again another. After a while, I was not sure which side of my mouth hurt the most. Pan said, "You wait here!" and disappeared in the tool shed. He returned with empty hands, sat down, pulled me between his legs, and said. "Now, let's see; which one was it again?"

I opened my mouth and watched him reach into his pocket and pull out small, needle-nosed pliers. I gasped, wrestled free, and hid in the barn the rest of the day. In the evening, I quietly sneaked into the attic. The next day, I announced that my toothache was gone. I lived in pain for several weeks, periodically resorting to our old medicine chest, testing the rest of the bottles and putting a healthy dent into all of them. They brought no relief. Then, one day, my toothache stopped as abruptly as it had started.

CHAPTER SEVEN

BY SPRING, PANI WAS FULLY recovered from her long illness, and she threw herself into the daily chores with renewed energy. She turned the much-neglected house upside down in a cleaning frenzy. Lice and fleas had moved in with us during the long winter and had found a cozy home on the thick-haired Ilowski women, as well as on me. Soap was in short supply. No one had been near a tub of water for as long as Henry and I had lived with them. We washed the dirt off our bare feet before going to bed, but that was the extent of our personal hygiene. Henry and I lived in the same clothes for weeks. If the Ilowskis afforded themselves the luxury of a periodic change, they did not include us.

Pani sent Kashia and me to the pump and had us scrub our heads with ice cold water. Then, she scraped our scalps with a fine-toothed comb to gather up the hangers-on, preventing the lice from forming a colony.

We had survived the winter, but food had become scarcer then ever. With the horsemeat long gone, we ate meatless meals again. But we had milk, eggs, and occasionally, even butter. Henry and I no longer ate with the family. Banished to the laundry kitchen, we waited there for the leftovers, never enough to still our hunger.

With spring planting on his mind, Pan returned sober from his latest disappearance. He shut down the vodka operation and concentrated on preparing the soil. He sent me over to the Germans to enlist their help.

I had not seen Frau Weber and Frau Leitzel since the thermometer incident, and I was anxious to renew contact. I often stood behind the stable and watched for signs of them. Occasionally, I saw some activity, but I did not recognize anyone. When I knocked at their door, a strange German woman appeared.

"Where is Frau Weber?" I asked, disappointed.

"They've gone to Germany."

I stood there, openmouthed, not knowing what to ask next.

"They've been gone a long time. They left during the winter," the woman continued. She scrutinized me and asked, "Who are you?"

I pointed to our property and said, "I live over there. Pan wanted them to come and help with the planting. "

"Tell him we'll come," the woman said.

The news of Frau Weber's and Frau Leitzel's disappearance devastated me. I had never stopped hoping they would come for Henry and me and would take us with them if they had a chance to get away. But they had left without us. Feeling totally abandoned and trapped, I regretted not having taken our chances with those jovial Russian soldiers, who had wanted to take us along to East Germany. How were we to know that the Russians were our friends now?

The new Germans living in the Weber-Leitzel quarters came from Elbing and were eager to work for Pan. Demoralized and hungry, they had migrated to the country, hoping to work on the Polish farms for food.

Henry and I worked alongside the Germans. We broke up clumps of dirt, spread what little dung the animals had produced over the winter, and planted seed. The conversation inevitably turned to food, while our stomachs growled. *Schlaraffenland* came alive, as we conjured up the wonderful delicacies from that magic land of roasted pigs, smoked sausages, and freshly baked bread, along with the finest jams, sweet cakes, and outrageous tortes drenched in heavy whipped cream. We left nothing out. I held my own during those wistful conversations while remembering our Sunday banquets. Somebody usually put an end to these visions of opulent feasts with such sobering comments as, "Why don't we quit fooling ourselves? It's been years since we've tasted any of those things," or, "That's what Hitler promised us, but did he deliver? He promised us the world, but he robbed us of the little we had. We have him to thank for our misery."

At the end of the day, Pani and Dorota usually doled out potato or cabbage soup, which the Germans wolfed down. They returned to work every morning. I joined them, pitchfork in hand, carefully avoiding Dorota, just in case she had other plans for me. I could barely lift the pitchfork, to say nothing of doing any good with it, but the women accepted my ineffectiveness with good humor and carried me along.

During this time, Henry and I received news through the German grapevine that a letter had arrived for us, the "Rapp children," in one of the neighboring villages. We were beside ourselves with anticipation. Pani had us wait until Sunday to go claim it. I could not sleep during those nights. Even my hunger pains disappeared. I had accepted the fact that our whole family might be dead. Now, I desperately hoped Father was alive, looking for us.

On Sunday, Henry and I flew to the village. I don't think our feet ever touched the ground, until we realized we did not know where to begin with our inquiries. We came upon two old women talking in German and said, "We're Henry and Eva Rapp. We heard someone in this village has a letter for us. Can you help us?"

They stared at us. "Who around here gets mail from anywhere? Where did you ever hear such a story?" one woman asked.

"Why don't you go over to that little house at the end of the road?" the other woman added. "Frau Schmidt lives there. She knows everything that goes on here. Go ask her!"

Frau Schmidt, a big, very pregnant woman, filled the entire doorway when she greeted us with raised eyebrows. She has a *Russenkind* in that huge stomach, I speculated, and wondered just how the Russians got it in there. Fraulein Gretchen and Frau Kehr had been raped repeatedly, and their stomachs never grew big. So that could not have been the cause.

Frau Schmidt knew nothing of a letter and asked, "Who is this letter supposed to be from, anyway?"

"From our father in Siberia," I blurted out.

She laughed. "Nobody gets mail from Siberia. There's no letter here for you."

A lot of Germans still lived in this village, which was much larger than Niederhof. We knocked on other doors, carefully avoiding the Poles, but always with the same results. People stared at us and shook their heads.

We returned, dispirited and dejected. News of the letter had been a cruel, cruel joke. I looked to Kashia for solace, but she had turned her back on me after my drunken verbal attack on the entire Ilowski family.

"You're just like all the other Germans," she had accused me. "I told Schotka about you. I don't like you anymore."

I did not know she had visited her aunt on the sly and was jealous.

"I'm going to tell your mother," I threatened. But Kashia did not care. I liked Schotka and wanted her to think well of me. Now Kashia had ruined it by telling her how I had wished all the Poles to hell.

One sunny spring day, our stork returned. It had escaped the war unharmed while wintering in some warm, exotic land and had had the sense to stay away until it could safely return. Our stork reclaimed its empty nest on the roof of our barn and announced its arrival with raucous clatter. I wanted to rush up to it, embrace it, and thank it for being so loyal. Since storks always return to the same nest, I knew it was our resident stork. Its faithful mate arrived the next day. All that summer, I held one-way conversations with these two relics from the past, and, when their babies hatched, I included them. They were good listeners while I unloaded some pretty heavy stuff on them. These monologues made my life more bearable.

When a farmer in a neighboring village lost his horse to a landmine while plowing a new tract of land, Pan received orders to put a crew together to clear the area of mines. An expert arrived and led the farmers to suspect sites. For days, we heard intermittent explosions reminiscent of the war, and everyone felt safer for it.

At the beginning of summer, relatives of Pani's arrived, an extended family of several adults and six or seven children, all cousins to the Ilowski offspring. They came by train, with their belongings, and planned to settle in a village some four kilometers away. They stayed on our farm long enough to unload their possessions from the freight car.

Dark curly-haired Olga, age fifteen or sixteen, was the oldest of the children. The others reached all the way down to a four-year-old retarded boy. I liked them all and secretly wished they would take Henry and me with them. Occasionally, one of them returned for a visit, but the four kilometers separating the villages kept the two families from a closer relationship.

One Sunday, Olga came to visit Dorota. Pan and Pani were not home, and Dorota was especially abusive that day. Everything I did irritated her. When Dorota started to pick on her cousin, Olga charged into the kitchen, red faced and fuming. She turned to me and said, "Come on, Eva! Come home with me! I don't have to take this, and neither do you."

I did not hesitate and ran after her. We stumbled on Henry in the yard.

"Henry, I'm taking Eva home with me," Olga called out. "Do you want to come too?"

He hurried after us, and we rushed out of the yard. I expected Dorota to chase after us and kept looking over my shoulder, but she did not come out of the house. All this time, I had thought there was no breaking away from the Ilowskis, yet here we were, escaping with no one stopping us.

We followed Olga like two docile lambs. I agreed with her whole-heartedly while she expounded on Dorota's shortcomings. She ended each sentence with, "I hate her." I punctuated it with, "Me, too!" By the time we reached her village, I adored Olga. As we got closer to her home, she turned subdued and edgy. I sensed that she had acted on an impulse to spite Dorota and now did not know what to do with us. However, her exuberant family welcomed us.

"Why are these German kids with you?" Olga's mother asked.

"Oh, Mother, Dorota was mean to Eva. She wasn't nice to me either. I hate her! I'll never go back there again!"

Olga's bitter words sounded sweet to me. I was tempted to help her out and list Dorota's mean traits in greater detail, but I thought better of it. The family treated us like relatives and made room for us at the supper table. Before bedtime, we all received a thorough scrubbing by the pump, which Henry and I badly needed. At night, we got to sleep in the same room with the children, sharing beds and huddling together. No one minded the extra crowding. We giggled and laughed. I felt myself surrounded by angels and took them into my dreams. For once, the demons of the night stayed away. I had but one wish before falling asleep: when I awoke in the morning it would all still be there, and I would not find myself transported back to our farm with the heartless Ilowskis.

Olga was the only child with regular chores, and I become her devoted slave. I wanted everyone to see how useful I could be. My greatest fear was that they would find me superfluous in this house-hold of so many women and would send me back to the Ilowskis.

But it was harvest time; the women were busy canning fruits and vegetables, and for the moment, we all helped.

Henry worked alongside the men and did men's work in the field. I spent hours with Olga, peeling and coring wormy apples, glad there were so many of them. Olga praised my unflinching diligence to her mother and aunts, and I blew my own horn at every opportunity by enumerating all the things I could do.

"I know how to knit mittens. I can sew on buttons, and I'm good at darning socks," I interjected and naively added, "I know how to read and write." If I could have carried a sign on my back it would have read, "I will do anything for food and shelter—with a little bit of love thrown in and no beatings."

But hard as I tried to win Olga's family over, my courtship with them was short-lived. One morning, a young woman appeared. Olga's mother called me into the kitchen and said, "This is Eva. She's a good worker." She looked at me and added, "You go with this Pani! She wants you to help her with her babies."

"What about Henry?" I asked. "Is he coming too?"

"He'll stay with us. You can come to see him any time," she consoled me.

Just when I thought my future was secure, this woman showed up and wanted me. From her swollen belly, I could tell she expected a baby soon, and I wondered how many other children she had. The woman had a kind face and a gentle way about her. When she saw my tears, she took my hand, smiled at me, and said, "Don't be afraid, Eva. You'll like my little girl." Her comforting words made me no happier as I walked alongside her. My reprieve with Olga's family had lasted barely a week.

My new mistress lived at the outskirts of the village by a small pond. They were very poor, judging from the sparseness of their furnishings. The couple's bedroom had nothing but a bed in it, and the baby's room contained no furniture at all. The infant slept on a mattress pushed into one corner. Without the confinement of a crib, she slept anywhere on the bare floor. Sometimes we found her blocking the door to the room. I slept on an old worn-out sofa in the kitchen.

The husband worked nights as a gate guard at the nearby railroad crossing. He left before dark, returned early in the morning, and slept most of the day. I kept the baby quiet and took her for walks mornings and afternoons while Pan slept and Pani rested.

Pani asked many questions. "Tell me, Eva, how come you know so much Polish? Were your parents Polish? What happened to your father? Did the Russians shoot him because he was a Nazi?" Then one day she asked, "Eva, where are your clothes? Don't you have any shoes? What are we going to do when winter arrives?"

"We left all our things at the Ilowskis when we ran away with Olga," I told her and added, "You know, that was our farm once. They have all our things, the furniture and our clothes. Only our animals were gone when they moved in. Dorota even has my mother's good china hidden in a room in the attic."

That caught her attention, "You've got to go there and ask for your things. Just tell them you need them for the winter. Tell them you're not coming back and you want your things!"

I had talked too much. The following Sunday, Pani said, "Today is a good day for you to get your belongings."

Just the thought of facing any of the Ilowskis turned my stomach into knots. But Pani was right. We had walked away barefoot and in thin, threadbare summer clothes. Now, in September, the nights had turned cold, the sun was less warm, and my new family was too poor to provide me with anything.

I walked the four kilometers to our farm, all the while thinking about how to approach the Ilowskis. I rehearsed out loud what to say. Should I beg, plead, cry, or demand? The closer I got to my destination, the more my resolve weakened. By the time I walked into the yard, all the courage had drained out of me. The yard was deserted, the kitchen empty. Music and young laughter poured forth from the living room. I stood by the closed door and listened to the words of an old, familiar German song. They even have our records, I thought. Then I heard Dorota arguing, her loud voice drowning out the music. Intimidated, I knocked at the door. I had a sudden urge to run, but the door flew open. Dorota stared down at me and snarled, "You've come back, ha? What do you want, you little piece of shit?"

All my rehearsed approaches evaporated into thin air when I saw the venomous expression on Dorota's face. A barely audible, "I've come for my clothes and shoes," passed my lips as I nervously wrung my hands and shifted from one foot to the other.

She glared at me and shouted, "Get out of here! Go back where you came from!"

I turned and ran, wondering all the while whatever made me think I would be successful. A girl's voice called after me, "Wait, I'll go with you!" But I was not about to stop. I ran out of the yard, crossed the street, and headed in the direction of Steglitz. I did not look back until I realized I had taken the wrong road. I slowed down and heard that voice again. "Wait for me! I'm going to Steglitz too."

I turned around and saw a young girl about Dorota's age.

"Why did you run? I wasn't going to hurt you," she said when she caught up with me.

"*Ja*, but Dorota was."

"Dorota is mean. I don't like her either," she blurted out.

I started to cry and opened up to this friendly stranger. She listened sympathetically and said, "Come home with me. My mother will give you something to eat, and then I'll show you a shortcut to your village."

Her name was Irena. She had the biggest dimples when she smiled at me. She had gone to Dorota's birthday party that day. She and Dorota had bickered all afternoon, and she was about to leave when I arrived.

Irena's family had claimed Aunt Liesel's farm as their own. Only the mother was home, with no other children running about.

"What happened to the Germans who lived here?" I asked the mother.

"There were no Germans here when we arrived this spring," she said.

She gave me an indulgent smile and handed me a slice of bread and a big red tomato. "Eat these on the way," she said. "So you make it home before dark!"

Irena walked me to the edge of their property and showed me the way. I pushed back the tears, threw my naked arms around her slim waist, and held on to her. She pried me loose and said, "You better hurry along."

I ran across the field. When I looked back, Irena was gone. What will my new Pani say or do when I returned empty handed, I wondered? Panicked, I ran as if my life depended on the time of my return. I cursed their poverty.

"So what happened?" Pani asked. "Where are your clothes?"

"Dorota threatened to beat me," I lied. I did not want to be sent back and quickly added, "Dorota said she would whip me if I ever showed up again."

I let go of the tears that always seemed to be close to the surface. Everything seemed so hopeless. I dreaded Pani's next words, but she consoled me by saying, "There are a lot of kids in Olga's family. Maybe they'll have some things they can spare. I'll ask them." Those words were like a stay of execution.

She gave me an old sweater of hers and said, "I'm going to talk to them tomorrow."

The next morning, Pan Ilowski rode up to the house with Henry in tow. "Eva, you get out here this instant. You're coming back with me," he shouted from his agitated horse.

Henry came running up the stairs and said, "You better hurry. He means it!"

I looked at Pani with pleading eyes, but she said, "You'd better go," and she removed the warm sweater she had given me only the day before from my shoulders. Naked anger flashed in Pan's eyes as he shooed us in front of him along the dusty road, cracking his whip around our bare legs and feet. We jumped, trying to avoid the stinging lashes coming from behind, and scampered along, driven by the determined rider on his beast. I wondered what awaited me once Pan turned me over to Pani and Dorota.

CHAPTER EIGHT

HENRY AND I NOW FELT like true prisoners. Our food rations shrank, and our hunger pains grew. Henry was back in the stable, feeding and watering the animals, mucking the stalls, and running Pan's official errands just like before. I was once again at Dorota's mercy. I could do nothing right or fast enough, and she was quick to kick me in the shins or jam her fist between my shoulder blades, sometimes hitting so hard it took my breath away.

The entire family became more and more mean spirited as their own situation grew more desperate. Pan and Pani were at each other's throats continuously. No one talked in a normal voice any more. The family was headed for hard times, as were all the Poles, and Henry and I would suffer even more.

The harvesting was not finished, and the fields needed to be prepared for the winter wheat. Pan could no longer summon the Germans to help. They had quietly disappeared one night, during the time Henry and I were gone. Only an elderly couple still lived in our farm workers' housing. They told Henry the others had gone to Elbing and had boarded a train headed in the direction of the German border.

"They must have gotten out. No one has come back. Pan Ilowski was plenty mad when he came looking for them," the old woman told Henry.

That left Henry and me to help Pan in the field. Walek, too, had to work, but somehow, he always managed to disappear when Pan was not around.

"No wonder Pan came after us," Henry said. "We're better than no help at all."

Pani banished us back to the attic for the nights. We still had no electricity, and I dreaded the dark more than ever. Every night, I wrestled with the demons of my imagination. Before long, I wet my bed regularly. When Pani discovered it, she pounced on me like a wild animal. I started to fear for my life. The same curse had befallen Henry. Every morning, Pani now came into our room, ripped the covers from us, and made her daily "bed check." Each day, we suffered a rude awakening and a harsh beginning. Our bladders developed lives of their own, and Pani threatened to throw us out. It was a meaningless threat. But then, one evening, she said, "Go sleep in the barn and stay there until you stop peeing in your bed!"

We went willingly. The barn, although drafty, provided shelter and put distance between us and our antagonists. We climbed onto the highest pile of the abundant straw and burrowed down, hoping to keep warm during the night. Grateful for Henry's company, I lay there listening to the voices of the night.

An eerie, cold movement of air swept across my face and startled me out of my nightmares. Fear crept up my spine as I held my breath and listened. The barn had come alive. The straw rustled, the beams creaked, and the wind whistled through the cracks. Something scurried over my face. I pressed my hands over my eyes. Henry shifted in his burrow, whispering, "What's the matter with you? Why are you whimpering?"

"The ghosts are coming to get us. Listen! They're all around us. They're hiding in the straw. One has already touched my face. Can't you hear them?"

"That's the wind outside. What's the matter with you? Haven't you ever heard the wind howl?"

"*Ja*, but what about the thing that just touched my face?" I said, trembling from fright. "It woke me up. This place is full of ghosts. Listen to them. They're hiding in the straw!"

"Eva, you're crazy! It probably was a mouse or rat. This place is full of them."

Relieved, I opened my eyes. Mice and rats I could deal with. Wide cracks between the old weathered boards let in a dim, filtered light, and the rafters threw long shadows across the empty expanse. A bright full moon shone in the sky somewhere above us. My fear slowly melted away, and I floated back into my tortured dreams.

Gnawing hunger remained our constant, painful companion.

Bread and potatoes were the mainstay for the Ilowskis, and if they ate any vegetables, they rarely appeared on Henry's or my plate. Obsessed with food, I paid closer attention to the slop in the pigs' trough and fished out an occasional piece of potato or other edible. Sometimes, I sneaked a handful of horse feed and picked out the grain. I ate anything I could get my hands on. If I could chew it and swallow it, I ate it. Hunger made everything taste good.

Pan finally made us return to the house to sleep, not in the attic, but in Oma's death room. I missed the barn and being away from the Ilowskis. Skittish as a young colt, I now jumped as though caught committing a misdeed every time someone called my name.

By fall, the first signs of scurvy showed up on Henry and me. Painful sores the size of quarters covered our arms and legs. The lice and fleas returned as well.

As the weather turned colder, Pani threw a worn-out pair of shoes at my feet and handed me the old green cardigan sweater Mother had knitted for me. I ran my hands over it. Part of Mother dwelt in every stitch. Kashia had worn it the winter before, and now most of the buttons were missing. I sewed the fronts together, making it into a pullover. It was tight. I had grown in the last year and a half.

Then, our storks flew away as suddenly as they had arrived. I mourned for them. They had been such good listeners all that difficult summer. I dreaded the approaching winter, with its relentless freezing rain and ice storms.

Food and fuel were now the Ilowskis' main concern. Father's stock had carried them through their first winter, but now they had nothing to fall back on. The harsher their life became, the harder they came down on Henry and me, as if the evil fairy had turned their hearts to stone. I accepted my chores as part of life and concentrated on keeping warm, allaying my hunger, staying out of the dark at night, and keeping out of Dorota's way. Thus, I survived each day. I was not connected to a higher authority and too young to question God about why these things were happening to me.

One dark and freezing morning, I got up and stepped into a yellow puddle by my bed. Mystified as to how it had gotten there, I thought of one of Grandmother's stories about a sleepwalker who terrified the countryside during moonlit nights. Had I become a sleepwalker, or worse, turned into a bad night spirit? I scrambled around frantically, looking for rags, but Pani was already there. Walek had discovered the puddle and called his mother. He stood in the doorway, grinning maliciously. Pani exploded. She looked for something with which to hit me. I ducked, flew out of the house, and hid in the straw in the barn. After an hour or more, the barn door sprang open and Kashia called, "Eva, come out! Mother wants you. Don't worry; she won't beat you."

Pani put me through a harrowing day. She withheld food and showered me with verbal abuse about my unfortunate mishap. By the time the day ended, I had scrubbed every room in the house, including the outhouse, filled the water cistern to overflowing, brought in enough wood to keep the fires going for a week, and completed whatever else Dorota could think of to add to my misery. Walek, too, joined in and seemed to derive sinister pleasure from watching me trudge through the chores.

By evening, I was numb from any feeling, physical or mental. I no longer cared what happened to me, and voluntarily headed for the barn just to get away from everyone. But Pani stopped me and told Henry, "Take her to the stable and lock her in with the animals! That's where she belongs."

I surrendered. It no longer mattered where I slept, the stable or the barn; there was little difference between the two. Tired and emotionally drained, I just wanted to sleep and forget, never to wake up again. Henry walked me to the stable. Before he locked the door, he whispered, "I stole a loaf of bread from the bakery today. I hid it. I'll bring you a piece."

"How did you do that without getting caught?"

"When I walked by the bakery, the door was wide open. I saw this loaf of bread on the counter, with no one in the store. I sneaked in, grabbed the bread, and ran. I ate half of it and hid the rest. I'll be right back with some," he promised and disappeared.

I looked around the stable. The dark room smelled of hay, dung, and leather. I felt unloved and unwanted. A shaft of light fell through the open door onto a pile of hay in a corner. I lined a feed trough in one of the empty stalls with it. That's where I would sleep, I decided, and made myself comfortable while waiting for my brother, salivating over the unexpected treat. I had just about given up on him when his silhouette appeared in the doorway.

"Where are you?" he whispered.

"Over here in the trough."

He handed me a chunk of bread and left quickly. The door shut, the key clicked in the lock, and the room turned black.

I lay in my cozy cradle, eyes squeezed shut, devouring the fresh bread. I had not tasted anything so gratifying for a long time. Forgetting my fear and isolation, I savored each delicious bite. I forced my eyelids open and stared into the darkness. The room came alive with shadows, and my heart beat faster. I could not escape; the door was locked. Cut off from the living made me doubly afraid of the dead. When I heard the animals' rhythmic breathing, I calmed down. A wave of well-being swept through me, and soon I fell asleep. After a week, Pani relegated me back to the attic, where Henry was sleeping again.

One night, I awoke to a strange clatter coming from the crawl space. I slid deeper under the covers and yelled, "Henry, wake up! The man with the wooden leg is back. He's come to get us."

"Oh, Eva," he said disgustedly. "It's a rat that's caught in a trap. It's probably trying to get free. Pan and I have set traps all over."

In the morning, he showed me a rat the size of a half-grown kitten. One hind leg had been caught in the wire trap, and it had tried all night to wrestle free. From then on, we usually caught at least two or three rats and would have gotten more if Pan had had more traps. The thriving pests ate everything—the paper off Pan's cigarettes, documents in drawers—and sprinted out of the pots and pans, making us jump. They even scurried across the kitchen table in broad daylight. They gnawed a hole through the storage room door and got into Pani's flour. When we found a nest of baby rats in the sock basket, Pani drowned them in a bucket of water the way Erwin used to do with our kittens.

The Polish government finally came to the rescue. A small truckload of rat poison arrived at our farm to be distributed among the farmers in Niederhof and the surrounding area. Pan called the farmers together and held a meeting. Some ten men came from several villages, inspected the deadly red kernels, filled their sacks, and loaded them on their wagons. They held a meeting over a meal Pani and Dorota prepared for them. Several of our chickens sacrificed their lives for the occasion. The kitchen had not emanated such delicious aromas in months. I greedily watched the large platters heaped with steaming food leave the kitchen and schemed how I might sneak at least one meaty bone.

I had my wish. Pani's presence was needed to read and explain the instructions that came with the poison. Dorota flitted in and out of the kitchen, more out than in, while I stayed in the kitchen to do the cleaning up. She piled the dirty plates in front of me. As soon as she turned her back, I licked each plate clean and chewed the chicken bones to a pulp. When she caught me in the act, she barred me from the kitchen. But by that time, my stomach was full, and it felt good.

I was sitting on the back steps when one of the men charged past me. He faced the wall, stuck a finger down his throat, and coughed up everything he had consumed just minutes earlier. Another guest followed close behind. I watched, puzzled, regretting the delicious food wasted on them. The meeting broke up abruptly, amid a lot of commotion. The men had handled the potent poison with their bare hands and then had eaten the chicken without washing up. Fortunately, they merely had a good scare. I figured they must have licked their fingers clean of the poison before their food scraps reached me, since I felt no adverse affects. But the poison shortened the rats' lives considerably and took its toll on the mice as well.

While he was out on Pan's errands, Henry got to know the Poles in Niederhof and the surrounding villages. I, on the other hand, was bound to the farm. I became more and more timid and shy, but my brother grew bolder. He had stolen another loaf of bread.

"Pst, Eva," he whispered. "I've swiped some more bread. Come with me. I'll give you some."

I would have followed him to the end of the earth for that bread but needed only to go as far as the barn. He pulled the half-eaten loaf from behind a rafter, broke off a piece, and handed it to me. "You better eat fast," he said. "If we're caught, it'll be the end of us."

I sat down on a pile of straw, relishing each mouthful. I admired my brother's boldness and hoped he would perfect his thieving ability so he would never be caught. Dorota brought me out of my reverie with her shrill impatient voice, calling, "Eva, get over here!"

I jumped, hid the rest of my bread behind a rafter, and ran to the house. My chores went easier and faster that day as I thought about what awaited me in the barn. I could not reclaim my precious gift before late afternoon. When I reached behind the rafter, the bread was gone. I probed deep into the straw, but without luck. The rats and mice had beaten me to it. Not even a crumb remained. I stood there, disbelieving, and pounded the rafters until my fists hurt. Then, I sat down and cried.

CHAPTER NINE

HUNGER, COLD, AND FEAR RULED Henry's and my life. Our arms and legs oozed with sores, and the pain became unbearable. Afraid of everyone and everything, my movements grew mechanical, and demons lived in my head. Then, one day, the electricity came on. For two years, we had been without, and now, suddenly, the whole house blazed with light. It was as though the sun had decided not to go down.

Winter came early. I shuddered as I watched the world turn white. Then, Henry vanished. Pan had sent him on an errand to another village, and he did not return. Furious, Pan jumped on his horse and went looking for him, but he came back alone. I missed my brother terribly and discovered how much his presence had shielded me from Walek.

I now became Walek's object of torture. At night, he waited for me in dark corners and behind doors, and jumped out, making eerie noises. I screamed and escaped to the safety of the house, while his ridiculing laughter echoed through the dark. No matter how much I anticipated his pranks, my blood curdled in my veins every time. I ran as if the devil himself pursued me, and perhaps he did, in the person of Walek.

After Henry disappeared, Pan made me help with the animals. The worst was the watering. Although we now had electricity, the Russians had dismantled the pump and taken it with them. I made many trips lugging half pails of water across the yard. Blisters, which quickly festered into painful boils, developed on my fingers. One finger became infected, swelled to twice its normal size, and hurt so much I could not use my hand. A red streak appeared along my wrist and slowly inched up my arm. When Pani saw the blood poisoning, she grated a raw potato, applied it to my throbbing finger and wrapped a rag around it. Her simple remedy amazed me and made the pain go away fast. By morning, the red streak had receded. I repeated the grated potato treatment every time a newly infected blister appeared; it always helped.

Snow fell for weeks, and a sharp wind blew across the barren fields. I longed for my brother. My life seemed to hang by a fragile thread. I escaped more and more into a world of fantasy and make-believe. I imagined Father and Erwin returning from Siberia and rescuing me, or Douglas appearing and beating up Walek. My sister showed up in a dream with a suitcase full of warm clothes. Life became a blur of reality and nightmare, and I had trouble distinguishing between the two.

I knew Christmas had arrived when Pani removed the silver Jesus from the wall above her bed and passed it around the table to be kissed. But it was another sad Christmas, sadder than the year before, because my brother, too, had abandoned me. I sat with my plate of food in the kitchen by the heating stove, while the family celebrated on the other side of the wall. Pani had been more generous with my portion, and I was grateful. Had there ever been a better life, a happier existence, I wondered. Or was I locked into one long fairy tale as the unfortunate, downtrodden character, never to escape?

All year, Pan's vodka still had stood idle. After Christmas, he spent an entire day in the attic, preparing it for production. Day and night, for a whole week, he guarded the room.

On New Year's Eve, a neighboring farm family invited the Ilowskis and Dorota to a party. The day passed in an atmosphere of excitement. The women washed their hair, dried it by the cooking stove, and ran the fine-toothed delousing comb across each other's scalp. Pani rolled Dorota's thick blond hair around paper strips and tied them into knots to hold the flimsy rolls in place.

When the much-awaited moment arrived, Dorota swept into the kitchen. She had been transformed into a real beauty, wearing a bright red party dress and with her hair piled high in tumbling curls. All those ringlets from a few pieces of paper, I marveled. She gave me a friendly smile when she noticed my stare and asked, "How do I look, Eva?"

"Like a princess," I said, and thought, I hope you prick your finger and fall into a hundred-year sleep tonight.

Pani made her entrance with fewer airs and lesser results. A wave of pain rushed through my anguished heart. She wore one of Mother's good dresses. Considerably smaller than Mother, she looked like she needed the assistance of a good seamstress. She was not in a happy mood. She and Pan had argued vehemently when he announced he was leaving early to start celebrating with the men. He had departed dapper and polished-looking in his riding boots, with his hair and mustache neatly trimmed and a bottle of spirits under his arm. I realized that the sudden resurrection of his alcohol factory was in preparation for this "bring your own bottle" party. The women left much later, reminding us to look after little Stashek.

Kashia, Walek, and Stashek huddled around the tile stove in the living room, which had been turned into Pan and Pani's bedroom for the winter, while I kept the fire going in the kitchen.

"Come tell us a story, Eva!" Kashia called from the other side of the wall.

"*Ja*, Eva, why don't you?" Walek chimed in.

Pleased, I piled extra wood on the fire and joined them. I taxed my imagination, trying to come up with a new slant to my worn-out old tales, but my numbed mind remained blank. I considered resurrecting the Russians and Oma from their graves, hoping to frighten Kashia and Walek. While I formulated new themes in my traumatized brain, Kashia said, "Father told us we'll be going to school in Steglitz as soon as a teacher arrives. I'm scared. Tell us about school!"

Thus, I began on a journey down memory lane and told them all about school, how much fun they would have and how smart it would make them.

We decided not to go to sleep but wait for the New Year to arrive. We weren't sure what to look or listen for, but there was a party going on nearby, and surely a sign would reach us from that direction. Stashek had long ago fallen asleep at our feet. We turned off the lights and sat in the dark. Walek pulled a feather pillow from his parents' bed, and with his head comfortably embedded on one end, he soon fell sound asleep, too. Kashia followed within a short time, claiming the other end of the fluffy pillow. Her deep rhythmic breathing mingled with Walek's and Stashek's. The moment held such peace and harmony that I wanted time to stand still. Soon, I also drifted off. And so, somewhere during that time, 1946 ended and 1947 began.

Shouting and door slamming jarred me out of my slumber. Pan and Pani charged into the room. The light never came on. He beat and kicked her while she screamed. It sounded as though he was dragging her across the floor. Walek and Kashia stirred but remained silent. I did not dare move and hoped my wildly pounding heart would not give us away. Pan's speech was slurred, but there was nothing slurred about Pani's loud screams. Kashia winced, dug her fingernails into my arm, and let out a muffled groan. I was sure he would kill Pani and regretted it was not Dorota he was manhandling. Where was Dorota, anyway? She had not come home with her parents.

Pan must have thrown Pani on their bed. The wire springs creaked as she landed on it with a hard thump. It sounded like he was ripping off her clothes. There goes Mother's beautiful dress, I thought, and was glad. Pani's wails weakened while Pan's breathing quickened to the accompaniment of the rhythmic squeaking of the bedsprings. Labored sighs, first from him and then from her, followed, and then I heard only heavy breathing. Kashia, Walek, and I crawled out of the room, leaving sleeping Stashek behind.

In the morning, Pan was gone and Pani sported a swollen black eye and spent the day in bed. Dorota appeared from somewhere still in her fine, but wrinkled, party dress. Her ringlets, no longer springy and tight, hung down on her shoulders in tired disarray.

Kashia and Walek barely acknowledged my presence. It was as though the night before never happened. If not for Pani's black eye and the bruises on her arms, I might have thought I had dreamt it all.

Pan stayed away for several days. When he returned, renewed friction filled the atmosphere. He called Pani a goddamned bitch, and I feared the evening would turn into a replay of New Year's Eve. Kashia and Walek vanished as they always did when things got too uncomfortable for them. Pani, too, was suddenly gone. She had quietly slipped out the back door. When Pan realized she was gone, he chased after her, shouting, "Damn you, woman. I'm going to kill you!"

He returned without her and stalked into the kitchen mumbling, "Useless bitch." He ordered Dorota to fix some eggs and potatoes for him and disappeared into the bedroom. I was in the kitchen with Dorota, who by now was in a state of frustrated agitation as well.

Wielding a wooden spoon in the air she yelled, "Eva, go fetch some eggs! And make it snappy!"

It was a dark, moonless night, and the chicken house was clear across the yard. I called out for Kashia to come with me. Instead, I felt Dorota's wooden spoon land on my head with such force it made me reel. The spoon split in half, and the pieces bounced to the floor. I stumbled forward, grabbed the edge of the table, and hit the floor, taking a few dishes with me. The walls started to spin, and the room went dark for a second.

Stupefied, I stumbled into the freezing, black night. An icy wind whipped into my face, and I could see the steam from my breath as I ran through the newly fallen snow. Another explosive outburst from Pan aimed at Dorota pierced the frozen stillness. I shivered.

The hens cooperated. I scooped up a mixture of seed and chaff from the ground and held it in front of their barely discernible, groggy heads. At the same time, I reached under their feathery warm bodies with my other hand and removed their eggs the way Charlie had taught me.

In my eagerness to get my hand out of harm's way, I cracked the first egg. I quickly licked up the slimy, warm mixture as it ran through my fingers, marveling at the delectable taste and the ease with which I was able to swallow it. Only two years ago, at home with my parents, being asked to eat a raw egg would have sent me on a hunger strike for several weeks. Now, it tasted like the most precious of all foods. I gulped down a second egg, this time a lot more skillfully and with less loss. After I found the next few nests empty, I collected the remaining eggs in my apron and brought them back to the house. Not all eggs would make it to the Ilowski dinner table from now on, I schemed.

"What's all that egg on your hand?" Dorota asked, raising her eyebrows.

"A chicken pecked at the egg when I tried to take it from her," I said, hoping there was no telltale evidence around my lying lips. But Dorota was distracted. Pan was waiting in the other room, and he was not in a good mood.

Pani stayed away for two days. Pan did not go after her. When she returned, her eye was still black but no longer swollen, and hatred and bitterness were written on her face. She now took firm charge of the household and called all of us useless brats. Only Dorota seemed to be in her good graces. Kashia, Walek, and Stashek tiptoed around the house, and for the moment, pernicious Walek left me alone.

CHAPTER TEN

WINTER HELD THE COUNTRY IN its firm grip, with one dark, dismal day following another. As January ended, I knew that somewhere during that passage of time my eleventh birthday had also come and gone, along with another year without school. But my survival skills were sharpening, and the weak threads by which my life hung were hardening into a strong rope. I now scored at least one egg a day and felt better for it. Mother's green wool sweater barely reached to my waist and was full of holes, but it kept me warm. Much as I wished, hoped, and willed for a prince to appear in the shape of my father, he refused to materialize.

A cold Nordic wind turned the house into an uncomfortable, drafty place. Pan resorted to pulling boards from the barn for fuel. A heavy, leaden winter sky continued to hang above us, and the sun abandoned us. Pani gave me Henry's old woolen pants after Walek had outgrown them. They hung on me and would not stay up without the missing suspenders. I pushed the suspender buttons through the holes in my sweater to hold them up.

Walek started to call me "Adam," because I was now in pants. Each day, he turned meaner. His pranks shifted from simple scare tactics to knocking the bundle of wood out of my arms, or yanking the bucket of water out of my hand—always when no one was looking.

One night, a shadow standing by my bed frightened me out of my sleep. I trembled, thinking Oma had finally come back to get me. I kept my eyes tightly shut, held my breath, and waited for her to grab me. Water splattered on the floor, and the smell of warm urine reached my nostrils. I pushed back my eyelids just in time to catch a glimpse of Walek disappearing through the open door. Deep rage welled up inside me. I wanted to charge after him and tear off his tinkler.

I could only guess what Pani would do to me in the morning. My head filled with troubling thoughts. I would run away and try to find Henry. I cursed my brother for not telling me where he had gone. For all I knew, he might have walked all the way to Germany, wherever that was. I resolved to go to the old German couple who had stayed behind in our farm workers' housing and beg them to help me.

In the morning, a bucket of freezing water thrown over my head sent shock waves through my entire body. I lay in a pool of water, not comprehending what had happened. Pani stood over me, empty bucket in hand, releasing a tirade of condemnations aimed at worthless me, my weak bladder, and the whole damned German race, with Walek glowering in the doorway. She pulled back my soaking bed cover, grabbed me by the arms, and yanked me out of bed. I broke free and tore toward the front of the house, with her in pursuit.

"What are you trying to do? You want to kill her?" Pan shouted, entering the house as I tried to rush past him. "Put her to work! She is of no use to us dead. And get some food on the table!"

He grabbed my arm and pulled me with him out of the house into the sunless, frigid morning. "Come on, Eva, we've got to chop up more wood!" When he noticed my bare feet, he added, "Go get your shoes!"

I stole back into the house, eyes glued to the floor, and snatched up my wet shoes, which had not escaped Pani's icy bath. I did not look beyond Pani's and Walek's feet as I rushed passed them, but I felt their hate-filled stares.

Pan chipped away at the barn. I wondered how many winters it would supply us with precious fuel before the entire building was gone. I gathered the wood and carried it into the laundry kitchen. When sober, Pan was a much kinder man. At breakfast, he handed me a slice of bread from his plate and sent me off to water the animals. Later, Pani made me clean up Walek's puddle and scrub all the floors. Blood seeped from the cracks in my chapped hands. At the end of the day, Pani said, "Eva, get your covers and take them to the storage room! That's where you're going to sleep from now on."

I broke out in goose bumps. Oma had lain there, very frozen and very dead, before her burial. Now, I was to sleep on the same cot. The room felt heavy with her presence. When Pani locked the door from the outside, I was petrified. Iron bars secured the windows. I was a prisoner, and I could not escape. I could not tell if my bedding was wet from the sweat of fear, or from Pani's icy shower.

Despite my fears, Oma's ghost never once disturbed my slumber. Exhausted, my weak body succumbed quickly to the sweet abandonment of sleep. By the end of each day, not enough fight remained in me to battle with a fly, let alone Oma's harmless ghost.

A whole week went by before I had a chance to seek out the old German couple, only to find no sign of life. I cautiously poked my head around the corner of the building and promptly bumped into a pretty, youngish woman. Surprised, she jumped and said in Polish, "What are you doing here? What's your name?"

"I come from over there," I said, pointing towards the farm. "I'm looking for the German people."

"There are no Germans here."

"Where did they go?"

"I don't know. There was no one here when we arrived."

I faced her, stunned. I had heard these same words so many times before and now took them in with the same helpless feeling. Big fat tears escaped first from one eye than the other. The woman looked puzzled and asked, "You're German, aren't you? Where is the rest of your family? What are you doing here anyway?"

"They're all dead," I said with emphasis on the word dead, hoping for compassion. She took me into the house and gave me a cup of warm milk along with a slice of dark bread. Young children appeared out of the corners of the room and watched while I ate.

"Can you read?" the woman asked.

"Yes."

"I've got something for you," she said and disappeared into the other room. She returned with a thin, yellowed book in one hand, wiping off the dust with the other. "I think you might be the right age for this. It's in German," she said, handing me the tattered volume. "It's yours. Take it home and read it! I think you'll like the stories."

My plans to run away had come to nothing. However, I now held a German book in my hands. I slipped it under my sweater to hide it from the Ilowskis. Clutching it protectively against my chest, I ran straight for the barn and hid it. No one would deprive me of this precious treasure. I waited impatiently for Sunday, my first opportunity to get back to the book. Would I still remember how to read after two years without school? I could think of nothing but the book and the mysteries it would reveal.

The week seemed twice as long. My hunger for food was second to my hunger to read. When Sunday arrived, I burrowed into the straw and held the book for a long time without opening it, relishing the moment. A big round knothole on one of the boards offered a full view of the yard and house. Safe from surprises, I stared at the bold title: *Children's Bible Stories.* Yes, I could still read, and I had a book to confirm it. A picture of a long-bearded, Santa Claus-like man sitting among puffy white clouds took up half the first page. He held one hand stretched over the wide earth and blue sea beneath him, pointing to a group of exotic animals. Under the picture stood the title, "The Creation," and the story followed: "On the first day God created …"

I devoured the stories, all with characters larger than life. Above them hovered a God greater than the whole big universe. There was Noah's Ark and all those circus animals, the Tower of Babel, Sodom and Gomorrah, the parting of the Red Sea, and many, many other miracles performed by God. The New Testament followed, describing Jesus and his magic deeds. Colorful, beautifully illustrated pictures accompanied each story. God looked benevolent but unreachable, peeking out from behind the clouds far above the earth. Jesus, on the other hand, walked among the people, performing miracles just for the asking. No wonder the Ilowskis prefer him, I thought. The book ended with a short paragraph on the power of prayer.

That Sunday afternoon, alone in our barn, under the shadow of the brutal Poles, I made my first acquaintance with God and Jesus and what they represented. Until then, "my God" and "Jesus" had been meaningless, empty expletives the adults often used for no reason at all. I knew nothing of heaven and hell in the biblical sense. Now, a whole new world opened up and gave me a lot to contemplate, with no one to turn to for explanations. I did not know if these stories were real or just another genre of fairy tales, although Oma had never mentioned them. I returned to my book often and memorized each parable. I planned to tell them to Kashia and see if she could throw some light on this uncharted territory.

But Kashia offered no help when I approached her with my many questions, carefully keeping my source of information from her. She did not know much more than I and could talk only about the prayer part. She often listened to her mother pray with that beaded necklace. "She never prays without it," Kashia said. "I'm learning the words. With the beads you can ask Jesus for things, and sometimes you get them," she explained.

I begged her to teach me after she learned. But she looked at me suspiciously and said, "Jesus doesn't like the Germans any more. He only helps the Poles now."

Her reasoning seemed perfectly plausible at the time. Even I could see that the miracle-working magician sided with the Poles.

"Do you need those beads when you pray?" I pressed on.

Kashia was not sure. So I decided to bypass Jesus and go directly to God with my wish list. The list grew longer each day. A plea for Father's return always came first. Occasionally, I inserted what seemed, at the time, a perfectly reasonable appeal that God resurrect Mother. After all, Jesus had done it, at least so it said in my book, and God, being even more powerful, could surely do it, too. I talked to this all-seeing, all-hearing God the way I did to the animals, making deals with him and childish promises. The Bible stories said that if you ask, you shall receive. Well, I asked for a lot, and not all of it was good. I made a few uncharitable requests for the Ilowskis as well. This newly discovered God ignited a renewed feeling of hope in me. However, much as I pleaded with him, nothing changed. But I never eased off and counted on wearing him down, just as I had so often done with my parents.

The weeks passed with no relief from winter's arctic winds and gloomy, gray days, and God still was not listening. Red fleabite welts covered my body, and my head teemed with lice. I scratched my scalp raw. Blood and dirt matted my hair. When Pani saw me scratching, she cried out, "My God, Eva, you've got more lice than hair on your head. No wonder we can't get rid of the vermin. You keep bringing them back into the house!"

The Ilowski women managed to keep the lice at bay with their weekly treatments using the fine-toothed louse comb, but they neglected to include me. Now, there was only one thing to do, Pani declared. My hair had to come off. She grabbed the scissors from the mending basket and pushed me into the freezing laundry room.

"Get on your knees!" she ordered and started to snip away. I watched the dirty clumps of hair fall to the cement floor and wondered what had happened to my blond hair?

When she had finished, she pointed to the floor and said, "Scoop up the filthy mess and bury it in the snow. Then, take some of that snow and rub it into your scalp until your head is frozen! That'll kill the rest of the vermin."

I pressed handfuls of snow against my sore head until my hands and scalp were numb. The cold snow brought unexpected relief, but it did not make the ugly, oozing sores go away.

Bald and in pants, I now looked like a real boy, and Walek took great pleasure in calling me such. I wished him dead.

CHAPTER ELEVEN

PAN CALLED THE SURROUNDING FARMERS together for another emergency meeting. Fewer men attended this time, and there was no accompanying feast. They gathered in the kitchen, the only room that still held a feeble semblance of warmth. I picked up mere fragments of their spirited debate, but it was clear they were concerned about the many shortages they faced—shortages of fuel, fertilizer, seed, food, and money. They also bemoaned the fact that no Germans remained to help with the spring planting. I wanted to shout, "That's not true. I'm still here!" and felt deeply disturbed to learn that all the Germans were gone. Where was Henry? What would happen to me now? Would I remain the Ilowskis' slave forever?

When the gathering broke up, one of the men hollered in my direction, "How about watering my horse, boy?"

I cringed and meekly asked, "Which one is yours?"

They all looked at me, startled. "What have we got here?" one of them asked. "Are you a boy or a girl?"

I blushed and felt a strong urge to cry. "I'm a … I'm a girl." I stuttered.

They roared with laughter.

"Well, I'll be damned!" the man said, turned to Pan, and added, "I could have sworn I was talking to a boy. What are you raising here, anyway?"

"She's not ours. The Germans left her behind. She was so full of lice, we had to shave her head and dunk her in the well," Pan explained.

They made allusion to my being too young to have been a Nazi and laughed some more. Somebody finally said, "Ah, leave her alone! She's only a kid."

Events accelerated, and the bad days outnumbered the good. Pani was sick again, and Dorota ran the household alone. Every morning, while it was still dark, she charged into my room, yanked off my covers, and yelled, "Get the fire started, Eva!" She then headed for the stable to milk the cows. Too tired to move, I often crawled back under the cozy covers and fell asleep again. My second wake-up call came equally as abruptly, but considerably more painfully. Dorota, now irate and angry, usually followed up with a slap across my head or a painful punch in the ribs.

What Kashia had told me about going to school happened all too soon. Pan came home one day and announced, "A teacher has arrived. School starts tomorrow."

I begged Pan, the more approachable parent, to let me go to school, too. But he laughed and said, "Only Polish kids get to go to school."

That evening, I asked God to make Pan change his mind.

In the morning, Dorota did not have to jerk the covers away from me. I was already sitting on the edge of my cot, rubbing the sleep out of my eyes, when she stormed into the room in her usual militant fashion. I hurried about—the straw, wood, and fire were done, and hot water for Pan's chicory coffee was already steaming when Dorota reappeared from the milking. The entire household came alive earlier than usual. When Pan appeared for his hot coffee, I had it ready and handed it to him. I looked beseechingly into his cold eyes and said, "I want to become Polish. I don't want to be German anymore. I want to go to school!"

This time Pan did not just laugh, he roared as if what I had said was the funniest thing he ever heard. I faced him, fighting back those darned tears. He looked at me, stopped abruptly, and said, "Eva, you can't ever be a Pole. Someone has to want you before you can become Polish."

He probably meant adopt me, but at age eleven "want me" or "adopt me" were pretty much the same. In a last desperate attempt, I offered to accompany Kashia and Walek to show them the way, but Pan, who had taken little interest in his children in the past, suddenly seemed to care. He would take them to Steglitz himself.

When Kashia entered the kitchen, I was struck dumb. Her silky blond hair shone with cleanliness, and she wore a new red wool knit dress. To her it was new, but to me it was one of my sister's hand-me-downs that had lain in Mother's cedar chest, waiting for me to grow into it. At that moment, I hated Kashia more than Dorota, and I wanted to tear the dress from her body and rip it into shreds.

Kashia and Walek walked ahead, while Pan saddled his horse. I walked with them to the railroad crossing, they eager, and I miserable. They wallowed gleefully in the advantage they were about to gain over me. I fought back. "You know my mother died in that school house. Her body lay out across those wooden desks for a whole week. Her ghost has haunted the schoolhouse ever since." Then I turned and ran back to the farm.

With Walek and Kashia in school, I felt the hopelessness of my situation more deeply. I dragged my tired body around, while my mind lived in the fairy-tale land where miracles happened. More tired than usual one day, I went to my hiding place in the barn and fell into a fitful sleep. I awoke to an explosion. A bomb had detonated somewhere, but as my mind cleared, I realized it had only been a door slamming. I peeked through my observation hole. Dusk had spread its heavy gray veil over the buildings, and it had started to drizzle. Dorota's hollow footsteps echoed through the deceptively peaceful silence as she hurried across the yard with milk pail in her hand. She disappeared into the stable, and all was quiet once more. I picked that moment to sneak back into the house. But despite my long nap, I felt drained of all energy. A fire burned in my head, and my gnawing hunger pains had disappeared. I crawled to my little room and collapsed on the cot before Dorota returned.

Kashia later told me that I did not leave my bed for more than a week, and that I talked nonsense most of the time. I must have drifted in and out of consciousness, because when the worst was over, my hazy memory of the episode was like a film with many missing frames. Only Kashia's caring face kept flashing across the screen of my foggy mind, with her standing by my bed, holding a cup of cool water to my thirsty lips. I do not know what I had come down with—typhoid, a severe case of the flu, some childhood disease, or simple exhaustion. Kashia had been my diligent caretaker, and I created a special place for her in my heart, even if she did wear my sister's clothes to school.

Each day, I felt a little stronger. Dorota let me sleep in the mornings, and it seemed like my food rations had grown more generous, or maybe my stomach had shrunk! Within a week, however, I was back performing all my old chores, and the hunger pains returned.

A week later, one of the cows stopped eating. Pan added extra grain to her fodder, but she refused even that. Two days later, she died. Pan tried to coax her back to life by kicking his boot into her stiff side, but she did not move. He fell to his knees, rested his head on her bloated belly, and wept. It was the only time I saw this so often hard and brutal man cry. I quietly tiptoed out of the stable.

When Pan recovered, he skinned the cow and saved the hide, while Pani and Dorota dissected the animal right there in the stall, amid the dung and waste. Pan rode off to the city and returned with a sack of precious salt, the only preservative available for use without refrigeration. We labored for several days and wasted nothing. We scraped and boiled the meat off the bones, turned the intestines inside out, and cleaned and salted them. We feasted for an entire week. The potato soup tasted of more than just starchy potatoes, and occasionally, the Ilowskis let a piece of meat slip into my ration. I thanked my newly discovered God and let him know that I would not mind if he let a little piglet or one of the calves follow the fate of the cow. My relationship with him was improving. I figured that perhaps he had been testing me all this time. My Bible stories spoke a lot about this irritating habit of his.

I noticed that after I had developed a taste for raw eggs, the hunger sores on my arms and legs started to shrink. And now, with the cow's unexpected death, my daily rations improved. I went for almost two weeks without breaking out in new sores.

One day, a wagon drove into our yard with Henry sitting next to the driver. I could not believe he was really my brother. While his new master talked business with Pan in the living room, Henry stayed in the kitchen and warmed himself by the stove.

"What are you doing here?" I whispered. "Aren't you afraid the Ilowskis won't let you get away again?"

"I'm not afraid of them anymore!" he said.

My brother had become surer of himself. Thirteen now, he seemed very grown up. We exchanged few words because Pani and Dorota were within earshot. He worked in a neighboring village for the man who had brought him along. Life was better, but not by much.

"Why don't you come back to us, Henry?" Pani suggested.

Torn between wanting him back and trying to protect him, I coughed and vigorously shook my head at Henry, silently moving my lips. "Don't do it, Henry! Don't do it!" He said nothing, but I sensed his uneasiness.

The man entered the kitchen and said, "Let's go, Henry!"

My brother looked my way and whispered, "I'll stay in touch."

I wanted to run after them. As I watched the vehicle pull out of the yard, I felt abandoned all over again.

A few days later, the storks announced their arrival with the usual clatter of their long beaks. They were the only constant in my life. I was grateful for their loyalty and resumed my one-way dialogue, telling them all the things that had happened to me during that long, cold winter and felt better for it.

Polish workers appeared from Elbing to collect the bricks from the rubble of the burned down buildings in Niederhof. The city was being rebuilt, and materials were scarce.

I climbed up the weather-cracked staircase that led to the *Gasthaus* facade one last time before they tore it down. While sitting there, I saw a man striding along the highway, his gait labored and his progress slow. "Father" flashed through my mind.

I jumped up and cried out, "Papa!" and flew toward him, every nerve in my body tense with excitement. I held out my open arms shouting, "Papa! Papa!"

Hot tears of happiness streamed down my cheeks. The man stopped and watched me, but I kept running. Then I, too, stopped dead and stared at him in horror. He looked grotesque. Big bulging eyes protruded from his emaciated face. His unkempt gray hair and matted beard reached his chest and slumped shoulders. His trembling arms and hands seemed to have a life all of their own. His head jerked as he addressed me in German, "Don't be afraid, little girl. I won't hurt you."

I wanted to run, but he had called me a girl when everyone else called me a boy. I stared at him, openmouthed.

"Don't be afraid," he repeated. "Are there any Germans in this village?"

"There used to be a lot of them, but they've all run away."

"Well, where are your parents? Where do you live?"

I pointed to the farm, "I live over there with the Ilowskis. My parents are dead."

"Do you think the Ilowskis will give me something to eat? I have not had any food in days."

"Maybe," I said, uncertain, and added, "They understand German."

I followed him as he shuffled toward the farm. Even from behind, he looked freakish, and I was relieved he was not my father. When he reached the back door, he straightened his stooped shoulders and knocked. Pani opened the door, gasped, and tried to slam the door in his face, but the man moved fast. With an agility and strength I did not expect from him, he pushed a knee and fist against the door and shouted, "May God's wrath come down on you if you don't give this poor hungry man something to eat." Pani crossed herself and relaxed her grip on the door handle. "May the whole Ilowski family rot in hell," he continued, "if you don't show mercy on this pitiable man." I had told him their name, and he used it effectively. He had tapped into Pani's superstitious nature and her fear of God. He frightened her into being charitable.

She gestured for him to sit down at the kitchen table. Dorota brought him bread and a cup of milk. He ate slowly. Milk ran down his tangled beard as he drank. He smacked his lips between bites and wiped his beard with his frayed sleeve. When he had finished, he rose with slow, deliberate movements, turned to Pani, and asked for another piece of bread to sustain him the rest of the day, which Dorota was quick to hand him. After he had gone, Pani crossed herself again and seemed relieved to have him out of the house.

Dorota grabbed a dishcloth and busily wiped the table and chair the man had occupied; as an afterthought, she gave the door handle a thorough cleaning as well. Pani fled into the living room and recited the Jesus and Mary prayers that went with those beads Kashia had told me about.

Around Easter, news spread in Niederhof that a high church official would be making a pilgrimage through the area. The entire Ilowski household was aflutter. Pani declared it an event of enormous importance. Nobody knew the exact route this "holy man" would take, but she hoped it would lead through Niederhof, past our farm. For an entire week, she stayed off her couch and helped wash windows, beat dust out of the rugs, and scrubbed and polished floors. Even the stable got a good cleaning. When the big day drew near, Kashia, Walek, Stashek, and I gathered wild flowers to scatter along the highway in the dignitary's path.

Then Pani heard that the bishop's route would end at the church in the village before Niederhof. She persuaded Pan to take the family there with his horse and wagon so that his holiness could bless them all. The problem was Stashek, who was in bed with a fever. He threw a tantrum when Pani told him he had to stay home with me. No bribe or promise pacified him, so Dorota had to stay home, too. I sensed it was not going to be a good day for me and fled to my storage room, but for once she took out her frustration on her little brother. Stashek screamed for his mother, but he was too sick to keep it up for long, and soon the house grew quiet.

"Eva, where are you?" Dorota called. She sat by the kitchen table and stared out the window, wringing her hands as if she did not know what to do. "I've never seen a bishop. I really wanted to go," she said. "You know, it's special to be blessed by a bishop. He is very powerful and helps our prayers get to God." She fought back her tears. I did not feel one bit sorry for her. But she had put a new twist on things. It was so confusing—God and Jesus, Pani's Virgin Mary, and now this bishop, who had a direct line to God. I was tempted to tell Dorota about my Bible book but held back.

As soon as I could get away, I headed for my hiding place in the barn.

"Is anyone home around here?" A female voice called to me from behind. I spun around. A woman in a long black skirt and frilly red blouse stood before me. She looked like she had stepped right out of my exotic fairy-tale books. A magic fairy, flashed through my mind; she's come for me.

"Well, can't you talk? Is there anyone home here besides you? The whole village seems deserted. Where is everybody?"

"They went to … to look at the bishop. Dorota's … Dorota's home," I stuttered and stared. If she was not a magic fairy, then she was an alien queen, at the very least, I thought, while I admired the sparkling silver chains around her waist and neck.

"What are you staring at?" she asked. "I won't bite you."

Dorota met her at the door, equally taken in.

"You want your fortune told? For some eggs I'll tell you your future," the gypsy woman said. She added, "Throw in a loaf of bread, and I'll tell you about the man you'll marry."

Dorota let the woman into the laundry kitchen but barred her from the house. The woman sat down on the hard cement steps, reached for Dorota's hands, turned Dorota's palms up, and took her on a journey into the future. The woman spoke so convincingly that I felt sure she was also some sort of sorceress who could make everything she said come true. When Dorota disappeared to get the payment she had promised the gypsy, the woman motioned for me to kneel in front of her and reached for my open palms. She studied my sore-covered hands and ran her palms over mine as though trying to wipe them clean for a better look.

"Tell me, tell me," I begged. "Will my father ever came back?"

"Oh, *Dziewczyna*, little girl. So young and so many tears." She shook her head, looked at me with her deep dark eyes, and said, "Your father won't be back, and neither will your mother. But don't worry; they'll come for you." She stroked my hands reassuringly but said no more, and I was too shy to ask. Dorota reappeared, pushed me aside, and said, "I'm not paying for her."

I puzzled over the gypsy's words. How could she have known Mother could not come back, and what had she meant by, don't worry they'll come for you? Did "they" mean my dead parents and would I, too, soon die? I shuddered at the thought of dying and realized how much I wanted to live.

CHAPTER TWELVE

WITH MY BROTHER GONE AND Walek in school, Pan now took me with him into the field. He usually disappeared for a while and returned, staggering, sometimes too drunk to lift the pitchfork. At those times, I feared him. But usually he just collapsed under a tree and slept it off.

When planting time came, the whole family pitched in. Even Walek and Kashia had to help after school, under much protest. Suddenly, they had mountains of homework.

Dorota let the cows out to pasture for the summer, and I no longer had to muck the stable. I had not yet graduated to the milking stage, but Dorota dropped hints that next winter she would teach me. Dismayed to hear her make plans for me that far into the future, I made up my mind that, if Henry showed up again, I would not let him get away without me. But almost three months had passed since I saw him, and it did not look like he would be back.

When Pani heard a traveling priest was coming to the neighboring village church to hold mass, she grew excited. Ever since the bishop's visit, when she had gotten close enough to his holiness to kiss the hem of his robe, she talked of little else. This time, Pan refused to hitch his tired horse to the wagon to take her. So she, Kashia, and Walek walked the four kilometers. Dorota had to stay home again because Stashek could not walk that far. After Pani left, Pan mounted his "tired" horse and rode off in the opposite direction.

More relaxed than usual, Dorota disappeared into her "treasure room" in the attic and returned with Mother's parlor curtains draped over her arm.

"Eva, in which room do these go?" she asked.

"In the parlor. They were Mother's summer curtains," I explained, resentfully.

"Well, let's put them up. I want to surprise Mother."

We had no ladder to reach the top of the tall, narrow windows. Dorota took a kettle from the kitchen, turned it upside down across the wide windowsill, and had me hold onto it while she climbed on top, holding a hammer in one hand. The kettle wobbled, she lost her balance, and she crashed to the floor. Scared, I ran for the door. Dorota, unhurt, jumped quickly to her feet. The hammer whizzed past me, skimmed my shoulder, hit the door, and landed on the floor with a loud thump.

"I'm going to get you for this! I'm going to get you for this!" she screamed, as though I had deliberately caused her to fall.

Terrified, I fled to the barn and crawled into my hiding place. I looked through my peephole and called on God to protect me from Dorota, certain she had not meant to miss. She did not follow me, and I did not come out of hiding until after Pani returned.

WEEDS STARTED TO TAKE OVER Mother's garden. A lone daffodil found its way onto one of the Russians' graves and made an indiscriminate stand. The sun worked its magic, and a new growing cycle began.

One Sunday, after a heavy rainstorm, Walek found a human skull in the ditch along the highway. I could not look at it without breaking out in goose bumps. Later, I heard Pan and Pani talking about how other farmers had made similar finds in their fields.

That evening, I saw the living manifestation of the invisible world of ghosts, spirits, and phantoms staring at me from the shadows of my cot. Walek's hollow-eyed, gray skull rested comfortably on my pillow. My blood turned to ice, and my legs stayed solidly anchored to the floor. I held onto the door handle and screamed as I had never screamed before, while Walek and Dorota snickered behind me. When life returned to my legs, I made a wild dash for the barn and buried myself deep in the straw.

I spent the night there. Kashia called for me several times, but I did not answer. In the morning, I felt everyone's curious eyes on me. Perhaps they thought I had gone mad. I probably was getting ever closer to that fine line between sanity and insanity. However, at the time, it seemed more like a nightmare from which I could not awaken.

I did not return to my room until Kashia swore the skull was gone.

Henry's continued absence convinced me I was the only German remaining in the area. But I was mistaken. A young German woman appeared at our door one day and asked Pan for work. She spoke some Polish, and he engaged her on the spot. I was beside myself with happiness when he brought a mattress from the attic and put it in my room.

I am not sure I ever learned the woman's real name, but the Ilowskis called her Niemiecka, the Polish word for German woman. Her meager possessions consisted of a red and white checkered pillowcase containing a few items of clothing. No more than thirty years old, she had that unkempt, neglected, drab look about her that all the young German women had tried so desperately to achieve when the first raping Russians had arrived. Finally, I had someone to whom I could pour out my heart.

That first evening, when we were alone in our room, the questions spilled out of me, but she interrupted me and said, "Tomorrow. I'm too exhausted to talk."

Niemiecka worked hard, and Pan was pleased. Every day we toiled side by side, and every night we had long, whispered conversations. She came from Elbing.

"There used to be a lot of Germans from Elbing here in Niederhof, but they've all disappeared. How come you're still here?" I asked.

"It's probably the same reason why you're here. It's a long story."

Night after night, we talked before going to sleep. She told me that there still were pockets of Germans scattered throughout the countryside, trying to survive by going from village to village and farm to farm, hoping to work for food.

One night, she told me her story. Although tragic, it did not differ from the many other horrible tales I had overheard the Germans in Steglitz tell. She had never married and had worked for the electric works in Elbing. She had two younger brothers, both soldiers, who had fought at the Russian front. The younger was reported missing in action just days before the Russians marched into the city. She knew nothing of the older brother but feared that he, too, had become a casualty.

The day the Russians entered Elbing, she was at work "trying to keep the city lit," as she sarcastically put it. When she heard shooting in the street, she abandoned her post and tried to get home. People screamed and ran in all directions. She threaded her way through back alleys of a city in flames, stumbling over dead bodies, animals, and turned-over wagons. It took her two hours for what normally was a thirty-minute leisurely walk. She made it home, terribly shaken but unharmed. She found her hysterical mother, who minutes earlier had witnessed a tank run over her husband. The father had escaped from mandatory service at the home front and had come home to round up the remnants of his family and flee. He had run into the street to rescue a screaming child from an abandoned baby buggy, when a tank, Russian or German, she could not tell, appeared through the dense smoke and ran over both. The mother and daughter had fled to the nearest underground shelter. The Russians showed up, dragged the women from the cellar, and mass raped them. Niemiecka managed to hide. When the city turned quiet, mother and daughter ventured above ground, only to find their home a pile of smoldering rubble. Then followed the painful struggle to find food and stay hidden from the raping Russians. The mother contracted pneumonia and died, leaving Niemiecka the sole survivor of her family. Within a period of three months, she had lost two brothers, her mother and father, her home, and all her possessions. The only thing of value she had hung onto was her wristwatch, and that she had kept cleverly hidden in the hem of her dress. She later traded it with the Poles for a bag of potatoes and a loaf of bread.

"So you want to know why I'm still here. Like you, I had nothing to sell to the Poles with which to buy my way out of here. I've roamed the countryside for many months and walked from village to village. It was always the same. They let me stay and work. You slave all day for one measly meal, and if you're lucky, they let you sleep in their barn, and the husband leaves you alone. If you're not so lucky, you get raped in the bargain, and then the wife finds out and kicks you out."

She stopped abruptly. I wanted her to keep talking and tell me more. So I talked instead. I told her what I knew about rape and made it sound like I knew a lot more than I did. She gave me a surprised look. "You mean ... did a ... did a soldier," she hedged around, "did a soldier ever touch you?"

"Yes, one of them put a hole through my dress with the dagger at the end of his gun. It went all the way to my skin. I was scared to death."

She sighed, relieved, and asked, "What do you know about rape anyway?"

"A soldier raped my mother before she died," I said. "I saw him do it." I reasoned that would remove her reservation about the subject, and it did, because she continued her story. "The last farm I worked on was the worst, even though the food was plentiful. I was starved and felt like I had arrived in *Schlaraffenland.* When I got my strength back and started to look better, the man of the house took notice. In the middle of one night, he slipped into my room, gagged me, and raped me. He said he would kill me if I told his wife. When he did it a second time, I did tell his wife and got away from there as fast as I could. I walked a night and a day until I was exhausted."

She had talked to the ceiling, but now she turned to me and asked, "What is Pan like?"

"He has a mean temper and beats his wife a lot," I reassured her, thinking that a man who beat his wife would not be interested in raping other women.

"Oh, dear. Here we go again. I hope he'll leave me alone. You stay by my side, Eva! You hear?"

Pleased that she thought I could protect her from Pan, I clung to her like a cocklebur.

We became a team. All day, we pulled weeds in the field, and in the evenings we sawed wood. The dull blade pinched and buckled. We struggled and made little progress.

"How long do you think it will take us to cut all those logs?" I asked Niemiecka.

"Too long for me. I don't intend to be around here that long."

"Will you take me with you?" I pleaded. "Please, please don't leave without me. I won't be in your way. I can do many things, and I know I can walk a whole night and day like you. I did it when the Russians took our cows and made us drive them to another village. I really can walk a long way. Please … I don't want to stay here."

She stopped and looked at me. She was thinking and took her time to answer. "Look, Eva, I'm not going to leave tomorrow. We'll wait until the time is right, and then we'll leave together."

"You promise?"

"Yes, Eva; don't worry. There is nothing we can do right now. We don't have any money or food, and Germany is very far from here. We can't get there without either."

That sounded believable, and I trusted her.

CHAPTER THIRTEEN

NIEMIECKA APPEARED AT A CRITICAL time in my life and helped me get my bearings back. I decided the gypsy woman had meant Niemiecka when she had said that someone would come for me.

One day, while weeding the potato field, we heard loud, ear-piercing screams coming from the house. Walek came racing across the field stark naked, arms flailing in the air, jumping from one foot to the other as though navigating a bed of hot coals. Both of his legs were beet-red from knees to ankles. What had happened to him? I wondered, with malicious joy in my heart.

Pani rushed him home and got clothes on him. The rest of the day, he stalked around the farm, calling on dear Jesus for help.

Later that evening, Kashia told me that Walek had decided to try out the new bathtub Pan had brought home the week before. He asked Kashia to boil more water for him, which she did and then poured over his legs.

The next morning, oozing blisters covered Walek's legs. Serves you right, I thought, and hoped he would be crippled for at least as long as I was there.

In the evening, I raised the issue of God with Niemiecka. I broached the subject carefully, because I sensed from our nightly conversations she did not have a good relationship with him either.

"Do you think God finally punished Walek for being so mean?" I asked.

She ignored me. I changed my approach and said, "I wish God had punished Dorota instead. She's a lot meaner than Walek. You know, she threw a hammer at me and almost killed me. If Kashia had poured that boiling water on her legs, it would slow her down a lot."

Obviously thinking other thoughts, Niemiecka responded with a short "Hmm."

"I have a Bible book hidden in the barn. It says in there that God punishes people for their meanness," I persisted.

That stirred Niemiecka into a response, but it was not what I hoped for. "Look, Eva, forget about God," she said, all agitated. "Do you think for one minute that if this God of yours cared about you, he would have let all these terrible things happen to you? You're only a kid. What have you done? He took your parents, your brothers and sister, and now he allows these people to beat you to a pulp and starve you to death."

Niemiecka sat up at the edge of her bed and worked herself into a bitter tirade, and I regretted having brought up the subject, for she was about to destroy the little faith in God I had so recently acquired.

"Eva, Eva," she pleaded. "God has forgotten us a long time ago. We mean nothing to him. Nothing. No one person should have to suffer and endure as much as we have. Your Bible book is a fairy tale, one long fairy tale. Remember that."

I understood what she tried to tell me. This God, Jesus, Virgin Mary, and prayer business required blind faith, of which I had next to none. The Ilowskis were real. My life with them was real. Their hatred of all that was German was real. Niemiecka was real, and I put all my faith and trust in her.

She got more and more upset every time we heard the key turn in the lock of our door. "Do they think we are prisoners?" she said one night. "If I wanted to get away from here, I'd just walk away in bright daylight. Isn't it enough that they make us work like field oxen and throw us morsels of food like animals? She's afraid Pan will come after me." She looked at me and added, "Where is that God of yours now? What if the house burns down during the night? Will she remember to unlock the door?"

I was tempted to remind her that I had not referred to God as my God, but merely wanted information. However, her mention of fire alarmed me. I remembered the last thunderstorm and asked, "Do you think there will be a thunderstorm during the night?"

"What does that have to do with all of this?"

"Oh, nothing. It's just that I'm scared of thunder and lightning."

As long as she did not make the connection, I was not about to mention fire again, which suddenly seemed a real possibility.

I lay awake for a long time, disturbed and troubled by Niemiecka's mounting reaction to being locked in during the night. I wondered if she planned to get away. Would she keep her promise and take me with her? I sent a little prayer to God. It was more a reminder that if he really was up there, and he really had forgotten us, to take another look and see that we were still around and needed help.

I slept fitfully and kept waking up from one terrifying nightmare only to get pulled into another, more horrifying predicament. My dreams centered on Niemiecka; she was always running and I was always chasing after her, with an ever-widening distance between us until she disappeared over the horizon. I woke up in a cold sweat and listened for her rhythmic breathing. Reassured of her presence, I slipped back into a helpless state of immobility, of running but not moving, of shouting but with the sound stuck in my throat, of putting my arms around her but having her evaporate in my embrace.

When night finally gave way to morning, Niemiecka let out a loud sigh. A stream of gray light revealed she was awake, tossing, turning, and periodically letting out an agonized moan. She got out of bed and tried the door, but she found it as locked as it had been the evening before. "Those damn people," she cursed. "How is one to go and pee?"

She pounded on the door and shouted, "Let me out of here! Unlock this door!"

She tried to pull the window open despite the iron bars, but it was stuck from years of disuse. She sat down on the edge of her bed and rocked back and forth, mumbling, "I've got to relieve myself. If they don't unlock that door, I'm going to have an accident."

She paced the floor like a caged animal and made another attempt to force the door open by slamming into it with her whole body. "Open the door," she screamed. "I'm desperate!"

The house remained quiet.

Niemiecka finally squatted between our beds and relieved herself on the floor. I watched, amazed, and wondered where all that liquid came from as the puddle under her grew into a small lake. A steaming rivulet inched its way toward the door, accumulated at the threshold, found the lowest, most worn-down part, and disappeared under the door into the hallway. Horrified, I wondered what consequences Niemiecka would have to suffer from this act of desperation and dreaded the approach of day.

Niemiecka fell back into bed, gave a relieved sigh, and talked to the ceiling in half sentences. "It's humiliating to have to … If they think they can keep me prisoner … It's not enough that they make you work like … I'm not staying here one more …"

I remained quiet and listened for clues as to what she intended to do once Pani unlocked that miserable door. Suddenly, the key clicked, Pani entered the room, stepped right into the ill-omened puddle, and all hell broke loose. She turned to me with a vile harangue of words and came down on me with her fists. Holding my arms protectively over my head, I cried out, "I didn't do it. I didn't do it. Niemiecka did it." Pani kept pouncing on me. Taken aback by the strength behind those powerful blows, I pleaded with Niemiecka, "Tell her I didn't do it! Tell her it was you!" But Niemiecka watched in silence and made no attempt to come to my rescue. When Pani had regained her composure, she pointed to the floor and said, "Now, clean up this mess, you pig!"

I did not move but stared at her defiantly, nodded toward Niemiecka, and said, "She did it. Let her clean it up."

To my astonishment, Niemiecka said, "Okay, okay. She's been punished enough. I'll clean up after her," and went for a bucket of water and a rag.

I watched Niemiecka mopping the floor, avoiding eye contact with me, saying nothing.

She did not talk to me all day. But I stuck to her side. After supper, we tended to the animals and finally ended up in our room. I hoped Pani would show up soon and lock us in so Niemiecka could not slip away while I slept. I asked her, "Do you think they'll lock the door again after what happened this morning?"

"They better not," she said and added, "but I suppose I should make another trip to the outhouse just in case."

She was gone a long time. I became apprehensive. Time stretched into eternity. Then the door opened, but it was Pani, checking on us.

"Where is Niemiecka?"

"She went to the outhouse, but she has been gone a long time," I said.

"Go look for her!" Pani ordered.

Niemiecka was nowhere to be found. She had slipped away without me. Hysterical, I paced the floor and admonished God, Niemiecka, Frau Leitzel, Frau Weber, Henry, and Mother for deserting me. With Niemiecka's disappearance, the last flicker of hope died within me.

I lay on my cot crying, waiting for sleep to carry me to the magic land of forgetfulness. Pani did not lock the door that night, and I hoped Niemiecka would still come back. When the first morning light crept through the iron bars, I listened for her breathing, but the room was silent, and her bed was empty. More tears welled up inside me, and by the time Dorota appeared to call me to do my chores, I had worked myself into another convulsive crying spell. I could not stop. Dorota glared down at me with a disgusted, puzzled look on her face, saying nothing. She turned her back on me and slammed the door.

Angry, Pan blamed Pani for the loss of Niemiecka's valuable free labor.

"You should have chased useless Eva out. Instead, you let a good worker get away. Now you and Dorota better work your asses twice as hard. I can't do it all myself."

Something happened inside me after Niemiecka's disappearance. I felt like a spectator rather than a participant in life. I spent hours in my hiding place in the barn and only came out for meals. With merely a tenuous grip on reality, I no longer worried about punishment or what form it might take. When Dorota found me in the barn, she threatened to drag me into the house if I did not come willingly. I stared her down, defiantly. When it looked as if she would beat me, I jabbered nonsense with profanities I had learned from Pan mixed in. She backed off and returned to the house.

Dorota's reaction surprised me. She had always been quick to get physical with me; now she not only left me alone, but she fled from me. Blabbering nonsense and acting like an idiot became easier and easier for me. By tapping into the Ilowskis' superstitious nature, I had stumbled into something very powerful.

A blaspheming lunatic in their midst proved too much for them. They made no demands on me. I showed up for meals, which usually were already set out in my room. I wandered around the farm, communicated with the animals, and talked to the storks more openly than before. I desperately wanted something to happen and, in a way, was challenging fate. I wanted the Ilowskis to act for me, because I no longer could. I knew they would not put up with my mutinous behavior for long.

I was sitting behind the stable, watching a few ragged clouds float gently across the incandescent sky, when Dorota's shrill voice pierced through the air and my heart. "Eva, get over here!" she yelled.

Standing in the doorway, both hands on her hips, eyes glaring, she said, "Get in the house! Mother has something to say to you!"

Pani was waiting in the hallway, and she pushed me into the storage room. A pitiful heap of tattered clothing, including my dirty green sweater and the baggy pants I had worn all winter, lay on the floor. Papers were scattered on top. They appeared to be legal documents. Pani pointed to the floor and said, "Pick up your stuff and get out of here!"

I glared at her and groped for something cutting to say, but my mind was a large void.

Pani stomped out of the room. I sat at the edge of my cot and stared at the papers. The names Herbert and Anna Rapp stuck out in bold letters. I picked up the document but could make no sense of the writing. Instead, I held it in my hand and kept repeating, "I am Eva Rapp—Eva Rapp—Rapp—Rapp."

Then, a voice inside me cried, "Get out of here, fast!"

I stripped Niemiecka's checkered pillowcase off her pillow, gathered up the things on the floor, slung the bundle over my shoulder, and walked out of the room. Kashia stood in the laundry kitchen and called out in a soft voice, "Good-bye, Eva." That was the only friendly gesture in this dark moment. I received it gratefully, like a blessing.

A bright sun stood above the rooftops as I sleepwalked out of the yard with an iron determination not to cry. I did not know where to go or to whom I could turn. The Germans were gone, and I had developed a deep distrust and fear of all Poles. I crossed the road. I stopped and looked back at our house and the Russian graves that had thrown such long, menacing shadows over my existence. I realized the dead soldiers under those weed-covered mounds had been harmless all along. They only represented a threat in my vivid imagination. A feeling of overwhelming lightness settled in my being.

I walked along the highway, sure of only two things. I was eleven years old and homeless, but I was free.

CHAPTER FOURTEEN

I HEADED IN THE DIRECTION of Elbing, knowing I could probably get there on foot. From there, I would try to find a way to get to Germany. All the Germans I heard of who had disappeared over the past two years went to Elbing and made their escape from there. None came back. Hopefully, I would not return either.

Hunger directed my feet as I turned into the road leading past the bakery where my brother had stolen the bread. Maybe there was another loaf sitting on that counter just waiting for me to snatch up. But the bakery door was closed. My mind raced. Where to go? How far exactly was Elbing? Would I get there before dark? Where would I spend the night? While thinking these thoughts, my legs developed a will of their own, and before I knew it, I was knocking on Schotka's door.

"My God, Eva, is that you?" she exclaimed, startled. She took a step back. "What have they done to you? What happened to your hair? Dear Jesus, you are a sight!"

She looked smaller than I remembered, her face narrower, and her features more chiseled.

"Pani kicked me out," I said, quivering, tears close to the surface. She reached for my hand and pulled me into her cozy kitchen. They had just finished their midday meal, and the seductive aroma of recently prepared food still lingered in the air. Her husband had returned to his job, and his sister was not home. I greedily eyed the empty plates and the loaf of bread on the table.

Schotka pushed me into a chair and said, "You look like you haven't eaten in months. Let's get some food into you. And your clothes! They're filthy!"

I gobbled the food down as if afraid someone would steal it.

Schotka watched in silence, finally shook her head, and said, "Slow down, Eva. There's more." But I did not slow down until she refilled my plate and handed me another slice of bread.

Then, she poured a kettle of hot water into the wash basin, peeled off my clothes, and gave me the most thorough scrubbing I had ever received. I savored the warm sensation of her strong, but gentle hands, and I closed my eyes, pretending it was Mother caressing me. So much time had passed since anyone had touched me without hurting me, I wanted to throw my wet arms around her and hold her close. When she wrapped a towel around me, I could no longer hold back the tears and pressed my face into her slim body. I could feel her ribs like the ruts in a well-traveled road. She had lost weight since I last saw her over two years ago.

"We'll have to wash everything," she said gathering up my clothes. "That's the only way we'll get rid of the lice you probably brought with you."

When her baby cried in the other room she said, "Come see my little boy. He's nine months old now. Isn't he beautiful?" He smiled, not at her, but at me. It made me feel warm all over.

She turned to me and said, "He likes you." Those were sweet words. Somebody liked me.

When Schotka's husband came home, he looked surprised to see me, but showed no sign of displeasure. He picked up his son, seeming not to give me another thought.

Their tight quarters consisted of the kitchen and two rooms, one buried under the sister's sewing aids, patterns, half-finished garments, and scraps of material; the other belonged to Schotka, her husband, and their baby. I could see there would be little room for me, and I was apprehensive as to how the evening would play itself out. When Schotka made a bed for me on the floor of their room next to the baby's crib, I was much relieved.

I awoke to Schotka shaking me at the shoulders. "Eva, stop crying. You're keeping us awake."

I threw my arms around her and could not stop sobbing. She held and rocked me back and forth.

"I want my mother," I whimpered.

Schotka wrapped a sweater around my shoulders and said, "Come, I want to show you something."

We went out into the moonless night and walked to the edge of the meadow. She put one arm around me and pointed to the sky with the other. "Look up there, Eva. See all those stars? They are the beautiful souls of the dead, and your mother is among them."

I now thought of nothing but how to please Schotka, her husband, and his sister. I polished the husband's shoes each evening, diapered and fed their boy, and helped the sister sew buttons and snaps on the garments she made.

However, dark clouds were gathering in Schotka's life. She had to go to the hospital for surgery.

She was gone a long time. When her husband brought her home, I could see both her breasts were gone. She spent the next few days in bed, and I worked hard to show her how useful I could be. I cleaned house, washed clothes, and took the baby for long walks. Schotka marveled at how competent and reliable I was, giving me a feeling of security.

One evening, a young pregnant woman knocked at our door. Schotka greeted her like a friend, turned to me, and said, "Eva, you go with Pani Kolski. She wants you to work for her!" She handed me my things in the checkered pillow case and said with averted eyes, "I'm sorry, but we just don't have room for you."

I wrapped my arms around the bundle, held it close to me, and followed the woman, feeling as if I had just been expelled from paradise, like Adam and Eve in my Bible stories.

I walked alongside the woman, wondering what awaited me. She was very heavy, but she was surprisingly light and fast on her feet. Her bulging stomach stuck out from under a much-too-tight dress.

"So your name is Eva?" she inquired as though she doubted what Schotka had told her.

I nodded.

"How old are you, Eva?"

"I don't know," I lied.

She gave me a startled glance and repeated, "You don't know?"

"I forgot. My mother is dead and my father has not come back yet. I can't ask them." I thought hinting at my father's eminent return would keep her from mistreating me.

The woman and her husband lived on the outskirts of Niederhof in a small, lonely dwelling near the railroad crossing. They were poor.

My heart sank as I surveyed the sparsely furnished room. A red brick built-in corner stove, used for cooking and heating, dominated the room. The worn wooden floors reflected years of neglect and traffic. Two plates and cups along with some utensils sat on a shelf next to the stove. A sooty cooking pot and cast-iron frying pan hung from hooks below. The austerity reflected in the room dashed my last hope for an easier life. Would I have to sleep in the stable again with the animals, I wondered uneasily?

Pani walked me through the work routine she expected of me. The drinking water had to be hauled from a well across the street. They had brought up human bones from the well behind their house. "We can't drink that water for a long time," she said. "We can only use it for watering."

A chill ran up my spine. Ghosts followed me everywhere.

Pan Kolski was just removing the harness from his only horse when Pani turned me over to him. A handsome man, even in his dirty, torn clothes, he looked as though he did not belong in the bleak surroundings I faced. I sensed him computing my worth as he quietly sized me up.

"You understand Polish?" he asked, chewing on a blade of grass.

"Yes."

"You're awfully small. How old are you?"

"I don't know."

"Where're your parents?"

"My mother is dead, and Father hasn't come back yet," I said, and added for emphasis, "but he will."

He studied me wearily but asked no more questions. Instead, he showed me how to care for the animals, a pitiful small and mangy-looking menagerie consisting of a horse, a pig, two goats, and a few scraggly chickens. I followed Pan around until Pani called us for supper.

A delicious aroma of fried bacon drifted from the house. The table was set for only two people. Pani heaped fried potatoes on the two plates and had me fill the cups with goat milk. They sat down to eat. I stood and watched, near tears and drooling. Please, God, don't let this be a repeat of the Ilowskis, I implored in my heart. After a while, Pani put down her fork, pushed the plate toward me, and said, "Here, Eva, you eat now!"

She rose, refilled the cup with milk, and handed it to me with a slice of bread. Then, I understood. Those were the only plates and utensils they owned.

The Kolskis had no electricity, and bedtime came early for them. When dusk gave way to night, Pani threw a pillow on the couch, spread a blanked over it, and said, "This is going to be your bed, but first go wash up by the well."

I shivered, thinking of the human bones. When I did not budge, she said, "Come, child, I'll go with you. We'll both wash up."

She brought up a bucket of water from the well and set it between us. She motioned for me to strip off my clothes, while she did the same. I was dumbstruck. She wore no undergarments and stood before me totally oblivious of her pregnant nakedness. I had never seen a nude adult, not to mention a pregnant woman. I stared at her huge, bulging stomach and enormous breasts. She handed me a cup, turned her back to me, and said, "Here, pour some water over me."

This ritual lasted but a minute. She picked up her dress, dried herself with it, and turned towards the house. Pan stood in the doorway, thumbs tucked under his suspenders and smiling. He put his arm around her heavy waist, and they disappeared into the house.

Left standing alone in the dark by that menacing well, I picked up my dress and ran after them. I heard Pan and Pani talking behind a closed door, which I had assumed to be a storage room but now realized was their bedroom. Their human presence so close comforted me.

Sleep would not come. One angry thought followed another. I felt helplessly bound to this state of indentured servitude because of my young age. I beseeched my Bible God to make me grow up fast. As I noticed a few stars through the little window above my bed, I felt grateful to Schotka. She had given me a precious gift by raising Mother to the heavens, where I could search for her among the stars. A whole legion of frogs sprang to life and took over the warm night. Finally, I fell asleep.

Pani shook me awake in the early morning hours.

"Get up, child. Get dressed and go help Pan."

A crackling fire burned in the stove while Pani prepared some kind of porridge. Pan had seen to most of the animals when I joined him. I merely had to haul water to their troughs. He was a taciturn man and gave his orders in grunts and single words rather than in complete sentences.

Like the evening before, Pan and Pani ate breakfast first, while I waited my turn. After breakfast, Pan hitched his horse to the wagon, and we all drove to the field.

I shivered in the misty, raw air, sitting among the potato sacks behind Pan and Pani. We stopped at a field that was already plowed and began the planting. Pan dug a hole with a hoe, Pani dropped a piece of potato into it, and I pushed the dirt back with my hands. We spent the entire day doing this; we did not return to the house until the sun started to edge down at the horizon, and the trees threw long shadows over the landscape.

We worked several days to get all the potatoes into the ground. After that, we planted turnips, sugar beets, and various kinds of grain. The weather held, and Pan seemed driven to get his crop into the ground before the next rain came and turned the fields into a sea of mud.

On Sundays we rested. I spent the afternoons at the railroad station. During my stay with Schotka, I had discovered that the station was not as frightening a place as I had thought. People stopped and talked to me, and sometimes they even wanted to know who I was and where I lived. I remained guarded, lied often, and never volunteered my German origin unless someone guessed it. I longed to join the children in their games but was not brave enough to approach them. My world was expanding, but fear remained deeply lodged in my heart.

CHAPTER FIFTEEN

THE KOLSKIS' PIG AND I started to eat well.

Pani's garden yielded a bountiful crop of tempting fresh vegetables and berries, and craving these things, I sneaked raw beans, peas, turnips, beets, radishes, carrots, onions, and greens. When the pig periodically escaped and ravaged the garden, I had a scapegoat and indulged even more freely.

However, the pig turned into a nuisance. No matter what contrivance Pan employed to keep it confined in its tight stall, it proved smarter than Pan and managed to get out and head straight for Pani's garden.

"You get out one more time, and I'll have your balls," Pan finally threatened.

I did not know what he meant, but from the sound of his voice it did not bode well for the stubborn pig. When I poured the slop into its trough that evening, I watched it guzzle down the gruel and felt sorry for it.

"You better behave, or Pan will cut off your balls," I reinforced his threat. It looked up and grunted with a hint of a grin on its snout. I was becoming attached to it.

WHEN SCHOOL LET OUT FOR the summer, Pani's sixteen-year-old brother arrived from the city to spend his vacation with us and help out on the farm. I disliked him instantly. He had a sullen disposition and shifty eyes. His shorn blond hair reminded me of the way the young Russian soldier recruits had looked. He was lazy. Pan had to prod him on to keep up with us in the field, and whenever he could, he shirked his chores off on me.

Pan set up a bed for him in the opposite corner from where I slept. I feared him and had trouble sleeping. Pan and he quarreled constantly. But Pani smoothed things out between them, only to have them start arguing again the next day.

When the pig got out during one night and trampled Pani's garden, she wept over the damage. We found it snoring between the vegetable beds, with a contented look on its snout. Pan picked the following Sunday for the "operation."

That morning, Pan added a whole cup of vodka to the pig's slop. It took only minutes before the pig fell on its side. Pan tied its front and hind legs together, handed the rope to the brother, and told him to keep the pig still. I was to hand him more vodka and rags when he asked for them. Then, Pan took the knife and reached between the pig's hind legs. I could not look. When the pig let out an ear-deafening squeal, I dropped the alcohol and rags, ran out of the stable, and hid behind the well. A few more squeals reached me, then silence. I thought they had killed the pig, just when I had started to befriend it.

After it stayed quiet for a while, I checked on my friend. The pig lay on its side, legs untied. Feeling sorry for it, I said, "At least you're still alive," all the while thinking it would probably end up on our dinner table eventually.

Two strong hands grabbed my shoulders, swirled me around, pushed me against the wall, and lifted me onto a wooden crate. I thought it was Pan, but it was Pani's brother. He held a pocketknife against my wildly pounding chest and pressed his strong body against mine. Memories of the Russian's pointed bayonet flashed through my mind as I felt the hard steel blade through my thin dress. I tried to scream, but he put his hand over my mouth and threatened, "You make one sound, and I'll cut out your heart!"

I could see the blood pulse through the temples in his red face. Breathing hard, he pressed one knee into my groin and held me pinned to the wall, while he lowered his pants with his free hand. He thrust his hard male organ between my thighs and I felt a warm liquid trickling down my legs. He released me within seconds, but I remained glued to the wall. He pulled up his pants and warned me, "I'll kill you if you say one word about this to them."

I looked into his cold, hard eyes and believed he would carry out his threat. He disappeared quickly and left me terrified.

He did not cause me any physical pain, and I did not know exactly what had occurred. Did it mean that I, too, would now have a baby grow in my stomach like Pani? I knew enough about procreation to sense this vile act had something to do with it, but I did not understand the mechanics. Panicked, I sat on the crate and joined the pig with my tears.

Pan was surprised to see me when he brought the pig's slop.

"What ... doing ... stable ...?"

I nodded towards the pig and said, "I'm keeping him company."

"Hmm ... house ... supper ... Pani ..."

Used to Pan's swallowing every other word, I followed him into the house. The brother was not there; he did not appear until much later. I looked at him accusingly. His face grew tense. I dreaded bedtime, knowing I would not be able to close my eyes with him in the same room.

"I'll slit your throat if you don't stop your whimpering," he later threatened from his bed. "You're keeping me awake."

I swallowed and, with every fiber in my body alert, kept careful watch on his corner of the room. Soaked in the sweat of fear, I lay ready to scream and run if he made the slightest move.

In the days that followed, I stayed close to Pani and Pan. My nights were living nightmares. As much as I watched out for the brother, he caught me off guard the following Sunday. He and Pan had gone to the neighboring village to check out some farm equipment for sale. Relieved, I revisited the pig. It was an attentive listener, and I appreciated that friendly grin on its face. Its occasional grunts made me think it understood my monologue. I did not notice the door open until I saw a shadow loom over me. I looked up, and there he was again, the devil. He pointed the shiny blade of his pocket knife against my chest and pressed one hand on my neck, constricting my breathing, and warned, "Don't you dare scream!"

I feared that if I made a sound he would surely use that knife and mutilate if not kill me. I submitted. He did not bother to drop his pants this time; he merely unbuttoned his fly and barely touched my thighs when it was all over. The act took only a minute, a terrifying minute. He vanished quickly with the same admonishment, snarling, "Don't you dare tell. I'll kill you for sure if you do!"

With rage in my heart, I sat on the crate, holding my knees to my chest, and vowed that the next time he came near me, I would scream so loudly they would hear me all the way at the station. However, I never had to act on my resolve. He came running out of the stable one evening, pants in hand, with Pan in pursuit with a pitchfork.

Pani rushed out of the house and stopped Pan from physically attacking her brother. The normally taciturn Pan would not calm down and continued to shout obscenities in full sentences after the long-gone offender. That night Pani went to bed crying. The brother did not return, and I spent a worry-free night. But in the morning, he was back in his bed. Pan did not speak to him, and we went to work in the field without him. When we came home, he was gone.

That evening, Pani went into labor. Pan hitched his horse to the wagon, swept her up, and raced to the hospital in Elbing, calling out, "Be sure to water and feed the animals."

They left while it was still light. As darkness slowly crept into the corners of the house, I panicked. I frantically looked for Pani's night candle; she had not used it in weeks, since it stayed light much longer. I could not find it.

The house came alive with creaks and moans, and all the prankish spirits of my imagination floated in through the keyhole. Even the rustling of the wind in the trees outside had an eerie quality about it. I saw those human bones assemble into a full skeleton and rise from the well. I crawled deeper under my covers. When I heard the clatter of a horse and wagon approach, I relaxed, thinking Pan was back. But the wagon passed the house, and the clop-clop of the horses hooves faded in the stillness.

I thought of the brother. What if he returned and found me alone? It was a notion more terrifying than all the ghosts and phantoms put together. I drifted in and out of sleep in a delirium-like state, and I prayed for the sun to rise and chase the demons away.

When dawn finally broke, I made up my mind that if Pan did not return during the course of the day, I would knock on Schotka's door, and if she turned me away, I would sleep on her doorsteps. But Pan returned in the early afternoon, the happy father of a little boy.

Pani's parents arrived while she was still in the hospital. They came by train, and Pan and I drove to the station with his horse and buggy to pick them up. We passed the time waiting for the late train in the crowded waiting room. Suddenly, I heard German spoken behind me. Startled, I shot around. A short, portly woman, who appeared to be the owner of the food concession, was giving orders in German to another woman who worked there. I wanted to approach the woman but was too shy and timid; I remained glued to the bench. The train arrived, and I had missed my chance.

The following day, Pan brought the new mother and infant home, and the grandparents went to stay with other relatives. I was surprised the Kolskis had kin in Niederhof. These relatives, a family of four, came to inspect the new arrival. They were Pani's aunt and uncle, and their two girls, Maria, who was about Dorota's age, and the much younger Magda were her cousins. I liked the girls right away. When they invited me to come and visit them the following Sunday, I was thrilled.

The grandparents came every day to help. The grandmother stayed with the mother and child while the grandfather helped in the field.

The brother's sexual assaults weighed heavily on my mind, and I pondered much about the mystery of conception and birth. I remembered the dead cow with a calf sticking half-way out of its rear and was petrified that such a thing might be awaiting me. I ran my hand over my stomach every day to make sure it had not grown overnight. I needed answers. Just how did a baby start in one's stomach? How did it get so big, and scariest of all, how did it get out? When I asked Pani, she seemed embarrassed and brushed me off with a blunt, "You're not old enough for those kinds of questions." So I continued to check my stomach for signs of expansion and lived with this new fear.

When Sunday came around, I rushed to the station where Magda and Maria lived. They seemed happy to see me. Their mother, a good natured, stout woman, handed me a piece of cake. It was not very sweet, yet it tasted like candy. Unfortunately, my visit was cut short. They expected company, and the piece of cake marked my dismissal.

Just knowing Magda and Maria gave me the much-needed confidence to face the other Polish children at the station. I no longer watched them from afar but walked boldly past them and sat on the cement steps, waiting for the German woman to come out of the building.

I sat there for what seemed like hours and watched people come and go, but she did not appear. A tall, dark-haired, kindly looking woman came out of the building, stopped, and asked in a friendly voice, "You've been sitting here all afternoon. Are you waiting for some one?"

"I'm waiting for the German woman who works here."

"She didn't show up for work today."

"Will she be back tomorrow?"

"Probably. Are you also German? Where do you live?" she asked, running her warm brown eyes up and down my person.

Ignoring her questions, I said, "Please tell her that I'm looking for her."

"What's your name?"

"Eva." Realizing the woman wouldn't know who I was, I added, "Tell her I just want to talk German with her."

"Hmm … I'll tell her when she comes back to work," she said and walked away.

I returned to the Kolskis full of hope and jubilant that a German woman actually existed.

Instead of going into the house, I went to a spot in the meadow behind the stable where the coltsfoot leaves grew tall. I lay down under the sheltering plants and watched the capricious sun disappear behind dark clouds. The giant leaves moved in the gentle breeze and tickled my face. Happy, I soon fell asleep.

I awoke to the sound of voices. Two boys stood over me. I did not move and feigned sleep. They deliberated over my identity. One voice said, "I think that's the Kolskis' German girl."

"German girl? Let's have some fun with her," the other voice said.

I felt a stick scrape my bare thighs as one of them raised my skirt. I pulled my knees close to my chin, moaned and groaned, and con- torted my body, faking pain. I pressed both hands into my stomach the way I had seen Fraulein Gretchen do with the Russians. I was about to add a few screams when one of them said, "Ah, leave her alone! She's just a heap of vermin."

One of the boys kicked me in my private parts before walking away. The blow hurt, but I silently thanked Fraulein Gretchen. Although I wasn't sure what kind of fun the boys had intended, I sus- pected it was of a sexual nature. I watched them disappear along the tree-lined highway and realized they were not little boys, but rather young teenagers.

New obstacles were appearing in my life. I missed the Patient. She would have given me the answers I needed. She had tried to enlighten us, but now that the terrible things she had talked about were happening to me, I could not remember any specifics. I sensed growing up would have drawbacks of a different nature.

CHAPTER SIXTEEN

WHEN PANI'S PARENTS ACCUSED PAN of having been too hard on their son, he blew up and shouted, "He's a lazy, good-for-nothing pervert. I don't ever want to see him under my roof again."

The parents departed that day.

Pan and I went into the field later than usual. Irritable, he cut the day short. When we returned, a car was parked along the highway by the house. My heart beat faster. I imagined Father had come for me in our Opel, and so I jumped off the wagon and ran into the house. A man much younger than Father sat by the table across from Pani, with papers spread in front of him. Deeply disappointed, I stopped in the doorway. Pani looked up and said, "Here she is. This is the girl."

Wild thoughts raced through my mind. A prince, an estranged relative, a caliph from *A Thousand and One Nights* has come for me just as the gypsy woman had predicted.

But the man had not come for me, only because of me. I needed to be registered. He looked at me and asked in a gruff voice, "Let's see now, your name is Eva Rapp?"

"Yes."

"What's your middle name?"

"I don't know."

"When is your birthday?"

"January twenty-one."

"What year were you born?"

"I don't know."

"How old are you?"

"Eleven."

He asked many more questions, some of which I could not

answer. Was Father a soldier? Did I have any living relatives in the area? How come I spoke Polish?

I started to cry.

My inquisitor softened, smiled, ran his hand across the short fuzz on my head, and asked, "What happened to your hair?"

"The Ilowskis cut it off."

He looked puzzled and asked, "Why did they do that?"

"I don't know," I said, too embarrassed to tell the truth.

"Ah, don't worry; it'll grow back," he said and reminded Pani not to delay having photos taken of me. He scooped up the papers and walked to his car. I ran after him and watched him drive away with a sinking heart.

Sleep would not come that night. Pani was evasive when I asked her what a registration was. I worried they were trying to adopt me.

On Sunday, Pani sent me to Magda's and Maria's house to ask them to take me to Elbing for the picture taking. She handed me a note and said, "I've written it all down. They'll know what to do. School's out, and one of the girls will take you."

I went to the station building first to seek out the German woman. Taking a deep breath, I kept my head down and entered the building. The friendly woman at the ticket counter sat behind the glass and said, "You're back. If you're looking for the German woman, she's sick. She hasn't come to work all week. Her girls came and told us."

"Sick?" I panicked, "How sick? When will she be back?"

"When she's able to get out of bed."

"Are you sure she'll be back?" I persisted.

She smiled and said, "I'm sure. What do you want from her, anyway?"

"I just want to talk to her."

A man with a hand full of money stood behind me. She pointed her chin toward the door and said, "Wait outside for me. I want to talk to you."

When she finally came out of the building, she said, "Come home with me. We'll have some cake."

She poured a glass of fresh milk and handed me a giant piece of cake with marble-sized streusel. She asked me to call her Roza, but without the polite form of Pani. I immediately felt closer to her, as though she were a relative. She told me about her little baby boy who was sleeping at a neighbor's house and invited me to come back the following Sunday to go walking with them.

I left feeling flattered by all the attention Roza paid me. On the way home, I dropped off Pani Kolski's note at Magda's house. The mother read it and stuck it into her apron pocket. She studied me for a minute and said, "If you're going to get your picture taken, we'll have to do something about your clothes. You can't go looking like that. Come back early tomorrow so the girls can fix you up. Magda will take you."

"Do you know why I have to get registered? Does it mean Pani Kolski will have to send me to school?" I asked, full of hope.

She gave me a blank look and shook her head. "I don't know about school, but you're German, and that's probably why you need to be registered."

The next day, I sneaked away immediately after breakfast. Magda and Maria were still in bed, but their mother said, "It's good you've come early. It'll take some time to clean you up."

Magda washed my hair and greased it with her father's pomade to get it to stay down. She reinforced it with two hairpins, one on each side, and glued them down with extra spittle.

The mother entered the kitchen with a red and white checkered dress draped over her arm and said, "Here, Eva, try this on. It should fit you."

I could not believe my eyes. It was such a beautiful dress with a pretty white collar and puffy short sleeves. I slipped it on and instantly felt transformed. Magda produced a pair of black patent leather shoes. They were too small and pinched, but I did not want to give them up. When Maria came into the kitchen, she exclaimed, "Eva, you look like a new girl."

"She does, indeed," the mother said. I blushed and felt my ego swell while I lapped up all the attention. I purred like a happy kitten and wanted to rub against all three of them, just the way Schnurribart used to do.

We boarded the train, and the wheels rolled towards Elbing. I watched the familiar villages fly by, familiar only on the surface. Underneath, everything was changed—the people, the language, even the fields. I caught a glimpse of my reflection in the window glass. Was that really me, that skinny girl, all neat and clean, in a beautiful dress with some semblance of hair? Every few minutes, I stole another peek to make sure I was not dreaming.

We pulled into the station. Although pockmarked with bullet holes, the building had survived the war. However, the heart of the city gaped like an open wound. Skeletal facades towered above deep holes and threatened to tumble down in the slightest breeze. We passed entire blocks that had no signs of rebuilding. Piles of broken concrete, shattered glass, twisted pipes, tangled wires, and metal lined the streets. Exposed inside staircases hung precariously from walls and were still used to reach the surviving upper floors. People coming in and out of partial houses made a ghostly sight.

The photographer's studio was in one of those half houses. A well-trodden path led over rubble. I feared the freestanding walls would collapse on top of us.

My photo session was short. Sit up straight, smile, click, done. The pictures would be ready the following week.

On the train home, I asked Magda, "Do you know why I have to get registered?"

"Because you're German."

"Do you think the Kolskis want to adopt me?"

"Why would they want to do that? They already have you."

When we returned to Niederhof, Roza sat behind the ticket counter and waved to us. Glad she got to see me in my fine clothes, I walked straighter and held my head higher. At Magda's house I had to give up my beautiful dress and shoes. All day, I had felt so proud and special, but now, back in my dirty, drab dress, I shrank back into my old, faint-hearted self.

On Sunday, I hurried back to the station, only to find the building empty and Roza not at her window. It was the time between trains. I stayed glued to the bench, waiting for the German woman to appear.

Two skinny, blond girls, younger than I, entered the building. Faces guarded, they tiptoed to the bench opposite mine. I guessed they were the woman's daughters that Roza had mentioned. Timid and shy, we sat in silence and scrutinized one another.

The door opened, and the mother came out. The girls jumped up and clung to her, while she squeezed them closer and put her arms around them. I, too, wanted to wrap myself around her. She looked up, smiled, and said, "You must be that little German girl who has been looking for me."

"I've been … I've been waiting for you. I … I just want to talk to you," I stuttered.

She appeared cautious.

"I work for the Kolskis near the railroad crossing. I just want to talk to you."

"Oh!" she said and invited me to walk a bit with them.

I accompanied them until we reached the narrow path to their village. I asked if all Germans had to get registered.

"There still are a lot of Germans around," she said. "But I never heard of anyone having to register. The Poles who come into the waiting room told me there are whole families scattered throughout the villages"

"I know my brother is in one of those villages. His name is Henry. Do you know him?"

"There used to be a couple of orphan boys in the next village, but I never knew their names. What's your name, anyway?"

"Eva."

"I'm Frau Leppe, and the girls are Gudrun and Gitte."

The girls promised to come earlier the next Sunday so we could play hopscotch behind the station, where the Polish kids would not bother us.

I returned to the Kolskis later than usual. Pani, busy canning, looked at me accusingly. "Where have you been? I told you we were going to can vegetables. I wanted you home."

I gave no excuse, but picked up her crying baby and walked him until he fell asleep in my arms. It earned me a forgiving smile.

CHAPTER SEVENTEEN

MAGDA DELIVERED MY PICTURES THE following week, three copies in all. The official did not come back for them, and Pani did not know what to do about it. I vacillated between anxiety and dread, uncertain what would happen to me if he did show up. Pani handed me one of the pictures and said, "Here, you can keep one. The man asked for only two."

"Why hasn't he come back?"

"He'll show up when he needs them," Pani replied. She shrugged her shoulders and added, "These things take time."

Meanwhile, Pani's garden flourished. The vegetables and berries needed to be harvested and preserved. We found a cache of glass jars and earthenware in the attic, a find more valuable than money, Pani said. We canned into the late hours each evening. But on Sunday, I slipped out after the midday meal while Pan and Pani rested.

"Where were you last Sunday?" Roza asked, happy to see me. "I waited for you."

"You weren't at the ticket window. I met Frau Leppe and her girls and walked home with them."

"Well, I'm glad you came today. Let's take Jurek for a walk," she said.

It was a warm summer afternoon with a cloudless sky. I felt light-hearted and happy in their company. While we walked along the deserted highway, Roza asked many questions about the Kolskis, why I was there, and what I did for them. She looked at her watch and said, "The next train will arrive soon. I've got to man the ticket counter."

Back at their apartment, she put Jurek in his crib and said, "Why don't you stay here and watch him until I'm done? I won't be long."

The fog lifted from my naive brain. Behind Roza's friendly kindness lurched a hidden agenda. When she noticed my hesitation, she said, "I really won't be long. We'll have some cake and milk when I get back."

I had a strong desire to please her, but I worried about getting back late and facing an angry Pan and Pani. I was relieved to hear the train pull out of the station and to see Roza appear shortly thereafter.

"I've been thinking, Eva," she said. "Why don't you come and stay with us? All you'll have to do is take care of Jurek while I work at the ticket counter. He likes you. I'll write to Mother and have her make new clothes for you. And shoes—you'll need shoes. Just think: you won't have to work in the field any longer, and you'll have time to play with Frau Leppe's girls."

To play again; those were magic words. I jumped at Roza's offer. We agreed I would get my things and come to her the next morning. I did not know how to tell the Kolskis. "I'm afraid Pan will beat me," I said.

"Just take your things and leave," Roza said. "They can't force you to stay."

She meant to reassure me, but would she come and rescue me if the Kolskis kept me locked up like the Ilowskis did? Roza did not know just how powerless I was.

The Kolskis had just finished eating, and the house smelled of cabbage. They looked at me, startled. Pan pushed his plate aside, jumped up, grabbed my arm, and started to pull me outside. "You come home … eat. You hungry," he shouted. "You want eat. You no want work!"

I dug in my heels, but he yanked hard on my arm. "I won't run away again," I cried.

"Leave her be," Pani called after him. "I'll talk to her. I'll see to it that she doesn't run from her chores again."

Pan let go of my arm and headed for the stable. Grateful to Pani, I said, "I won't do it again," and I thought, I'll be gone by tomorrow. Pani refilled her plate with cabbage soup, pushed it in front of me, and said in a conciliatory tone, "You can't just take off whenever you feel like it. There's too much to be done right now. We've got to put up these vegetables for the winter."

Pan returned, considerably calmer, and said, "The weather ... changing. I think ... rain ... night." I looked out the window and could not distinguish between rain clouds and the approaching night, but I hoped he was wrong. How would I get away during a storm?

I lay in bed, forcing myself to stay awake as I waited for the night to pass. At dawn, when it was just light enough to chase away the demons of the dark, I would take my bundle and run. But much as I tried to resist, sleep embraced me and freed me of my anxiety.

A loud noise jarred me out of my dreams. Tree branches whipped against the roof. The stable door banged against the wall. Maybe the pig had gotten out again. Jagged lightning lit up the room, and claps of thunder reverberated through the darkness. It not only rained, but it stormed. The night seemed endlessly long as I lay waiting for it to pass.

In the morning, Pani shook me awake. The storm was over and Pan had already tended to the animals. Feeling trapped, I thought hard about what to do. When it was my turn to eat, I ate slowly, very slowly, stalling for time. Pan hitched his horse to the wagon and called for me.

"Hurry up, Eva," Pani urged. "Pan is waiting."

I did not look at Pani, nor did I move.

"Hurry up! Pan will get angry," she warned.

"I'm not going into the field. I'm leaving you," I said in a shaky voice.

Pani stared at me for a minute and then called after Pan, "Eva wants to leave us!"

"Give her a kick in the ass and send her scrambling!" Pan shouted back.

I heard the crack of his whip and thought he was coming after me. I froze. My legs would not move. Then, the wagon rumbled off and Pan was gone.

"Why do you want to leave us?" Pani pleaded. "Haven't we treated you right? We've fed you and given you a bed to sleep in. There're plenty of Germans around who would gladly trade places with you."

I stared at my feet and said nothing. When life returned to my legs, I grabbed my bundle and fled without looking back. I am free, I am free, kept racing through my mind. I am free at last.

Roza sat on the steps waiting for me. She hugged me and said, "See, I told you the Kolskis couldn't stop you."

I nestled my head against her warm, soft body and cried. She stroked my back and ran her hand through the stubble on my head. "They didn't beat you, did they?" she asked.

"No, but I thought Pan Kolski was going to."

"Well, you're here now. No one will beat you here." She took the bundle from me and lifted it up and down as though guessing its weight. "Are these all your things?" she asked.

"The Ilowskis kept my things when they chased me away."

She shook her head. "I'll see what Mother can do. She'll sew something up for you. You'll need clothes for the winter."

So I graduated from field hand to nursemaid. Little Jurek was a sweet child and easily entertained. Perhaps he recognized the child in his "child nanny," and he only fussed when hungry. I bathed and diapered him and prepared his bottle. I walked him for hours, enjoying my newfound freedom. Roza praised me, and I lapped up each kind word like a hungry puppy. The more she stroked my ego, the more my confidence grew. I no longer feared the Polish children; I often talked to them and sometimes even joined in their games.

Roza was not married and lived with Jurek's father. He worked in Elbing and commuted. Tall and princely handsome, he had a light-hearted, flirtatious attitude toward everything. Whenever he and Roza fought, and they fought often, it usually ended with him staying in Elbing with his married sister for a night or two. When he returned, he teased her mercilessly about her quick temper until she caved in under his charm. When things were good between them, a peaceful harmony ruled their lives.

When Jurek napped and after I had done my chores, Roza let me play with Gudrun and Gitte. During one of those carefree afternoons, Gudrun casually remarked, "You know, we're going to flee to Germany as soon as we have enough money saved. Mother is keeping it a secret from the woman she works for, but that's what we're going to do."

"When?" I blurted out, surprised.

"I don't know. Mother said we won't be here another winter."

"Where does your mother get money? Do they pay her for working in the waiting room?"

"No, but the people she waits on sometimes give her money, and as soon as we have enough to buy train tickets, we're leaving."

My world threatened to collapse again. Frau Leppe was my last hope. If she disappeared one day like all the others, I would never get away.

I needed money, but I had no chance of getting my hands on any. Money was short in Roza's household. Money, or the lack of it, caused most of their fights. But the longer I lived with them, the more I felt on solid ground again and slowly shed my infantile inse-curities. Soon, I knew every Pole in Niederhof. I still visited Magda and Maria, and once I asked them if the official had ever come back for my pictures. They did not know. He remained a mystery. When I cried, Magda gave me a coin and whispered, "For some candy." But I held on to the money.

I took courage and told her about Pani Kolski's brother. Not sur-prised, she called him a lewd creep who was always in trouble. I asked her point blank, "Did he put a baby in my stomach? Am I going to get a big belly like Pani Kolski had?"

She laughed, shook her head, and said, "Oh, Eva, you're so dumb. He'd have to do a lot more than that. And besides, children can't have babies."

She meant to reassure me, but that uneasy feeling would not go away.

My favorite time at Roza's was Saturday evening after Jurek was down for the night, and they brought up a metal bathtub from the cellar for their weekly bath. I waited downstairs on the steps until they called me for my turn. I lingered in the tub until the water turned cold and listened to Roza and Pan make love in the other room. The first time I heard her moan and groan, I thought he was beating her. But then she giggled and laughed, and I knew they were just playing.

I tried to visit Schotka, who lived right next door, but she was not there. Roza told me she was sick and staying with her in-laws in the city. Then, one day, she came out of her entryway and called after me, "Eva, what are you doing here?"

"I live with Roza now. I take care of Jurek."

She held out her arms and I ran into them. "I'm glad to see you," she said. "I'm sorry we couldn't keep you. But I see you've found a good home with Roza."

Train traffic increased considerably that summer, and Roza's work schedule turned hectic. Sometimes, she left the ticket window unmanned until finally a young woman arrived to share the job with her. Roza now had more time for her son, and I had more freedom. I ventured out even farther and got to know more people. I spent many hours at the station and a great many more with the Polish families who lived in our farm workers' housing. The woman who had given me the Bible storybook still lived there with her children. I befriended all of them. I asked her if she had any more German books. She shook her head and fished a coin from her apron pocket, handed it to me, and said, "But I have this for you."

I turned it over and over and contemplated its value. I now had two coins and thought a lot about how I could acquire more.

Roza often sent me to the bakery to buy a loaf of bread, or to the kiosk, a flimsy wooden hut, for sugar, salt, and soap. She gave me money, and I brought back change, which she carelessly dropped into an empty ashtray. Eventually, she put the money away, but not before I made one or two coins disappear. I was cautious and went for the smallest coins, not realizing that the smaller ones did not necessarily have less value. Then, one day, Roza looked at me suspiciously and asked, "What happened to the rest of the change?"

I felt like cornered prey. But I was quick, looked straight into her eyes, and suggested innocently, "Maybe Pan took it."

To my surprise, she accepted my explanation with that dawning look on her face that said, why didn't I think of that? But she no longer left her money lying around.

I got away with my lie, but it dried up my meager source of income. However, fighting for my survival made me inventive. If people at the station sometimes gave money to Frau Leppe for her services, I would make myself useful too. I now went to the station every chance I got and waited for arriving trains. Occasionally, passengers let me carry their suitcase for a coin or two. Sometimes, someone just slipped me a coin and shooed me away. I did not realize that at the slow rate my pennies were accumulating, years would pass before I reached my goal.

CHAPTER EIGHTEEN

LIFE WITH ROZA WAS GOOD. My sores healed, the pain in my joints slowly disappeared, and my hair was growing back. However, I missed my parents, my siblings, and the comfortable rhythm of my all-too-short childhood. Memories of their faces dimmed, and I lost all sense of time.

Just when I had given up all hope of ever seeing my brother Henry again, he reappeared in Niederhof. Someone had told him where to find me. Months had passed since our last strained meeting under the watchful eyes of Pani Ilowski and Dorota. Now that we could talk freely, we had very little to tell each other. Separated by adversity, we were resigned to fighting for survival in our individual ways.

Henry moved between villages and worked on various farms. At fourteen, he now did a man's work. He had enough to eat and usually slept in the stable with the animals. A Polish official had come looking for him as well and had left forms, but they were in Polish, and he could not make any sense out of them.

I was thrilled to have my brother back in my life. Sometimes he came two Sundays in a row, and then he would not show up for several weeks. After a while, he stopped coming altogether.

ROZA LOCATED A WOMAN WHO offered to knit a sweater for me. We unraveled what was left of my frayed green sweater, and by adding some yarn remnants of Roza's, we had enough for a new one. Roza also sent my measurements to her mother, but the occasional package that arrived was filled with little things for Jurek and never contained anything for me.

The sweater knitter lived some distance away. Every other Sunday, I walked to her village, but she never had anything for me to try on.

She consoled me with, "Be patient. Wait until the harvesting is over. I'll have more time then." Undeterred, I continued my pilgrimages with nine-months-old Jurek in tow, if for no other reason than to remind her that I was waiting.

I rediscovered nature during those last days of summer. With so little beauty in my life, I took renewed notice: birds singing in the trees, storks wading in the lowlands, the smell of the earth after a light rain, and trees rustling in the gentle breeze. I loved it all.

I always brought an extra bottle along for Jurek so I would not have to hurry home, and we often took the more interesting side paths. One day, I came past a tall yellow wheat field sprinkled with red poppies and blue cornflowers. I left the stroller holding the sleeping Jurek at the edge of the road and rushed into the field to pick flowers for Roza and my sweater knitter. I went deeper and deeper into the wheat, while all around me the flowers winked me on.

I heard playful laughter and a low male voice coming from among the stalks. Edging closer, I stumbled upon a man and a woman frolicking on a blanket behind a screen of wheat. The woman was naked on her hands and knees, while the man, stripped from the waist down, rode her like I had seen our bull do with the cows. I stopped and watched, fascinated. They were deeply engrossed in their act. They do it like the animals, flashed through my mind. The woman turned her head, just slightly, her eyes closed. Dorota, I thought. I dropped the flowers, backed away quietly, and made a wild dash for the stroller.

With the field safely behind me, I slowed my pace and thought about what I had stumbled upon. Had it really been Dorota? Without her clothes on, I no longer was sure. But I had witnessed human sexuality in a new form.

All this time, I had avoided going near our farm. Now I wanted to see Dorota again, laugh at her, and tell her I saw her naked in the wheat field with a man.

I saw Pani Ilowski picking cherries in the garden as I passed the house. She had an enormous belly and looked just like Pani Kolski had before her baby was born.

Dorota, Kashia, Walek, and Stashek suddenly appeared by the road as though waiting for me. My heart skipped several beats, and all courage drained out of me. But I did not turn around and run. I raised my head higher, straightened my shoulders, and pushed little

Jurek's stroller ahead of me like an iron tank. All kinds of frightening thoughts flashed through my mind. They watched my approach, and I met their stares. Then Kashia called out, "Oh, hi, Eva; whose baby do you have there?"

I slowed and said, "He belongs to Roza. I live with her and Pan." I said it like a warning that implied, if you touch me, you will have to deal with them. I eyed Dorota's stomach, looking for swelling and hoping she, too, now had a baby in there. Kashia smiled and said, "Why don't you help me round up the cows for Dorota?"

"I don't think so," I said, feeling triumphant that I had stood up to them.

I looked at Walek's scarred red legs, and I hoped that they still hurt. I felt no malice in my heart for Kashia, but I could not conjure up one kind thought for the rest of the Ilowskis. It was a good thing God was not listening to me.

During the course of the summer, a man named Oleg moved into the apartment unit directly below us. His young family was to join him in time for his twin girls to enroll in school in Steglitz. A kind, gentle-mannered man, he paid attention to me. In the evenings, he often joined me on the front steps while we waited for the stars to light up.

"Why don't you come into my kitchen? I'll teach you how to play solitaire," he said one evening. Starved for love and attention, I was delighted. Our relationship developed into a partnership. Soon, he invited me every evening to come down and play the game with him.

The game became our game. He never moved a card without my presence, thus guaranteeing my nightly visits. He pulled me between his legs, or had me sit on his knees with the cards spread out in front of us. Gentle and affectionate, he stroked my arms and ran his calloused hands up and down my back under my dress. "Your skin is so soft," he would say. Occasionally, when I discovered a clever move, he gave me a peck on the cheek. I enjoyed the physical closeness with him, savored every kind word he had for me, and yearned for more. I felt loved and thought of Father.

Oleg became more and more physical, until one day, while sitting on his knees, I felt him rub his stiff male organ against my bare back. He tried to distract me, but I knew what he was doing. "Move the black queen onto the red king," he said. "Take the nine and move it over."

When I felt warm liquid trickle down my spine, I slid off his knees and headed for the door, confused. He held me back by the arm, pushed a Zloty note into my hand, and said, "Here, go buy yourself some candy at the kiosk tomorrow." I understood. He was buying my silence.

He need not have worried about my exposing him. If I had told Roza about the incident, she probably would not have believed me. If she had and confronted Oleg, he would have denied it. I remained silent and avoided him. However, I owned a whole Zloty, which I carefully added to my coin collection. I hid my treasure on top of a rafter in one of the unused stalls in the utility building. I had no idea what the value of my sparse savings was, but I felt rich nonetheless.

I did not know how to behave around Oleg. That Zloty was like the apple that tempted Eve in my Bible stories. I worried more and more that Frau Leppe would disappear without me because I had no money. When she did not come to work one day, I thought they had disappeared like all the others. But Roza put my mind at ease. She told me that the girls were sick with some type of contagious childhood disease. It must have been serious because she warned me not to go near them with Jurek.

I no longer played cards with Oleg and sat alone on the steps. He came out one night, leaned against the fence, and asked, "Why don't you want to play solitaire any more?"

"I don't like the game," I said. "It's boring."

"I'll teach you other fun games."

Tempted, very tempted, I envisioned a sequence of Zlotys passing into my hands, but I was cautious and finally said, "No, I don't want to come into your house any more."

I missed our warm relationship and would have gone back to him if I had not been afraid that he would hurt me with time.

One Saturday evening, however, as I came down to wait on the steps while Roza and her man bathed, Oleg stood by his door, grabbed me by the arm, and pulled me into the kitchen. He kicked the door shut with his foot and locked his arms around me from behind. He lifted up my skirt and rubbed himself against my bare back, just like he had done before, but with more force. Within seconds, warm liquid squirted on my back and trickled down my legs. He never looked at me when he opened the door and pushed me out, this time without giving me another Zloty.

I sat on the front steps, looked for Mother among the stars that were beginning to light up, and cried.

By the end of summer, the Polish children prepared to return to school. I was not among them and asked Roza, "When Jurek gets old enough for school, will I be able to go with him?"

"You'll be much too old by then," she said.

Food became scarce again, and Roza rode to the neighboring villages on her bicycle to buy potatoes, root vegetables, and apples. She usually returned empty-handed and irritable. She and Pan fought a lot, and he stayed away from home more often and longer.

When she found a letter from Pan's mother in his coat pocket asking when he was getting rid of that woman he lived with, Roza exploded. "What kind of mother is she?" she shouted. "Doesn't she know she has a grandson?"

Pan just shrugged his shoulders.

"Answer me, you bastard!" Roza screamed.

When he said nothing, Roza carried on like a mad woman.

"Okay, okay, I'm leaving, and I'm not coming back," Pan said calmly.

"You can't leave me," Roza shouted between sobs. "I'm going to have another baby."

"Oh, no!" he said and sat down, resting his head between his hands.

Feeling sorry for Roza, I picked up Jurek and left the house. I did not want her world to fall apart, because my world would collapse with it. I could not tell where their relationship was headed, even with another baby on the way, and I was no longer sure where I fit in. The only positive thing I had going for me was my fluency in Polish. People often mistook me as belonging to Roza. I had learned to speak the language by osmosis, but it did not appear I would ever have the chance to learn to read and write it. I felt the lack of schooling like the deficiency of vital nutrients in my diet.

The next day, Roza and her man made peace, but it was an uneasy peace. I feared she would take Jurek and go home to her mother, as she had threatened to do, and leave me behind.

Whenever I ran errands for Roza, I befriended the woman at the kiosk, who always had a little treat for me. One day, she presented me with a colorful skirt and said, "Here, try this on. I bet it'll fit you."

I reached for the garment, unable to express my feelings of gratitude, not just for the pretty skirt, but for her generous spirit. Hers was a gesture of genuine compassion without expecting something in return. Anxious for love, I would have done anything for her to guarantee her continued fondness for me.

So it was that for each setback and disappointment, I also made new discoveries, and my faith in humankind slowly reawakened.

After two weeks, Frau Leppe returned to work with Gitte and Gudrun in tow.

Fall arrived. The trees turned a brilliant yellow, the pungent aroma of dried grass permeated the air, and a feeble sun hinted at darker and colder days to come. The knitter had barely started my sweater, and Roza's mother had not yet sent any clothes for me. I still ran around barefoot. Roza tried to buy shoes for me in Elbing, but without success.

Help came from the kiosk woman. One chilly morning I stood by her hut, shaking from cold. "My God, Eva, you're running around barefoot," she said. "Don't you have any shoes? And what about warm clothes?"

"Roza tried to buy shoes for me in Elbing, but she didn't get any, and the woman who is supposed to knit a sweater for me has barely started. The Ilowskis kept all my clothes."

"Oh, yes, the Ilowskis," she repeated and let the rest of her thoughts trail off. "You come back in a few days. Maybe I'll have something for you."

I did not tell Roza about the kiosk woman's promise, but I waited anxiously for the days to pass.

Roza did not have any luck with the farmers in obtaining food for the winter. She finally went to the Ilowskis to buy potatoes and had a long visit with Pani and Dorota. They gave her an earful about me, telling her they kicked me out because I stole, told lies, and wet the bed. Roza looked hard at me and asked, "Is it true?"

I blushed under her steady gaze and said, "Yes, I stole food from the pigs' trough and lied about it," Then she dropped the real bombshell, "Well, it doesn't matter. They promised to sell us milk. You're to pick it up evenings after the milking."

"I'm not going there," I said, with a defiance that surprised her. "They're mean people. They beat me. They'll do it again. Please, please don't make me go there. Kashia is nice. Ask her to bring the milk to us."

"You won't have to do it right away," she said. "Our regular milk people won't cut us off for another week or so."

Roza did not mention the Ilowskis again for the next few days.

All signs pointed to another long, cold winter with extreme food shortages. I worried about Frau Leppe. When would she make her move? I pumped Gudrun and Gitte for information, but they suddenly were tight-lipped and merely shrugged their shoulders.

The kiosk woman kept her word. The following week, she handed me a pair of shoes and a wool sweater. The shoes had holes in the soles and were too big. She stuck paper in the toes and handed me a pair of coarse woolen socks. "They fit perfectly," I quickly declared. But they felt strange on my feet after having gone barefoot for so long. The sweater was warm and soft like my cat.

When I showed up in shoes, Roza accused me of stealing. I explained how I came by them, but she chided me for having gone begging behind her back. I did not know she and the kiosk woman were not on friendly terms. Perhaps the woman wanted to get to Roza through me. I had gained a pair of shoes but had also lost something. Roza no longer trusted me.

I ran over to Schotka's to show her my shoes. She looked troubled and was in the process of packing to go to her in-laws. "I have to go to the hospital again," she said.

"I'll miss you a lot. Will you be gone long?"

Her eyes glistened with moisture. She shrugged her shoulders and said, "I don't know."

She left the following day, and I never saw her again.

CHAPTER NINETEEN

A CAPRICIOUS FALL WIND BLEW from the icy north, warning of worse weather to come. Roza and Pan continued to fight, and she threatened to flee to her mother. A feeling of doom settled in my heart. Roza now was irritable all the time. The slightest thing set her off, and she found fault with everything I did. My spirits sank.

To get away, I took Jurek for longer and longer walks, and I spent every free minute with Gudrun and Gitte. One day, I asked their mother, "How much does a train ticket to Germany cost?"

"More money than we'll ever have," she said with such resignation that I felt reassured they would not be leaving soon.

Then, one day, Pan Ilowski rode up to the station. "Come over here, Eva," he called waving his whip in my direction.

I repressed my impulse to run; instead, I pushed Jurek between his horse and myself and waited. He dismounted, a good sign, and said, "Eva, I have important news for you. All Germans must report to Elbing. You'll be shipped out of Poland in two or three days."

I heard the words, but nothing registered. I was to be shipped out of Poland? How was that to happen? How would I get to Elbing? Didn't he know I had no money? My mind raced. Never in my wildest fantasies did I think that Pan Ilowski would be the bearer of such monumental good news. I stood glued to the ground and stared at him. He grabbed my arm and said, "Go find the German woman who works in the waiting room. I told her to take you with her to Elbing!"

I left Jurek in his stroller and ran inside the station past a puzzled Roza, who called after me, "Eva, what's the matter? What's happened?"

I ignored her and shouted across the room, "Frau Leppe, Frau

Leppe! Pan Ilowski told me that all the Germans have to be in Elbing by tomorrow. He said you have to take me along."

"Yes, I know. He told me." She hesitated. I could tell from the puzzled expression on her face she wasn't sure what to do about me. But I was determined that this time I was not going to be left behind. "Pan said you have to take me with you to Elbing," I repeated, and to reinforce my position I whispered so Roza could not hear, "I have money." It came out more like a desperate plea.

"*Ja, ja,* you can come home with me after I get through here," she said. "We'll leave for Elbing in the morning."

I rushed to the ticket window and called out to Roza, "I'm leaving for Germany with Frau Leppe. We have to be in Elbing in the morning. I'm going to leave Jurek in his crib." I talked fast as if every minute counted.

"Calm down, Eva," Roza said. "Don't worry. I just talked to Pan Ilowski. Go home and wait for me. We'll have to get your things together, and you'll need food. I'll make sure Frau Leppe comes for you when she is through working."

"She'll leave without me if I don't wait for her right here on the steps."

I was panicked. Frau Leppe had become my lifeline.

"Eva, it's all arranged. Go home and wait for me!" Roza insisted.

After three years, the time of my liberation had finally arrived, and my desperate desire to get out and be free overrode every other emotion. For the next hour, which seemed like an eternity, my feet never touched the ground. I could barely contain my impatience and kept walking to the window, watching for Roza and Frau Leppe. To my relief, Roza finally appeared and brought a sense of reality with her. I had already stuffed my scant belongings in the red and white checkered pillowcase and had retrieved my pathetic savings. Roza handed me some money and said, "Here, go to the Pani at the kiosk and get a loaf of bread and as much sausage as the rest of the money will buy. You'll be on the road a long time, and you'll need food. If she isn't open, go to her house and tell her you need these things right away!"

The woman was at the kiosk. "I need some bread and meat," I called out all excited, still running. "I'm leaving for Germany." She had already heard and asked, "Where are you going in Germany? Who will take care of you there?"

Her questions cut deep. For the first time, I realized that no matter where I was, I would remain an orphan, with no place to go. I knew nothing about my father and brothers. Surely they were dead, or they would have come looking for Henry and me. And where was my sister? My parents had sent her away, but I did not know to where. And what about Henry? Did somebody tell him he needed to be in Elbing?

Blind hope swept me along. Nothing could stop me now. Even if Frau Leppe did not come for me, I would walk to Elbing and knock on every door until I found the place where the Germans were to assemble. I was determined to be among them.

The woman at the kiosk gave me a loaf of bread and a piece of smoked sausage. She cut off a chunk of cheese, handed it to me along with a box of hardtack, and said, "This is a gift from me, Eva. I wish you good luck. I'm sure you have living relatives somewhere."

She came out of her hut, gave me a hug, and kissed me on the forehead.

I rushed back to Roza's, eager, anxious, excited, tense, worried, afraid—all wrapped up in one big knot in my stomach. Roza had not been idle and had repacked my things in an old rucksack. She added my purchases and the gifts from the kiosk woman and said, "This will be much better for your trip." She handed me an old faded jacket and added, "This is a present from my partner at work."

When Frau Leppe came for me, Roza pulled some Zloty notes from her wallet, handed them to me, and said, "Use the money to buy more food if you need to."

She put her arms around me as she had done when I first came to her, and it felt just as good. We both had tears in our eyes. She slipped a piece of paper into my pocket and said, "This is our address. Write to me from wherever you are."

Frau Leppe was in a hurry to get home, and we quickly departed. I trailed behind the woman, with Roza's rucksack slung over my shoulders.

Gitte and Gudrun waited by the front door, surprised to see me. Two packed suitcases along with some boxes stood in the corner of the room. It dawned on me that Frau Leppe must have known about the German "roundup" for a day or two and had prepared for it. I wondered what would have happened if Pan Ilowski had not come to tell me and insist that she take me with her. I preferred not to know the answer.

Frau Leppe had everything planned. A farmer would drive us with his horse and wagon to Elbing in the morning. For his service, she had promised him the things they could not take with them. He showed up in the evening and told us to be ready by five o'clock in the morning.

"Why so early? You told me eight," Frau Leppe reminded him.

"I need to get back and work in the field," he explained, casting a calculating look around the room.

Frau Leppe cooked up an enormous batch of potatoes and mashed them with bacon grease. "Eat as much as you can," she urged us. "There'll be no breakfast in the morning. Heaven only knows when or where we'll have our next meal."

She spread a feather bed on the floor for me and counseled us to sleep hard and fast. I lay back, held on to my rucksack lest the mice get to it, and waited for sleep. The night dragged. I felt the magic of the moment in every fiber of my body. I was about to begin a fairy-tale adventure and hoped that this time it would have a happy ending. When sleep finally came, it brought sweet dreams.

Frau Leppe awakened us before the night ended. She rolled up two feather beddings, wrapped a sheet around them, and added them to their baggage. She handed each of us a chunk of bread, the last food she was to share with me, and we were ready. The farmer arrived shortly thereafter. He loaded Frau Leppe's belongings on the wagon. I refused to let go of my rucksack and held on to it as if my life depended on it.

We made ourselves comfortable among Frau Leppe's things, while the driver sat in the front and urged his horse on. As we pulled out, shadows appeared from the bushes and headed for the house.

"So that's why he came so early," Frau Leppe mumbled under her breath. "He was afraid somebody else would beat him to the plunder. Well, they're welcome to it. I just hope he doesn't dump us along the way and take off with the rest of our things."

I tightened my grip on the rucksack.

A thin sliver of a moon accompanied us as we drove through the chilly autumn morning. We could see the steam of our breath in the semidarkness, and I was glad to have the kiosk woman's sweater and the jacket Pani's colleague had given me. Our driver did not speak. When the terrain turned hilly, the wagon dug into the sand, and the horse struggled up the incline. The Pole cursed the animal. After a while he stopped, descended from the wagon, and motioned for us to do the same. Alarmed, Frau Leppe said, "Grab what you can. This is where he'll dump us." But she had guessed wrong. He told us to leave everything on the wagon and walk.

We reached the outskirts of Elbing by late morning. A policeman directed us to an immense abandoned German military complex. A guard stopped us at the gate. Our driver could not proceed beyond that point. He helped us unload Frau Leppe's things and took off without saying a word. An official directed us to one of the buildings. Bullet holes honeycombed the outside walls, a reminder of the heavy fighting that had taken place around Elbing only three years ago.

Some thirty people, mostly women and young children with a handful of old men, lay crowded together on beds of hay in our designated room. Most had arrived the day before. We remained holed up in those tight quarters for three days, forced to rely on the food we had brought with us. Frau Leppe quickly disassociated herself from me. She told everyone I did not belong to her, that she had merely brought me along because I was all alone. That evening, I reached into my rucksack, broke off a piece of bread, took a bite or two of the sausage, and thought of kind-hearted Roza and the generous kiosk woman. Thanks to them, I did not go to sleep hungry.

I made the painful discovery that our mutual misfortune may have brought us together in that place, but for our survival, we each stood alone. Only the immediate family members shared anything, and I had no family.

CHAPTER TWENTY

EXALTATION RODE HIGH IN THE barracks. Germans came from all directions. Many had walked for two days and slept under the stars along the road. They had been told to get themselves to Elbing. East Prussia, our homeland, belonged to the Poles now. All Germans were being expelled.

Some families had hoped they would be allowed to stay on their land. But when the Allies had met at Yalta and had decided Germany's new borders, they had forgotten about us, and the Poles did not want us; they just wanted the land.

"This has been our home for generations. I don't want to die in some refugee camp," an old man lamented.

"It isn't our land any longer. If you get buried here, the Poles will trample all over your grave. Is that what you want?" a woman asked.

By the second day, we still did not know what would happen to us. Tempers flared. A few more Germans trickled in. We had no facilities for washing or bathing. The latrines overflowed, the stench spread. Contradictory rumors circulated. We did not know whether we would be sent west to Germany or east to Russia, synonymous with labor camps and death. "I'd rather hang myself right here," a woman said.

And where was Henry? I combed the corridors and looked in every room in hopes of finding him. At the far end of the building, I discovered several Polish women selling bread and smoked meats to the Germans. I hurried back to our room, gathered up my money, and returned. The women were not supposed to be in the building. I overheard someone say the guards had chased them away earlier, but they had returned.

The news of this forbidden activity had not yet spread. I watched the furtive transactions for a while, trying to gather the courage to approach them. The merchants kept their goods hidden in boxes and sacks and charged outrageous prices. I zeroed in on the woman who conducted her business mostly in sign language. I walked up to her, held my Zlotys in her face, and said in my best Polish, with all the self-assurance I could muster, "I want a sausage and as much bread as I can have with this money."

She hesitated. I quickly added, "Schotka, auntie, told me I could buy a whole sausage and two loaves of bread with this money." I figured by hinting at a Polish aunt and letting her know I had some idea of the value of my Zlotys, she would be less inclined to cheat me. She took all my money, including the change, and gave me half a sausage and a loaf of bread. I had no way of knowing how well I had done. When I returned to our room, I told the others about my discovery. Now everyone sent a member of their group to deal with the merchant women, but they were too late; the women were gone. I felt secure and safe in the knowledge that I would not go hungry for several days.

In the morning of the second day, an official appeared and told us to follow him to the documentation office. "Bring with you all papers in your possession," he said and warned us that our things would be searched in our absence. We better not be hiding anything, or we would be punished. I fished my bundle of papers that Roza had carefully tied together out of the rucksack and followed the flow of people into a large assembly room. Stern-faced Polish officials sat behind a row of pushed-together tables. We stepped up one at a time to be interrogated. I handed my packet to the man and trembled, afraid he might find something irregular that would hold me back. He carefully pulled the papers apart, scrutinized the documents, and laid each piece on separate piles for bankbooks, property titles, and the like. He pulled out my picture, the one Pani Kolski had given me, and asked, "What happened to your parents?"

I thought for a few seconds and said, "They're dead."

"Do you have any brothers and sisters?"

"Yes, but I think they're dead too."

A smile erased the frown on his face as he handed me a document, my official ticket to freedom. He placed the photo on top if it and said in a kind voice, "You're a cute little girl. Maybe somebody will adopt you."

His remark alarmed me. I did not want to be adopted. I wanted my family back.

In the hallway, I saw Frau Leppe and her girls in the corridor talking to a woman quartered next to us. I recognized her as Frau Schmidt, the same woman Henry and I had approached about the nonexistent letter while we were still at the Ilowskis. At that time, she had been very pregnant. Now her big belly was gone, but she had no baby with her. The child would have been over a year old. Remembering Pani Ilowski's dead baby, I asked Gitte and Gudrun, "What happened to Frau Schmidt's baby? Did it come out dead?"

"Oh no, she had a baby boy, but she refused to feed it, and it died," they enlightened me. Then Gitte, being the older, added with an air of confidentiality, "Mother said that she killed it because the father was a Russian soldier, and so she couldn't love it. Now, she sometimes acts crazy, talks to her dead baby, and then cries."

Frau Schmidt was not the only one suffering and haunted by arguments of conscience. Many others sometimes escaped into a world of fantasy, and while hallucinating, tried to erase the horrible memories of the past. People talked in their sleep and cried out. We all had our private demons, the common denominator that bound us together.

The merchants returned in the afternoon, and a long line formed. Frantic buyers besieged the women. Those with no money offered personal items of clothing, bedding, or an occasional piece of jewelry they had managed to hold on to, which quickly became the preferred currency. Soon, the merchants would not deal in money at all.

In the evening, two officials came into our room and told us to be prepared to leave by eight o'clock in the morning. They did not reveal our destination. The optimistic embraced and hugged one another. "Has the time of our liberation finally arrived? Has God decided we have done enough penance?" I heard somebody say.

I was nervous about what lay ahead for me. I overheard Frau Leppe tell someone that the "Rapp girl" would probably end up in an orphanage, and the interrogating official had implied the same. Was I going from one form of bondage to another? Now that the much-longed-for moment of liberation had arrived, I no longer had a clear concept of what to expect.

That night, a disturbing restlessness filled the air. By morning, the excitement and anticipation had reached a new high. A guard came to tell us to take our possessions and line up behind the waiting people outside. The guards emptied the rooms methodically. We stood around for a long time, nervous and anxious to get going. One guard told us we would be marched to the station. That meant we would be leaving by train, whatever the destination. A few people cried. They did not want to go to Russia. When the line started to move, everyone calmed down. Curious onlookers assembled along the sidewalks and watched our procession crawl along. A few spectators jeered and showered us with Polish and German curses. A woman sprang out of the crowd, stepped in front of Frau Leppe, and spat into her face. An armed guard pulled her away. Most of the onlookers, however, watched in silence, hatred and contempt written on their faces. Occasionally, someone waved a fist at us, and we were grateful for the guards. When we reached the center of the city, the crowds increased and became more hostile. Our procession picked up speed. The column tightened, and we pushed into the station like a giant steamroller. The soldiers led us to the freight yard, where empty cattle cars awaited us. The old and disabled had to be lifted on board.

We settled into our new environment and sighed with relief, knowing that at least we would not be forced on a long foot march. The loading did not take long, and by midday we were ready and most anxious to start rolling. But we had to wait for a locomotive. In the midafternoon, a water tank drove up, and pandemonium broke out as the people stormed it. The guards pushed the crowd back and established order by having us line up by cars.

Restless Germans milled around the grounds. As long as there was no engine, there was no threat of the transport leaving without them. Someone counted twelve cars and commented that there had to be over four hundred refugees on that transport.

I stood by the open cattle-car door and watched the people siphoning water from the tank. An older girl joined me. The Polish spectators had dispersed. We saw a young boy walking down the main highway parallel to the railroad tracks. The girl nudged me and said, "I know that boy. He's German. That's Henry Rapp."

"Henry Rapp? That's my brother!" I strained my eyes and stared in his direction. I saw only a bedraggled, unkempt, beggarly waif, with a deflated rucksack on his back.

The girl repeated, "That's Henry," and called out to him, "Henry, over here. We're over here on the train!"

Then, I too, recognized my brother. He ran over to us, and we pulled him into our car. I immediately felt reinforced and stronger. From here on, we would find our way together.

The people reluctantly agreed that Henry could stay in our car, but he did not have the necessary official permit allowing him to be on the train. Rumors had reached him about the roundup of the Germans. He immediately embarked on foot for Elbing and stumbled on our train by accident. Had a locomotive been there earlier, we would have been long gone, and he would have stayed behind.

Henry approached every officer, guard, and soldier and explained he was German, that his sister was on the train, and that he arrived late and had no papers. They told him to hang around; someone would come and take care of it. We waited nervously. Nothing happened. No one showed up.

By late afternoon, a locomotive finally hooked onto our boxcars. We felt a jerk, the cars set into motion, and we slowly moved out of the station. Someone cried out, "We're headed west! We're going home!"

"No, we're leaving home," another voice called out.

"And I have no papers," Henry said.

THE NEW GERMANS

CHAPTER ONE

TORN BETWEEN HOPE AND DREAD, we stood by the open cattle-car door and watched the jagged outline of the skeletal facades of war-ravaged Elbing recede in the distance. We were leaving behind our ancestral homeland and everything that had once belonged to us. Stripped of our possessions and the documents that tied us to the land, crowded together in a cattle car, we were a group of disowned and displaced women, children, and old men.

A lone church steeple towered brave and tall above the ruins of Elbing. It bade us farewell until it, too, vanished from view. New vistas opened up, and hope for a better life filled my heart. I had found Henry or, rather my brother miraculously had found me, and I no longer felt so abandoned. Only one oppressive dark cloud hung over us: Henry's lack of documents. But for the moment, the train was moving, and the staccato rhythm of the turning wheels along the tracks comforted both of us. I wanted the train to take us away, far, far away, from all that tragedy and suffering.

As dusk settled over the landscape, the engine jerked to a sudden halt. An armed Polish guard shouted, "All of you, out! Go relieve yourselves in the field! We won't stop again."

When the engineer blew the warning whistle, I scrambled for the train and climbed back into our car. The wheels started to roll and set the train into motion, while panicked stragglers ran and screamed, "Stop! Stop! Don't leave us behind!"

The train kept moving. They ran frantically, arms waving, yelling, shouting, and beseeching God for help. This lasted several minutes, the locomotive moving just fast enough to stay ahead of the stranded. No one was missing in our car. "Are the guards deaf?" someone said. "Why won't they stop?"

"I'll pee in my pants," Frau Leppe said, "or worse, before I'll leave this car again."

A gunshot pierced the air and brought the train to a halt. It waited long enough for those left behind to reach their car and get pulled in by their worried loved ones.

When we regained our composure, we discovered that many of our bundles had been rummaged through, and things were missing. People blamed the guards. My rucksack sat where I had left it, with its contents untouched.

When the light started to dim, we brought out our provisions and ate hunched over the food, hiding it from our neighbors, afraid we might have to share what little we had left. We did not know how long our journey would last, but it appeared we would have to rely on our own resources or go hungry. "Go easy on your food!" Frau Leppe warned us. "Save some for tomorrow and the day after!"

We ate sparingly. The farsighted had filled their containers with water. Henry and I did not have anything other than our two hands to drink from. Now we had to do without.

When it turned dark, we prepared for the night. The women unrolled bedding and arranged their space. Henry and I had nothing. Frau Leppe spread a feather bed on the hard floor and said, "Eva, you can lie at the end next to my girls." Henry had to make do on the bare floor. He huddled close. Comfortable, with a full stomach, I let the gently swaying car rock me to sleep.

I awoke in the middle of the night. I dreamt the Polish woman had finished my beautiful green sweater. But she would not give it to me unless I gave her all my food. I held on to it with all my strength. When she tried to yank it away from me, I awoke shivering, clutching my rucksack. A cold draft blew through the cracks of the boards. My mouth was dry; I was thirsty. Henry had pulled a corner of the cover over himself, leaving me exposed. Four little openings, two by each side of the closed doors, let in beams of moonlight and raw air. Someone stirred and let out a pained moan. I listened to the rhythmic breathing around me. Feeling secure and safe, I pulled the covers back over me and fell asleep again.

In the morning, I awoke to find the train stopped. We sat on a sidetrack outside a small town. Frau Leppe said we had been standing there half the night, and that the Poles had removed the engine. The guards told us to take care of nature's call in a nearby field. We took turns, some of us staying behind to watch our things. People complained of thirst and begged the guards for water. A few hours later, a horse-drawn metal tank filled with water pulled up alongside our boxcars. The women rushed over and almost trampled the driver. A guard fired a shot to restore order. When I finally got my turn, I greedily gulped down the stream of water flowing from the spigot. A woman pushed me aside and said, "You're wasting our precious water," and sent me back to the end of the line.

In the late afternoon, just as we started to turn restless, a locomotive slowly backed into our waiting cars. The engineer blew the whistle, waited a few minutes, blew the whistle again, and set the train in motion.

We crept past villages and towns with Polish names, leaving us guessing as to where we were. The landscape changed to undulating hills, and the adults passed the day conjecturing about our final destination. Occasionally, someone recognized a town. We were headed southwest. "As long as it isn't east, we're safe," a woman said. "I don't want to go to Russia. I'll throw myself under the train first."

We spent that evening much like the previous one. The train made another "relief" stop. Fearful of being left behind again, we jumped out of the car and took care of our business in full view of one another, casting aside all inhibitions and preserving some sense of dignity by simply closing our eyes.

Frau Leppe spread out her bedding but did not make room for me this time. I put on all the clothes I had in my rucksack and huddled close to Henry, eyeing Frau Leppe's feather covers with bitter envy. The night turned cold again. My mood dropped faster than the temperature outside. I spent hours in a state of half sleep, edging ever closer to Frau Leppe's warm bedding. The wind howled, and the night felt twice as cold as the one before and seemed many times longer.

By morning, everyone was agitated. Where were they taking us? Henry's and my provisions had dwindled to a quarter loaf of bread. An odor of perspiration, urine, and feces permeated the air. People suffered from dysentery and dehydration. Word spread that an old man in another car had died during the night. One of the "left behind" on the first stop, he had suffered a heart attack. Now we sat on a sidetrack again in some nameless town, waiting for the body to be removed. Guards brought water, a lot of water, and left the container for us to empty. The women refilled their vessels several times, and Henry and I drank as much as our bellies would hold.

According to rumors, our destination was Goerlitz, an East German city on the Neisse River. Our spirits lifted. The adults calculated that we could not have much farther to go and hoped to cross the border before evening.

The Poles did not come for the body until late afternoon, and we did not start moving again until after dark. We spent another freezing night huddled together. By early morning, the train stopped moving again. We saw the ruins of a large city on the other side of a river. "That's the Neisse, and that has to be Goerlitz. I'm sure of it," someone said.

The Neisse River marked the border between bondage and freedom. The sudden jerk of the car told us they were exchanging locomotives. As the train crawled across the bridge, I looked down on the smooth ribbon of water, a layer of mist hovering above it. This is what a border looks like, I thought. This is what separated us from the *Reich*.

We arrived in Goerlitz by midmorning and were left standing on a sidetrack. Russian soldiers appeared and ordered us to get out of the cars and line up in front. We stood on German soil, but the Russians' stern, unsmiling faces and their cold, deliberate manner made me tremble with fear that the brutal past might repeat itself. They checked our papers against their master list. My brother's name was not on it.

"Where are your papers?" one official asked. "What are you doing on this transport?" He pulled Henry away from us and added in a gruff voice, "Are you a Pole, trying to run away?"

With his command of the Polish language, Henry could have easily passed for a Pole. He tried to explain to the officials what had happened. They seemed to be in a quandary. Words flew back and forth. One of them finally motioned for us to get back into the car. He turned to Henry, and said, "You wait here! I go check at the office."

Henry looked helpless and forlorn as he stood alone. "I'm going to run away if they won't let me stay," he called up to me. "I'm not going back."

"Oh, no, Henry! They'll shoot you if you run."

"I don't care. I'm not going back."

A lump formed in my throat. Would they really send him back to Poland? It made no sense; we had just been expelled from there. Much to our surprise, one of the men returned after only a minute or two and told Henry to get back into the car.

Later, two nurses' aides, dressed in white, appeared and led us to a delousing station. We lined up single file and waited to be dusted with a white powder. A woman equipped with a hand sprayer, similar to those used for bug spray, aimed it at me and said, "Close your eyes and mouth! Take off your jacket! Lift up your arms! Turn around!" The powder had a metallic odor and tasted bitter. My body came alive, my skin tingled, and my head crawled with little things. Feeling ashamed, I avoided the woman's eyes. But she gave me a sympathetic smile and said, "Don't feel bad. Everyone has lice when they arrive here. Now, go to the soup kitchen and get something to eat!"

I waited for Henry, and we joined the food line. Two women in white aprons stood by a giant kettle and doled out hot soup, providing metal bowls for those of us who had no containers. The thin green liquid had an indefinable flavor, but it tasted wonderful.

Then things happened fast. Armed Russian soldiers told us to get our belongings and start marching. The sun warmed the earth, and the air smelled of dried leaves and fall. It felt good to be mobile after the long confinement. We soon arrived at our destination, an old German military compound, now a refugee holding camp. Rows and rows of wooden barracks overflowed with people. The soldiers separated the females from the males and ushered us into a long, one-story building where empty bunk beds awaited us. After settling into our space, we stood in line for more soup. I stayed close to Frau Leppe and her girls.

That evening, I fell into my bunk, tired and relieved. The coarse mattress smelled of hay. I pulled the blanket over myself and slept the sleep of the dead.

We spent the entire next day standing in long lines. A young woman in uniform, Russian or German, I could no longer tell, guided me to various areas. I stood before many officials, who asked a lot of questions. I was being "documented." My last interrogator, an older motherly woman, motioned for me to sit, not across from her, but next to her. "Now, Eva Rapp," she said in a familiar tone. "That's your name, isn't it?"

I merely nodded.

"Listen very carefully. I'm going to read back to you all the things you have told us about yourself. You stop me when something isn't right. It's very important that everything is correct. You see, Eva, we're going to try to find your family so you can be reunited. If any of your people are alive, we'll find them. For all we know, they may already be looking for you."

So the search for our family began. I felt euphoric. Back in the barrack, a young nurse told me to gather up my things and follow her to another low, wooden building. "This is where you'll be staying until they take you to the orphanage," she said.

My stomach did a somersault. One person had just told me they would look for my family, and now this nurse was sending me to an orphanage.

Alarmed, I said, "I don't want to go to an orphanage."

"That's where all the children without parents go. Don't worry; it's only temporary." She introduced me to an older girl and her two younger sisters who were already settled there and said to them, "You look after her! She's also an orphan."

Most of the bunks stood unoccupied. I chose one next to the sisters. I did not know where Henry had landed on this large compound, but I assumed he had had a day similar to mine. The older sister told me they kept boys and girls, and men and women, separated in camp, even if they were brothers and sisters, or married.

An older woman and her nineteen-year-old son sat on their bunks at the other end of our long room. The male roommate surprised me. The next day, I asked the nurse if my brother could move in with us. She answered with an emphatic no. "The boy in your barrack is a special case," she explained.

"He's not right in the head," one of the sisters told me later. "He's suffering from shell shock. He needs his mother to take care of him."

"What's shell shock?"

"It's something that happens to soldiers when they become afraid of getting killed in battle. They snap." She rolled her eyes and continued, "They go berserk. All day long, he sits at the edge of his bunk and whittles with his pocketknife. The nurse brings him pieces of wood, and he carves little animals. She says he's gifted. But he's still crazy if you ask me."

He looked normal to me. In fact, he resembled my brother Erwin, the way I remembered him, and I decided to befriend him. Watching him gently rub a piece of wood between his fingers, I asked, "What are you going to make out of it?"

"What do you want me to make?"

"A cat."

"Well, I don't know if there's a cat hiding in here. But if there is, I'll find it."

I kept my eyes peeled on his skilled hands as he whittled away, waiting for a cat to emerge. He stopped abruptly, glared at me, and shouted, "What are you staring at? Get away from me!"

I dashed from the room, puzzled by his angry outburst.

At bedtime the following evening, I found a curled-up little cat, crudely carved and sanded smooth, resting on my pillow. Thrilled, I ran to him to throw my arms around his neck and thank him, but his mother grabbed me by the elbow and said, "He doesn't like to be touched. He's a good boy with a big heart, but don't ever touch him."

That night, I went to sleep holding on to my tiny wooden cat and dreamed of Schnurribart.

The next morning, Henry showed up. He had investigated the entire compound.

"Do you remember those Russians at the Ilowskis?" he asked. "The ones who wanted to take us along when they were pulling out of the area? Well, this is where they would have brought us. We were pretty stupid not to have gone with them."

"*Ja*, but we were scared of the Russians. They had guns. How do you know they would have brought us here? Maybe they would have shot us instead, just as they did with Kurt and Herr Weber."

"It's different now. The Russians are our friends."

Henry grimaced while scratching his head. "The lice are driving me crazy. The powder just stirred them up."

"Why don't you let me cut off your hair," I suggested. "That's what the Ilowskis did to me. It got rid of the lice."

I borrowed the older sister's scissors and attacked Henry's head the way Pani Ilowski had done with mine. When the sister saw his shorn head, a solid raw wound with little black dots scurrying in the festering sores, she said, "You better find a nurse and get help."

Several more girls moved into our barrack. One day, someone carelessly left a door wide open. Suddenly, it slammed shut with such force that I jumped. The whittler sprang from the edge of his bunk and charged toward me, his pocketknife pointed at me. His face contorted into an evil grimace, he shouted obscenities through clenched teeth. I rushed out the opposite door, screaming, and ran into the nurse who was delivering two new arrivals to our barrack. I flew into her arms.

"That boy in there," I cried out. "He's trying to kill me."

"Calm down! Calm down! He's harmless. Just stay away from him. He's been badly hurt in the war."

"He tried to kill me. He really did. He came after me with his knife." I said, not letting go of her.

"No, no, Eva. He just wanted to scare you. He doesn't like to have anyone come too close to him."

If he tried to scare me, he succeeded. I gave him a wide berth from then on. I later overheard the nurse tell his mother that she needed to keep a better watch over her son or else they would put him away. The mother called me a troublemaker and accused me of trying to make life difficult for her poor son. I had trouble sleeping nights and worried I would start wetting my bed again.

CHAPTER TWO

TROUBLESOME THOUGHTS ABOUT OUR FUTURE filled my head.

I saw my brother every day at mealtime, but Frau Leppe and her girls had vanished. Each day, more girls, most between the ages of six and fourteen, moved into our barrack until no empty bunks remained. One of the later arrivals, an older girl, overheard that we would be moved to an orphanage within a day or two. We did not know if it would improve our situation or worsen it. The shell-shocked whittler's mother put things into perspective when she said, "Look girls, you're orphans. You don't have anyone to take care of you. This is only a temporary camp. Where else could you go but to an orphanage?"

"What's an orphanage like?" someone asked.

"Better than this. I promise you. Now go to sleep!"

The following evening, the nurse told us to gather up our things. "Tomorrow morning, I'll be taking you to the orphanage in Bautzen."

"What about my brother?" I asked, alarmed.

"He's coming, too."

The next day, after breakfast, we grabbed our bundles and gathered in front of the building. The whittler stood by the door and said good-bye to us, calling everyone by name. I waved to him, glad to have my little cat. It turned out that he had carved something for each of us.

Henry and I boarded the train together, restless and excited. Traveling in a real passenger train and sitting on real seats instead of riding in a cattle car bode well. I watched the countryside pass with its forests, red-roofed villages, and the many church steeples. It looked peaceful and untouched by destruction.

But Bautzen quickly reminded us of the war, especially as we walked past blocks and blocks of ruins to the orphanage, old army barracks at the outskirts of town. The nurse deposited us in a large dining hall.

Two women in gray, nunlike attire wheeled a kettle of steaming soup into the room. Ravenous, we pushed and shoved to get to the head of the line. With the first spoonful we gulped down, we realized we had not entered *Schlaraffenland*. The soup consisted of potato skins floating in hot water, and it smelled and tasted like earth. An older girl sitting next to me said, "If this is a sign of what it's going to be like here, we're in for more hard times."

"You mean it's going to be really bad?" I asked.

"*Ja*, really bad. This is the worst stuff I've ever eaten, and I've eaten some awful things."

After the meal, we were separated again from the boys and led to the medical building. "Strip off all your clothes and line up!" a nurse ordered.

I was sure we were going to receive shots, and not in the arm. Still afraid of needles, my hands turned clammy and my heart beat faster. I edged to the end of the line and checked the room for emergency exits. Just then, an older man in a white coat appeared.

"The doctor will give you each a physical examination," the nurse explained.

He sat down on a swivel chair next to a table lined with threatening-looking instruments. When the first girl stepped forward, the nurse pulled a curtain across the room, blocking my view. Waiting, I took a better look at my naked peers and discovered that some of them had protruding stomachs just like mine. I had put the incident with Pani Kolski's brother out of my mind, but now, as I ran my hand over my swollen stomach, I was absolutely sure that a baby was inside. I had not yet learned about the effects of malnutrition. Would they cut open my stomach and remove the baby?

By the time I stood before the doctor, I was numb with fear. He placed his stethoscope over my rapidly beating heart, looked at me kindly, and said in a calm, soothing voice, "Don't be afraid. No one is going to hurt you. Tell me your name. How old are you?" While his hands pressed here and there and rested on my round belly, he gave the nurse a silent look that only adults understood.

Then he examined me for venereal disease. I did not know if it was another form of sexual molestation or a real medical procedure. Before I could draw any conclusion, the nurse told me to get dressed and wait with the other girls. When comparing my experience with them, I learned that everyone had undergone the same treatment. Later I learned this examination was routine for females of all ages, even the very young, because many had contracted venereal disease after being raped or sexually abused by the Russians or the Poles.

With the medical ordeal behind us, we were separated into groups of twos or threes and taken to our assigned buildings. A young, dark-haired nurse with a kind face came for me, held me by the hand, and said, "There are a lot of nice girls where I'm taking you. You're going to have a really sweet bunkmate."

A chill hung in the late evening air, and the grounds were dimly lit. My new home looked just like the barracks in Goerlitz, except for the double-decker bunks. Two cast-iron stoves, one at each end of the room with wide metal pipes suspended from the ceiling, emanated welcome warmth. Shafts of moonlight streamed through the bare windows and illuminated the inside enough for us to find our way. A peaceful stillness greeted us. Only rhythmic breathing gave away that the beds were occupied. The nurse pulled me over to one of the lower bunks and whispered, "This is going to be your little corner. You can store your things under the bed. Your bedmate's name is Agnes. She's ten. I think you'll like her."

At the mention of her name, Agnes stirred and called out for her mother. The nurse went to her, held her, and rocked her back and forth, whispering, "It's all right, Agnes. No one is going to hurt you. I'm here. Now go back to sleep!"

I watched and listened with such a deep sensation of envy that I could feel the pain in every part of my body. I wanted to cry out, "Come and love me, too!"

Before she left, the nurse turned to me, smiled, and said in a soft voice, "Sleep well, little Eva."

I relished those sweet words and cried myself to sleep. In the morning, Agnes shook my shoulder and said, "Hey, wake up! You better hurry, or you'll miss breakfast."

Coming out of a deep sleep, disoriented and befogged, I focused on the strange face staring down on me and asked, "Where am I? Who are you?"

We studied each other. Her round face and thick tousled hair looked familiar. I glanced around the room, and then it all came back in time frames: the physical exam, the train ride to Bautzen, the days in Goerlitz, the long and terribly cold trip in the cattle car, the Poles, and the Russians. They were flashes of the past, and memories of places where I did not want to be. My stomach cramped with fear.

"Is it nice here?" I asked, and then I realized I felt hunger in my stomach, not fear.

Agnes sat at the edge of her bunk, watching me, and said, "I'll wait for you if you hurry."

I had made my first friend.

The dining hall across from our barrack served two buildings. We sat at long wooden tables with attached benches. "All the bunks in the buildings are full," Agnes explained. "As soon as someone gets adopted, the nurse brings a new girl to fill the empty bed."

"Adopted? Will we all be adopted?"

"*Ja.* Every other Sunday is adoption Sunday."

"But they told me they're going to find my father and brothers. I also have a sister. I just don't know what happened to them." Not at all happy with how this conversation was going, I added, "So I'm not really an orphan."

"I don't know about you, but my parents are dead, and I'm going to be adopted."

"How do you get adopted? Do you get to pick your new parents?"

"You'll see. They're coming again this Sunday to look us over."

"Quiet, children! Come get your food!" A sister, that was how the girls addressed these nurses in gray, handed each of us a slice of dry rye bread and a tin cup of hot chicory milk-coffee. No further talking was allowed during mealtime. The bread and coffee tasted delicious, but it did not satisfy my hunger, and I wondered how long it would be until the next meal.

Once I adjusted to this new life in the orphanage, I liked it. Girls my age with similar experiences surrounded me. Our barrack was spacious and warm, my bed was comfortable, and I did not have to work for the food they served. Above all, I had Agnes. Each day, we received one slice of coarse rye bread and chicory milk-coffee for breakfast and supper. Our main meal at noon consisted of a one-pot stew, made up of potatoes or cabbage with a few other vegetables thrown in. They called these concoctions by their meat base, but we never found a sign of meat in them. Twice a week, the thin, watery potato-skin soup appeared. We constantly talked about food and what it felt like not to be hungry.

Erika and Frieda, ages sixteen or seventeen, shared a room at the end of the building and were in charge of our barrack. They made sure the lights went out at the designated hour, oversaw our hygiene, and kept the peace. Petty fighting and accusations of one kind or another occurred daily, stealing usually being at the bottom of most arguments. At first, the group shunned the perpetrator. But tears of remorse and apologies from the guilty party quickly restored harmony. No one could bear to be alone. We all longed for love and acceptance.

Before adoption Sunday, we had inspection day. Officials checked the barracks for neatness and cleanliness. On those occasions, Erika and Frieda drove us twice as hard. We had to stand by our bunks until the inspectors left the building. I trembled every time I saw a Russian in uniform. I could not think of them as friends.

However, these Russians were different. They walked through the barracks, hands clasped behind their backs, with expressions of indifference on their young faces. They showed a lot more interest in Erika and Frieda. At the end of their routine, they stopped for a short visit with them, flirting and making small talk in perfect German. Frieda's and Erika's lack of fear baffled me.

I asked Agnes, "Are these Russian soldiers different from the ones who did all the killing and raping?"

"The Russians have always been kind to me, and these soldiers are really nice too." She moved closer and confided, "You know, Frieda has a crush on the tall one."

"Really?" I gasped. "How can she like him? Doesn't she know about all the people they've killed? They shot Herr Weber and Kurt for no reason at all. They beat and raped Fraulein Gretchen and Frau Kehr and my mother, and they killed all those people on that train in Niederhof."

Agnes shrugged and said, "Things are different now. They don't do that anymore."

Much had changed over the past three years, but I did not understand how Erika and Frieda could forget so quickly.

That night, I awoke to Agnes's heart-rending crying. Embroiled in a nightmare, she thrashed about wildly, beat down on her pillow, and shouted, "I can't find mother's head! Where's mother's head?"

Erika came running in her nightgown, took Agnes in her arms, and shook her. "Agnes, it's all right. It's all right. Wake up! No one is going to hurt you."

But Agnes could not stop crying. "Don't be afraid," Erika said. "You're with us. Eva is right next to you. You're not alone."

Comforted, Agnes reached for my hand. "What happened to your mother's head?" I asked after Erika left.

Wide awake now, the words spilled out of Agnes. Her family, mother, grandmother, and younger brother had fled on their wagon with other villagers. When their vehicle had broken down, they had been separated from the group and had gotten caught between the two fighting factions. They had hidden in a ditch to escape the shooting. Grenades had exploded around them, blowing the wagon to pieces. When Agnes had looked up, her mother was lying lifeless in a pool of blood, with her head missing. Other body parts had been scattered everywhere. "I wanted to look for mother's head, but the shooting wouldn't stop. When it got all quiet, I screamed, but no one answered. They were dead, all of them. Then a Russian tank drove up."

"Were you scared?" I interrupted.

"I was so scared, I couldn't move. I thought the tank would roll right over me. But it stopped. A soldier jumped down and picked me up. I was terrified. When we arrived at a village, that same soldier carried me to the first farm house we came to. He pointed his pistol at the women and children who lived there and said, 'You! Take care of girl! Her people dead. *Germanski Soldat*, German soldiers, kill.' You should have seen the women. They looked like stone statues, afraid to breathe. The soldier set me down and handed me a piece of chocolate. Then, he climbed back into the tank, and they drove off."

"Do all the Russians speak German now?"

"This one did. He was really nice, too. He held me the whole time until we got to the village. He kept repeating, 'We no shoot your family, little one. Germans shoot at us. You just in way.' He said he was really sorry."

"Did the German women keep you, or did they leave you with the Poles?"

"They kept me until we got to Goerlitz. Then, the camp people brought me here. They have been looking for my relatives. But I've been here a long time. I think they're all dead. I know that some of them got killed during the bombing in Koenigsberg. Now, I'm in the adoption pool."

"Adoption pool? What's that?" I asked, alarmed.

"You'll see on Sunday. I hope somebody nice picks me."

"Do you have to go with them even if you don't like them?"

"Yes. Even if I tried to come back, I'd never find my way. Most people come from really far away."

I started to have mixed feelings about this adoption business and ardently hoped Father would turn up, or my brothers, or aunts Elsbeth and Gertrude, before it was too late.

When adoption Sunday arrived, the girls scurried around nervously. A group of people, mostly women, arrived shortly after breakfast.

"All children up for adoption gather between the heating stoves, so these people can have a good look at you!" the sister called out, clapping her hands.

I watched from my bunk. The adoptive parents looked joyless and grim.

"Tell these people your name and age," the sister instructed as she pulled one of the girls toward an interested couple. "Tell them what you like to do!"

The girl fixed her eyes on her feet and said nothing.

"What happened to your parents?" the woman asked.

The girl did not look up and remained silent.

To my relief, they bypassed Agnes. That evening, in our bunks, she said, "I didn't like any of those people. They all looked mean." She started to cry and added, "I want my mother back."

I, too, missed Mother and joined Agnes with my tears.

CHAPTER THREE

LIFE AT THE ORPHANAGE TOOK on a semblance of normalcy, and we followed a loosely structured routine. Henry came to see me almost every day. Knowing I had at least one living relative comforted me. I often saved some bread rations for my brother, just to ensure his visits.

After a few days, I started school. Excited and apprehensive, I followed Agnes on that Monday afternoon, my first day back to school after three years. How would I bridge the gap? All that time, I had not held a pencil or a piece of chalk in my hand. I practiced writing in the dirt and discovered I still knew my letters, small and large, from beginning to end.

Separated from the boys even in school, Agnes and I were placed in a class consisting of ten-, eleven-, and twelve-year-olds. Our teacher, a young beauty who spoke with a lisp, seemed as much at a loss about where to begin as we were. Agnes, having been through this routine for several months, turned to me and said, "It's always the same. Each Monday we start all over again with the same lesson because there are so many new girls."

Despite the disruption in continuity, I did learn and appreciated school more than ever. Although I was almost twelve, I felt as if I was starting at a first-grade level. Intimidated by my ignorance, I resolved to learn and to learn quickly. My empty mind greedily absorbed everything. However, the shortage of teachers, books, and paper slowed our learning. The two hours of school every afternoon turned catching up into a tedious exercise. At the end of each session, we had to turn in our pencils for the children in the morning classes, which meant we had no homework.

That same week, our barrack sister told us, the Protestant girls, to dress warmly. The vicar was coming after breakfast to take us to the nearby church for our religion lesson. Finally, I would learn religion. The vicar would teach me to pray the right way so God would better understand what I was asking of him. I almost exploded with impatience and compiled a new list of requests, careful to get my priorities in the right sequence. Bring back Father, find my brothers and sister, and find my aunts Elsbeth and Gertrude headed the list, followed by more food, warm clothes, books so I could practice reading, a doll to love, and shoes. I needed shoes the most.

The vicar was a young woman. Unlike the old pastor at Oma's funeral, she wore layman's clothing, which reduced my faith in her ability to help expedite my prayers. Even so, she offered an opportunity to negotiate with God.

Inside the immense church, I felt as if I had entered heaven, and I expected God to appear in person at any moment. Music floated out of long pipes somewhere in the loft above us and echoed through the vast, hollow space. The vicar put her finger to her lips, indicating silence, and motioned for us to sit down in the front pews. We listened piously. Peace and tranquility settled in my soul and transported me into a world filled with angels, Mother, and everything beautiful and good. Tears welled up inside me from deep within. This, I thought, was what the world should be like, instead of what it had been. I did not want the music to stop, ever. But it did. The organist finished playing, and my indoctrination into religion began.

I remember little of my lessons. But that first visit to a church, a towering cathedral as it turned out, left a lasting impression on me. If God existed on earth, he lived in that church. I looked forward to Wednesday mornings and entered the cathedral with awe and reverence. I wanted so much to believe in an all-powerful God, who according to the vicar saw and controlled everything. Why had he been so unrelenting in his punishment and deaf to my cries for help? When I asked the vicar, she explained it away as a lack of faith. "You have to trust God. He has his reasons," she said.

Her answer troubled me greatly. It made little sense. What had Kurt and Herr Weber done to deserve their fate, to be brutalized and killed as they had been, and Oma, the gentle spinner, who had died such a painful, lonely death? And Mother, who died with a drunken Russian soldier in her bed. What crimes were my abducted Father and young brothers guilty of? And all those people whose corpses lay rotting in the fields around Niederhof after that terrible massacre, their flesh eaten off the bones by wild animals—what had they done to deserve such a cruel fate? I feared for myself and did not see salvation as the vicar promised. I could not conjure up that blind faith in God's benevolence about which the woman preached. I questioned everything. We all did, but we received no convincing answers. It was always "God's will" and "he has his reasons." We began to see God as someone capricious, who just toyed with our lives. We had seen too much violence and experienced trauma beyond our capacity to comprehend. We asked many thought-provoking questions. The vicar tried hard to bring us around to God's side, but our memories of what seemed a godless world could not so easily be erased.

We learned the Lord's Prayer, listened to Bible stories, and sang religious songs. Often, the organist stayed after his practice sessions and accompanied us. The music made me look forward to those lessons in religion. I learned by rote, while my spirit soared to the heavens on the uplifting notes coming from the organ. Music is God's language, I thought. Maybe I needed to learn to play an instrument.

Other than Wednesdays, I did not like the mornings, usually dedicated to fresh air and exercise. A raw October wind blew through the city streets, and it rained leaves. Like many of the girls, I did not have enough warm clothing. No amount of exercise could keep the cold at bay. By the time we returned to the warmth of the barrack, our hands and feet were numb. I started to warm up to the prospect of adoption, if only for the sake of a comfortable home and warm clothing. I wished for a soft, cuddly sweater along with a thick winter coat with a hood, fur-lined shoes and gloves, and a shawl to wrap around my face. I dreaded the arrival of winter, with its endless dark and dreary days.

One freezing morning, the sister announced that all new arrivals would be going to the garment storehouse to receive warm clothing. Excited, I envisioned myself wrapped in a wardrobe of pleasing softness and happy, bright colors. I would emerge from this garment paradise a changed person, and no one would recognize me.

Reality proved quite different. I scanned the storeroom shelves stacked with inventory sadly lacking in color. We had to declare what we owned, and from that the sister determined what we were entitled to receive. From my position at the back of the line, I listened and learned that none of the girls told the truth. Everyone suddenly owned next to nothing, and what little they did have was badly worn or too small. When my turn came, I adjusted my conscience and sense of truth accordingly. Starting out with the truth, I lifted my foot and said, "These are the only shoes I have. My feet are always wet and cold."

But luck failed me. There were no shoes left in my size. I would have to wait until a new shipment arrived from the Swiss Red Cross. "God only knows when that will be," the sister said.

I did get everything else I asked for: a set of woolen underwear, long stockings, a dress, and a sweater. The sister gave me a choice between a pretty gray and white short-sleeved dress and a drab, long-sleeved warm one. I changed my mind several times until she said with some impatience in her voice, "Now, which one is it going to be? This is your final choice."

I wanted so much to own something pretty, just one pretty thing. But I had grown practical and wise, and so I opted for the ugly but warm long-sleeved one.

As I started to leave the storeroom with my bundle draped over my arm, the sister held me back. She pulled the coveted dress from the shelf, pushed it under the clothes on my arm, and said, "Those sad blue eyes break my heart. Here, take it. It's a present. But don't talk about it!"

She kissed me on the head and pushed me out the door. I don't know what thrilled me more, the kiss or the dress. For the first time since Mother's death, I felt like someone really cared about me.

With my new and better-fitting clothes I discovered how much I had grown over the last year.

The days passed harmoniously. I attended school and owned warm clothes. The meals, although sparse, were regular. I had found a friend in Agnes and nurtured hopes for a better life.

Over time, I befriended our wardens, Erika and Frieda. I told Frieda, who always primped for her Russian inspector friend, that I knew how to create curls with paper strips as I had seen Pani Ilowski do with Dorota. She immediately made me her personal hair dresser. Many an evening she came to my bunk and whispered, "Eva, come and roll up my hair!" Although I had never done it, my skill improved rapidly. Soon Erika said, "Do mine too!" I darned socks, sewed on buttons, and polished their shoes as well.

Even in this new and better life, worries about the future continued to plague me. What would happen to Henry and me if the search for our family turned up empty, or worse, if they were all dead? Then, we would be real orphans. I often awoke from bad dreams, drenched in the sweat of fear as I relived my life with the Poles. I had nightmares within nightmares and longed for a protected life with parental love. Yet, I sensed I might never have such a life again.

Another adoption Sunday arrived. Agnes was not among the available girls. She had come down with measles two days earlier and was in the infirmary.

A storm raged outside and heavy rain beat against the window panes when the camp director drove up in an army jeep with only one couple. They chose a big girl, the older of two sisters. She begged the adoptive parents to take her sister as well or to choose someone else. But the couple remained unmoved.

"Times are hard," the man said. "No one can take in two children." He exchanged glances with his wife who added, "You can write to your sister as often as you like. When she has found a home, you can visit each other."

The older sister pleaded with the director, but his face remained a frozen blank. "You've got to go with these people. You're lucky they want you," he said.

The sisters' teary goodbye made me glad Agnes was safely tucked away at the infirmary.

After that, the younger sister cried herself to sleep every night and sometimes called out for her sibling in her dreams.

Then, late one evening, the adopted sister stood at our barrack door in tears. The siblings fell into each other's arms. "What happened? Did you run away?" we all asked, wanting to know. "How did you find your way back?"

"Those people wanted a maid," she told us. "They never let me out of their sight. At night, they locked me up. One of them was always with me. I worked all day, and when I asked about going to school, they said that first there was work to be done. School would come later."

The couple was starting up a small plant nursery, and they had adopted her strictly for free labor. "One day, a man came to see them," she continued. "They argued about money. Things got real heated. They shouted at each other, and it looked like the men were going to have a fistfight. I think they forgot about me. I just walked away. I knew the direction to Bautzen, and I started to run and kept running. I got a ride with some Russian soldiers, who dropped me off at the edge of town. I told them I was visiting relatives here."

No one had ever come back before, and Erika and Frieda did not know what to do. They summoned the camp director, who had allowed the separation of the sisters only two weeks before.

"Please, don't send me back," the older sister pleaded. "Please, I want to stay with my sister."

Touched, he regarded her kindly and said, "I'll put through a special order for you two not to be separated again. Now, back to bed, all of you!"

Another week passed. Agnes still had not returned from the infirmary, and I was not allowed to visit her. I missed her terribly. Afraid she might die, I faked sickness. I went to Erika with my hands pressed into my belly and told her I had a really bad stomach ache. She took me to the infirmary and turned me over to a nurse, who, after taking my temperature, looking at my stretched-out tongue, elicited the usual ah, shook her head, and sent me back to my barrack.

After leaving the medical office, I noticed that passport-size photos of all the children at the orphanage lined the reception hall walls in alphabetical order. I stopped, studied the faces, and read the first and last names, ages, sex, origin, and other identifying particulars. I easily found Henry's and my pictures. The personal information was correct, Eva Rapp, Steglitz, East Prussia, born January 21, 1936. No physical marks. The small print next to an asterisk surprised me. It read, "Arrived on last transport out of the Elbing area." I shuddered, thankful that chance had gotten Henry and me to the right place at the right time. There also were pictures of young children with nothing but their first names under them and where they had been found.

Agnes did not die. She recovered and returned to our barrack two weeks later. I was thrilled, but my happiness was short. Someone adopted her the following Sunday. She disappeared from my life like all the others, and our barrack sister no longer lingered by Agnes' empty bunk during her nightly rounds.

A new kind of loneliness seeped into my heart.

CHAPTER FOUR

ENDLESS STORMS SWEPT ACROSS THE fallow fields; the trees stood naked and bare. The sun disappeared, and the skies remained a dismal gray for days on end. The iron stoves in our drafty barrack were no longer a match for the freezing cold nature thrust upon us. Fuel shortages kept our allotment of coal to a minimum. We hovered around the two stoves like moths seeking light. Our outdoor exercise sessions stopped because few of us had warm winter coats.

Nearly two months had passed since Henry and I arrived at the orphanage. Our barrack had emptied out with the many adoptions and few new arrivals. Agnes' bunk remained vacant. Then, one day, our barrack sister came looking for me, waving a letter in one hand. "Eva, look! I have a surprise for you. It's from your family," she called out.

I stared at the envelope addressed to Henry and Eva Rapp. On the back, it read from Elsbeth Rapp. I turned it over and over, squeezing it between my nervous fingers, rereading our names several times to convince myself it was real. Tears trickled down my cheeks, and my hands trembled as I unfolded the letter, one of those wartime pieces of stationary that folded together from the four corners, forming its own envelope on the outside. I noticed it had been opened.

"We read all the mail before we give it out," the sister volunteered. "We need to make sure your relatives are real, and that you are not misled." She hesitated and asked, "Would you like for me to read it to you?"

"I can read. It's from Aunt Elsbeth. She started writing to me when I was in first grade," I boasted.

I sat at the edge of my bunk and deciphered the first line: "*Mein liebes Evelynchen und lieber Henry,*" my dear little Evelyne and dear Henry. I spelled it out. E-v-e-l-y-n-e, the added "chen" represented merely the diminutive form. Evelyne … it sounded so familiar. The name had always been in the deep recesses of my mind. Now, Aunt Elsbeth had committed it to paper and recalled it to my memory. Much as I tried to squelch my tears, they refused to stop. They were tears of happiness.

Waving the letter in the air, I ran over to Henry's barrack and shouted, "Henry, Aunt Elsbeth is alive. We have a letter from her."

We sat on the steps, and Henry, much calmer than I, read out loud.

My dear Evelynchen and dear Henry,

We can't tell you how happy we are to know you are alive. We searched and searched for you. Yesterday we heard from the Angehoerigensuchdienstzentrale [loosely translated, search for lost relatives service headquarters] *that you are in an orphanage in Bautzen. Aunt Gertrude and Uncle Eduard are here with me in the American Zone. Your sister, Vera, and Frau Teichert made it out safely ahead of the Russians. They are living with Aunt Kaethe in Singfeld; so is your brother Douglas. The Russians released him within a few months when they realized how young he was. He is attending the Gymnasium* [private High School] *here in Klosterburg. Erwin returned—a mere skeleton—from a Russian prison camp only a few weeks ago. He suffered many hardships during his three year incarceration and is lucky to be alive. As yet, we have no information about your father. He and Erwin were separated shortly after the Russians took them prisoner. But we have found you, and we won't give up until we find him. We know that your mother died. People who got out of Steglitz earlier left that information at the Lost Relative Search Headquarters. As soon as the authorities in Bautzen can manage to put together a transport, they will send you to us along with all the other children who are waiting to be reunited with their families in the western zones. They told us it wouldn't be until some time in January. But we are hoping they are wrong, and we will have you with us for Christmas. Until then, I embrace both of you and kiss you.*

Your Aunt Elsbeth

I asked Henry to help count the days until Christmas, but he said, "It's only November. Christmas is a long time away."

I was euphoric. Our life was about to take on a whole new meaning. We would be a family again. Aunt Elsbeth not only had thrown us a life preserver; she had lowered the whole lifeboat to carry us into a safe harbor. Just knowing someone cared and wanted us made me come alive with a feeling of well-being. It dominated my every thought.

That evening, I asked Erika about the *Angehoerigensuchdienst,* what it meant and how it functioned.

"It's an organization that has sprung up after the war for the purpose of reuniting families such as yours. Your aunts sent in your names as missing persons, and the people here at the orphanage sent in your names as looking for surviving family members. It was only a matter of time for you to get matched up. A lot of kids have been reunited with their families that way. Soon, those of you who are going to the Western zones will be leaving here."

"When?" I was bursting with impatience.

She shook her head. "I don't know. They're trying to find as many relatives as they can before putting together a transport. The children who have families in the Russian Zone are picked up immediately, but you'll have to wait. You'll all go out together."

"What's a zone? Why can't we just take a train, even a freight train?"

She shrugged her shoulders and struggled with her answer. "I just know that Germany is now divided between several countries. We're in the Russian part. My soldier friend told me so."

I did not understand Erika's complicated explanation, nor did I really care, as long as the aunts and my brothers and sister were waiting somewhere for us.

I thought of nothing but our family reunion, what it would be like to be together again. I had struggled so long to conquer my deep-seated fear of continual abandonment; now, one loving letter swept it away.

Henry and I quickly replied to Aunt Elsbeth. Our barrack sister supplied us with a pencil and paper. Painfully aware of my lack of schooling, I struggled to put together the words and labored carefully over each individual letter. I wanted to bare my soul to her, to write of the joy and happiness I felt, but my hand failed me. Too much time had passed since I had written anything. I condensed my part of the reply into two sentences. "Dear Aunt Elsbeth. I have missed you so much. Please come and get us quick."

Time dragged on. The weeks passed without further word from anyone. I longed for a letter from my sister. Every day, I asked our barrack nurse, "Was there mail for us today?" She would shake her head and say, "No, nothing today. Don't worry, Eva; if anything arrives, you'll get it. The mail between the zones is very slow. Be patient!"

I counted the hours and the days. Finally, we received a long letter, three whole pages, from my brother Erwin. Once more, I raced over to Henry's barrack, pressed the letter into his hands, and prevailed upon him to read it to me. Surely this letter would reveal all the secrets to our future life. It would tell us what wonderful things awaited us once we crossed into this other zone, the American Zone.

I plucked the words from Henry's lips as he read out loud. However, my spirits sank and a pit opened in my stomach as my mind tried to make sense of the strung-together words. Erwin, Vera, and Douglas were leaving for America within two weeks, and they would be long gone before we got to Aunt Elsbeth's. He wrote to say good-bye. Devastated, I lay awake nights, wondering what my brothers and sister looked like, and whether they would like me better now that I was older and so much wiser, as I thought myself to be. Erwin held out one promise that kept my spirits up: we would follow them to America, the land of Father's dreams, as soon as they were settled.

Winter arrived with vengeance. Snow fell for several days, covering the city's ruins with a pristine sheet of white, as though trying to hide the shame of defeat. The wind whipped across the compound and made the powdery snow dance in the air. Cold crept into every corner of our barrack and left us shivering under our blankets.

Another letter arrived from Aunt Elsbeth. My brothers and sister were on their way to America. So it had come to pass. They were floating on a big ship somewhere on a huge ocean. In my child's mind, I had looked to my sister to take Mother's place. Now she was gone, without knowing how much I longed for her. But with disappointment came a ray of hope. The officials in Bautzen notified Aunt Elsbeth that we would arrive before Christmas.

I got to go one more time to the clothing storage house—to fill in the missing pieces, as the sister had said. This time, they had shoes my size. My rucksack barely held it all, and I felt rich.

For our last religion lesson, the vicar took us to her place in a partially bombed-out building. We climbed over rubble, up a shaky, half-exposed stairway to her one-room flat on the second floor. An iron stove nestled in one corner. She added wood and coal to the dying embers, and soon cozy warmth embraced us. She lit three candles on the advent wreath, the only sign that Christmas was near, and passed out a plate of the traditional *Pfeffernuesse*, a spicy Christmas cookie, that she had baked especially for us.

That morning, the vicar did not speak of religion; she asked instead about our families, and where we were going.

"I'm going to America," I proudly announced. "My brothers and sister are already there."

"Where's America?" a girl asked.

"It's on the other side of the ocean." That was all I could tell them, and I realized how little I knew about my future home. Suddenly, I was frightened.

The vicar pulled an old atlas from a shelf, opened it to a map of the entire world, took my hand, and said, "It's a long journey." She guided my finger across the Atlantic Ocean and added, "But it's worth it. You're a very lucky girl, Eva."

"What language do they speak in America?" one girl asked.

"American," someone volunteered.

"No, they speak English. My brother wrote that I will have to learn English," I explained.

"Eva is right," the vicar said. "They speak English in America." Then, she gave us a short history lesson about America, while I hung on her words. America had become a subject very dear to me.

Before she took us back to the orphanage, she gave each of us a picture postcard, the kind Aunt Elsbeth used to send to me.

"Write to me when you're reunited with your families and tell me how you're doing," she said.

I never did write to her, but I used the card as a bookmarker all these years and still have it.

When the vicar said goodbye to us at the gate, she said, "You see, God is looking after you. You'll be with your families for Christmas."

After the midday meal, our barrack sister announced that we would leave that evening.

All afternoon we waited, each of us lost in our own fantasies. Time seemed to stand still. Henry came over after lunch to tell me Aunt Elsbeth had written to the orphanage officials that Uncle Eduard would be waiting for us at the border. Erika had been right. Germany was divided into different sections, and we had to cross more borders. This time, Henry was included on the passenger list, and we had nothing to fear.

I sat by the window at the edge of my bunk and watched darkness gently descend over our camp. My heart sank when our barrack sister told us to assemble for our evening meal. But once we returned to our barrack she announced, "Put on your warm clothes and get your things. Your train is waiting at the station. You'll be traveling all night."

Erika and Frieda accompanied us to the front gate. Several groups were already waiting with their plump little bundles, including Henry. Erika nudged me on the shoulder and said, "We'll miss you, Eva. Nobody can roll up hair the way you do."

I smiled inwardly. I would be missed. It felt good.

I searched the clear, star-filled sky and wondered if Mother was watching from up there. Concentrating on the brightest one, I said, "Good-bye, Mutti." I bade farewell not only to her but also to a life of rejection and immense loneliness.

Our group was much smaller than I had expected, with no more than fifty of us, the girls outnumbering the boys. At the station, an empty passenger car awaited us on a sidetrack. We piled in, pushing and shoving for a window seat. That we would be traveling all night and not be able to see anything did not occur to anyone.

"Calm down," one of the sisters said. "You arrived in a cattle car. Be glad you're not leaving the same way."

Henry eyed the net luggage rack above us and announced, "I'm spending the night up there. It'll be like sleeping in a hammock."

"Try to go to sleep," the other sister said. "Soon, we'll get hooked onto a passenger train. You want to be rested when you meet your families in the morning."

None of us intended to sleep. This train ride would change our lives for the better, and we wanted to experience it to the fullest.

However, I did not even stay awake long enough to feel our car go into motion. When I awoke, the wheels were rolling, and the stars were already dimming. I kept my eyes glued to the window. The sky turned a purplish blue as the sun edged up at the distant horizon. A thin layer of snow blanketed the quiet, frozen land as far as my eyes could see, and lifeless trees threw long, skeletal shadows across the white plains. Occasionally, a lonely village swept by. Used to disappointment, I no longer cared that my brothers and sister would not be there to meet us, as long as the aunts and uncle awaited our arrival somewhere in the American Zone.

CHAPTER FIVE

I DO NOT REMEMBER THE name of the city on the West German border where our families picked us up. Only one thing stands out in my mind. The wheels were still turning when I spotted Uncle Eduard among a crowd of people. A whole head taller, he towered over the group like a giant among dwarves. My heart filled with joy at the sight of him.

Henry and I jumped off the train and shouted, "Uncle Eduard, over here!" elbowing our way through the anxious gathering. "Over here!" we kept shouting. "We're over here!"

My uncle did not move. He looked in our direction and waited for us to reach him. He had always been nearsighted and now had been declared legally blind. Yet, he had come to meet us and bring us home. I threw my arms around his waist, pushed my head into his stomach, and cried with happiness. He felt so good, so comfortable. His familiar voice reached my ears like an echo of home, the home no longer ours. Even his smell evoked memories of a happier past.

The formalities at our destination were few. Uncle Eduard signed a document assuming responsibility for Henry and me, and we were free to go. After that, things became more difficult. Train travel in all the zones was a nightmare. We sat for hours on our bundles in an overcrowded waiting room. Aunt Elsbeth had had the foresight to send sandwiches along. Food concessions in railroad stations did not yet exist, and the German people were still on ration cards. The sandwiches took care of our hunger, but not our thirst. We could not even buy water.

The train arrived hours late, packed with weary travelers. Only a few people got off. Uncle Eduard pushed us ahead of him. He pressed me into the people until I thought I would suffocate. Someone forced the door shut behind my uncle and cursed us. Couldn't we see the compartment was already packed full? Were we blind?

My uncle pointed to the black and white band on his sleeve and said, "Yes, I am."

The tension eased. Someone rose and offered my uncle his seat, assuming his affliction was the result of a war injury. "We've all suffered from this damned war," he said. Uncle Eduard neither confirmed nor denied the man's assumption, while making himself comfortable in the vacated seat. Henry and I slid onto the floor next to him in a forest of legs and feet. And so we rolled towards Klosterburg, in a train warmed only by body heat.

Twice more we changed trains, hours late and overcrowded. Pushing and shoving, I held my breath each time, letting the crowd carry me along.

Shortly before midnight, we arrived in Klosterburg, a small provincial town with no more than eight thousand inhabitants. The station loomed dark and deserted. Only minutes separated us from our reunion with Aunt Elsbeth and Aunt Gertrude. I wondered, with some misgivings, whether I would be able to keep all the promises I had made to God if this ever came to pass.

"How much farther is it to their house" I pestered my uncle. "How much longer?"

But Uncle Eduard concentrated on navigating the slippery sidewalks on that cold winter night. Occasionally, he asked, "Tell me. Is that ice in front of us?"

I realized how restricted his vision was and wondered how he had ever found his way to get us. I never had had much feeling for this uncle, who, unlike his sisters, had paid little attention to me when they had visited us on the farm. Mother often referred to him as a ladies' man, which I interpreted as not liking children. But now, as I watched his unsteady groping steps, my heart filled with love for him.

Klosterburg was asleep, and snow glistened in the moonlight. Nothing hinted of Christmas being just days away. No colorful lights decorated the streets, not even a cheerful candle in a window. Yet it seemed like Santa Claus walked beside me, in the guise of my uncle. The closer we got to the center of town, the faster my heart beat and the lighter my steps became until I no longer felt the ground under my feet. Powerful emotions swept me along during this moment of our final liberation after three dark years with little sun and too many tears.

When we came to a three-story, red brick building, Uncle Eduard stopped, pointed to a little Mansard window in the steep roof, and said, "That's where Elsbeth and Gertrude live. They have a room in the attic above the post office."

After walking through the dark entranceway, we climbed the three flights of creaking stairs, dimly lit by weak moonlight peeking through the tiny windows above each landing. Uncle Eduard guided us down an unlit corridor. On familiar ground now, he walked with steady feet, while Henry and I felt our way along the wall in the dark.

A door flew open at the far end, and there stood Aunt Elsbeth, framed in a glow of light like an angel descending from heaven. Tears of joy glistened in her eyes. I flew into her open arms and felt her embrace like a tightening band around me as she pressed me close to her heart. I wanted her to crush my bones so I could feel the sweet pain of her love more deeply.

"Evchen, *mein kleines Affchen*, my little monkey," she said. "Finally, you are here."

Aunt Gertrude stood behind her in her nightgown, looking equally angelic, tears running down her cheeks, repeating, "*Zuckermaeuschen! Zuckermaeuschen*, sugar mouse." That was all she could master between sobs. I just cried, and so did Henry, while Aunt Elsbeth embraced him, too.

"We've waited for you all day," Aunt Elsbeth said, "and had just about given up on you."

"You can't believe the delays," Uncle Eduard complained. "The endless waiting for trains that we weren't even sure would materialize. I don't know where all the people were coming from, or where they were going. It's like a mass migration out there."

We learned his journey to meet us had taken two long days, a journey that should have lasted less than a few hours under normal conditions. He spent the night sleeping on the floor in a crowded waiting room. He looked at Henry and me, smiled, and said, "But it was worth it."

While Uncle Eduard related his experiences, Aunt Elsbeth rekindled the fire in the stove and heated a pot of soup for us. I sat on a chair by the table, dazed and tired, not sure I wasn't dreaming. Everything looked out of focus. I felt like I had suddenly returned from another planet to a world I had known a long, long time ago. I inhaled that wonderful special smell of fresh paint, firewood, the lingering aroma of recently prepared food, and the familiar scent emanating from the aunts.

Looking around the room, I realized it contained all their possessions. No doors led to additional space. A bed and a chaise lounge tucked under the slanted roof served as their sleeping place. An old-fashioned washstand with a porcelain bowl and a cracked water pitcher stood between them. The cooking stove and a small workbench-type table took up one corner of the room, and an oversized wardrobe with glass doors took up the other. Books lined the shelves behind the glass and added a touch of luxury. My eyes rested on Aunt Gertrude's piano next to the stove, the only familiar piece of furniture in the room. She had crated it up, filled the hollow spaces with her most precious books, and shipped it to Aunt Kaethe the summer before they had fled. Now, it graced the wall of this otherwise very functional room and looked out of place. Sparse living quarters for the aunts who loved their oil paintings, antique furniture, oriental rugs, and their many books, I thought. I wondered where we would sleep. Uncle Eduard solved the mystery when he said to Henry, "Come, my boy. You and I are sleeping in the attic." I got to crawl in with Aunt Elsbeth. Never did I sleep better nor dream sweeter dreams.

When I awoke in the morning, both aunts were already up, and the room smelled of freshly brewed coffee. Aunt Gertrude had rolled up her bedding and stored it in the attic, their extended living space. Everything ended up there eventually: firewood, left-over food, pots and pans, dishes, clothes, and whatever else was in the way.

I watched Aunt Elsbeth put bread, margarine, and brown syrup made from sugar beets on the breakfast table. Everything seemed so strange. Someone else was doing the things the Poles had made me do. Now, here I sat, listening to the happy household clatter, inhaling the delicious coffee aroma, while luxuriating in Aunt Elsbeth's cuddly warm bed. She looked my way and asked, "*Na, Affchen*, little monkey, did you sleep well?"

Aunt Gertrude sat at the edge of my bed, stroked my arm, and said, "*Mein armes Zuckermaeuschen*, my poor little sugar mouse, what you must have lived through." I simply lay there and let the attention wash over me like the gentle surf of the sea.

We spent the morning sitting around the table, the aunts asking questions and Henry and I providing answers, shyly and cautiously at first. But once the floodgates opened, the words poured out of us.

"Those brutes! You are children. How could anyone mistreat innocent children like that?" Aunt Gertrude occasionally interjected.

"The Poles hated us because we were German," Henry said. "They hated all the Germans."

"How could Frau Weber and Frau Leitzel leave you at their mercy? They must have known that the Poles would mistreat you. How could they be so heartless?" Aunt Elsbeth persisted. "I'm going to write to Frau Weber and give her a piece of my mind. You know, it was Frau Weber who reported your whereabouts to the organization for missing persons. I wrote to you in care of the Polish official in charge of the Germans in the Elbing district. We also contacted the American Embassy in Warsaw. But we never heard from either."

One by one the pieces came together. That mysterious letter Henry and I had been told about existed after all. The official in the shiny black car, who had came to the Kolskis looking for me, was real. The same man, perhaps, had found Henry and had given him forms to fill out. Henry still had the documents, written in Polish. We could only make sense of the heading: *Amabasad Amerykanska, Warszawa, 17 Marca 1947*, American Embassy, Warsaw, March 17, 1947. The American Embassy in Warsaw had started the search for us, but it had not followed through.

After breakfast, Uncle Eduard left for Singfeld some three kilometers away, the same small village where their sister, Aunt Kaethe, lived. He had a room in the attic above the schoolhouse. Aunt Gertrude reported for her shift at the telegraph office downstairs, and Henry and I accompanied Aunt Elsbeth to the stores on her daily hunt for food. Peace may have come to Germany, but the store shelves remained empty.

We stopped first at the butcher. Seduced by the delicious aroma of smoked sausage and meat, I decided that as soon as I was old enough, I would get a job in a butcher shop and eat my way through mountains of sausages. People waited in line while the two women carefully weighed out the different meats. When it was our turn, Aunt Elsbeth pushed Henry and me in front of the older woman and said, "These are my dead brother's poor children. Their mother is dead too. They just arrived from Poland. Oh, how they have suffered. The Poles beat and starved them. Then, they kicked them out on the street. I don't have ration cards for them yet. Can you do anything for us? I mean for them?"

The store turned quiet. I felt everyone's eyes on us and blushed with shame. Aunt Elsbeth was begging! I realized we had not arrived in *Schlaraffenland*.

Nonetheless, Aunt Elsbeth's ploy worked. The woman handed a healthy slice of sausage to Henry and to me, and then she said to Aunt Elsbeth, "Show me what ration cards you have. Let's see what we can do."

Aunt Elsbeth used this approach everywhere, not always with the same success. Shortages of every kind still existed, housing being the most acute. The rebuilding of the country had not yet begun, and refugees from the Russian Zone and the lost eastern territories continued to pour in, with no place to go. Jobs were scarce, and the black market thrived. Aunt Gertrude traded in her jewelry, which opened doors for us that otherwise would have remained shut.

On Christmas Eve, Uncle Eduard came with a tiny evergreen tree tucked under his arm. It was no more than two feet tall and perfectly shaped. We decorated it with tinsel and tied little red bows made from narrow strips of fabric to the ends of the branches.

"That used to be Hitler's flag," Aunt Gertrude explained when I examined the frayed edges. "That's all it's good for now. You should have seen the little girls in their red dresses the first year after the war. All out of the old German flag, with red skirts, white blouses, and black trim. There was no mistaking what it was." She laughed and added, "It was funny to see. They looked like they belonged to some kind of youth cult."

The dresses sounded wonderful to me. I would have loved to own such a colorful outfit.

And so we celebrated Christmas. Aunt Kaethe had sent cookies from her store, along with a few other goodies. Aunt Elsbeth made sandwiches with meat for our supper and surprised us with cups of cocoa she undoubtedly had extorted from one of the merchants with her "those poor children, how they have suffered" act. Henry and I even received presents. Writing paper, a pencil, and a book for each of us lay under the tree. We lit all four candles, and Aunt Elsbeth said, "We have a lot to be thankful for tonight. If only your father were here."

That was also my most ardent wish.

On Christmas morning, I awoke to the sound of tolling bells, summoning the people to church. Aunt Elsbeth had answered their call and left a note for us to eat breakfast without her. I inhaled the smell of fresh pine mixed with the aroma of roasting meat and spices that hung in the air, and I felt good all over.

The week after Christmas was a busy one. Both aunts had arranged to have time off work. The need for ration cards for Henry and me kept us sitting in overcrowded waiting rooms. Aunt Elsbeth tried to get extra coupons for us, but the official shook his head and said, "I can't do anything for you without a doctor's certificate stating the children are malnourished."

With that in mind, Aunt Gertrude took me to her private doctor the next day. A retired gynecologist, he still took patients willing to pay for his services outside the socialized medicine system. His waiting room was empty. Aunt Elsbeth had coached her sister well. She recited the rehearsed litany about these two abused orphans while the good doctor listened.

He stroked his gray goatee beard, and said, "Well, let me examine her."

He led me into an adjoining room and closed the well-padded double doors behind him. My heart pounded, and my temples throbbed. Was that protective door meant to muffle the screams from the pain he inflicted on his patients?

He sat down on a stool next to the examination table. Never taking his eyes off me, he said, "First we'll have to x-ray your lungs. Take off your dress and undershirt and go stand behind that machine."

I quickly stepped behind the big glass plate of his x-ray equipment, trying to hide my nakedness. The light went out and the room turned dark.

"Don't be afraid," he said. "It has to be dark for x-rays."

I relaxed. He sounded convincing. Suddenly, I felt his cold bony hands on my breasts.

"We have to hold these cute little things to the side so we can get a good picture of your lungs," he said. When he started to massage "those cute little things," my heart threatened to jump out of my chest into his busy hands. I wanted to scream, but I doubted Aunt Gertrude would hear me through those well-padded doors.

"Hold still. I'm almost done," came his labored voice. Not sure what was normal any more, I just held still. Finally, the lights went on, and he said, "Now, take off your panties and climb on that table!"

I froze and, with a shaking voice, said, "I've already had that examination." I grabbed my dress, slipped it on, and headed for the door. My aunt looked up startled. "*Na, Maeuschen*, is everything all right?"

"*Ja*," I said, avoiding her eyes.

"Why are you holding on to your underwear?"

"Oh, I forgot to put them on."

After several minutes, the doctor appeared, handed Aunt Gertrude the much-desired document, and said, "This is good for six months. You'll have to bring her back to get it renewed."

"I'll never go back to him," I said to my aunt on the way home. Probably thinking adolescent modesty caused my revolt, she said, "I know, I know. But he's my private doctor. He's not such a stickler with formalities. We had a better chance of getting the extra ration cards."

I wanted so much to tell her about the doctor's behavior and about Pani Kolski's brother and the man who had lived below Roza, but since I was shy about the subject, I could not find the right words.

Before bedtime, I climbed on a stool in front of the little mirror and checked my chest. I discovered that, indeed, I had entered puberty.

Aunt Elsbeth, too, had succeeded in getting extra ration cards for Henry. Shoes were another matter. I desperately needed shoes. The ones I had received at the orphanage were so poorly made that I had wet feet only minutes after stepping out in bad weather, and winter had barely begun. Aunt Elsbeth said, "You'll catch pneumonia if this continues."

But Henry and I had become inured to the elements.

The shoes displayed in the store windows all had "sold" signs by them. We found the same thing in all the stores, whether shoes, clothing, furniture, or any type of household goods. Each piece of merchandise, although temptingly displayed, had a "sold" sign next to it. We tried all three shoe stores in town with the same results: "We're sorry, but we don't have her size."

"Won't you go and check again," Aunt Elsbeth pleaded. "We'll take a bigger size. She'll grow into them."

In desperation, she asked to speak with the owner of the last store and recited her "poor orphaned child" routine. The woman shook her head and said, "Fraulein Rapp, I really would like to help you, but our shelves are empty. I don't know when we'll get new stock."

"What about all those shoes in the window?" Aunt Elsbeth persisted. "What about them?"

"I can't do anything for you," the woman said and turned away.

Once outside the store, Aunt Elsbeth complained, "They've got shoes. They're holding out for better times. Our money isn't worth anything these days. Let's hope we won't get a heap of snow this winter." She looked at the display window and added with bitterness, "Next, there will be sold signs on the food as well. Then, we will freeze and starve."

In the meantime, whenever I was not wearing my shoes, we set them on the kitchen stove to dry out.

"We need to talk about your schooling," Aunt Elsbeth said to us the next day. "You sound like a couple of Polish immigrants. Your German is sprinkled with Polish. Sometimes, I can hardly understand you. How are we going to get you to make up those lost years?"

Her comment surprised me, because I had no trouble understanding my aunts and uncle.

"Get your pencils and writing paper!" she said. "At least we can do something about your spelling. Let's see how much you remember." She dictated random sentences with well-chosen, difficult words.

"When will we go to America?" I asked.

She sat down and put her hand on mine. "I need to tell you something. You can't follow your brothers and sister to America until they're settled. It will take time for them to learn the language, get jobs, and find housing. They'll not be able to take care of you. We're going to keep you here as long as we can."

Although anxious to be with my siblings, I liked the idea of staying with my aunts for a time. They felt like home, and there was no doubt they loved Henry and me.

However, we lived in tight quarters. The aunts decided Henry would stay with them, and I would room with the Schade family in Singfeld where Aunt Kaethe lived. Herr Schade taught the upper grades in the village school and had agreed to tutor me outside of class to help me bridge the gap of those lost years. I would move in with them after Christmas vacation. Weekends I would spend with the aunts in Klosterburg.

"We'll all go to Singfeld the day after tomorrow," Aunt Elsbeth said. "I'll take you to meet the Schades and Aunt Kaethe, and you'll see Frau Teichert again."

"Why can't I live with Aunt Kaethe?" I protested. Living with an aunt, although I did not know her, sounded a lot less frightening than living with a teacher who probably was a strict disciplinarian. At least that was how I remembered the only male teacher I had ever had.

"You can't live with Aunt Kaethe. Your cousin, Kurt-Heinz, has tuberculosis. He's in and out of the sanitarium. It's very contagious. Besides, she really doesn't have room for you."

My cousin's advanced TB served as an excuse; Aunt Kaethe did not want Henry or me. I later overheard her say she had had enough of the Rapp clan. She had taken in the aunts and uncle, as well as Vera and Douglas. Then Erwin returned from Siberia, starved and in rags. "I'm finished with that family," she told Aunt Gertrude. "You deal with these two."

I did not like Singfeld. A little village with small farms, narrow streets, and a smelly manure pile in front of each house, it looked like a scene from the middle ages. When I pointed to the dung heaps, Aunt Gertrude, with her dry sense of humor, said, "They must be very proud of their dung to be displaying it right by their front doors."

After I met Aunt Kaethe, I was more than glad Aunt Elsbeth had made other living arrangements for me. I felt uncomfortable under her sharp, appraising gaze when Aunt Elsbeth introduced us as her remaining niece and nephew. She greeted us with an empty smile and gave no sign she was glad to see us, nor did she attempt to hug or embrace us. Her husband, Uncle Kuno, disappeared immediately after the introduction, saying he had to tend the store. I threw my arms around Frau Teichert, thinking she, at least, would be happy to see me. But she, too, remained cold and aloof. I felt her body stiffen when I tried to hug her. She pushed me away, studied my face, and said with a hint of disdain, "My, how you've changed."

"*Ja*, hasn't she turned into a beautiful young girl?" Aunt Gertrude asked.

"I don't know. She has the same black bags like you under her eyes."

Her poisonous words stung. I had hoped Frau Teichert, who had lived with us on the farm that last year before we had fled, would be an intimate connection to my missing family and maybe even a friend. But I sensed she saw me as another Rapp intruder.

On our way home, Aunt Elsbeth took me to meet the Schades and their teenage son, Gerhard. They lived in one wing above the schoolhouse. Herr Schade did not look like the stern disciplinarian I expected him to be. Frau Schade, on the other hand, was a solemn-faced, small woman. Dressed in black from the shoes on her tiny feet to the combs holding her prematurely gray hair in place, she appeared stoic and grim. I could not warm up to her. I hoped Gerhard, although not at home this day, would help lighten the atmosphere once I lived with them. Since he was the same age as my brother Douglas, and they had attended the *Gymnasium* in Klosterburg together, I felt a kinship with him.

"In a year or two, we'll try to get you into the girls' *Gymnasium* in Klosterburg," Aunt Elsbeth later consoled me. "You have a lot of catching up to do. That's the whole idea of your living with the Schades. Herr Schade can supervise your homework, give you extra assignments, and help prepare you. You're going to have to work hard, very hard."

"Why does Henry get to live with you? Why do I have to stay here? I don't like this place. Why can't we stay together?" I started to cry.

"I wish we had room. You know how crowded we are. Besides, we'll be together every weekend. You'll come to Klosterburg, and we'll come to Singfeld whenever we can."

We stayed the weekend with Uncle Eduard in the other wing of the schoolhouse, in the same attic room the aunts had originally shared with him before they obtained housing above the post office in Klosterburg. For an entire year, they had walked the three kilometers to and from work, in good weather and bad. Now, living in Klosterburg, their commute was reduced to a flight of stairs, a badly needed relief, since Aunt Elsbeth was not well. She had already contracted pneumonia twice and always seemed to be suffering either from a severe cold or debilitating bronchitis.

CHAPTER SIX

BEFORE THE AUNTS RETURNED TO Klosterburg, Aunt Elsbeth accompanied me to the Schade family. I carried the suitcase she had carefully packed with things my sister had left behind for me. The clothes I had brought from Poland quickly found their way into the garbage bin. Finally, I got to wear my sister's clothes.

"Be a good girl now," Aunt Elsbeth instructed on the way. "Don't give the Schades any trouble. Do your homework and be helpful around the house."

Their son, Gerhard, a red-cheeked, gawky adolescent, was home this time. He politely shook our hands and listened attentively while Aunt Elsbeth told Frau Schade, in great detail, about Henry's and my ordeal with the Poles. I sat embarrassed, wishing she would stop. I was acutely aware of how self-conscious and timid I had become around strangers. I wanted to forget the past and leave all that ugliness behind me, but she kept bringing it up.

Frau Schade took my suitcase and led me into the parlor, a room usually reserved for visitors, now to be my bedroom. It contained her most precious treasures: crystal vases, good china, and fancy knick-knacks. Houseplants stood scattered on special stands, and empty flowerpots lined the outside windowsill. A colorful Oriental rug covered the well-waxed parquet floor. Frau Schade pointed to the grey velveteen couch and said, "That's where you'll be sleeping."

She pushed two chairs together and placed my suitcase on top. "Keep your clothes neatly folded in here and don't touch any of my things!" she warned.

After Aunt Elsbeth left, I accompanied Gerhard to the bakery to buy a loaf of bread. At age seventeen, he might just as well have been an adult; I was that intimidated by him. When he talked to me, I could not verbalize a simple sentence beyond a weak yes or no. Probably thinking me dull and uninteresting, maybe even retarded, he soon gave up. When people stopped us in the street and talked to us, I stared at the ground.

Back home, he said to his mother, "There's something wrong with her. She acts funny."

"Just give her time." Frau Schade said, with a mother's innate insight. "This is all new to her. She's been through a lot. She'll come around."

My first day of school was a day of torture and embarrassment. Thrown together with fourth through eighth graders, I felt lost. I could barely add, spell, or read. My mind was as empty as the blackboard in front of me. When Herr Schade called on me for answers, the words stuck in my throat, and my tongue refused to move.

That evening, Herr Schade handed me the multiplication tables and said, "Don't leave the house until you've learned each one by heart."

Where would I have gone? To visit Aunt Kaethe, who had shown no interest in me? My cousin Kurt-Heinz, whom I was most anxious to meet, was still away at the sanitarium. That left Uncle Eduard in the other wing of the building, but he had turned into a cranky recluse.

I learned the multiplication tables and did all the extra assignments Herr Schade gave me. He drilled me every afternoon, and eventually some of it stuck. On Saturday afternoon, I took off for the aunts in Klosterburg. Always anxious to be with them, I felt better the minute I entered their little island of love. They provided an anchor and gave me a sense of belonging.

On one of my weekend visits, Aunt Elsbeth handed me a letter from Erwin. "Your siblings are doing fine," she said. "The Gervences found them a place to live and helped them get jobs. Vera is living with them."

"Does that mean we'll get to go to America sooner?" I asked

"Oh, Evchen, Evchen, don't be so impatient. It'll be a long time before you'll be ready. You're much better off here with us."

"Who are the Gervences. Are we related to them?"

"*Ja*, the Gervences. We're lucky to have them and grateful that they have taken such an interest in you children," Aunt Elsbeth said.

"They're just good friends from a long time ago. Herr Gervence is from Elbing. I dated him in my youth. When I turned down his marriage proposal, he immigrated to the United States. I've corresponded with him all these years, even after he married."

"That sounds so romantic," I interrupted.

"It was a one-sided romance. But luckily for you kids, they remained childless and volunteered to help your brothers and sister," Aunt Elsbeth said. Then, she added, "While I'm at it, let me explain some confusing facts about your American citizenship status. Since you were all born outside the United States, you fell under different immigration laws. Erwin, Vera, and Douglas had to be in the States before age twenty-one to keep their citizenship. That's the reason for their quick departure. Both Henry and you have to live in the States at least five years before you turn twenty-one."

"Does that mean I'll have to stay here another four years? Will I have to wait that long to see my sister and brothers again?" I asked, disappointed.

"Yes. Henry will leave in two years," Aunt Elsbeth said. "After he's gone, we'll have room for you here. In the meantime, we need to go to the American Consulate in Frankfurt to get your paperwork started. Right now, you don't even have a birth certificate. Everything was lost. We'll do that during your summer vacation."

I divided my time between Singfeld and Klosterburg, making the weekly trek on foot in good and bad weather. Aunt Elsbeth persevered and managed to find a pair of shoes for me. In desperation, she wrote to an old family friend from Elbing who now owned a shoe store in Hamburg. A package with a pair of shoes arrived on time for my twelfth birthday. Although not new, they fit and kept my feet dry.

Keeping food on the table remained a daily challenge. The lines at the markets were long, and many times the shelves were empty when we reached the counter. While the locals sometimes got their needs taken care of at the back door, we often came home empty handed. Aunt Kaethe rarely sent anything from her store. To augment our food supplies, Aunt Elsbeth sent Aunt Gertrude, Henry, and me begging in the country at the "kind nuns" whom they had befriended through work. Equipped with a handcart, we made our way to their convent in a nearby village on a cold, wintry Sunday. Hoping for a warm meal, we timed our visit accordingly. The nuns received us in a friendly manner but did not invite us to partake in their midday meal. Instead, they served us hot tea and biscuits. They listened to Aunt Gertrude's "these are my poor dead brother's hungry children" tale, with extra emphasis on the hungry. It was an embarrassing moment for all of us. Aunt Gertrude broke down crying. She apologized for having been reduced to begging. "We're desperate," she explained, wiping the tears from her cheeks.

"Fraulein Rapp, believe me, we would like to help," one of the nuns said, "but look at us. We're all living from day to day. The refugees keep coming. We can't feed them all."

Her speech sounded well rehearsed. However, the nuns did not let us leave empty handed. We returned with a few potatoes, turnips, and rutabagas. I wondered if there ever would be a time when we would not have to worry about food.

Darkness fell early on our way home, and we felt the bite of the icy wind in our faces as we came over the last hill. A dimly lit Klosterburg lay at our feet. It looked deceptively peaceful under the vaulted, star-studded sky. But I knew things were not always what they seemed to be.

Big, fat bedbugs moved in with us and disturbed our sleep. In the evenings, Aunt Elsbeth set the alarm clock for midnight to counterattack. We pulled the bedding apart, turned the mattresses upside down, and looked under the rugs, killing them by the hundreds. Aunt Elsbeth suspected Henry and I might have brought the pests with us. When there seemed to be no end in sight, she went on the offensive.

"The walls are crawling with them," she said one weekend. "We can't be the only ones plagued with these pests. But they'll blame us, the dirty refugees, for bringing them into the building. I'm going down to talk to the postmaster and complain." She looked at me and added, "You come with me. We'll show him the welts on your body."

The postmaster lived in the wing below us. His wife answered the door.

"Frau Kueber, please excuse my intrusion," Aunt Elsbeth said with great self-assurance and extra courage in her voice. "May we come in? I've something very unpleasant to discuss with you."

"Of course, please do," Frau Kueber said, puzzled, and showed us into her parlor.

Aunt Elsbeth went straight to the point. "This is really quite embarrassing, and I hope you won't be offended," she said with false concern. "But we're being inundated with bedbugs. Look at the welts on this child. Each night they come crawling up the wall. We've sprayed for them, but they keep coming."

Frau Kueber fidgeted uncomfortably with her hands while I was dying of embarrassment, sure we were going to be evicted on the spot. Instead, Frau Kueber looked at Aunt Elsbeth and said, "I know, I know. We have the same problem down here. I think the whole building is infested. The refugees, you know." She halted, realizing she was talking to a refugee, and quickly added, "Oh, Fraulein Rapp, please excuse me. I didn't mean it that way. But we live in such close quarters. You know what I mean."

I did not know what she meant as I surveyed the spacious, beautifully furnished room. It looked like a palace to me.

"My husband is already looking into the matter to see what can be done," she continued. "I think the whole building needs fumigating. It's so embarrassing. But what can we do. We have to put up with all kinds of unpleasantness these days. Please be patient. It'll be taken care of."

Frau Kueber's response amazed me. Aunt Elsbeth had only hoped to divert blame from us, and now she had the woman not only accepting the responsibility but apologizing as well. Back in our bug-infested room, Aunt Elsbeth said, "You see, Evchen, sometimes you have to fight fire with fire. I'm tired of seeing all that's bad being blamed on the refugees. I'm tired of being treated like scum. They know nothing about us. We can't prove anything when we talk about the good life we once enjoyed and our spacious homes that were filled with beautiful things. It's all gone forever. We don't even have pictures to show them."

She turned to me and asked, "Are you listening, child?"

"*Ja, ja*, I'm listening."

"Even Kaethe has turned her back on us," she continued. "We used to be the rich *Erbtanten*, the inheritance aunts, from whom her children would inherit. She could not do enough for us when we still had everything. Now that we have lost it all, we are the undesired burden, and she would just as soon we disappeared so that her conscience would not be bothered. All we can do is demand respect by our actions, by how we talk, by our manners, and by how we dress. You've seen it work. Let that be a lesson to you."

Duly impressed, I remembered the lesson well.

When the weather turned warmer, the aunts and Henry came to Singfeld more often, and I spent most of my time with them in Uncle Eduard's little attic room. Sunday mornings, however, were reserved for church with the Schades. The school curriculum included religion again, and church attendance was required. Much as I tried, I could not feel God, not in the people who sat in their pews, divided by status, the titled in a private section and the school children in the front under the pastor's watchful eye, or in the church itself.

During services, Herr Schade played the church organ, and his son, Gerhard, often accompanied him on his trombone. Although nothing like I had experienced in the cathedral in Bautzen, Herr Schade knew how to make powerful music come out of those shiny pipes. I liked to listen to father and son perform. Their music provided welcome diversion from the obtuse Bible verses and sermons I could not relate to.

Singfeld, with the exception of a handful of refugees, was staunchly Protestant. Klosterburg, on the other hand, although only three kilometers away, had been one hundred percent Catholic before the refugees arrived. Religion played a deeply integral part in the lives of both communities, and intolerance and prejudice divided the two. The people wore their religion on their sleeves but not always in their hearts. That lesson came to me slowly.

At age twelve, I began to see life through a thinking mind. I realized I was an aberration among the village children who had remained untouched by tragedy and trauma. Although some of them had lost a father or brother, they always had had a home and never missed a day of school. I had experienced a darker side of life. It set me apart.

Sitting among fertile green hills, Singfeld looked like an idyll out of Oma's fairy tales. Entrenched in the old ways that had been passed on from generation to generation, where trivialities often became major issues and everyone knew everyone else's business, Aunt Gertrude called it a cultural backwater. The village still had a town crier just as it had since the Middle Ages. Every evening, he made his rounds and rang his big bell, while people gathered around him or hung from their windows between the geranium pots and listened to his monotone announcements.

Dating back to the tenth century, Klosterburg, too, appeared an idyllic medieval town, set among rolling hills, untouched by war and forgotten by time. On my weekends with the aunts, Henry and I explored the town and delved into its history. Situated on top of a hill with many church steeples, all Catholic with the exception of one, it greeted a visitor with a picture-postcard face from every direction. With parts of the old wall and watchtowers still intact, it was my fairy-tale world into which I could escape. Returning to Singfeld, when the weekend ended, became more and more difficult.

Much as I tried to befriend Frau Schade, she stayed distant and aloof. I remained an outsider with no close friends. Life was better, but I was troubled.

Hoping to find a friend in my cousin Kurt-Heinz, I looked forward to meeting him when he came home from the sanatorium. The aunts took Henry and me to see him one warm spring Sunday. He was not cured; in fact, he was worse. He received us in their little garden behind the store. The air was heavy with the sweet smell of lilac from the neighbor's yard. As he lay in a hammock between two old apple trees, he studied Henry and me.

"The last time I saw you, Eva, you were still in diapers," he joked.

"Oh, my dear Kurt-Heinz, what is happening to you?" Aunt Gertrude asked, little teardrops forming in the corners of her eyes.

"Don't cry, Aunt Gertrude. I know I'm dying. I'm tired." He turned to me and added between coughs, "If you need any school supplies, come to me! Don't go to my mother. I'll see to it that you get them."

Aunt Kaethe and Uncle Kuno did not join us, and Kurt-Heinz, being tired, cut our visit short. When I saw him again, he was back in the sanitarium.

Letters arrived regularly from America, always written to us collectively but addressed to Aunt Elsbeth. As the head of the household, she ruled over all of us. Aunt Gertrude dutifully handed over her paychecks and left the decision making to her sister. Aunt Elsbeth answered each letter individually and made Henry and me write notes to be included. This proved to be more difficult for me than school. I stared at the blank paper and could think of nothing to say. I no longer knew my brothers and sister.

When my siblings sent a photo of themselves taken among a group of friends, I could not pick out my brothers or sister. I remembered long-legged, awkward youngsters in short black corduroy pants, while the camera had captured images of handsome young men. My sister was transformed into a movie star, as Aunt Gertrude put it. I took Uncle Eduard's magnifying glass and studied every detail of her even features, her long blond hair, the fashionable clothes, and the glittery jewelry, while my heart ached with envy.

CHAPTER SEVEN

AUNT GERTRUDE HAD GIVEN MY sister a diamond ring and bracelet to sell in America. With the money, she was to send care packages. I was in Klosterburg when the first parcel arrived. Sewn into an old white bed sheet, it looked like it had come out of an Egyptian tomb. Henry and I watched, flushed with excitement, as Aunt Elsbeth cut open the stitches and unpacked coffee, cigarettes, cocoa powder, chocolate bars, chewing gum, and a box containing a dozen rolls of colorful little round candy rings, labeled LifeSavers. The root beer candy and peanut butter left us guessing what to do with them. We had never tasted either and disliked both. Thinking the root beer candy to be some kind of cough medicine, we saved it for that purpose, but we found no use for the peanut butter. Stuffed among the items was the remainder of my sister's discarded German clothes.

Henry popped a stick of gum into his mouth and said, "I bet you I can chew it for hours and still have it at the end of the day." I did not believe him and lost the bet.

Some time that spring, Kurt-Heinz was rushed to the hospital in Klosterburg. He was losing his battle for life. Every other day, after school, Aunt Kaethe had me take clean sheets and towels and his favorite foods to him on his bicycle. When I was riding his bike, I felt as if I suddenly had grown wings, and I would have gladly made several trips a day to my cousin's bedside. But since he was now bedded in the isolation house, I was allowed to see him for only five minutes each visit. His tuberculosis had progressed to the most contagious stage. He would look at me, give me a sad smile, and say, "Here, you eat this chocolate bar," or "You take these cookies, but don't tell Mother!"

I hoped my devotion to my cousin would soften Aunt Kaethe toward me, but instead, she turned even more taciturn and bitter.

My short visits with my cousin became highlights in my lonely life and paid dividends. I got to ride his bicycle and often took a more circuitous route for the sheer pleasure of pedaling through the countryside. Also, I knew some of the things I brought to him would end up in my stomach. But most of all, I loved being with my cousin, for however short a time. When he could no longer talk, he motioned for me to take one of the chocolate bars accumulating on his nightstand, winking at me with a conspiring smile. On my last visit before he died, he looked younger, almost boylike. The shadow of death had already settled on his face, He turned to me and said, "You remind me of your sister. I wish she were here."

Always my sister, I thought with resentment.

Kurt-Heinz died peacefully in his sleep that night. I did not learn about his death until after they brought him home in a coffin. For one entire day, it stood in the kitchen with the double doors wide open to the outside world so the villagers could deliver their condolences to my somber-faced aunt and uncle, who blamed their son's death on that devastating war. The visitors brought flowers until the room overflowed. Much to my relief, the casket remained closed.

Aunt Elsbeth and Aunt Gertrude arrived the morning of the funeral. Aunt Elsbeth pressed a small bouquet of flowers into my hands, and together we followed the procession to the cemetery. Ten pallbearers carried the coffin to its final resting place, while the villagers walked behind, singing religious hymns. Aunt Gertrude cried hard as they lowered her beloved *Bubchen*, little lad, the favorite of all her nephews, into the yawning earth. Aunt Elsbeth tried to calm her, while Aunt Kaethe's face remained tearless and expressionless. I wondered what a friend I might have had in my cousin if he had lived. He might have provided a bridge to my estranged older brothers. Instead, he joined the world of ghosts, the same world that had haunted me for so long.

I hoped Aunt Kaethe would let me have Kurt-Heinz's bicycle. But my many trips to her son's sickbed brought me no nearer to her, and the bicycle stayed locked in the shed.

The weeks passed, and I grew ever more lonely. I wanted so much to be like everyone else, but I could not get closer to my peers. We lived worlds apart. They accused me of making up stories when I merely hinted at my dark past.

Gerhard and I did not become good friends either. He was well mannered but spoiled. His mother doted on him to the point where he would exclaim in exasperation, "Mother!" I would have gladly taken his place. Every act of love between mother and son only served to remind me of my own losses. I resented it. Sometimes I resented the entire world. I struggled to understand the past and God. How did he decide who was to suffer and who was to be spared? On many a night, I pondered this question, while a refugee family's screaming baby next door kept me awake.

I befriended Fraulein Heise, a young widow who lived with her parents in the other wing of the schoolhouse and who taught the lower grades. Her husband, a Singfeld native, had been reported missing in action at the end of the war. Having waited in vain for his return over five years, she reverted to her maiden name and the status of *Fraulein*, Miss. After my cousin's death I spent more and more time in the Heise household and did my homework there. Fraulein Heise and Herr Schade had had a falling-out some time in the past and barely spoke to each other, but since I felt very much at home with the Heises, I ignored Herr Schade's disapproval.

The school year ended, and I spent the summer with the aunts in Klosterburg. There was room for me during the warm months because we used the attic for sleeping. I came to regard caring Aunt Elsbeth as our mother. As sure as the sun rose every day, her love shone brightly in our lives. Occasionally, a few clouds gathered and obscured the warmth, but never for long.

I realized how lucky we were the aunts had never married and had no children. As for Erwin, Douglas, and Vera, my memories of them faded more and more. Separated even in childhood when my parents were still with us, I now recalled very little about them. They had never paid much attention to me then, so I did not feel their absence as strongly as I might have. I wondered if we would ever be able to bridge the gap of those lost years and be a family again.

In Klosterburg the merchants' "sold" signs in their display windows multiplied.

"They are holding out for the new currency," Aunt Elsbeth complained.

I paused by every display case, longing to own some of those pretty things and fantasized how one day one of those "sold" items would mean sold to me.

One day, a letter from Frau Weber arrived. Aunt Elsbeth had written to her, accusing her of heartlessly abandoning us, her poor brother's children, and leaving us at the mercy of the cruel Poles. The tone of Frau Weber's letter hinted that my aunt had not spared words when telling her what she thought of her and Frau Leitzel.

Frau Weber demanded a meeting with Aunt Elsbeth. She wanted Henry and me present so we could not make false accusations. I was horrified and realized Aunt Elsbeth, although well-meaning, did not fully understand the circumstances of the times. No one had wanted the extra burden of two strange children when self-preservation and survival were first and foremost on everyone's mind.

We convinced Aunt Elsbeth not to respond to Frau Weber and to let the past rest. A meeting would change nothing, nor gain anything. It would merely upset everyone. Instead, we concentrated on getting our immigration papers to the United States in order. Since we were considered American citizens, we needed to obtain American passports at the American Consulate in Frankfurt to prove we existed. Our birth certificates, proof of who we were, had stayed behind with all the other documents the Polish official took away from me in Elbing. I often wondered what they did with the papers they forced us to surrender. Aunt Elsbeth, however, having gone through this with my siblings, prepared notarized documents, attesting to our date and place of birth.

We departed for Frankfurt early one morning and spent the entire four-hour trip standing in an overcrowded train. We arrived irritated and tired. Rubble, the fallout from the war, still lined the streets. The embassy, however, was located in Frankfurt's impressive villa quarter, an area the bombs had not reached. The imposing buildings stood far apart, surrounded by spacious gardens. The lilacs were in full bloom and smelled wonderful.

We did not have to wait long. An attractive young woman came out and escorted us into her office. We followed in the cloud of her exotic perfume, hinting of *A Thousand and One Nights*. Dressed in bright red, with lipstick and nail polish to match, she lit up the room. She asked us to sit down while she filled out a form on the typewriter. I studied her blond hair, her elegant dress, her every graceful move and thought of my sister in America, who probably had transformed herself into something quite similar to this alien princess.

After a short while, the consul, an imposing man with gold-rimmed glasses, joined us. Already tongue-tied, I now was speechless. His skin was the color of dark chocolate, and he spoke perfect German. Immaculately dressed, he reminded me of the kind Moor in my children's book. When he smiled, his teeth resembled Aunt Gertrude's string of pearls. His cologne mixed with the young woman's perfume and turned the air into a field of flowers, sprinkled with a dust of exotic spices. I kept my eyes glued on him and drank in the essence of his foreignness. When we left, he shook our hands and wished us good luck in America.

On our return trip, we managed to get seats on the train. Our good luck put Aunt Elsbeth into a talkative mood. She explained to us the lengthy ordeal she had gone through to get our U.S. citizenship reinstated.

"You know, everyone is trying to get to America these days," she said. "It's difficult enough with the proper documents. But you children have nothing, no birth certificates, no baptismal papers, and no registration of any kind. You don't even have a permanent address."

She pulled a photo from her purse, the same family portrait for which we all had gone to Elbing that summer of 1943, one of the few family pictures that had survived, thanks to Aunt Elsbeth.

"Well, this is the magic photo that got things rolling," Aunt Elsbeth continued. "When your sister worked for the Americans here in Germany, she enlisted their help. Somebody finally found the mate to this picture buried in Washington. It took almost two years of letter writing to the American Consul in Switzerland. Thank heaven he was still alive. A true friend to your father, he was very instrumental in getting Washington's attention. We owe him a lot."

What would we have done without Aunt Elsbeth, Father's favorite sister and confidante, I wondered? Immigration to America was equivalent to entering paradise during those years immediately after the war. People said that it was easier getting into heaven than getting to America, and everyone wanted to go to America.

"And there's another thing," Aunt Elsbeth continued. "Haven't you wondered about your English names? Your father prepared you for America the day you were born. Your mother fought him. She wanted German names. So they compromised with something that didn't sound so foreign."

"What about Douglas's and my name? They sound foreign," I asked.

"Douglas was the exception. Your father held fast on that one. He was an ardent admirer of Douglas Fairbanks, the movie star."

Since I had never been to a movie, I did not know this Douglas Fairbanks, but he sounded important and I asked, "What about me? Am I named after a movie star too?"

Aunt Elsbeth did not know.

But I liked my name, unusual in Germany. Grateful to Father for picking it, I tried to get people to call me Evelyne, but I remained Eva.

That summer, Henry and I recaptured a little bit of our lost childhood. Aunt Elsbeth never wavered in showing her concern for our well-being. To be regarded once again with the eyes of love felt special.

Free of chores and responsibility, we explored the countryside. We bathed in the little river flowing through the valley below the town and climbed the medieval ruins sitting on a small volcanic mound some distance away. Klosterburg was steeped in history and rich in legends about robber kings, local feuds, and religious myths, all the stuff fairy tales are made of. I especially loved Sunday mornings, when the many church bells rang out in unison. Aunt Elsbeth usually heeded their call and went to church. She did not insist that Henry and I join her, or Aunt Gertrude, who did not believe in a personal God.

"God is too busy trying to clean up the mess we've made of the world," she said in her dry sarcastic way. "He doesn't have time for selfish prayers."

I understood what she meant.

CHAPTER EIGHT

During the summer of 1948, Germany converted to new currency. People lost their savings in the old Hitler-era currency, now declared worthless. New bills went into circulation, and each person received forty Marks with an extra premium of twenty Marks per family. Suddenly, cigarettes, coffee, tea, pastries, and meats of every kind became available, even exotic fruit like oranges, lemons, and bananas. The "sold" signs in the store windows disappeared overnight, and the merchandise on display doubled. Everything could be bought, but now we had no money.

I went from store window to store window and vowed that some day I would be able to buy anything I wanted. Above all, I would own many pairs of shoes in every color and style. In the meantime, I just looked through the glass windows and drooled.

The currency reform also marked the beginning of the end of ration cards. Aunt Gertrude decided to go to the nearby city on our first major shopping trip, and I finally received a brand new pair of shoes.

With Aunt Elsbeth's coaxing, I did write to Roza in Poland. I had good memories of her. She had done the best she could with what she had, and I now had a better understanding of the past. Happy to hear from me, she replied immediately. However, she wrote in Polish, and we needed a translator. The woman read the letter to Henry and me in Polish, while we translated each sentence for Aunt Elsbeth.

"My goodness, you're fluent," Aunt Elsbeth said, surprised. "I had no idea your Polish was that good."

"Yes," the woman said. "They may not be able to read it, but they certainly understand it."

The letter contained much news. Roza had had another boy, and her man was still with her. Pani Ilowski also had had another boy and was expecting again. I counted. That would make six children, between miscarriages. And lastly, Pani Kolski, too, was about to have another child. I shuddered at the thought of all those babies. If I had still been there, no matter whom I was with, I would be taking care of a bunch of infants instead of going to school. I looked at Aunt Elsbeth and almost cried with gratitude.

Roza dwelled on their hard times and concluded her letter with a long wish list. "Send coffee, tea, sewing needles, baby clothes, cigarettes, and razor blades for Pan." Although pleased to hear from her, I was equally annoyed. "They're still trying to take advantage of me," I said to Aunt Elsbeth.

"Roza may have used you," she said, "but she also saved you from much worse. Think of what might have happened to you if she had not taken you in."

Aunt Elsbeth had a generous heart. Roza got the razor blades for her Pan as well as coffee, tea, and some of the aunts' dresses, but no cigarettes or baby clothes.

I corresponded with Roza off and on for some time, and she kept us informed about the people in Niederhof. Pani Ilowski produced a baby, dead or alive, almost every year. The Kolskis moved away. Their try at farming had failed, and he took a job in the city. Schotka, to whom I had run after the Ilowskis had kicked me out, died from breast cancer two years later. Her death touched me deeply, and I mourned for her. When Roza's wish list grew too long even for charitable Aunt Elsbeth, I stopped writing to her.

We, too, still suffered from shortages, and we begged and hunted for the many items that made life bearable. The simplest chores were an ordeal without the proper tools such as pots and pans, warm bedding, a good broom, silverware, or a reading lamp, not to mention furniture—all the items we once took for granted.

"We lived in the wrong part of Germany and paid a higher price for the war," Aunt Elsbeth complained. She looked at Aunt Gertrude and added, "You should have shipped out our bedding and dishes and rugs instead of that useless piano and all those books. All they do is take up valuable space. They don't keep us warm or feed us."

Aunt Gertrude's books, however, were worth more than Aunt Elsbeth was willing to admit. Klosterburg had no library, and word soon spread among the aunts' co-workers that Aunt Gertrude had quite a collection of written works. She freely loaned out her books, and they usually were returned with a glass of preserved fruits, jellies, pickles, or vegetables in exchange for another book.

On a larger scale, Germany underwent major changes during 1948. With the establishment of a new government, its revised borders became more clearly defined, and it became clear that Germany's former eastern territories were lost forever. Western farmers were forced to sell a percentage of their land to the refugees, who bought the property with reduced government loans. The program was only moderately successful. Many farmers divided their property among family members and friends before the law took effect, resulting in bitter resentment on both sides. The refugees who had relatives in the West fared better. The rest often ended up in camps that during the war had been army barracks or prisons, the residence of last resort. Much later, these same compounds accommodated the many foreign guest workers Germany attracted during the rebuilding years.

At the end of August of that year, the Russians lowered their iron fist on West Berlin, which stood totally surrounded by Russian territory and isolated from the West. They hoped to choke the city by blocking its land supply line and thereby annexing all of Berlin into their sector. The Americans and British flew supplies to the beleaguered city around the clock, every day of the week. Fear of another war on German soil panicked the people. Aunt Gertrude cried at the news and said, "Oh, God, please not another war."

People followed the news with nervous apprehension. The blockade lasted almost a year. Thousands of new refugees kept arriving in the West, taxing the housing shortage to the limit. I spent many a sleepless night, worried we might get separated from the aunts if another war broke out.

At the end of summer, I returned to the Schades in Singfeld with a heavy heart. In school, I struggled with every subject. Skipping from third to sixth grade after three years of no school proved too great a leap to overcome quickly. I ran to Fraulein Heise at every opportunity. Patient and generous with her time, she helped me work out math problems, gave me spelling exercises, and even taught me some English.

Aunt Elsbeth promised that if I passed the entrance exam in the spring, I could transfer to the private *Gymnasium*, in Klosterburg. She would pay the tuition, and I would get to live with them despite their tight quarters.

An unexpected death in the family took the Schades away from Singfeld, and I moved in with Aunt Kaethe.

"Your aunt Kaethe is expecting you, Eva," Frau Schade said one day. "Pack all your things. Don't leave anything behind." She explained nothing, not even how long they would be gone or when I could return. I sensed something was amiss and wondered if Aunt Elsbeth and Aunt Gertrude knew about this latest development. Having no telephone, we had no means of quick communication.

My reception at Aunt Kaethe's was cold, almost hostile. I thought Frau Teichert would share her room with me, but my aunt took me upstairs and deposited me in a narrow storage area. The room held a bed, accessible from the foot end only, with boxes and crates staked high against the walls. I worried they would tumble down and crush me during my sleep. A single naked bulb suspended from the ceiling provided light, too weak to read by at night. A tiny window occasionally let in a few rays of sun, but on cloudy days the cubicle remained in semidarkness. I quickly realized I would live with my aunt as the poor, unwanted relative and would have the status of a household servant. Aunt Kaethe and Uncle Kuno barely acknowledged my existence and took their meals alone in their office, while I ate with Frau Teichert and their maid in the kitchen. The three upstairs bedrooms were off limits to me. My cousin Kurt-Heinz's room remained locked. Only once did I get a glimpse of it when the maid cleaned it. I never saw the inside of my aunt's bedroom during the entire year I lived with them, not even when she was sick. I did, however, get a peek into Frau Teichert's sanctuary. Pink satin comforters covered the pushed-together twin beds. I wondered which one my princess sister had slept in and felt deeply hurt that I was not good enough to enjoy the same privilege.

After school, I helped in the kitchen, made deliveries, ran errands for the store, and continued to spend my free time with Fraulein Heise. My weekends in Klosterburg became fewer. They always turned into emotional episodes. I cried and threatened to kill myself if I could not come and live with aunts Elsbeth and Gertrude soon.

Aunt Elsbeth, in her patiently wise way, consoled me and said,

"Be patient, Evchen. Do your homework. Keep your nose in the books. Go to Fraulein Heise whenever you can. Learn, learn, learn! Next fall, the *Gymnasium*. I promise."

"I don't like Aunt Kaethe, and I know she doesn't like me," I complained.

"Try to understand. She's a very unhappy woman. She can't accept the fact that she has buried all three of her children, while you and your siblings lived."

"That's not my fault. I can't help that," I protested. "She's bitter about Erwin, Vera, and Douglas because they won't write to her. She calls them an ungrateful bunch and takes it out on me."

"A lot happened here before you arrived," Aunt Elsbeth said. "We all piled in on Aunt Kaethe with nothing. She fed us and housed us, grudgingly, but she did it."

"*Ja*, but Vera got to sleep in Frau Teichert's room. I have the dark old storage room."

"Look, I don't want to dwell on the past. Aunt Kaethe is simply tired of us. She's had her disappointments. Do what she asks of you. A year is not that long."

But it was a long and very lonely year. I had little contact with my siblings in America during that time. Firmly settled in the New World, they had jobs, made friends, and sounded happy. I had no place in their new lives. Aunt Elsbeth insisted I write to them. I stared at the blank sheet of paper and could think of nothing to say. Not wanting to be hurt any more, I carefully guarded my emotions and inner life. In the end, Aunt Elsbeth took over, dictated a few sentences, and enclosed them in her letters.

Emotionally, living with Aunt Kaethe resembled my life with the Ilowskis, without the hunger, hard work, and beatings. The untimely death of all her children had, indeed, turned her into a bitter woman, and the door to her heart remained tightly shut.

Always dressed in black now and always chewing on something, she moved about the house with a grim expression on her puffy, round face. She was a closet eater, and her ample figure and sausage fingers reflected it. She and Uncle Kuno never had visitors, nor did they invite aunts Elsbeth and Gertrude or Uncle Eduard for an occasional meal. They seemed to have no close friends. The villagers, while not prone to entertain or give parties, did celebrate important events, such as weddings, silver and golden jubilees, and special birthdays. On these occasions, most of the villagers were invited, and the celebrations lasted into the early morning hours. Aunt Kaethe and Uncle Kuno never participated in any of these festivities.

"Is it because they're in mourning?" I asked Frau Teichert.

"No," she said. "They don't like parties."

Every evening, after supper, grim Aunt Kaethe and solemn Uncle Kuno walked to the cemetery with their ill-tempered dog and me in tow. I grew to hate this nocturnal ritual. Half a head taller than her husband, Aunt Kaethe waddled beside him in stoic silence, holding on to his arm. I tried to at least win over their spoiled dog, but he always growled when I got too close to him. When I attempted to pet him, he sank his teeth into my hand. That ended our relationship. He now growled at the mere sight of me, and I showered him with a few unkind words whenever my aunt was out of earshot.

"Leave him alone" Frau Teichert said. "Can't you see he's jealous of you? He's used to being the big cheese around here."

"Jealous of me?" I asked. "I am nothing to Aunt Kaethe. She barely speaks to me, while all day long she showers the dog with loving words. If he is jealous of me, I'm twice as jealous of him."

With time, I befriended Mila, a Baltic refugee doctor's daughter. We shared the same troubling secret. She, too, had been sexually molested by an uncle, her mother's brother, who later was killed in the war. She had tried to tell her mother, but his tragic death made the mother unreceptive to the subject.

With the aid of Mila's father's medical books, we finally found answers to the many questions we had about sex and procreation, questions the adults brushed off with generalities. The text in these manuals was not always clear, but the pictures and graphs more than made up for the obtuse medical terms. Although I still had a slightly protruding belly, I now knew for certain I had nothing to worry about.

CHAPTER NINE

AUNT KAETHE DID NOT APPROVE of my frequent escapes to Klosterburg, and I saw Aunt Gertrude and Aunt Elsbeth less and less. Instead, Mila and I explored Singfeld's countryside and forests. We picked wild flowers and occasionally surprised a foraging deer. But life in this pastoral setting had a disturbing undercurrent. After a few weeks, when I decided to make a social call on Frau Schade, she barely spoke to me. Feeling awkward, I stood in the doorway and waited to be acknowledged. She did not even look up from peeling potatoes.

"What do you want, Eva?" she asked.

"I just came to say hello."

"What for?" she asked. "You've been telling the whole village that ten horses couldn't drag you back to us. I have no time for you."

I felt as though lightning had struck me. I had never even heard the "ten horses" expression, nor did I know any adults well enough to confide in, had I wanted to. Near tears, I looked at Frau Schade and felt sad for her and myself. I knew her to be a religious woman who never missed a Sunday service and observed all the rules the church imposed on her. She devoted Sundays to the Lord by not doing any housework and often had chided me for doing homework. But she seemed unable to find enough compassion in her heart to give me the benefit of the doubt.

"I never said such a thing," I said meekly and walked away like a badly beaten child. I did not tell my aunts in Klosterburg about the incident. Instead, I withdrew more and more into myself. As soon as school let out for Christmas, I headed for Klosterburg and celebrated the holidays in the comforting presence of Aunt Elsbeth and Aunt Gertrude and my brother. Uncle Eduard joined us on Christmas Eve, just as he had the year before, and brought with him another little evergreen. Aunt Gertrude had traded one of her precious books for a box of cardboard ornaments covered with glittery sprinkles. We decorated the tree, added the wax candles from the year before, and lit them. Aunt Gertrude parted with another book for me, and Aunt Elsbeth gave Henry and me each a refillable ink pen, more notepaper, and the next day, more dictation. She was relentless when it came to catching up on our education. A package from America included our favorite puddings and Jell-O, as well as chocolate bars and Lifesavers.

I returned to Singfeld with a heavy heart. Snowbanks lined the sides of the path. A strong Nordic wind blew thin flurries across the road. The moon hung pale and cold in the night sky. Still afraid of the dark, I looked for Mother among the zillion stars that sparkled above me like precious diamonds, and I wondered if she could be up there watching over me. With her in my thoughts, I always felt less lonely and afraid during those long night walks back to Singfeld.

I returned to Klosterburg for my thirteenth birthday. Aunt Gertrude parted with yet another book, and Aunt Elsbeth delivered more dictation with the promise, "It won't be long and you'll be attending the *Gymnasium*." And I shed more tears of impatience.

Winter continued to hold the land in its icy grip, and snow whipped across the soundless, frozen land. Not being allowed to bring friends home, I saw less of my friend Mila during those dark winter months. I yearned to go sledding with the village children and hinted at Kurt-Heinz's sled to Aunt Kaethe, but like the bicycle, it remained locked in the shed.

I did, however, find unexpected diversion. I discovered Aunt Kaethe's attic full of long-forgotten and now forbidden Hitler paraphernalia. I found a bag of lead soldiers with swastikas painted on their uniforms, an old Hitler flag neatly stored in a cardboard box, and a pile of Hitler Youth magazines. I pored over the publications and learned who Hitler was, this lover of youth and one-time friend of the German people. At least that was how he was represented on those mysterious pages. Cheering masses surrounded him in every picture, whereas I did not even get a glimpse of him on that train coming through Niederhof some years ago. Handsome young soldiers stood at attention, proudly saluting their *Fuehrer*. I hid for hours behind old trunks and boxes and read this forbidden literature, trying to make sense of it all, trying to find answers to the many questions the adults evaded with a mute shrug of the shoulders. No one wanted to talk about Hitler, the Nazis, or anything connected with that time.

In the spring, I crammed for the *Gymnasium* entrance exam. Fraulein Heise doubled up on my English lessons so I could skip the first year and be with girls closer to my age. A stern drillmaster, she constantly reminded me I had only three months to make up the first year of English. When she saw my tears of frustration, and there were many, she would say, "You want to get into the *Gymnasium*, don't you? Besides, you need to learn English for America." That was the ultimate motivator.

Fraulein Heise also taught me how to do embroidery and appliqué work. Aunt Elsbeth marveled at my talent and said, "You're gifted, just the way your mother was. You should think of becoming a sewing teacher."

However, I had other aspirations. I would become a librarian and read my way through every book in the library. For practice, I started with Aunt Gertrude's private collection. Thanks to her, I developed a love of reading.

On Easter Sunday, Mila and I took up the age-old local tradition of going from house to house to wish the inhabitants a happy Easter. They, in turn, gave each of us a beautifully colored egg for good luck. Our pockets full, we headed for the woods and played Easter egg hunt, quickly reducing our inventory to half by hiding them too well. We ate the rest and ended up with bellyaches, my first since I had devoured all the marzipan from my siblings' Christmas cookie plate years ago.

Each year, on Confirmation Sunday, when Singefeld's fourteen-year old children were confirmed, Aunt Kaethe had me deliver little gifts to them. For my trouble, their parents handed me pieces of pastry, often inviting me to sit down and eat with them.

"I'm saving the cake for my aunts," I said.

"No, you eat it! Your aunt has the whole store. She doesn't need our cake," they would say.

"No, my aunts from Klosterburg are here. I'm saving it for them," I explained. Then, they usually softened and often gave me extra cake to take to the aunts.

I ran from Aunt Kaethe's to the newly confirmed, to the visiting aunts, and back to Aunt Kaethe's for the next delivery, while the pieces of cake accumulated on Aunt Elsbeth's platter. I finished, exhausted and too tired to eat. Aunt Gertrude, though, relished the feast and said, "I wish kids would get confirmed more often."

Over Easter vacation, Fraulein Heise went to Frankfurt to help take care of her sick sister's three-year-old twins. She returned with Werner, one of the twins, to give the mother a break. Rumors quickly spread that he was Fraulein Heise's own child, fathered by an American soldier. The villagers referred to him as the "Ami [slang for American soldier] child." Fraulein Heise, however, continued to refer to Werner as her nephew, her ailing sister's boy.

One afternoon, when I sat over my English lesson at her kitchen table, there was an impatient knock at the door. "Come in!" the grandmother called out. The door opened, and an unshaven, emaciated German soldier stood before us.

Fraulein Heise looked up, stopped in midsentence, and exclaimed, "Helmut! Oh, my God! We thought you were dead."

"Well? Is that all the greeting I get around here?" he said, inviting her into his open arms.

The grandmother turned pale and stared at the man in tattered rags. Fraulein Heise closed my book, handed it to me, and said, "That's enough for today. You'd better go home now."

Fraulein Heise's long-missing and presumed-dead husband had been in a Russian prison camp all these years. He was one of the few survivors to come home. Within a week, the husband moved back with his parents and filed for divorce. Fraulein Heise stopped my English lessons, and, the day after the school year ended, she, Werner, and her parents moved away. I missed them, but my time in Singfeld also came to an end. I would take my *Gymnasium* entrance exam during summer vacation.

On my last visit to my cousin's grave, Aunt Kaethe turned to me and said, "We'll miss you, Eva, and so will Kurt-Heinz. I'm sure he liked seeing you here each day."

These sentimental words surprised me. I wanted to throw my arms around my aunt's ample body and say something equally as kind, but I could not think of anything to say. All year I had waited for her to open her heart to me. Now, it was too late.

When I departed for Klosterburg, I left no friends behind. Mila had moved away a few weeks earlier when her father took a job in a clinic in the city. Finally, I would live with aunts Elsbeth and Gertrude and my brother, and we would be a real family.

Reality, however, often is the killer of dreams. Aunt Elsbeth explored every possibility to obtain larger housing but without success. For the time being, we squeezed together in their one room and the attic. We learned to control our tempers and deal with the lack of privacy. Henry and I were teenagers now. Aunt Gertrude suffered the most and preferred to sleep in the attic behind a screen until it turned so cold that the water froze in the wash basin. Living in such closed quarters felt like living in a cage, but I loved it. I no longer had to make those lonely trips back to Singfeld.

For his fifteenth birthday, the aunts thrilled Henry with a second-hand bicycle. Plagued with envy and feeling left out, I complained a lot about it.

"Be patient, Evchen. The bicycle will be yours when Henry leaves for America," Aunt Elsbeth promised.

"But I'll have to wait a whole year," I protested.

"A year is not so long. Let him enjoy it," Aunt Elsbeth consoled. "You'll get your turn."

While Henry had his bicycle, I continued my remedial academic lessons. Aunt Elsbeth had made arrangements with Herr Bruchner, a widower who lived below us, to tutor me in English and advanced math. Every day for an entire month, he drilled me in English grammar and spelling. When the long-awaited entrance exam day arrived, I was prepared. Because I would skip two grades, I did not participate in the group testing but stood alone and trembling before my inquisitors. At the end of that grueling day, the sister superior handed me my acceptance slip and said, "You did well. School starts the end of August."

I raced home, stood under Aunt Elsbeth's window at work, and shouted, "Aunt Elsbeth, I passed! Aunt Elsbeth, I got in!"

She leaned out the window and said, "I knew you could do it. I never had a doubt. You're just as smart as your brothers and sister." She threw me a coin and added, "Go buy yourself an ice cream cone. You earned it."

I desperately needed to hear those words of praise. Both aunts were diligent at building up Henry's and my badly damaged self-esteem.

Without friends in Klosterburg, I tagged along with Henry whenever he was not pedaling through the countryside. We headed to the recently opened swimming area along the river on the outskirts of town, joined other kids in their water games, and learned to swim. Few of us owned bathing suits. We paraded around in our underwear and had just as much fun. By the time school started, we were as brown as the earth, and I was happier than I had been in a long time.

Sometime during that summer, the Berlin blockade ended, and the political climate normalized. Later statistics reported that the Allies made over 200,000 flights into the beleaguered city and delivered some two million tons of food, medicines, fuel, and other basic materials. Peace seemed guaranteed once more, but it was an uneasy peace as East Germany tightened its borders.

When Aunt Elsbeth read about a refugee gathering in Singfeld, we attended. "Maybe we'll run into someone who has information about your father," she said, "someone who might have been with him in Siberia. We might even meet people from Elbing."

Several hundred people, mostly women and young children, came together, hoping to reconnect with old friends and find lost family members. People gathered by place of origin, and we easily found the "Elbing and vicinity" group. We did not encounter any familiar faces while the aunts exchanged information with the people. We children played games, listened to the adults' stories, learned funny refugee songs, and sang *Heimatlieder*, songs that hailed the beauty of our lost homeland. Tears flowed easily that day, tears of nostalgia and shared losses.

Herr Bruchner proved to be an unrelenting taskmaster and prepared me well for the school of higher learning. Fortunate for me, the aunts valued education above all else and sacrificed to pay for mine. Henry, at an awkward age, had missed too much and did not have time to catch up. He needed to concentrate on the more practical things the public schools taught, because he would have to start working immediately after he arrived in America.

Nuns, along with only two or three lay teachers, taught at the *Gymnasium*, which was a convent school. For two and one-half years I had the privilege of learning from "the good sisters," as we called them. They taught us history, biology, geography, arithmetic, algebra,

physics, English, French, and German literature. Strict disciplinar-
ians, they did not tolerate laziness, tardiness, absenteeism, or bad
behavior. Above all, they regarded themselves as the guardians of our
chastity.

They divided our large classes into two groups. Class A consisted
of local Catholic students, and class B included out-of-town com-
muters and Protestant refugee girls.

I felt an immediate kinship with the refugee girls who, like me,
were a year or two older than the local girls and had a lot of catching
up to do. They, too, had faced many adversities and had lived through
horrors the locals could not come close to imagining or believing. I
felt less isolated. But the separation by faith made me acutely aware of
the many prejudices we faced. Lines of division fell not only between
the haves and the have-nots, those with homes and the homeless, the
locals and the aliens, as we were sometimes referred to, but also along
the age-old intolerances for others' religions. With the nuns, I learned
that one's belief was not so much a personal relationship between
one's self and God, but more a divider of people.

Nevertheless, I thrived in this new environment, made friends,
studied hard, and played harder. I read Aunt Gertrude's books, staying
up into the late hours. While my classmates still read innocent teenage
romance novels, I learned about distant lands, foreign cultures,
strange customs, and most fascinating, forbidden love. I escaped into
my aunt's world of literature, which transported me beyond Oma's
phantoms and ghost-infested world of the supernatural. I traveled
across the vast world and thirsted to see it all one day.

Giesela, also a refugee from East Prussia, became my best friend.
Her family owned the concession at the railroad station, where we
sneaked sodas and sweet cakes. She received pocket money, whereas I
did not. Every Saturday afternoon, she treated me to the movies. We
got into most of them, not all that easy since they were rated "youths
under fourteen, or sixteen, or eighteen years of age, not admitted,"
and we were barely fourteen. Giesela applied her older sister's lipstick
and arranged her long, curly hair on top of her head in an adult
fashion. Straightening her shoulder for extra effect, she walked up to
the ticket window and demanded, "Two, please," without as much
as a hint of guilt in her voice, while I watched from a safe distance.
We waited until after the movie house went dark before we entered

to avoid being recognized and left before the lights came on. We were confident we would not run into any of the nuns since they did not attend movies, or the good Catholic girls, because if they had attended, they would have had to go to confession.

If any of Giesela's pocket money remained, we bought movie magazines, cut out pictures of our favorite stars, and pasted them into an album. Occasionally, we got hold of her older sister's naughty magazines and read them from cover to cover. We were young teenagers, shedding what was left of our innocence.

CHAPTER TEN

WE MANAGED IN OUR CROWDED quarters, but Aunt Gertrude had a
hard time and complained bitterly about the lack of privacy. With
nowhere to escape to, we had difficulty staying out of each other's
way. We did not even have a little garden. On Sundays, we often
took walks in the quiet cemetery among the well-tended graves and
studied inscriptions on old tombstones.

When the postmaster's wife came to borrow another book from
Aunt Gertrude, she looked around our cramped room and said, "You
know, my daughters are away at the university now. Maybe your niece
would like to come down and use their room for sleeping and doing
her homework."

Aunt Gertrude called Frau Kueber a saint and almost kissed her
hand to express her appreciation. But Aunt Elsbeth stopped her and
said, "Frau Kueber, that's most generous of you. It will be quite a
relief for us." She swung her arm around the room and added, "As
you can see, we're trying to live like civilized people. Believe me, we
have known better. We did not ask for this."

Embarrassed, Frau Kueber apologized for not having thought of
it sooner. I marveled at how Aunt Elsbeth always had a unique way of
turning a situation around in our favor.

"How kind of that woman to offer to take Evchen in," Aunt
Gertrude said.

"Don't be so naive," Aunt Elsbeth said. "The housing commis-
sioner has been snooping around, making sure people are telling the
truth about their housing situation. Since the Kueber girls are no
longer living at home, she's afraid they may have to take in more
refugees. With Evchen, they're getting a child. They won't have to

share the kitchen with another family. Believe me, she's thought it through very carefully."

I did not care what motivated the woman, and I would have kissed her feet had she asked. To have my own room, a place of escape, sounded like paradise on earth. I might even be allowed to bring friends home now, I hoped.

Meanwhile, my brothers and sister prospered in America. Vera found work in a German travel agency, and Erwin and Douglas apprenticed in the trades. After barely escaping the clutches of Hitler's war, Erwin now had to register for the draft. At the same time, he announced his engagement to Ruth, a German girl. The aunts were happy; I was not. I saw a rival for my brother's affection and attention. He sent pictures of Ruth. Pretty and petite, she looked like a little girl, which made her even more of a rival. I could not hide my jealousy.

"Don't pout! Be happy for him!" Aunt Gertrude said with her black humor. "I would much rather see a woman get him than a bullet."

The monthly care packages continued to arrive and were now augmented with contributions from the future bride and her mother. Aunt Gertrude's diamonds put food, even delicacies, on the table. Root beer candy and peanut butter were no longer included.

Vera's letter announcing a visit over Christmas threw us into a state of frantic excitement. She would bring a slice of America to us, and Henry and I would finally reconnect with our sister after five years of separation. I lay awake during the night, trying to recall memories of her.

We turned our one-room quarters upside down in a cleaning frenzy in preparation for my sister's visit. Frau Kueber agreed to let Vera have my room downstairs, while I moved back upstairs.

The day of my sister's arrival, we headed to the station, dressed in our finest. The closer we got, the faster my heart beat with excitement. When we came around the last corner, the clock above the building struck one. Aunt Gertrude slowed her pace and said, "*Ach*, we have plenty of time. No need to rush."

"What took you so long?" my sister called out to us. I recognized her voice immediately. "I've been standing here for almost an hour."

She leaned against a stone wall amid a heap of luggage, looking the princess I had always imagined her to be, only twice as regal and grand. The teenage girl I remembered had been transformed into an elegant woman and a stranger.

Vera had caught an earlier train out of Frankfurt, and with no telephone, taxi or porter available at that time, she was stranded at the station. From here, my actions turned mechanical. I embraced and hugged my sister, and I am sure we exchanged some awkward dialogue. I did not know this person walking next to me as we struggled with her many suitcases. I kept throwing shy, sideways glances at her, trying to catch a glimpse of the face under the netting of her black hat. She looked like an apparition out of one of my movie star magazines. I was totally awed by her presence. I had hoped to find a little bit of Mother in her, but she did not resemble a mother, not in the slightest. I could not read her emotions under the carefully applied makeup masking her face, but I hoped she liked me. By the time we reached home, my fragile ego had shrunk to the size of a pea.

I stayed home from school the next day and became my sister's shadow. My mouth hung open continuously in astonishment over what she said, what she did, and what came out of those jam-packed suitcases. She brought gifts for all of us and many Christmas sweets, including the traditional fruitcake that had been "baked by angels in heaven," Aunt Gertrude declared.

Vera's wardrobe left me in awe. She brought enough clothes to stay a year or longer, it seemed, with one dress more beautiful than the next. She had gone to modeling school in America and glamour clung to her. She knew how to face the world with her best side, her photogenic side. For two weeks, I hung on her words and followed her every move like an understudy. I vowed that someday I, too, would work for a travel agency, attend modeling school, and conquer the world with many pouches of makeup and trunks filled with gorgeous clothes.

I floated through those two weeks in a trance-like state. After she left, her visit felt like a film in which we all had had a role, and when it ended, the parts we played ended too, and life continued unaltered. My sister had come to us a stranger, and I felt no closer to her when she departed. We had missed growing up together and lived vastly different lives for too long, lacking the shared experiences that bind a family together. We were a family of broken lives.

In the spring, Henry ventured farther and farther from home on his bicycle. On weekends, he often stayed overnight at youth hostels, extending his excursions by miles. The more adventures he had, the more I coveted his bicycle. I could hardly wait for him to leave for America.

Giesela did not have a bicycle either, which helped me get over my jealousy. However, she was about to be ejected from my life. She got kicked out of the *Gymnasium*, and I almost went with her. She brought a condom to school one day. During break, we all gathered around her and watched her unroll it over her thumb, demonstrating how it worked.

Only two days later, word of the incident reached the sister superior, who ordered Giesela to pack up her things. As her best friend, I, too, had to appear before the good sister and submit to intensive interrogation.

"How long have you been friends with Giesela? What do you do when you're together? Does Giesela see boys?"

Faced with loaded questions, I turned coward and disassociated myself from my friend as best I could. I turned pale with fear and finally let go of the tears building up. Not quite sure where I stood, I said between sobs, "I didn't do anything. I don't know what she does." With a flash of inspiration, I asked with an air of innocence, "What did Giesela do? She didn't bring the balloon into class." I tried hard not to blush.

The sister stopped probing and said, "It would serve you better to find new friends," and she let me go. I left the room relieved, thinking if they only knew what murky waters I had navigated during my time with the Poles. I was debased by past experiences and probably would never have gotten into their school in the first place had they known more details about my dark past. From then on, I guarded my secrets carefully.

Some time later, I asked Giesela, "How did you get a hold of that thing anyway?"

"I found it in my sister's drawer. She got into trouble with my parents over it. She won't even talk to me now. It took a while for things to settle down at home."

"What made you bring it to school? Weren't you afraid of what would happen?"

"I don't know. I thought it was funny."

"You should have known somebody would snitch on you. You know how prudish the nuns are. I almost got kicked out too. I don't know what my spinster aunts would have done to me. I bet they've never even seen a condom."

Shortly after her fall from grace with the nuns, Giesela's parents enrolled her in a private school in another city, where she commuted. Then, the family moved away.

After Giesela left, I made new friends at school. With the approaching spring and warmer weather, we had the entire outdoors for our playground. Even though I now could bring friends home, I was too embarrassed to let anyone see how we lived. It was the one oppressing cloud hanging over us. Aunt Gertrude, whose nerves were easily rattled, often unleashed her cooped-up frustration with a harangue of bitter words at Henry and me, reminding us of the sacrifices her weak sister and she were making for us.

Her outbreaks usually ended with me in her arms and both of us crying. No matter how stinging her tirades became, I never doubted her love for us. With time, our relationship matured into close friendship. She sealed it by often taking me to the movies, especially the "under sixteen not admitted" category, and I was not even fifteen.

For my confirmation, Aunt Elsbeth had the required black dress made for me. Our large group included boys and girls from the surrounding area. We knelt in front of the altar while the pastor put the symbolic bread on our outstretched tongues and held the wine-filled chalice to our lips. I waited for God to enter my heart, but I felt no different.

After my confirmation, I no longer had to attend church regularly. Instead, I decided to attend a Catholic mass with one of the local girls. I slipped into the back pew while she dipped her fingers into the font and crossed herself before she joined me. When the sermon started, I was mesmerized by the melodious voices echoing through the cathedral. I concentrated on the words and finally turned to my friend and whispered, "I can't understand him. What is he saying?"

"It's Latin. They always talk Latin in church."

I sat next to my friend who seemed to know when to read out loud from her book and when to stand and kneel. Everything felt so alien, yet so mysterious and beautiful. I told her I wanted to come back as long as I did not have to go to confession. I could not conceive of telling a total stranger, whom I could not even see, all the sinful thoughts living in my head.

When I suggested we go to a Protestant service for a change she said, "Oh, no, I can't. It's forbidden. I'd have to go to confession. It's a sin for me to go to your church."

"Why?" I asked, surprised.

"It just is."

That ended my experiment with the Catholic religion, a religion so rich in tradition but short in tolerance.

The following two years were the happiest years of my young teens. Steadfast Aunt Elsbeth guided Henry and me along with her unshakable love, devotion, and a strong sense of family. However, the hardships of the early postwar years had taken their tolls on her health. She came down with double pneumonia again and spent six weeks in a sanitarium.

When she came home, the color was back in her cheeks. She had gained weight and looked rested. Things ran more smoothly with her around, and we were calmer.

That summer was Henry's last in Germany. We both counted the weeks before his departure. He was anxious to be with our brothers, and I wanted his bicycle more than anything.

One morning, I awoke with an excruciating toothache and one entire side of my face swollen. "It's the same tooth Pan Ilowski almost pulled," I told Aunt Elsbeth.

She looked at her sister and said, "You take her to the dentist!"

The dentist's waiting room was crowded with patients. When the nurse called our name, my hands started to perspire. She pushed me into the dentist's chair and said, "Now, open wide so the doctor can see the tooth. Show him which one."

I just pointed to a tooth, any tooth, and said, "This one."

The nurse held on to one of my arms and motioned for my aunt to hold on to the other, while the doctor looked into my mouth and clamped an instrument around a tooth and started to yank it free. I kicked my feet and screamed louder than our pigs when being butchered. Another assistant appeared and helped hold me down. I had never experienced such pain, ever.

"Do you want the tooth?" the doctor asked, waving it before my tear-filled eyes.

I swallowed a mouthful of blood and could only think of escape. But they held me down while the nurse pushed wads of cotton into the hole. By morning, I still suffered pain, and the swelling was not gone, although the doctor had promised. The following day, it became obvious I had the mumps, something no one had even remotely considered. I had sacrificed a perfectly healthy tooth to ignorance and backwardness. Two weeks later, Henry came down with the mumps, but he kept all his teeth.

CHAPTER ELEVEN

THAT SUMMER, I BEFRIENDED VERONIKA, a new classmate who lived with an aunt in Klosterburg. Luckily for me, the aunt had two grown daughters who had moved away and had left their bicycles behind. This aunt, more generous than my Aunt Kaethe, let me borrow the extra bicycle any time she did not need it, provided I returned it with inflated tires. "No flat tires!" she warned.

Thus, a season of adventure and exploration began for Veronica and me. We pedaled to every point of interest, every castle, and every lake reachable within a day. Before the summer ended, we even stayed overnight at youth hostels. When Henry accompanied us, we were extra daring and swam in forbidden waters, sneaked into castles through the back door without paying, and snatched apples from people's gardens. Only the on-going private lessons with Herr Bruchner slowed me down. He not only promised Aunt Elsbeth to help me bridge those lost three years of school, but also to make a star student of me. Thus, I started my second year at the *Gymnasium* better prepared and on a more even level with the other students.

English was my favorite subject. I divided my spare time between memorizing vocabulary and reading Aunt Gertrude's forbidden novels, forbidden as far as the nuns were concerned.

Henry did not return to school at the end of that summer. Instead, he toured southern Germany on his bicycle. Erwin and Douglas sent the necessary funds and wished him a great time. Although not even sixteen, this would be his last fling before entering the world of self-supporters; he would sail to America on the *Queen Mary* the middle of October.

The aunts and I walked him to the train station on the day of his departure. Aunt Elsbeth accompanied him to the city, where he would transfer to a direct express to Paris, France. There, he had to catch a train to Le Havre, where his ship was docked. I could not conceive of making such a long journey through a foreign land alone. The world suddenly seemed enormous and frightening, and my brother so grown up.

However, my concern for Henry lasted about as long as it took to return home from the station when I could lay my hands on his bicycle. Excited, I rode over to Veronika's and announced, "My brother is gone! I have my own bicycle now!"

Shortly after Henry left, a letter arrived from Erwin with disappointing news. He wrote he had been drafted into the army to fight in Korea. Aunt Elsbeth, upset and bitter, had a difficult time dealing with the thought. "Erwin should have stayed here in Germany," she said.

"*Ja*, and the next thing we'll hear, it will be Douglas, and then Henry. They'll get them, too," Aunt Gertrude chimed in. "Those poor boys. They've already lost so many years. Will there ever be an end to war?"

"We should have kept them here," Aunt Elsbeth said, with a hint of regret in her voice. "We should have never let them go."

"Elschen, the sad truth is there is nothing here for the boys. This still is a country in ruins. Their future is in America. They'll just have to ride it out. Let's hope a bullet doesn't find them." Aunt Gertrude turned to me and added, "Maybe you'll stay with us. By the time you're through with your schooling, things will be better here. Germany will be rebuilt, and we'll have a home again."

Aunt Gertrude's optimism for Germany's future had no basis in positive evidence. Our standard of living still resembled that of a third world country. We had only recently gotten rid of the final ration cards except for sugar, coffee, and cigarettes. Although goods filled the stores now, money and jobs remained in short supply. People's wish lists grew, with little hope of getting any of the things they wanted. The common threads of everyone's dreams were a well-paying job, enough to eat, peace, a reunited Germany, the release of all prisoners of war—and for the East Prussians, to return home. People had yet to come to terms with the fact that Germany's lost territories were lost forever.

At the end of 1950, the Search for Missing Persons Organization issued a final edict: "Register or be declared dead!" The Russians announced that all prisoners of war had been released, which left hundreds of thousands still missing, Father being one of them.

During that time, we received a letter from an acquaintance who had been with Father in a labor camp in Novosibirsk, notifying us that Father had died there in the fall of 1945. Aunt Elsbeth sent an inquiry to the American Consulate in Moscow for confirmation. She received a reply several months later, stating no record existed of such a person ever having been in that camp. But we knew through Erwin, who had spent two years in a labor camp outside Moscow, that the Russians had never kept records. He told the aunts that every day they gathered up the dead, hauled them away, and buried them quickly, without recording their identities. The Russians' only concern was to get the bodies into the ground fast to prevent an outbreak of cholera, typhoid, or any other decay-related diseases.

Erwin had been lucky. He had come down with double pneumonia in Russia and, for nine days, lay semiconscious in a primitive dispensary, while a German prison doctor kept his heart going with extra-strong coffee. As soon as my brother could stand up, the doctor declared him unfit for heavy labor and singled him out for transport back to Germany. He may well have saved my brother's life.

Aunt Elsbeth followed the edict and applied for Father's death certificate. But I kept fantasizing he might yet surprise us. One day, there would be a knock at the door, and he would be standing there, a skeleton in rags, but alive.

A subsequent letter from Erwin brought happy news. He had received a six-month deferment through his company because of a big navy contract.

"At least Henry will get a chance to spend some time with his brother," Aunt Elsbeth reasoned. "You children have lived apart more than you've been together. All those missed years of a happy childhood. It's something that can never be recaptured. They're lost forever. How sad for you." It sounded sad, but I did not feel as sad as I might have. I did not really know my brothers and sister, and so I did not know what I had missed.

With a room all to myself, I now could occasionally bring a friend home, provided I cleared it with the aunts first. Forced to work long, irregular hours, including night shifts, they often took naps in my room during their lunch period, or between work schedules. So much shift sleeping was done in my room that we referred to it as the "rotating bedroom."

Academically, I made progress. However, my private lessons with Herr Bruchner, came to an abrupt halt. He did not answer my knock at the door one afternoon. I did not think much of it. He had forgotten our lessons before. When he did not report for work the next morning, Frau Kueber checked and found him dead in his bed. He had had a heart attack the day before and had lain there for many hours. I felt shudders up and down my spine, relieved I had not tried the door and walked in on a dead man.

"Why didn't you tell us he didn't answer the door yesterday?" Aunt Elsbeth said, accusingly. "He might have still been alive. We could have gotten him to the hospital."

"I thought he forgot my lesson. He's forgotten before," I said, on the defensive. But I could not rid myself of the uneasy feeling of guilt that I might have been partially responsible for his death. His room was directly across the hall from mine, and during moonlit nights, I now saw the reflection of his accusing ghost mirrored on the transom window. I sensed him standing by the door, checking his pocket watch the way he used to do during our lessons. I pleaded with the aunts to trade places with me and let me sleep upstairs. The past had come alive again, and I was afraid.

"Don't worry, Evchen," Aunt Elsbeth said, "I've talked to Frau Kueber. She's agreed to let us have Herr Bruchner's room. His spirit is long gone. Once we're moved in, there will be no room for ghosts. They don't like to be where people are."

Weeks passed before I could walk into that room without the eerie feeling of Herr Bruchner's presence.

When Aunt Gertrude converted the extra room into a little doll house, I felt more comfortable. She bought a bed, a sofa, an easy chair, and a beautiful mahogany cabinet for her books, our first new furniture. Pictures of bucolic landscapes and fluffy throw pillows added a cozy ambiance.

We now had three rooms, separated by one floor and a long corridor.

"I feel like I'm living in a hotel," Aunt Gertrude said. "I'm always packing a bag for upstairs or downstairs, for eating or sleeping."

No matter how hard we tried to organize our lives, the things we needed were always in the other room on the other floor. But we joked about it and reveled in the luxury of the extra space, enjoying once more the sweet comforts of life. We now had a place to escape to, a haven for dreary rainy days, and an island of peace when we needed solitude.

I enjoyed being alone, if just to lean from my window and watch the bright golden sun slip into the crack between heaven and earth and set the sky on fire. Sometimes a dense fog drifted in and made the world disappear below. In winter, the dance of the snow kept me listening to the silence as the flakes piled up on the frozen earth. The window became my peephole to God.

During my conversations with Aunt Elsbeth about religion, she once said, "If you need God to be in your life, he'll come to you in the way you need to perceive him, and you'll know he is there."

I knew what she meant when I observed the wondrous world outside. God put all his efforts into creating beauty around us, while we blindly destroyed what he had created. I could not see the hand of God in man, but I saw it in nature.

A light, thin snow began to fall as another winter approached. Letters arrived from Henry. Apprenticed to become a carpenter, he lived with Erwin and Douglas. He was in good spirits because, at sixteen, he was already self-supporting and not dependent on anyone. Erwin announced he and Ruth planned to get married before he had to report for basic training in March. Vera still worked for the travel agency and announced another visit in spring. Douglas, still unattached, wrote that he, too, would soon be soldiering.

By the middle of December 1950, Klosterburg put on its Christmas face. For the first time since the end of the war, decorations appeared in the store windows, and a few extra lights hung across the street at the entrance of town to welcome visitors. The Christmas market opened, and booths filled with tempting merchandise lined the medieval town square around Klosterburg's oldest cathedral. The holiday spirit appeared everywhere. Exotic foods, colorful ornaments, and alluring toys lined kiosk shelves. Merchants praised their wares, luring the patiently saved pennies from the prudent shoppers' pockets. I, too, was seduced when I spotted a kiosk with celluloid dolls of all sizes, heaped on a collapsible table. I begged Aunt Elsbeth to buy one for me. I wanted nothing more for Christmas if I could just have a doll.

"My goodness, girl. You're going to be fifteen next month. What do you want with a doll? They don't even have any clothes on."

"I'm going to sew the most beautiful wardrobe for her. You'll see," I said, and to help persuade her, I added, "Do you remember that precious doll Uncle Eduard brought me on my ninth birthday at home? The Russians killed her too. I only had her for a very short time. I still miss her. Did you know I named her Elsbeth?"

That hit her tender spot. She turned to the merchant and said, "Give her the biggest one you have!"

I held the doll in my arms and looked at the people gathered around us. Suddenly, embarrassed to be seen with a doll, I handed her back to the man and said, "Please wrap her in newspaper."

I spent the entire next day locked in my room with needle, thread, scissors, and scraps of fabric from Aunt Elsbeth's mending basket. By evening, my baby wore "designed by Evelyne" clothes, and I was cured of playing with dolls. I discovered that, indeed, I no longer was the little girl who, long ago, loved and mourned her precious Elsbeth.

On Christmas Eve, Uncle Eduard showed up with the traditional tree, the biggest one yet. "We have to cut it down to refugee size," Aunt Gertrude joked. We opened the package from America with the usual sweet cakes, chocolates, and a pile of hand-me-down clothes from my future sister-in-law, Ruth. Thrilled, I started to warm up to her.

Before going to sleep in my room that night, I opened the window and let the cold winter air caress my face. The moon stood bright and golden among the stars, and the snow glistened below like a million tiny glowworms. Church bells pealed in unison across the white rooftops, calling the faithful to midnight service. Deeply moved by the beauty of it all, I felt happier than I had been in a long, long time.

CHAPTER TWELVE

THE WINTER OF 1951 BROUGHT more cold than snow. The pond outside town froze over, and Veronika and I headed out with our skates. The days grew short, but when the full moon hung in the dark void like a bright lantern, it lit our way. I never thought I would ever like winter again, yet I not only enjoyed that special season, but I also wished the ice would not melt for a long time.

After my fifteenth birthday, the aunts talked more and more about the possibility of my staying with them in Germany.

"We'll send you to the university after you graduate from the *Gymnasium*. You can study whatever you want. I'll help pay for it." Aunt Gertrude prodded and Aunt Elsbeth added, "You're still so young. You'll be better off here with us. Your siblings are busy with their own lives. Germany is starting to rebuild. There's a future here for you. We would love to keep at least one of you. Think about it."

But America, my brothers' and sister's new home, pulled me like a strong magnet. I still hoped that once we were reunited, we would have a chance of becoming a family again and making up those lost years. However, events continued to pull us apart. Erwin married Ruth. By the middle of March, he would be in the military for two or three years. Douglas, too, warned us that the same fate awaited him. Vera announced her marriage in spring. She planned to spend her honeymoon in Italy with a side trip to Germany. Not happy about a man in my sister's life, I was not at all anxious to meet him. Chances of our becoming a family again in the way I envisioned were diminishing.

Aunt Gertrude liked to talk in monologues, and I served as her patient listener. Deeply disturbed when the facts about the holocaust and the atrocities Hitler and his gang had committed became public knowledge, she could not forgive her countrymen for putting that horrible blemish on the entire German nation. But most of all, she blamed God.

"How could God have allowed it to happen? Did he abandon us just to see how low we would sink without his divine intervention? Until someone can give me the answer, I cannot believe in anything. I'll never understand God."

She jumped from one subject to another and rarely noticed that I did not participate in the conversation.

"Look around you. This is a country of widows and disfigured men. Hundreds of thousands, no, millions have died because of one madman's greed for power, while God watched."

After a long silence, she continued, "There's another thing. The war has deprived us of our men. Two whole generations of men, and more, have been wiped out. Who will rebuild this country? The boys should have stayed in Germany. There'll be endless opportunities here if the Allies ever allow us to rebuild."

"Why won't they?"

"They're afraid we'll make war again. It'll be years before what we did will be forgotten. And forgiven? Maybe never."

When Aunt Gertrude had to go to the hospital to have a tumor in her lower abdomen removed, she befriended a nurse who slipped her a pass to the hospital's bath facilities in the basement of the building. Every weekend, Aunt Gertrude and I now luxuriated in the bath, a privilege so coveted we did not tell anyone for fear of losing it.

With the arrival of spring, we prepared for my newly married sister's visit. Once again, we turned our three rooms upside down in a cleaning frenzy. Herr Bruchner's room received special attention, since it had been designated as the honeymoon suite by Aunt Gertrude. She even sacrificed a portion of her pay for new lace curtains. I had other ideas. I wanted my sister to share my room with me and have "him," Harold, sleep in Aunt Elsbeth's room. But I did not have my way.

I had lost my attractive sister to a man and a different type of love. I made up my mind to hate Harold but ended up liking him. Dark-haired and handsome, he had a well-rounded, well-fed figure and an amicable, easy-going disposition to go with it. He looked very American. He was Jewish, a fact that troubled Aunt Gertrude greatly. Would he not look upon all of us as the murderers of his people?

However, things went well and everyone was happy, except me. My sister had eyes only for "him," while I wanted them on me. A new life lay ahead of her, with a future family of her own. I realized I would have very little part in it.

When school let out, three classmates joined me in a three-week bicycle trip across northern Germany during my last summer in that country. We were four young teenagers, experiencing our first real freedom away from protective parental eyes and policing nuns. It was a time of discovery and awakening. We discovered boys! We met them along the way, often headed for the same youth hostel. We talked and bantered with them, told stories, and practiced flirting. We stopped and swam in the lakes we passed, and in the evenings we played cards and games. We parted the next morning, only to run into the same boys somewhere along the road a day or two later. We returned home browned, windblown, more fit, and full of innocent secrets.

Aunt Elsbeth remained preoccupied with Erwin's draft into the military. "That poor, poor boy," she said. "Three years of back-breaking labor in a Russian prison camp where he almost died. And now, just a couple of years later, they send him right back onto the firing line in Korea. Let's hope a bullet doesn't find him, or Douglas, for that matter."

I realized, for the first time, that I might never see my brothers again.

"How long are they going to be in Korea?" I asked.

"Two or three years."

"Three years?" I counted. "That'll make it ten years since I last saw my brothers. I don't think I would recognize them if I passed them in the street."

"They would not recognize their pretty little sister either," Aunt Gertrude said. "They'd be surprised at what a young lady you've grown into. You know, you were the cutest of all of Herbert's children. You liked to run around naked and looked like a little marzipan piglet," Aunt Gertrude continued, chuckling. "I always threatened to take a bite out of you."

"*Ja*, I remember. I took it literally and hid from you."

During one of our long conversations, I learned that the aunts and uncle had tried to get on the ill-fated refugee ship, the *Wilhelm*

Gustlaff. Russian torpedoes had sunk it with some eight thousand women, children, and wounded soldiers aboard.

"We might have been on the *Gustlaff.* It was docked in Danzig when we fled to there in January 1945, but it was full and we could not get on," Aunt Gertrude said. "Just think, we would not be here today if they had let us on board. There were very few survivors."

"God saved us for you children," Aunt Elsbeth said.

"Nonsense!" Aunt Gertrude raised her voice. "If God really cared, he could have saved himself the trouble by simply letting Herbert and Annchen live."

We talked a lot about the past and the cruel fate we had been dealt, but it no longer mattered against whom we made our charges or accusations. God seemed far away during those dark times, and we all had to find our own way back, while vacillating between believing and not believing. Aunt Elsbeth, whose faith remained unshaken through it all, was one of the fortunate ones.

CHAPTER THIRTEEN

THE NEXT MONTHS PASSED QUICKLY. With the gentle guidance of my loving aunts, I regained solid ground under my feet. But in my heart, I felt a painful loneliness and a sense of loss, perhaps for those skipped years between childhood and adulthood. We all had to grow up fast and leave those missing years unfinished. Sometimes, I longed to turn back time, to be a little girl again, at home on the farm with my loving parents, brothers, and sister. I wanted to look into their faces as they were then and imprint those images on my consciousness forever. Instead, I was preparing for a new life in America with strangers. Overcome by sadness, mixed with fear of the unknown, I had no clear idea of what to expect. With the nostalgia of a final farewell not too far off, I saw my German past and life with the aunts in a new dimension. Beyond a doubt, Aunt Elsbeth and Aunt Gertrude had saved my emotional life. I came to them badly scarred, and they gave me what I needed most. They loved me, unconditionally.

Life continued its rhythmic pattern. I caught up in school and learned English, the language I would soon speak every day. Veronika and I took to the road with our bicycles whenever we could, and we added hiking to our weekend activities. Klosterburg with its undulating hills, verdant fields, and many forests became especially beautiful in the fall.

A letter arrived from my brother, Douglas, telling us he had to report to basic training and duty in Korea. He would be gone by the time I got to America. Painfully, I realized with Erwin already in Korea, a family reunion lay somewhere in the far-away future, if at all. I might never see either of my brothers again.

My siblings made arrangements for me to live with my new sister-in-law, Ruth, and her mother when I arrived in Chicago. Douglas committed to help pay for my upkeep, so I could at least finish high school. My sister financed my passage. I never gave a thought to the fact that I might be a burden to my siblings, until I saw it in writing. I vowed I would become independent and self-supporting as quickly as possible, without a clear idea of how I would accomplish this, other than to concentrate on taking command of the English language, the key that would open doors.

When a traveling dance school came to Klosterburg, Aunt Gertrude thought it would be an opportunity for me to learn some poise, although the admittance age was seventeen. She signed the required parental permission papers and paid the tuition. "It's my going-away gift to you. Every young girl should know how to dance," she said.

And so I learned to waltz, polka, fox trot, and tango—all in preparation for my early transition into adulthood.

When I bragged in school about my dance lessons, it took only a week before I stood before the sister superior again.

"What is a fifteen-year-old girl doing in dance classes?" she asked pointedly.

"I'm going to be sixteen next month," I corrected her. "It's my aunt's going-away present." This time I did not tremble and worry about the outcome of the meeting. I was leaving soon, real soon.

"Exactly when are you leaving for America?" she asked, giving me a stern look over her big, round glasses that had slipped down her nose.

"Right after Christmas. I won't be back to school after vacation," I said, smiling confidently.

She looked at the calendar on the wall, studied it a few seconds, and then said, "You're much too young for such a frivolous activity. But you're leaving. Just don't talk about it in school!"

For my Christmas present, Aunt Elsbeth took me shopping for traveling clothes. I had outgrown my new sister-in-law's garments long ago. It was obvious I would not be as petite as she was. Clothes became an obsession for me, perhaps as a subconscious desire to cover up my imagined deficiencies.

The day before school let out, I made the rounds, said good-bye to my nun teachers, and left with their good wishes and those of my friends. I did not visit Aunt Kaethe to take leave of her or the Schades, and I probably gave them all the more reason to call me ungrateful. Young and immature, I could not put my personal feelings and hurt aside and do the proper thing. The aunts, tired and weak, did not battle over it with me.

Uncle Eduard came a few days before Christmas, without the traditional tree, to say good-bye. Aunt Elsbeth had bought a little tree at the local market instead. We put it up and decorated it early. We shared a subdued Christmas. Aunt Gertrude parted with several of her books and wrote a dedication in each one of them, and Aunt Elsbeth had a small wooden case made to hold my start-up library, my most precious possession.

When the much-awaited day of my departure finally arrived, I was exited about the adventurous journey but afraid of what awaited me. Aunt Gertrude accompanied me to Bremerhaven, where my ship was docked. Aunt Elsbeth walked us to the train station. She held me to her breast, squeezed hard the way she always did, and said, "Remember, Evchen, if life gets too difficult in America, you always have a home here with us."

Just knowing I had a way back made the parting easier, although deep in my heart I knew I would not return.

I left, reconciled to the fact that my brothers would not be there to meet me, and that there would not be a family reunion. Departing with a heavy heart, I envied my older siblings, who had made this long journey into uncertainty together.

When the train started to move, I hung out the lowered window and watched Aunt Elsbeth shrink to a mere dot on the platform. Only the naked church steeples remained visible for a long time, and then they, too, disappeared from view. I had been very happy living with my aunts the last two years. My eyes welled up with tears, wondering if I would ever see them again. Aunt Gertrude looked at me, disturbed, and asked, "*Na*, Evchen, are you having second thoughts?"

We arrived at the central gathering point in Bremerhaven in the late afternoon. Masses of immigrants scrambled around while waiting to be processed. Since I was traveling with a U.S. passport, we did not have to wait long. We spent the night in a barrack with many other women and children, many of them GI brides. One woman cried all night, no longer sure she loved the American soldier waiting for her in New York.

We did not board our ship until late afternoon the next day. Aunt Gertrude did not want to come aboard to see the room in steerage I would share with five other women. "It's too sad," she said. "You go and put your things away, and then come back on deck and wave to me."

Finding my room deep in the bowels of the ship among all the confusion took a while. My suitcase and little trunk were already there. Three double-deck bunk beds lined the walls of the small quarters. A young woman sat on one of the lower bunks and looked up at me, crying. I put my tote bag on the bed above her and left the room, thinking she was another bride with second thoughts.

On my way back to the promenade deck, I got caught up in the excitement around me. I walked through the lounge with a half-dozen crystal chandeliers suspended from the ceiling and could not believe the luxury of it all. In the dining room, I glimpsed a Christmas tree reaching all the way to the ceiling, lit with hundreds of colorful electric lights. I felt as if I had been dropped into a fairy tale. Finally, I was leaving for America, the destination of all my hopes and dreams. Although ill prepared, I hoped to create a new life for myself. I would leave Eva behind and become Evelyne, future princess like my sister.

Great crowds were gathered on the pier by the time I reached the promenade deck. I searched for Aunt Gertrude but could not find her among all the heads looking our way. People leaned over the railing and called their good-byes back and forth, waving their white handkerchiefs when not using them to wipe away tears. Aunt Gertrude was not among them. Perhaps she had planned all along to slip away, to escape the pain of that final good-bye.

Darkness gathered by the time the ship pulled away from the pier and slowly edged into the waiting sea. I was sailing to America with a small trunk filled with books, a single suitcase of clothes, and an unrestrained optimism only the very young are capable of.

EPILOGUE

CHAPTER ONE

I NEVER THOUGHT I WOULD stand by Mother's grave again, or revisit our farm, or walk my childhood's paths. Yet, I did.

In the late 1980s, a miracle happened. The Iron Curtain raised, the Berlin Wall crumbled, and the former communist countries opened to tourism. East and West Germany became one, and divided families reunited. Euphoria ruled every German heart, even as far away as in America.

I had the good fortune to make the journey to Steglitz with Georg, who had lived with us through the Russian occupation. He was the young boy who, with the help of his pious mother, had put the identifying crosses on the many typhoid victims' graves, including Mother's. I could not have wished for a more informative companion. Five years older than I was, he helped fill in missing pieces in my sometimes sketchy memory.

In the summer of 1995, we made the trip together with his wife and a German tour group consisting of mostly East Prussian expatriates. It was a pilgrimage—a holy experience. Coming from Reno, Nevada, I was the only American in the group. Our shared place of birth and similar experiences quickly bridged national and geographic differences. All forty seats in the coach were occupied with impatient souls, anxious to set foot on the earth that had borne them, the land that had nurtured them and then cast them out. Never getting enough and never being rid of that special homesickness for what had been lost forever, the Germans kept returning to their place of birth and eventually befriended the Poles who now lived on their properties.

They came laden with gifts of good will for these new occupants of their one-time homes, hoping to break down the Poles' lingering hostility against the "evil" Germans they remembered. To set foot on the ground that linked them to the past and to walk through the rooms of an all-too-short childhood helped make the painful memories finally go away.

Georg and his wife, Hanne, had made the trip many times before. This time, they came laden with coffee and cigarettes for the adults on their farm and chocolate bars for the children. I brought coffee, ballpoint pens, baseball hats, and tee shirts with slogans. Georg warned me that the Poles in our area were very poor. Most of the old farm buildings were crumbling, and in some cases they were gone altogether.

"Don't expect to find things the way you remember them," he reminded me.

Our coach trip took two days, with an overnight stop near the Polish border. It gave Georg and me a chance to get reacquainted. I remembered him as one of the boys who had kept the Russians' vodka still going.

"It was a mixed blessing," he said. "The alcohol made the soldiers crazy. However, the village nurse saved many a life with it. But let's talk about you. You told me about your experience with the Poles. What about America? Was it the paradise we all thought it to be?"

"Yes and no," I said. "It was a difficult adjustment. The roads were not paved with gold, but there were unlimited opportunities. It took me a while to realize that." I reflected upon my arrival in Chicago, the initial disappointment and loneliness I had felt, and said no more. How could I make him understand the loss of all sense of belonging and the feeling of isolation, of being a stranger in a strange land?

"I think my siblings didn't know what to do with me," I finally continued. "I lived with Erwin's wife, Ruth, and her mother for a very short time. It did not work out. They were strangers to me. I needed to be with the family I knew and had longed for. But Erwin and Douglas were in Korea. Vera was newly married and working; they had no room for me in their little studio apartment. Henry lived in a one-room flat and was as lost as I was. I missed the aunts. I don't remember what happened, but I ended up with my sister, who put me up in a rooming house. The nightly fighting and screaming coming through the walls reminded me of life with the Ilowskis. Douglas contributed to my upkeep from his meager soldier's pay so I could at least finish high school."

"*Ja*, what about school? How did you manage the language barrier?"

"I made perfecting English my top priority. But my rooming house stay was a most unpleasant experience. When my sister found a room for me with an older couple who lived near my high school, I felt more at home. They were childless and often invited me to sit and visit with them. They never ridiculed the way I butchered the English language. It was different with the kids in school. They made fun of my heavy accent, and there was a strong anti-German hostility among some of the Jewish teachers, which did not help rebuild my badly damaged self-confidence."

"People can be cruel everywhere," Georg responded, shaking his head. "Even we experienced some of that right here in our own country. It must have been terrible for you."

"It was, but I had grown tough skinned under the Poles."

"So, when were you finally reunited with your brothers, Erwin and Douglas?"

"Before Douglas went to Korea, he got a special weekend leave to meet his little sister, who wasn't so little any more. I did not recognize my brother. He was in uniform and had grown into a mature man. The boy I remembered was gone. We were unable to bridge the lost years in the short time we had together. I had the fewest memories of our family life on the farm and the shortest childhood. Too many years devoid of shared experiences had passed. The surprising thing was that we never talked about the past. It was too painful."

"I would have thought adversity would have brought you closer together."

"It might have been different had our parents lived. They would have provided the center pole around which we could have re-gathered. Had we stayed in Germany, the aunts would have provided that pole. But they were thousands of miles away. We missed a whole decade and a half of growing up together at a very critical age. We lost our sense of family. At least I did."

"Were you sorry you didn't stay with your aunts?" Georg asked.

"I liked America, but I was homesick for my aunts. I missed the steadfastness of their life, with its security and predictable, everyday routine. I moved around too often in those first years in America. I lived with my sister for a while, but when she expected their second child, they needed my room. By then, I was out of high school and working as a secretary. I didn't earn much money and ended up in another rooming house for single women. It was not the best environment, but it was interesting. We never had a dull moment, between the police chasing down shoplifters, angry parents looking for runaway daughters, and rueful husbands trying to talk their fed-up wives into coming home."

We fell silent for a while.

It was late afternoon when we drove into Elbing. My heart pounded with excitement. Threatening black clouds blanketed part of the sky, while the bright sun made a valiant stand on the other side of the river. A perfect rainbow arched over the entire city to greet us.

"A good sign," Georg said.

The city had been rebuilt. Only an occasional gaping hole in the rows and rows of newly erected buildings scarred the skyline and served as a reminder of the war, a war only the old remembered.

We checked into a large hotel in the center of town, occupied by mostly German tourists. There was no denying Elbing looked beautiful again. Young, well-dressed men and women rushed about the streets. I looked into their happy, smiling faces; they were too young to remember the war. To them, it had happened an eternity ago and did not concern them. Elblag, the new Polish name, belonged to them now. Elbing had been erased from the map. It existed only in the memory of those of us who returned to relive the long-ago past. For me, it felt like returning to the grave where my missed childhood lay buried.

Equipped with an old German city map and filled with a burning desire to recapture some of those lost years, I headed for the old part of town. My family's apartment buildings had survived the war; they stood tall and alone in an area where almost everything had been obliterated.

I took picture after picture of the time-battered buildings from all angles and zoomed in on the still-visible bullet holes in the crumbling stucco. It seemed as if time had stood still here. In my mind, I saw a frightened little girl sitting on the front steps, watching the busy city life. Now, the street was quiet and deserted. An elderly woman appeared in the doorway and watched us. I could not tell if she was hostile or friendly. "*Dzien dobry*, good day, Pani," I called across the street, indicating with my camera that I would like to take her picture. She smiled and waved me on.

"You come from Germany?" she asked in perfect German and offered me her hand. When I told her my family had once owned the two buildings, she asked, "You want to come in and see my place?"

I could not believe my good fortune and quickly entered the building before she changed her mind. She led me into her apartment on the third floor, the very same one the aunts and my grandmother had occupied. I walked through the rooms and took more pictures. In contrast to the raw cement walls in the neglected hallway and the worn-down, bare stairs, her apartment was clean, cozy, and beautifully furnished with old-style furniture. I closed my eyes and could almost feel and smell the aunts' presence. My head filled with memories, and the years washed away.

"I live here with my daughter and grandson," she said.

"Do you own the apartment?" I asked.

"The buildings belong to the government. We pay rent to them. But they won't do anything for us. If something breaks down, we have to fix it ourselves. They have done nothing for as long as we have lived here."

For years, I had dreamed of revisiting these places of the past, and now that the dream was reality, it felt as if I was still dreaming.

The next morning, Georg, his wife, and I hired a taxi with a German-speaking driver. An older man, he was not only familiar with the former German names of the little villages around Elbing, as I still thought of them, but he also knew the back roads. The graceful, old linden trees that had once lined the streets were gone. The highway had been widened. Cars zoomed by. The slow horse-and-buggy days of my childhood were no more.

Shortly before Niederhof, I asked to be dropped off and got out of the car. "I need to be alone," I told Georg and his wife. "Please go on to Steglitz and come back for me in an hour."

I felt as if I was in another world—nothing seemed real. Wild emotions welled up inside me as the past came alive, and I let my feet carry me along. Landmarks had disappeared; old country roads were overgrown with weeds. A ripe wheat field covered the grounds where the Kolskis' little homestead once stood. Not even a trace remained. Nature had reclaimed it all.

A stork poked for frogs in the meadow near our farm. I wondered if he was a descendent of the stork family that had listened so patiently to my tales of woe. Then, suddenly, I stood in front of our farm, and I could no longer hold back the tears. The Russian graves were gone, and so was Father's fruit orchard. Not one tree had survived. The house had lost most of its stucco. The stable roof was close to collapsing, and tall weeds grew where the barn once had stood. I wondered if Pan Ilowski had torn it down board by board to keep his family warm during those cold, long winters.

A chain-link fence divided Mother's flower garden and picked up again in the back yard to where the barn had been. Large and small trucks filled one side; the other was empty. It was a house divided. I noticed there was a new entrance where the kitchen window once had faced out, and the doorway to the kitchen where cruel Dorota had ruled over me had been bricked up. I still could feel her powerful presence on the other side and shuddered.

An older man working on the window casings of Soscha's room upstairs waved to me. I waved back. Although he seemed friendly, I waited for Georg and the driver to return to help break the ice with the new owners before venturing onto the grounds.

CHAPTER TWO

GEORG AND HANNE TOOK THEIR time returning, and I grew impatient. I noticed no sign of activity on the empty yard side of the house and edged closer to the building. Cobwebs and grime covered the bare windows. I peeked through the glass, half expecting one of the Ilowskis to stare back at me. Instead, I saw our old parlor, filled with broken-down furniture. A thick blanket of undisturbed dust lay on everything. The living room was empty, with the exception of an old, thread-bare rug on the floor. I wondered if it was the original from Mother's time. The green tile heating stove, that hungry monster, stood in the corner, just as it always had.

I walked over to where the barn once had stood and stopped in my tracks. There, among waist-high weeds, sat Father's old hay rake, perhaps the very same from which I had kept a careful eye on our aggressive rooster before he jumped on my head and pecked a piece of skin from my forehead. Rusty and broken down, it had, over the years, stood its ground against the elements.

"Pani," a voice jarred me out of my reverie. A young, friendly-looking man stood behind me and kept talking. Although I once spoke Polish fluently, I now could pick out only a word or two. Too many years of disuse had passed. I shrugged my shoulders and turned to leave the premises.

At that moment, our car came into the yard, and the channels of communication opened. The young man had nothing to do with the house. He owned the stable, where he operated a carpentry shop. Pleased and eager, he offered to show us his business. The entire inside had been gutted. Workbenches, sawhorses, and piles of wood had replaced the stalls.

He had been there only a few years and knew nothing about the Ilowskis.

I asked the driver to inquire about the people who owned the empty side of the house. The young man could only tell us that no one had lived there for a long time. "Someone comes around occasionally to check on things," he said.

"What about the people on the other side of the fence? Are they friendly?" I asked.

He called across the barrier. A middle-aged man in a greasy uniform appeared, wiping his hands on a rag. He smiled and invited us into his yard. He operated a truck and car repair garage, from all appearances a successful one. Father's workshop, the pigsty, and the old stable, where I had spent several frightening nights sleeping with the animals, had been converted into a new business.

"Pan Novak," the man introduced himself and extended his hand to me.

"How long have you been here?" I asked.

"I bought the place two years ago. The previous owner was a drunk and ruined the business. I'm trying to build it up again."

"Do you own the house too?"

"Only half of it. We want to buy the other half, but the owner is very difficult," he explained. Then, he added, "Do you want to see the inside?"

"Oh, yes ... yes," I said.

"We've not had time to do any work on the house," he apologized. "We had to rebuild the business first. The place is run down. The rooms were piled high with garbage. I mean real garbage. We used shovels to get it out. We have an apartment in Elblag and work on the house on weekends."

Our beautiful house—desecrated and neglected beyond belief. I wondered what horror stories the walls would tell if they could talk. The rooms smelled of filth, the floorboards had rotted away, the walls were crumbling. I was glad Mother and Father were spared the pain of seeing their one-time beautiful home so defiled.

I would have given much to have a glimpse of the kitchen, where Dorota had ruled over me with her powerful fists, but the door to that part of the house was bricked up.

Upstairs, in Soscha's room, we met Pan Novak's father-in-law, the friendly man who had waved to me. He was removing dry rotted wood around the windows. "We're trying to save the house," he said. "A lot of work here. Much patience."

"How can they save half a house, while the other half is disintegrating right under their eyes?" I asked Georg.

"Beats me," he said and shrugged.

As we walked through the rooms, I felt very connected to Mother—the mother, who over the years, I so often had tried to resurrect in my tortured dreams. I closed my eyes and could almost hear her suppressed weeping the night before we fled. I felt her presence everywhere and was glad she had been spared much pain by dying without knowing the outcome of the war. Would life have been worth living for her after losing her beloved mate and everything they had tried so hard to hold on to?

An elderly couple now occupied the room in which our English prisoner guard once lived. They allowed me a glimpse of their quarters. A big bed, a table, two chairs, a cooking stove, and a few pots and pans and dishes made up their lives' possessions. It reminded me of the Kolskis' sparse ménage. The couple sat at the table drinking coffee out of big mugs. In my mind, I saw a hungry little girl waiting to get her turn to eat.

I took a picture of them and the room, which I later sent to them. When I held the developed photo in my hand, I noticed a television set on a night table, the only modern change in an otherwise unchanged world.

Pan Novak's pretty young wife joined us, and I took pictures of them as well. They had two teenage sons, she told us.

"I have something in the car for your boys," I said. They walked to the vehicle with us, and I handed them two baseball hats and tee shirts with the "Reno, Biggest Little City in the World" slogan. "That's where I live," I said, pointing to the words. "I hope your sons will like them."

Pani Novak smiled and said, "They're crazy about anything American."

When we were leaving, the woman from upstairs came running after us. She pressed a piece of paper with a name and an Elblag address into my hand. I read the name—Evelina Skaluda. Evelina— goose bumps formed on my arms. After an excited back and forth between the woman and our driver, I learned that this Evelina had lived in our farm workers' housing many years ago. I pondered over the coincidence of our shared name, and I asked the driver if he would find out who this Evelina was when we returned to the city.

"There were seven Russian graves here in this front yard," I asked him. "Do you know anything about them?"

"In the early 1950s, the Russians came around and exhumed the remains," he said. "They reburied them in a military cemetery in Russia. There were Russian graves all over this area. They dug them all up."

I felt a great sense of relief knowing those menacing graves were no longer there.

At the railroad station, the entrance to Roza's apartment was boarded up. No one could tell us anything about her. A younger generation had replaced all the inhabitants who once had lived in the complex. Tall weeds thrived among the decaying buildings. The freshly white-washed station building looked out of place. Inside, the bench where I anxiously had waited for Frau Leppe was still there. Boards covered the ticket window. "The passengers buy their passes on the train now," our driver explained.

Roza had lost her job and probably had moved away, I thought, disappointed. She was the one person I would have liked to meet again, if only to thank her for lifting me from a life of drudgery with the Kolskis and giving me a taste of a better existence.

Before we headed to Steglitz, I walked to the place where the friendly merchant woman's kiosk once had stood. Nothing was left of it, not even a sign to mark the spot. The grounds of the burned-down *Gasthaus* now housed weeds and tall grass. Tree roots snaked around the weathered foundation and had broken it apart. In my mind, I saw that little girl sitting on the tumbledown stairs when she beheld, for one brief but happy moment, the image of what she had thought was her father—the father for whose return she had wished for so desperately, and who then had turned into a grotesque old stranger and nearly broke her heart. As I thought of her, my heart broke all over again and tears welled up from deep inside me where that little girl still lived.

The memories of the past overwhelmed me. The faces of the people who had inhabited my life during those unhappy, lonely years stayed frozen in time and remained young. I had to remind myself that they, too, had aged, and many of them had probably died long ago.

We decided to walk the two kilometers to Steglitz and asked the driver to meet us there. The potholed dirt road we had navigated as children was now paved. The old chestnut tree under which we so often lingered and played on our way to and from school still stood at the half-way point and offered welcome shade. Georg pointed across the plowed fields in the distance and said, "Look over there. Those fields were covered with the dead from that train massacre. I helped bury them. It was terrible." He stopped and studied the landscape. "Somewhere out there is an unmarked mass grave. Maybe a hundred years from now, some farmer will dig up the bones and wonder what happened here. He won't find the answer in any history books. The secret will die with us."

"I heard so much talk about that bloody incident when I was a little girl in Steglitz and Mother was still alive. It frightened me terribly and gave me wild nightmares."

"Me, too," Georg said. "I found identification documents on two soldiers. I hid the papers in a split rafter in our barn, intending to take them with us when we got out of here. But when the time came, we were afraid to have anything on us that hinted of German soldiers."

"Maybe they're still there," I suggested, excitedly. "You've befriended the Poles on your property. Tell them about it. They might even help you look for them."

I thought of my children's Bible story book and wondered if the Ilowskis ever found it when they tore down our barn. I realized how much that little book had helped me through some very tough times, and the hope the stories had given me.

Steglitz looked deserted. Our driver stood in front of a weather-beaten cottage, conversing with two old women. They smiled at us, eager to talk.

"Ask them if they knew the Ilowskis," I told the driver.

The women had gone to school with some of the Ilowski children. However, the family had moved away years ago. "The Ilowskis had a hard life, with too many children and a drunken husband," one of them said.

"Did you know the Ilowskis?" one asked.

"I lived with them in 1945 and 1946."

The women studied me for a second. "Are you that little German orphan?" one asked. "There was a boy, too. Was he your brother?"

My first direct link to the past—my first connection to the Ilowskis!

I studied the women's wrinkled faces. They looked so old, and I realized that could have been me had I not gotten away from that life of drudgery and deprivation.

Georg read my thoughts and said, "The Polish farmers in these villages barely eke out a living. Look at the buildings. Nothing has been done to them in fifty years. The people have no money for repairs—for anything. They are the last generation to farm this land. Their children will end up in the cities. These buildings will collapse, weeds will grow over the ruins, and soon you won't even know that once there was a village here. A cooperative will plow it over, plant crops, and a new age will begin."

"It's all so sad," I said. "Look how our lives have changed for the better. And we started with even less than these people. It feels as if time has stood still here. Nothing has changed. I found Father's old hay rake buried deep in weeds, all rusted and broken down."

"That's nothing," Georg said. "Let me show you something." We approached his farm from the back. Behind the barn, which miraculously still stood, was assembled a whole array of rusty old farm equipment—hay rakes, hay spreaders, seeders, harrows, a broken-down thresher, and much more. "Look at all this equipment. This is just the stuff the Russians left behind when they pulled out. It's been sitting here all these years. My guess is it's never been used by the Poles. Instead, they do everything by hand with their one horse, maybe two, a plow, a shovel, and a pitchfork. They're working themselves to death. Their children see it and want no part of it."

"I suppose that's what drove the Ilowskis off our farm. I'm glad. I like the thought of their no longer being on our land," I said.

The people on Georg's farm seemed happy to see us and invited us into the house. Hanne emptied her bag and lined the table with coffee, tea, cigarettes, and chocolate bars. The woman offered to make tea for us, but Georg refused. I took pictures of the old kitchen stove, just like the one Father had replaced on our farm. In the newly installed bathroom under the stairway, you had to duck to wash your hands, but it had running hot and cold water. The toilet, however, was still the outhouse.

Later, when I showed Georg the developed pictures, he said, "I like the family on our farm, but it pains me to see all our furniture in those rooms. Mother's credenza is still standing in the same spot. They have everything of ours—pots and pans, Mother's good china, and our silver. I swear even that milk can in the corner was ours. It just serves as a reminder of how we were stripped of everything. That's why I refused the tea. I would have choked on the bitter memories. I know it's not their fault, but it's still painful."

In the stable, Georg tried to remember where he might have hidden the German soldiers' identification papers. "It's useless," he said. "Too much time has passed. It all looks so different. They've removed beams and changed things."

"Perhaps it's better to let the past rest," I said. "What would you do with the information after over fifty years?"

"I've always regretted not having written down the victims' names when we fled. I could have done some good with them then."

Our next stop was the mayor's vegetable garden, where Mother lay buried along with all the other typhoid victims. The gravesites were gone, and the land had been plowed over. But it did not matter. For me, it was enough to know that the little plot of earth on which I stood held Mother's bones. Healthy, young potato plants covered the ground, hiding what lay beneath.

"Do the villagers know this was a cemetery once?" I asked the driver.

"They do. They know a lot. They just don't like to talk about it," he said.

"What does it matter?" Hanne changed the subject. "Those graves meant nothing to them. This land holds many secrets, secrets that will never be told."

"But it still means something to us," Georg said. "This is what keeps calling us back."

"That's so true," I said. "I was a young child when I lost my parents and know nothing personal about them—their hopes and dreams, their loves and hates, their thoughts and tastes—all the things that make a human being what he or she is. Children don't recognize those qualities in their parents until they become adults themselves.

My parents remain a mystery to me. It is my greatest regret not to have known them better. I feel very much in touch with the past right now and close to my roots. I suddenly have a better understanding of the need for cemeteries. Somehow, they make us feel closer to our lost loved ones."

Georg nodded at Hanne and the driver, then turned to me and said, "Why don't you spend some time alone here."

"I would like that," I said and watched him take Hanne's hand and walk away.

I sat down on a patch of grass at the edge of the potato field, picked a spot where Mother's grave might be, and sent my unspoken thoughts her way.

I WANT TO TELL YOU about my life. If there is anything after death, you probably already know everything, but I'm going to tell you anyway. I missed you terribly after you died and was angry with you for leaving us. I didn't realize then that you had fought hard to stay alive for Henry and me. I'm no longer sure which was the more difficult to overcome, your death or the feeling of total abandonment. Maybe there is little difference. It must have been extremely painful for you to let go and leave us in the care of Frau Weber and Frau Leitzel, who dumped us at the first conve-nient opportunity. In my heart, I blame them for our journey through hell, not the Ilowskis. The Ilowskis just happened to be there. They did not ask for us to come into their life. Our presence probably represented but a second in the eternity of their own harsh experience, while for us it was the other way around. It was a time of singular agony and exclusion. I forgot what was normal and came to look upon the Ilowskis' behavior as normal. Not until I got away from there did I learn that not all Poles were evil. I forgave them a long time ago. But you know all that.

The pain of missing you became less painful after Schotka told me to look for you among the stars. I was no longer so lonely after that. I sensed your presence all around me. I still do at times.

Erwin, Douglas, and Henry were here last year. So you know they survived Korea and returned with all their body parts intact. Henry was lucky and served his military time in Germany. All three boys married women of German background.

You have many grandchildren and great grandchildren, who all speak English just like Father did. You'll live on through them.

As for me, I have made mistakes. After not finding the nurturing family environment with my siblings, I married too young, barely twenty, and for all the wrong reasons—a comfortable warm home, economic security, and a new family. Love was not one of them. But what did I know about love, when there had been so little of it in my life. I mistook my deep desire for stability for love.

However, I have two wonderful children from that marriage. They're beautiful, both inside and out. I know you would have loved them, and maybe you do from out there. I hope that some day I can bring them, their wonderful mates, and their children to visit you here. They each have two little girls and are good parents. They are better parents than I was, but then, I didn't have you to teach me.

It was my children who made life worth living and kept me from succumbing to bouts of depression. More than anything, I needed to come to terms with the past. The emotional wounds were slow to heal. Determined not to be hurt any more, I built a shell around myself and guarded my innermost life and feelings. I even shut out my siblings and, later, my husband. What I needed most was someone to help me work through my stormy past and put it to rest. But what do you do when even your own mother-in-law, this mother who I so wanted to love me, tells you, "You can tell a lot of stories, but how much is true?"

Maybe it was too terrible to believe when you merely read about the horrors of war rather than lived them. It is difficult for those whose lives remained untouched and who have lost nothing to empathize with those who not only lost everything but also suffered a lot. That was the hardest to accept—the doubting stares when I as much as hinted at my troubled past.

You, Mother, know the truth. Aunts Elsbeth and Gertrude did, too. They saw in our eyes the fear and suffering Henry and I had endured. Coming to them was like stepping out of a deep, cold darkness into a warming, bright light. We were lucky to have them. They loved us unconditionally and taught us many valuable lessons. For a short while, they were each like a mother to us—the mother you could no longer be. I remember the time with them as the best years of my early teens.

I missed them terribly after I left for America. Fifteen years passed before I was able to return to Germany and visit them. By then, they had moved away from Klosterburg. They had bought a beautiful, spacious villa near Heidelberg with the war reparation money they finally had received from the German government. Returning to them was like a homecoming. I visited them every year after that and always felt renewed, recharged, and treasured. I deeply felt their loss after they passed away.

I cannot deny that I was troubled and angry during those early years. Angry with you, Mother, for having left us, angry with my brothers for not coming to look for us, angry with Vera for having escaped. I was desperately looking for someone to take the role of my parents and expected too much of my siblings, who were still children themselves. Later, I was angry with my husband and his family for not recognizing what set me apart. I was even angry with God, in whom everyone but I seemed to trust.

I felt singled out. It took a long time for me to make peace with the world and myself. Only with age did I have a better understanding of my siblings' nature and my own, for that matter. Time and distance have smoothed out our differences and helped us accept each other for what we have become. We live scattered in all four corners of the United States and rarely see each other. Maybe you've looked upon us, your children, with sadness for not being closer and sharing our lives' experiences.

For years after I divorced my husband, my brothers and their wives would have nothing to do with me. They liked my husband, and to them, I had committed the unforgivable. They did not ask what happened or why. They only saw the facade of a good marriage, a marriage of eighteen years that, in their eyes, I had carelessly destroyed. They did not see the lonely woman who felt trapped in the consequences of a wrong choice. I was alone. Only Vera stood by me. But that was so long ago, and you need not mourn for me. I'm very happy and content now.

I am happy and content because Richard, my beloved companion, came into my life. We have been married over twenty-five wonderful years. He gave me the love and understanding I needed and yearned for. One by one, he opened the doors to my inner self and helped me find myself. He has been and still is my best friend, my father and brother, my confessor and liberator, and my teacher. He broke down that protective wall around me, brick by brick, until there was nothing left to protect. He made me feel loved and restored my badly damaged self-esteem. We have traveled across the world and made many visits to aunts Elsbeth and Gertrude. They loved him. In fact, he is the one who sent me to you. 'Go find your mother's grave,' he told me. 'Go to your farm and visit the places of your dark memories and make peace with the past.' And I have.

I hope you, too, Mother, have found peace. If the man who informed us about Father's death in Siberia was right, you did not have to wait long to be reunited. I like to think that you are together, and that you take pleasure in occasionally looking down on us, your children, and seeing that all is well.

I loved you more than I knew. Not until you were gone did I learn how much. And I will always love the memory of you.

CHAPTER THREE

"Let's go and find the Hagen farm today," Georg suggested the next morning. "The old road from Steglitz is gone, but if our driver is willing to take us along some unpaved country lanes, I can get us there from the opposite direction."

Bribed with an extra premium for his fee, our driver was more than willing to take us wherever we wanted to go. Although we were not far from Niederhof, I was unfamiliar with the area. Georg called out the old German names of some of the villages we passed through. When we arrived at the edge of a forest, the car's tires dug into the sandy road and threatened to get stuck. We parked the vehicle and walked the rest of the way.

"We're not far from our destination," Georg said. "We had forest land near here. It was close to the Hagens' farm."

We covered another kilometer or so along the edge of the woods. Georg stopped by a grove of mature pines and said, "Father and I planted these evergreens among the oak and beech trees. I'm sure of it. The Hagens' property was to the left of here."

We craned our necks to look across the tall wheat covering the land all the way to the horizon, but saw no sign of any buildings.

He pointed across the yellow field. "See that copse of trees? If they're fruit trees, we have found the Hagen farm. Even if it is no more, we should find the foundation."

We crossed the field, our heads barely visible among the tall stalks. Our driver followed, eager to learn more history about the area, he told us.

"Look! Gnarled old apple trees," Georg said, when we reached the clearing. "This is the place."

The farm was gone. Crumbling concrete foundations confirmed

that buildings once had stood on that spot. Tall grass, spiky thistles, and stinging nettles reached to our chests. A few brave cosmos competed for the sun, adding a splash of color to the landmark.

We poked around among the weeds and found rusty pieces of harness and farm equipment.

"This is where the stable must have been," Georg said.

"The house was directly opposite it," I suggested.

And so it was. We found pieces of white tile from the heating stove and a big hole in the ground where the cellar had been.

"Many times Fraulein Gretchen and Frau Kehr hid in here from the Russians," I said, excitedly. "I've often dreamt of returning to this spot, but I never thought it would come to pass."

I let my eyes comb the landscape. Nothing looked familiar. Old paths, fences, and landmarks were gone.

"I'm not surprised," Georg said. "You probably were afraid to leave the house."

"I came to know bone-chilling fear here. No ... terror. The blind terror of hatred. We all did. What you experience under those conditions stays with you forever."

As we were leaving, I stumbled over a pile of rusted debris and laid bare a perfect horse shoe, thick with rust.

"Take it back to America," Georg said. "Hang it over a door with the open end facing the sky to catch your luck. Believe me, it really works."

I smiled and said, "I'll do just that. When I was little, I believed in fairy tales, and now over time, I've become a believer in miracles. Look how well our lives have turned out, despite all this. But I do have trouble reconciling my good fortune with the misfortunes of those whose blood was so brutally spilled over this land. What had they done to deserve less?"

"There is no simple answer," Georg said. "At least I don't have one. War doesn't differentiate between the innocent and the guilty."

"Tell that to the dead," I said.

On our return to Elblag, we made a short stop in Steglitz and walked the streets one last time.

"We were forced to grow up too fast," I said as we walked along. "We were not prepared for what awaited us. I have often wondered how our lives would have turned out if the war had not come along."

We passed the house where Irena had lived and where her kind mother had given me a big red tomato after venomous Dorota had chased me from our farm. An old woman was pulling weeds in the vegetable garden.

"Let's go and talk to her," I said to the driver.

She greeted us with a big smile, exposing her toothless gums. Deep lines furrowed her weathered face, but her kind eyes sparkled like stars in the night sky. She's too old to be Irena, I thought. I told our driver to ask her name.

"Irena," she said, shielding her eyes from the sun while she studied us.

"Irena!" I exclaimed, recognizing the name without the need for further translation. She did not remember that little German orphan girl. But then, why would she remember anything so trivial? The incident represented but an inconsequential second in her life; yet, it had meant so much to me.

"That's how life is," I said, turning to Georg. "We don't realize how far reaching our casual acts and mindless words, good or bad, can sometimes be."

Irena could tell us very little about the Ilowskis. Life had been hard for the family. "Too many children," she said. "Eleven in all. Pani Ilowski died after the birth of her last child. Pan Ilowski moved away after that." She did not know to where. Some of the older children had been married by then and no longer lived at home. She thought the oldest girl, Dorota, had moved to what was now Elblag, but she did not know her address.

Although a simple woman, Irena was as generous as her mother had been. When we turned to leave, she said, "Wait! I'll kill a chicken for you. You can fix it for your dinner."

We declined, barely able to conceal a chuckle. She insisted that we at least take a few apples, which she quickly picked and placed in our hands.

Oh, Irena, I thought, how I wish I had fallen into your family's midst. How different those terrible three years might have been.

CHAPTER FOUR

THE FOLLOWING DAY, OUR TOUR program took us to Kahlberg. The little steamboats that had sat idle for nearly half a century ran again. We walked from the hotel to the pier, where our ship was docked. We were the only passengers, giving us room to move about freely on the small vessel.

"This is very exciting," I said to Georg, as the boat pulled into the river's course. "I feel like I'm reliving my childhood. Of all my happy memories, these are the most vivid. Kahlberg was always special to me."

When we entered the open sea, the tour guide spoke. "Thousands and thousands of Germans perished in these waters, trying to escape the advancing Russians," she said. "This inland sea was frozen solid and crowded with vehicles of all types, people pulling sleds, pushing baby buggies, or just walking along with bundles on their backs, while the Russians bombed them relentlessly. More people drowned or froze to death than made it across. For years, the eels were twice the normal size. I think if you were to dredge along the bottom of these waters, you'd still bring up more human bones than sand."

"Ours might have been among them," I said to Georg, remembering Father's plan to take the shortcut across the ice that fatal winter of 1945.

I watched the waves lap at the base of the lighthouse as we passed, listened to the pained cries of the gulls in the wind, and thought of Grandmother's dead sailors. "Do you think they're the souls of all those drowning victims?" I asked, pointing to the sky.

"What do you mean?"

"My grandmother filled my head with strange stories. Every time we came by the lighthouse, she referred to the gulls as being the souls of dead sailors who had drowned at sea. To this day, I don't know where she got her stories. To me, the stories were as real and frightening as the outside world. Then, overnight, this mysterious world came to meet me, with all the ugliness humankind was capable of. I learned what terrible things the mind can do when I started to confuse the real with the imagined."

When we reached the long narrow strip of land where Kahlberg once spread from the inland sea on one side to the Baltic Sea on the other, I did not recognize anything. Much smaller now, the resort's hub had shifted to the Baltic Sea side.

Despite the many changes, I found the sandy path through the woods that lead to Aunt Elsbeth's summer home.

We located two surviving cottages, but I could not tell if either one was Aunt Elsbeth's. The geranium flower boxes were missing, the weeds were high, and the undergrowth was dense among the tall fir trees. I could not help thinking of the Hansel and Gretel tale. "Weeds, weeds! Doesn't anyone ever cut them down?" I asked.

"It's all so depressing here," Georg said. "Let's go to the sea and find the beach."

We heard it and smelled it before we saw it. The violent surf called to us like an approaching storm. Then, behind the shifting white dunes there it was, spread along the horizon as far as the eye could see. Heavy grey clouds covered the sun, and a strong, cold wind blew across the dunes, making the sand dance in the air. Tall, foam-crested waves collapsed on the shore, leaving a scalloped border of bubbles along the beach.

"This is not at all the way I remember it," I said. "Did we really bathe in these turbulent waters? I didn't even know how to swim."

"The Baltic Sea is not always like this. But these are perfect conditions for finding amber along the shore," Georg explained.

"Or the bones of the dead," I added.

"Let's take a walk along the dunes," Georg suggested. "I want to show you and Hanne what used to be my favorite stretch of beach." And so we walked in silence along picturesque coves and inlets, mourning the loss of this little piece of paradise with its many warm memories.

We rested under the wide branches of an old pine tree overlooking the beach, watching fishermen repair their nets and naked children playing in the churning surf.

"Tell me, Georg, how did it all happen? How could our parents sit and watch our country being destroyed without raising a hand? Sometimes I feel it all was just a dream, a long, bad dream."

"You of all people shouldn't be asking that question. Don't you remember what happened to your father?"

"It might have been different if more people had spoken out and rebelled."

"Evelyne, you're a dreamer. We both have seen and lived through enough to know that those times tested everyone's capacity for good and evil. We had a leader who allowed the dregs of society to rise to the top, and they were most willing to carry out his evil schemes."

"Well, they gave the Russians good cause for the violence they unleashed on us," I said. "It's just too bad that we, the innocent, ended up paying for their crimes."

"The cruelty of war spares no one," Georg said. "Good and evil have no nationality. In war, atrocities are committed on all sides. Go back in history and you'll find that every nation has its skeletons to live with. What Hitler and his gang did is unforgivable. As Germans we have to live with that stigma." Georg picked up a shell and caressed it between his fingers. "We were young and did not understand what was happening in our country," he continued in a sad and remote voice. "We were born into a situation that seemed normal to us. We were brainwashed. That's what the Hitler Youth was all about in the end. We had no yardstick against which to measure what we were told. We believed everything and accepted the world around us as it was. I don't know what I would have done as an adult if the war had lasted much longer."

"Let's be glad we never had to find out," I said. "Looking back, I have no regrets. My experiences taught me a lot about human nature. I've learned not to judge people, but to wonder what has happened in their lives to mold them into what they've become. Even Dorota. She was the product of abusive parents. As the oldest girl of a large family she, too, was robbed of her childhood, while being forced to be the surrogate mother to so many children. Today, I understand what made her into the mean-spirited, abusive person she was. In retrospect I also met with a lot of kindness when I needed it most. It's just that at the time I did not always recognize it as such."

Back at the hotel, I asked our tour guide to accompany me to

Evelina Skaluda's place. She lived in one of those ubiquitous cement-block apartment houses that had sprung up all over the communist countries. Colorful laundry and red bedding hanging from windows and balconies added splashes of color to the gray behemoth of a building. Evelina lived on the first floor and was waiting for us in the doorway. An older, attractive woman, she did not take my hand in greeting. Instead, she threw her arms around me and kissed both my cheeks. Then she took my hands, put them to her lips, and kissed them too. Taken aback, I almost forgot why I was there. "Ah, *Amerika*! Ah, *Amerika*!" she kept repeating. "I remember you," she said. "You used to come around to play at our house when you were taking care of that ticket woman's little boy at the station. I have a son in America. In New York. I've visited him once. I love *Amerika*."

I learned it was Evelina's mother who had given me the children's Bible. It was difficult to get the woman to stop raving about America and to talk about the Ilowskis. She knew them, but her own family had moved to Elblag when she was still a child, and she lost track of the Ilowskis. However, years ago, for a short time, she worked with Dorota at the post office.

"Dorota is a widow now," Evelina said. "She married young and has two children. She lives here in Elblag, at the other end of town."

She wrote Dorota's address on a piece of paper and handed it to me. "Maybe you'll go and visit her."

"What about Roza?" I changed the subject. "Can you tell me anything about her?"

"Roza? Who was Roza?"

"The ticket woman."

"She moved away, too. Everybody left there. It was too difficult to make a living in the villages."

"Tell me about your name. We share the same name. Is it a common Polish name?"

"My grandmother was English," she said.

I had come full circle and delved into the past enough. Life had gone on for these people as it had for me. The constant aching drive to return to the setting of all those stored memories was finally satisfied. I realized that acceptance, not time, is the healer of all emotional wounds. I always knew that; I just didn't know I knew it.

"Write to me," Evelina said, embracing and kissing me. I promised

I would, but I never did. I wanted to close this chapter of my life for good. When we reached the street, I crumpled the piece of paper with Dorota's address and threw it in the drain.

Breinigsville, PA USA
26 August 2009

222967BV00002B/13/A